Contending Visions of the Middle East
The History and Politics of Orientalism

Zachary Lockman's informed and thoughtful history of European Orientalism and US Middle East studies, the "clash of civilizations" debate and America's involvement in the region has become a highly recommended and widely used text since its publication in 2004. The second edition of Professor Lockman's book brings his analysis up to date by considering how the study of the Middle East has evolved in the intervening years, in the context of the US occupation of Iraq and the "global war on terror."

ZACHARY LOCKMAN teaches modern Middle Eastern history at New York University. His previous publications include *Comrades and Enemies: Arab and Jewish Workers in Palestine, 1906–1948* (1996). He has served as president of the Middle East Studies Association, speaks and writes widely on current events in the Middle East and US foreign policy, and is a contributing editor of *Middle East Report.*

The Contemporary Middle East 3

Series editor: Eugene L. Rogan

Books published in **The Contemporary Middle East** series address the major political, economic and social debates facing the region today. Each title comprises a survey of the available literature against the background of the author's own critical interpretation which is designed to challenge and encourage independent analysis. While the focus of the series is the Middle East and North Africa, books are presented as aspects of a rounded treatment, which cuts across disciplinary and geographic boundaries. They are intended to initiate debate in the classroom, and to foster understanding amongst professionals and policy makers.

1 Clement M. Henry and Robert Springborg, *Globalization and the Politics of Development in the Middle East* hb 0 521 62312 X pb 0 521 62631 5
2 Joel Beinin, *Workers and Peasants in the Modern Middle East* hb 0 521 62121 6 pb 0 521 62903 9

Contending Visions of the Middle East

The History and Politics of Orientalism

Second Edition

Zachary Lockman
New York University

CAMBRIDGE
UNIVERSITY PRESS

CAMBRIDGE
UNIVERSITY PRESS

University Printing House, Cambridge CB2 8BS, United Kingdom

Cambridge University Press is part of the University of Cambridge.

It furthers the University's mission by disseminating knowledge in the pursuit of education, learning and research at the highest international levels of excellence.

www.cambridge.org
Information on this title: www.cambridge.org/9780521133074

© Cambridge University Press 2010

First published 2004
Sixth printing 2008
Second edition 2010
4th printing 2013

A catalogue record for this publication is available from the British Library

Library of Congress Cataloguing in Publication data
Lockman, Zachary.
Contending visions of the Middle East : the history and politics of Orientalism / Zachary Lockman. – 2nd edn.
    p.   cm. – (The contemporary Middle East; 3)
Includes bibliographical references and index.
ISBN 978-0-521-11587-2 (hardback) – ISBN 978-0-521-13307-4 (paperback)
1. Middle East – Study and teaching.   2. Orientalism.   3. Islam –
20th century.   I. Title.
DS61.8.L63   2009
956.0072'01821 – dc22   2009036355

ISBN 978-0-521-13307-4 Paperback

For Maya

Contents

Maps

Acknowledgments

It will be obvious that this book draws on the work of many other scholars. They are (I hope) all properly cited in the notes and listed in the bibliography, but I thank them here for the thinking and writing that helped make this book possible. I would also like to thank Joel Beinin, Juan Cole, Brandon Fine, Bill Madsen, Eugene Rogan, James Schamus and the anonymous reader recruited by Cambridge University Press for their perceptive comments on my manuscript. I must also thank Eugene Rogan for editing the series in which this book appears, and Marigold Acland for supporting the series, and my contribution to it, with patience and good humor. As has often been the case over the years, Robert Vitalis has been a most careful reader and energetic critic. I suspect that he won't agree with everything in this book, but I hope that he will like at least some of it and recognize his influence on how it turned out. I am, as always, especially grateful to Melinda Fine, for her thoughtful readings of draft chapters and for her exceedingly generous love and support throughout this project.

I committed to writing this book soon after my younger daughter, Maya Michal Lockman-Fine, was born; by the time the first edition was published she had turned eight years old. I promised her many years ago that I would dedicate this book to her, and among the many reasons that I was happy to be done with it is that it allowed me to fulfill that promise. I have been, and always will be, grateful for her great spirit, intelligence and energy, and for the joy she brings into my life.

Preface to the second edition

On October 17, 2006, the *New York Times* published an op-ed essay by Jeff Stein, the national security editor at *Congressional Quarterly*, entitled "Can You Tell a Sunni from a Shiite?" Sectarian violence and ethnic cleansing were convulsing Iraq, US military forces there were confronting a growing insurgency, and observers were voicing concerns about the prospect of rising tensions between Sunnis and Shi'is across the Middle East. But Stein reported that many of the top counterterrorism officials he had been interviewing in Washington, along with many of the members of Congress supposedly overseeing their work, could not offer even a rudimentary explanation of the difference between Sunni and Shi'i Islam or reliably identify whether Iran, Hizbullah or al-Qa'ida were Sunni or Shi'i. "After all," Stein asked, "wouldn't British counterterrorism officials responsible for Northern Ireland know the difference between Catholics and Protestants?" His conclusion: "Too many officials in charge of the war on terrorism just don't care to learn much, if anything, about the enemy we're fighting."

In the Afterword to the first edition of this book, written half a year after the US invasion of Iraq, I noted some of the illusions and delusions that have frequently informed US policy in the Middle East, and the forms of knowledge and interpretive frameworks (some of them with long pedigrees) that have underpinned them. As I write these lines more than five years later, it would not seem that a great deal has changed. There remains a substantial gap between vision and reality, between policy and consequence, along with a great deal of the kind of willful ignorance Stein uncovered, itself perhaps best explained as a byproduct of imperial hubris. The very fact that one or another variant of the term "war on terror" is still widely accepted as a useful and accurate way of describing what the United States is actually engaged in around the world indicates that not all that much progress has been achieved; indeed, in his op-ed piece Stein himself refers to "the war on terrorism" and "counterterrorism" as if these were self-evident or unproblematic terms.

It is of course true that the Bush administration's original vision of transforming Iraq into a docile (and happily oil-rich) client of the United States lies in ruins; a majority of the American people long ago turned against the war; and much of the political and media elite now understands that the United States must find a way out of the disastrous situation it has gotten itself into in Iraq and engage more intelligently with the rest of the Middle East and the world. As I note in Chapter 7, since September 11 many Americans (including college students) have also manifested a genuine desire to learn and understand more about the rest of the world (including the Muslim world) and their country's role in it.

Yet it is not at all clear that the more fundamental lessons have been learned, despite the many trenchant critiques of US foreign policy that have been published and the wealth of resources on the Middle East and the Muslim world – and US relations with them – now widely available. Most critics of the Iraq war, at least among politicians and in policy-making circles, do not question the need to maintain US hegemony in the Middle East and beyond; they only criticize the specific means the Bush administration has employed to maintain that hegemony, as well as its spectacular incompetence. Nor do they generally ask whether the deployment of US military personnel and facilities in more countries around the world than ever before really enhances either the national security of the United States or the prospects for global security and stability. So, however the United States eventually extricates the bulk of its military forces from Iraq, the stage seems set for a continuation of many of the same policies, and thus for future interventions that will have profoundly unhappy consequences for those on the receiving end of American power.

Iraq has already provided us with an all-too-graphic demonstration of what that can mean. Hundreds of thousands of Iraqis have died as a consequence of the US invasion and occupation, many others have been wounded or maimed, millions have been displaced from their homes, and Iraqi society has been devastated. Afghanistan, where since September 11 the United States has once again become deeply involved, continues to suffer from a bloody (and currently escalating) insurgency and the apparent absence of an effective state, and neighboring Pakistan is now being sucked into the maelstrom. Meanwhile, a range of other internal and interstate conflicts in the Middle East, including the Israeli–Palestinian conflict, continue to fester, with sporadic explosions of violence, even as the social, economic and political situation in much of the region deteriorates.

In the meantime, the fraught relationship between scholarly knowledge and the needs of the state continues to demand attention, as it has since at least the Second World War. On this front there is perhaps hope that scholars have learned some useful lessons. For example, in 2007 news surfaced of the "Human Terrain System," a $40 million Pentagon program that involved "embedding" social scientists with counter-insurgency units in Iraq and Afghanistan so that the military could more effectively benefit from scholars' knowledge of local societies, cultures and languages. The American Anthropological Association (AAA) promptly investigated and issued a report highlighting the serious ethical issues raised by the direct participation of anthropologists in military operations and intelligence activity. The AAA and other organizations and individuals also voiced concerns about the Pentagon's Project Minerva, announced in 2008 and designed to promote and fund research by university-based scholars on issues deemed important to national security, for example the development of the Chinese military and the "strategic impact of religious and cultural changes within the Islamic world." This immediately evoked memories of the Project Camelot fiasco, discussed in Chapter 4, and led to calls that such research be funded and managed through institutions that are independent of the military/intelligence establishment and that adhere to standard academic procedures, including peer review.

Many of the issues discussed in this book concerning the relationship between knowledge (of the Middle East and the Muslim world) and power (largely American, in this period) thus continue to be all too relevant today, and I therefore continue to hope that a better understanding of the origins and development of the study of Islam and the Middle East in the West, and particularly in the United States since the Second World War, may remain useful. In revising this book for a second edition I have focused on Chapter 7, where I now discuss the atmosphere in which US Middle East studies has operated in recent years, particularly the wave of politically motivated attacks on scholars of the Middle East and Islam and on the institutions at which they are based. Limitations on space have prevented me from delving into the spate of scholarly work on the history and politics of Orientalism, Arabic and Islamic studies, and Middle East studies which has appeared since the first edition was published. However, I cannot resist briefly mentioning three relatively recent works on Orientalism.

The first is Robert Irwin's 2006 book *Dangerous Knowledge: Orientalism and its Discontents*, published in the United Kingdom under a more lurid and provocative title, *For Lust of Knowing: The Orientalists and their Enemies*. I find this a quirky, indeed rather odd, book, though also quite entertaining in its own way. Irwin offers a comprehensive survey of individual Orientalist scholars through the centuries but is largely uninterested in interpretive paradigms and their links with power, imperial or otherwise; and he displays an *ad hominem* animus toward Edward W. Said that strikes me as both excessive and intellectually counterproductive. *Dangerous Knowledge* is nonetheless worth reading, particularly for its lively portraits of scholars, their idiosyncrasies and their milieux.

Then there is Daniel Martin Varisco's *Reading Orientalism: Said and the Unsaid* (2007), which the author describes as "judicious satirical criticism" directed at the "polemicized rhetoric" of Said's *Orientalism*. I find this book neither judicious nor successfully satirical, and too much of it rehashes (often tendentiously, if in great detail) the many useful critiques of *Orientalism* advanced over the past three decades. Finally, in contrast to both Irwin and Varisco, *Genealogies of Orientalism: History, Theory, Politics* (2008), edited by Edmund Burke III and David Prochaska, offers a set of thoughtful essays that engage critically but productively with aspects of Said's intellectual legacy and illuminate ongoing scholarly conversations about Orientalism, colonialism, nationalism, modernity and the writing of history.

There is certainly a good deal of other work, published or on the way, on the histories and issues addressed in this book, and there is much more research yet to be done before we will be anywhere near an adequate scholarly understanding of the development of the kinds of knowledge discussed in this book, and of the politics with which they have been enmeshed. As I freely acknowledge in the Introduction, this book is meant only as an introduction; it makes no claim to offer the final word on any subject.

Meanwhile, despite the grim situation that prevails today in much of the Middle East and the rather uncongenial climate in US academia, scholars writing within and on the field of Middle East studies broadly defined continue to produce much excellent work, teach their students and train new cohorts of scholars and teachers. I hope that this new edition will be useful for them, as well as for a wider public interested in understanding how a part of the world in which the United States remains so deeply entangled has been studied and portrayed.

January 2009

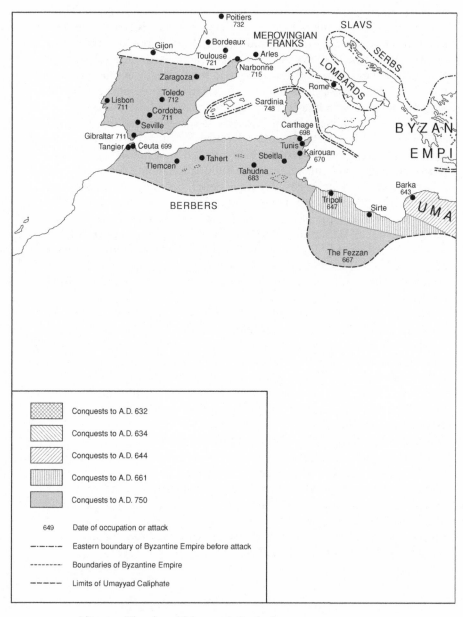

Map 1: The rise of Islam and the Arab conquests

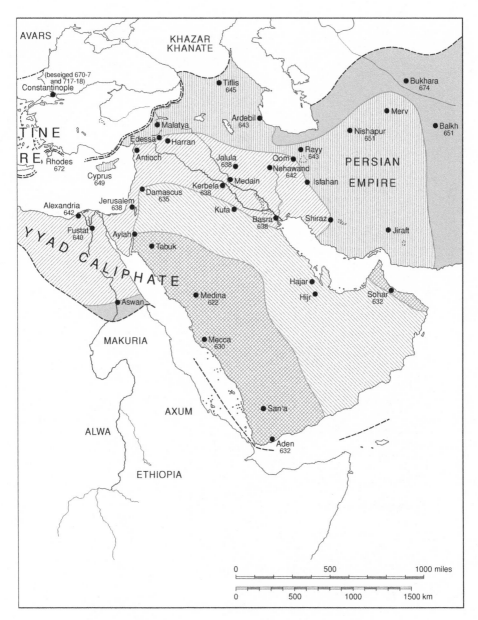

Map 1: (*cont.*)

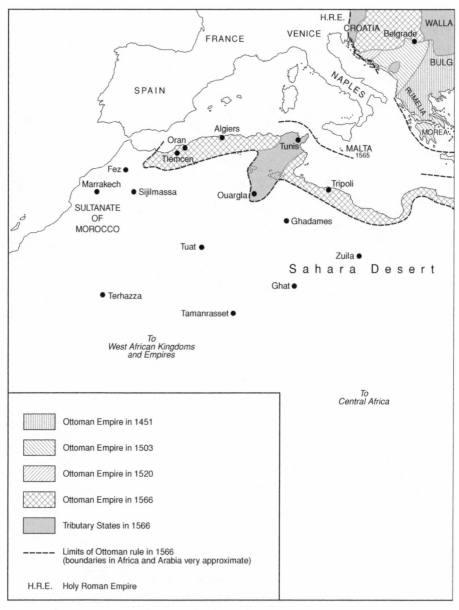

Map 2: The Ottoman empire to 1566

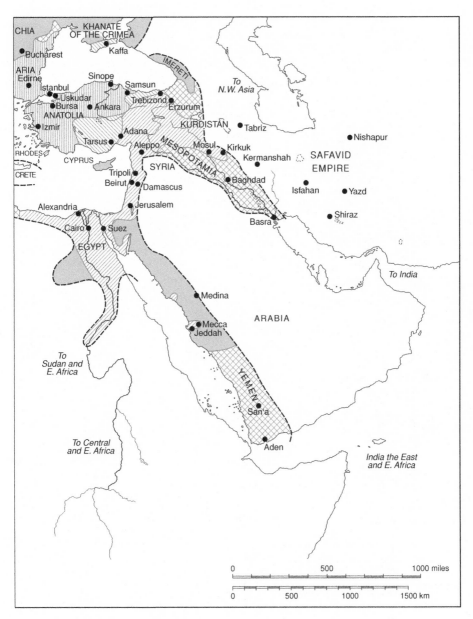

Map 2: (cont.)

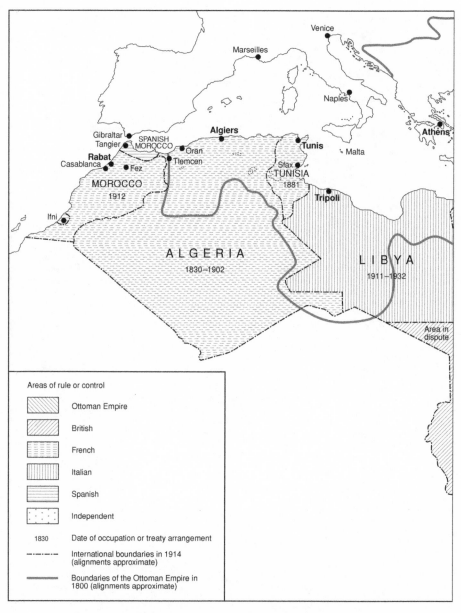

Map 3: The Middle East and North Africa on the eve of the First World War

Map 3: (cont.)

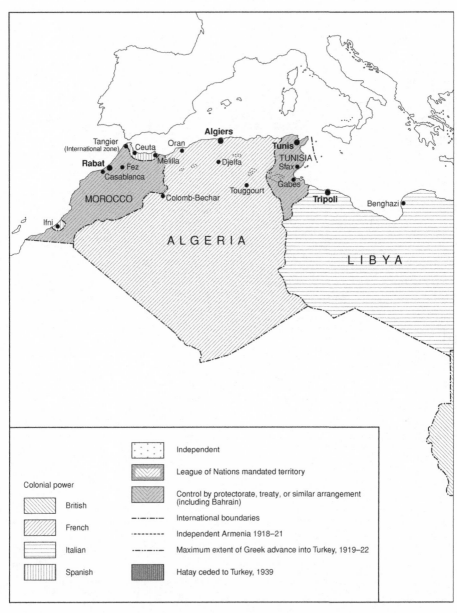

Map 4:   The Middle East and North Africa between the two World Wars

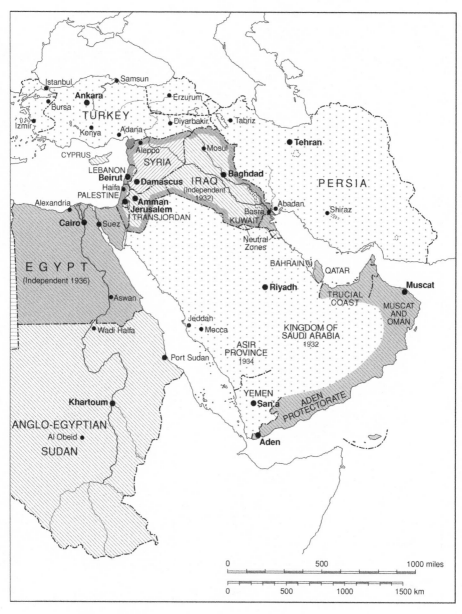

Map 4: (cont.)

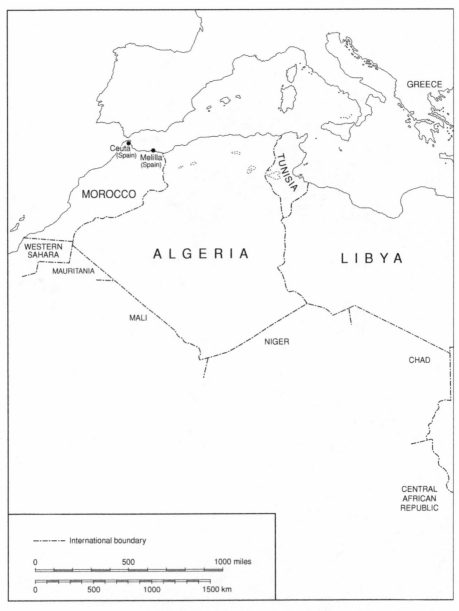

Map 5: The Middle East and North Africa – boundaries

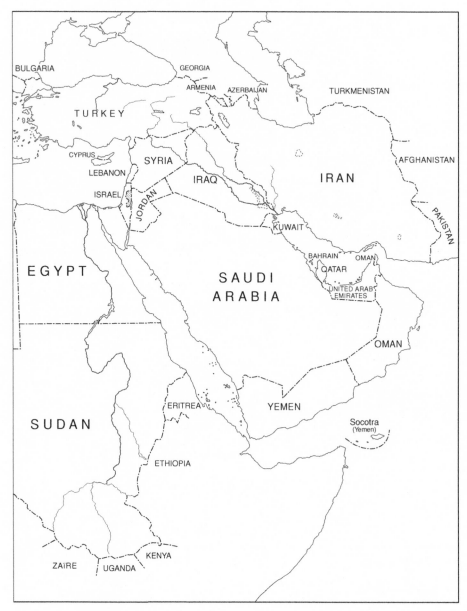

Map 5: (*cont.*)

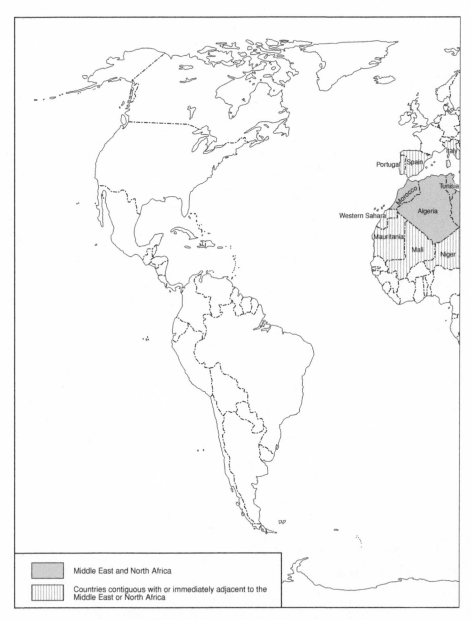

Map 6: The Middle East and North Africa in the world

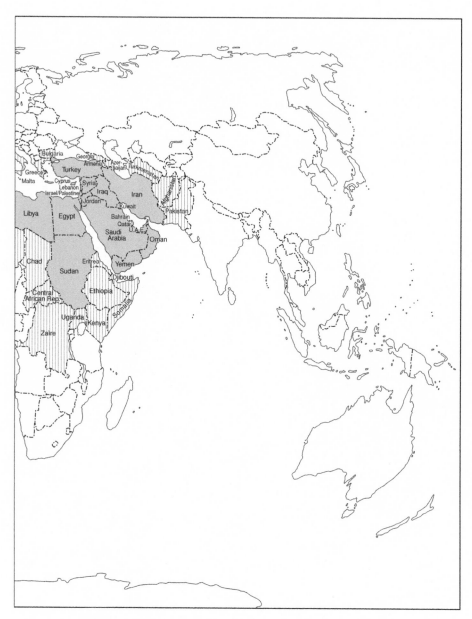

Map 6: (*cont.*)

Introduction

Perhaps it would be best to begin by explaining what this book is *not*. It is not, and does not purport to be, a detailed, comprehensive history of the study either of Islam or of the region that has come to be called the Middle East, as conducted by scholars and others in what has come to be called the West. Nor does it claim to be a full-scale, in-depth scholarly analysis of the origins, development, character and implications of Western perceptions of, and attitudes toward, Islam, Muslims, Arabs, Iranians, or the Middle East.

This book's purpose is much more modest. It seeks, first of all, to introduce readers to the history of the sometimes overlapping enterprises known as Orientalism, Oriental studies, Islamic studies and Middle East studies as practiced in the West, with particular attention to the United States from the mid-twentieth century onward. It does not attempt to identify or discuss all the scholars, writers, artists, travelers, texts, schools of thought or institutions involved in studying, commenting on or depicting Islam, the Middle East or the broader Orient over the past millennium and a half. Rather, it explores broad trends, some particularly influential interpretive paradigms and theoretical approaches, important debates and significant transitions, along with their political, social and cultural contexts, largely by focusing on a selection of representative individuals, illustrative texts, key institutions and important developments.

A better understanding of how the Middle East and Islam have been perceived, understood, studied and depicted would seem to be more important today than ever before, especially for Americans. The United States is in our time very deeply engaged in the Middle East and in other predominantly Muslim parts of the world. That engagement, which goes back more than half a century, has had complex political, military, economic and cultural dimensions and powerful consequences, not only for the peoples of the Middle East but also for ourselves, as the events of September 11, 2001 brought home all too tragically. Those events, but also much else in the tangled, often painful history of US involvement in the Middle East over the past six decades, demonstrate that Americans cannot afford to remain as uninformed as they have generally been about the histories, politics and cultures of that region. Nor can we any longer trust blindly in the assurances, predictions and promises of those in power or in the kinds of knowledge about the Middle East and Islam which have often been used to shape and justify the policies they have pursued.

As this book seeks to show, there has been over the past several decades a great deal of criticism of, and controversy over, the ways in which the peoples, politics and cultures of the Middle East have been studied in the United States, the kind of knowledge that has been produced about this part of the world, and the implications and consequences of that knowledge. These disputes among scholars who study the Middle East or Islam often stem from fundamental disagreements over which approach, concepts, interpretive framework or methods should be used in order to best understand what it is they are studying; indeed, as we will see, there has even been substantial disagreement over how scholars should define what it is that they are studying.

As in other academic fields and disciplines in the humanities and social sciences, scholars studying the Middle East or Islam have, explicitly or implicitly, drawn on one or another interpretive framework, model or paradigm – often rooted in a broader vision about how the world works (or ought to work) – in order to make sense of whatever historical period or social institution or event or process they were seeking to understand or explain. Each of these approaches has its own (often unacknowledged) premises, analytical categories and preferred methods, and each defines what is being studied in a different way. Each approach or interpretive framework thus tends to treat certain aspects or features of the society or culture or place or period they are studying as important while ignoring or downplaying others; each explains how and why things change (or do not change) differently; each prescribes certain types of sources, and methods for exploring them, as most useful or relevant for the scholarly task at hand. Moreover, these differing (and sometimes diametrically opposed) paradigms always take shape within, and are thus influenced by, complex historical and contemporary contexts, involving (among other things) personalities and personal networks, generational inclinations and shifts, political contention, cultural trends and conflicts, and institutional developments.

Scholars who study the emergence and development of scholarly fields and disciplines often refer to the contexts, arguments, conflicts and processes which affect the production, dissemination and reception of knowledge in a particular field or discipline as its "politics" or its "politics of knowledge." Understanding something about the politics of knowledge in Islamic and Middle East studies, and the alternative ways of understanding Islam and the Middle East in the modern world which scholars advocate and argue about, is important for several reasons. For one, scholars and students engaged in this field would, one might think, benefit from a better understanding of its origins, history and debates. But I would also like to hope that a better grasp of the politics of contemporary Middle East studies might enable ordinary Americans to make better sense of what is going on in the Middle East, and to more effectively assess the policies advocated by government officials, politicians, pundits and "talking heads" on television, since those policies are often rooted in, and justified by, certain (often much disputed) ways of understanding the Middle East and the wider Muslim world initially elaborated by scholars.

That is why, after offering a largely narrative account of the emergence and development of what would eventually be called Islamic or Oriental studies that takes us from ancient Greece down to the twentieth century, this book narrows its focus to explore in greater depth the politics of knowledge in US Middle East studies over the past half-century. After a chapter centered on the emergence of the new field of Middle East studies in the United States and its Cold War contexts, I turn to the critiques of the key intellectual paradigm that initially underpinned that field, but also of Orientalism as a scholarly discipline, that gathered force in the 1960s and 1970s. There follows a chapter devoted to Edward W. Said's very influential 1978 book *Orientalism*, its critical reception and its longer-term impact and consequences. A final chapter discusses subsequent developments in US Middle East studies, bringing us to the aftermath of the attacks of September 11, 2001 and the US occupation of Iraq in 2003.

My chief concern in this part of the book is how different theories, models or modes of interpretation have shaped the kinds of questions scholars have asked about the Middle East or Islam (and therefore what answers they have come up with), the methods and sources they have used, and the meaning they have given to the results of their inquiries. In so doing the book also calls attention to the historical contexts, and the specific political, social, cultural and economic forces and factors which have contributed to the emergence and acceptance – among scholars and in society at large – of certain interpretive paradigms, as well as to the social and political interests which have been served by the adoption of one way of construing reality rather than another.

Having argued for the importance of paying attention to the politics of knowledge in this field, I hasten to add that we need to be very careful not to conflate a particular theoretical or interpretive approach with, or to explain it solely or even mainly in terms of, bias, prejudice, stereotyping or racism. As we will see, for many centuries – indeed, down to the present day – a good many people in the West, including the ostensibly learned, have embraced and espoused crude prejudices about Islam, Muslims, Arabs and others. However, for purposes of analysis at least, we need to distinguish clearly between such sentiments, however repellent or pernicious, on the one hand, and on the other the interpretive framework embraced by an individual scholar or by a group of scholars in a given field. As we will see, there have been a substantial number of scholars who were highly respectful of Islam and empathetic toward its adherents' beliefs and aspirations but who nonetheless produced work which critics have argued is implicitly or explicitly informed by a questionable interpretive framework. So while I will certainly be noting instances of prejudice, stereotyping and racism in scholarship on Islam and the Middle East, I will also be insisting that it is important to distinguish such attitudes from the interpretive frameworks which scholars use; these are, analytically at least, two different things, though they all too often coincide and can be hard to separate.

I should also acknowledge at the outset that there have been, and continue to be, scholars of the Middle East and Islam (as well as scholars in other fields and disciplines) who reject the entire notion of a politics of knowledge and insist that their own scholarly impartiality, critical faculties and good judgment, along with the use of tried-and-true scholarly methods, allow them to produce knowledge that is not informed by any implicit or explicit theory, model or vision of the world but is simply and objectively true. They might be said to take their motto from police sergeant Jack Webb's favorite line in the old television series *Dragnet*: "Just the facts, ma'am."

Adherents of this epistemological position, which (depending on how it is formulated and implemented) may be characterized as empiricism or positivism, insist that they simply examine the facts, which are deemed to "speak for themselves," and derive their analyses directly from them, without allowing any presuppositions, theory, political viewpoint, social values or personal prejudices to affect their judgment. In contrast, they tend to see their epistemological opponents – those who see the production of knowledge as always involving some degree of interpretation and judgment and as always influenced by historical contexts – as wrongly injecting a distorting political and subjective element into what should be the politically neutral, objective world of scholarship.

Of course, scholars who see knowledge as socially produced or constructed respond by insisting that what we believe we know about the human world, what we take to be true about whatever aspect of human social life past or present we are interested in, is never simply the product of the direct observation of reality and our capacity for reasoning. Rather, attaining such knowledge always entails resort to some (often implicit and unacknowledged) theory, interpretive stance or exercise of judgment. Nor do the facts ever really speak for themselves in any simple sense. What we deem to be a fact, which facts we deem to be significant, which questions we want our data to help us answer, and how we go about producing an explanation of something – all these involve making choices, which again means interpretation, judgment, some notion or theory or vision of how the world is put together and can be understood. Facts thus do not stand entirely on their own: they come to make sense within a theoretical or interpretive framework which specifies that they are indeed facts, that is, true statements about reality, and that it is *this* set of facts and not some other that counts, that tells us what is really going on. And the emergence, dissemination and decline of the contending scholarly frameworks of interpretation, the many alternative possible ways of comprehending the social world, are always bound up, if in complex ways, with broader contexts and developments.[1]

Given this book's title and its substance, it will be obvious that I share the perspective outlined in the preceding paragraph. However, to argue that the facts do not simply speak for themselves, that knowledge and truth are not immediately and self-evidently available to us but are embedded within systems of meaning generated and embraced by human beings and human societies, and further that social interests have something to do with how knowledge is produced and received, is not necessarily to argue that facts mean absolutely nothing or that all the different stories one could tell about reality are equally true or valid. Even as we recognize that how we interpret reality is not the simple outcome of direct and unmediated observation (or of experimentation, for the "hard" sciences), we are entitled to establish, and demand adherence to, what we might call community standards for truth, broadly agreed-upon ways of selecting and treating relevant data and of making, supporting and challenging arguments, as well as procedures for avoiding gross distortion, not to mention fabrication.

This is something scholars in specific fields and disciplines have long done, and it is what makes it possible for them to talk with one another and collectively judge (or at least constructively argue about) the accuracy and utility of alternative interpretations and narratives. I certainly believe that my interpretation here is a reasonable one that conforms to the procedures and standards my fellow historians and other scholars have established in order to advance knowledge and avoid the production and dissemination of tendentious distortions and outright falsehoods, and I hope that those who read this book will agree.

Because I wanted the nonspecialist audience for which this book is intended to find it as accessible as possible, and because it could not be too long, I had to make a great many decisions about what to discuss and what to leave out. Among other things I opted, once I got to the twentieth century, not to address work by, and debates among, French, German, Russian/Soviet or other scholars of the Middle East or Islam who were (or are) neither American nor British, or their political and institutional settings. This is not to suggest that those scholars and settings are unimportant; it is simply that, linguistic constraints aside, one of my chief goals for this book was to provide an introduction to how the Middle East, Islam and related issues have been studied and argued about in the United States over the past half-century and thereby to help Americans acquire a better understanding of the implications and consequences of some of the kinds of knowledge which have over recent decades framed both US government policy in the Middle East and popular perceptions of the region and its peoples.

Nonetheless, I expect that some of those who read this book will deem some of my choices, as well as my overall approach and specific interpretations and judgments, idiosyncratic, wrong-headed, inaccurate or even perverse. I am in fact not so concerned with those who fundamentally reject this book's basic approach, from which its specific analyses and arguments flow: it is clearly written from a particular intellectual, disciplinary, political and moral standpoint. It also reflects my two decades of experience as a university-based teacher of modern Middle Eastern history and my sense of what American college and university students know (or what is sometimes worse, think they know) and don't know about the Middle East and Islam, and what *I* think they need to know. In addition, it has been shaped by what I have learned from the time and energy I have invested in trying to help Americans outside the academy acquire a better understanding of the Middle East and the Muslim world, and of the role of the United States in them, a commitment which this book seeks to further.

I will not be surprised if those who understand the world in ways that are diametrically opposed to my own do not like this book. In fact, I would feel as if I were doing something wrong if they were not unhappy with what I had to say. But I do regret any annoyance or disappointment that this book may engender among those who may be broadly sympathetic to its thrust or purpose but are unhappy about what they see as my failure to deal with, or properly treat, what they believe to be critical scholars, texts, trends and debates.

In response I can only hope that disgruntled readers will keep in mind what I said at the outset: this is an *introductory* survey, intended primarily not for scholarly specialists but for students and for a wider reading public. There is clearly much more to be said about the issues I have addressed here (and about many others I have not), and I hope that other people will go ahead and say them – though I would also point out that a great deal more research is needed before we have anything like an adequate scholarly understanding of the histories of Islamic studies and Middle East studies as they have developed in Europe and the United States. If this book helps generate discussion, stimulate intelligent and constructive criticism, and encourage further research and writing, I will feel as if I have done something right.

Because this book is itself something of an extended historiographical essay, it would be redundant to devote space in this introduction to a systematic review of the extensive literature on Orientalism and related topics. But I hope that readers will compare, at their leisure, this book's similarities with, and differences from, other relatively recent synthetic works on the Western study of Islam and the Middle East. At the risk of offending the authors of the many other works which I have found useful, I will mention here only Maxime Rodinson's *Europe and the Mystique of Islam* and Thierry Hentsch's *Imagining the Middle East*. Both are very valuable contributions to the literature, but my specific purposes, interests and intended audience have led me to produce a rather different kind of study. The same applies to Alexander Lyon Macfie's *Orientalism*, which I first read only after I had substantially completed the manuscript of this book. Though Macfie covers some of the same ground as I do, especially with regard to the material in Chapters 5 and 6, this book ranges much more widely, is much more concerned with historical, political and institutional contexts, and deploys a very different analytical framework. I would also call readers' attention to *Orientalism: A Reader,* the very useful collection of readings on Orientalism which Macfie has compiled.

In the end, of course, in addition to assuming responsibility for any factual errors, I must leave it to my readers to render final judgment on the virtues and defects of this book, in its own right, in relation to comparable work and, last but not least, in terms of its avowed purposes.

1   In the beginning

In this chapter I explore some of the ways in which Christians living in the region that we think of today as western Europe during the medieval period came to perceive Islam, the new faith that emerged in the Arabian peninsula in the third decade of the seventh century and rapidly spread across much of the world as it was then known to them. As we will see, even the initial western Christian perceptions of Islam and of its adherents did not come out of nowhere or develop in a vacuum. Seventh-century "Europeans" – of course they did not think of themselves as Europeans at the time – already possessed concepts and categories through which this new and frightening phenomenon could be made sense of. Some of these concepts and categories, and the images they generated, would prove quite durable over much of the medieval period, though by the end of this period a handful of scholars had begun to lay the basis for a somewhat better understanding of Islam.

To adequately understand the development of western Christian images of Islam, it is helpful to go even further back in time, to ancient Greece and Rome, and there begin to explore the origins and evolution of the idea of a "Europe" and a "West" often deemed essentially different from an "East." Over the succeeding centuries these and other ideas and images would be drawn on, in different ways and in changing contexts, to underpin certain ways of dividing the world and categorizing its parts, and thus of understanding Islam.

To begin with ancient Greece and Rome and to discuss medieval western European understandings of Islam is not to suggest that there was any continuous or monolithic Western image of, or attitude toward, the East or Islam stretching from antiquity through the medieval era down to the modern period. But as we will see, at various points over that very long span of time, some European scholars, writers and others appropriated certain images and notions about the East and Islam from what they had come to perceive as Europe's distinctive past, refashioned them in keeping with their own contemporary concerns, and propagated them as relevant for their own time. It is this process of selective borrowing and creative recycling, which goes on even today, that makes delving into early images and attitudes useful for understanding how Islam and the Middle East would come to be understood and portrayed even in the modern era.

The cradle of the West?

"Ancient Greece" is itself a term that requires some unpacking. What would much later be given this label, as if it were a unified and coherent entity, more accurately denotes a rather diverse collection of city-states, principalities, towns, villages and islands inhabited largely (but not exclusively) by speakers of some dialect of Greek. After centuries of expansion this zone encompassed a large geographical area, from Athens and Sparta and Corinth and Thebes and other city-states located in what is today Greece eastward to the many Greek ("Hellenic" would be better) settlements in Asia Minor ("Little Asia," today Anatolia in Turkey), south and east to the islands of the Aegean and Mediterranean seas, northward into southeastern Europe and along the coasts of the Adriatic and Black seas, and westward to the settlements established by Greeks in what are today Italy and southern France.

Many centuries later, Europeans would come to identify ancient Greece, and particularly Athens in its "golden age" (about 500–400 BCE), as the source of core components of the thought and culture of what they had come to call "Western civilization," indeed as the "cradle" of that civilization, the time and place in which it originated. This identification rests on the notion – popular in the nineteenth century and still powerful today – that over the past four or five thousand years the histories of the myriad peoples and cultures of the world can be most usefully grasped in terms of the successive rise and fall of various civilizations. In this view, each civilization constitutes a more or less coherent entity with its own distinctive core values, beliefs and principles, its own unifying spirit or essence, which clearly sets it apart from other civilizations with different core values and beliefs, different spirits or essences. Furthermore, civilizations are often deemed to have a life cycle similar to that of human beings: they are born in some specific time and place; when young they are vigorous, flexible, creative, able to absorb new ideas; they grow to maturity and reach the height of their cultural and political powers in a "golden age"; then they gradually lose their cultural energy, they grow less creative and innovative, more rigid and insular; and finally they decline toward social stasis and cultural senescence, until they disappear from the scene or are absorbed by some other younger and more vigorous civilization.

I will discuss this conception of history and of how humanity can best be divided up, and how Islam fits into it, more fully later on. For now let us keep in mind that the ancient Greeks did of course not see themselves as Europeans or Westerners, much less as the originators of anything resembling "Western" or "European" civilization. Rather, they regarded themselves as a distinctive and culturally superior people surrounded by less advanced "barbarians," by which the Greeks meant all those who spoke not Greek but some other language, disparaged as gibberish. Moreover, though many European scholars would later depict Greek culture in the "classical" period of antiquity as wholly new and unique, as an achievement of incomparable genius which the ancient Greeks created virtually out of nothing, we know that in fact the Greeks were very much influenced by, and borrowed from, the cultures of their older, richer and more powerful neighbors to the south and east. These included mighty Egypt, the various empires which arose in the fertile and densely populated lands between the Tigris and the Euphrates rivers (Mesopotamia, from the Greek for "between the rivers"), and the Phoenicians, who originated along what is today the coast of Lebanon and who, like the Greeks, ranged far and wide across the Mediterranean Sea as traders and settlers.[1]

This is not to say that the philosophers, poets, playwrights, historians and scientists of ancient Greece did not create anything new and distinctive; of course they did. But it is also clear that ancient Greek culture did not exist in a vacuum, that it was always influenced by the cultures of the surrounding peoples (and vice versa), and thus that what the ancient Greeks achieved rested on, and was interwoven with, the achievements of other peoples and cultures. Similarly, while our culture, language and politics are still influenced by elements of classical Greek culture, we need to be very careful about tracing the historical origins of ideas and institutions back into the distant past. We may be able to find what appears to be a familiar idea or institution in some earlier historical setting, but it probably meant something very different in that setting than it would later.

For example, Athens of the fifth century BCE is often depicted – indeed, revered – as the first democracy, the ancestor of today's western democracies. But in fact the political institutions of ancient Athens, and what those institutions meant to Athenians, were in many important ways different from what we understand by democratic political institutions today. As a result, to trace a more or less direct link between fifth-century Athens and today's United States or Britain is to distort history by projecting our own conceptions onto the past and assuming that they were shared by the ancient Greeks, whose vision of the world and conception of themselves were in many ways radically different from, indeed alien to, our own.

As I will discuss later with reference to Islam, this is precisely why treating the West or Islam as self-evidently distinct civilizations has come in for such heavy criticism in recent decades. This way of thinking about the world presumes that the West and Islam each has its own unique and unchanging essence or character which gives it its coherence and continuity across time and space. In this way it becomes plausible, for example, to link the fifth-century Athenian city-state and twentieth-century American democracy as if they were both essentially the same thing, that is, merely different stages in the evolution of the same Western civilization, or to explain today's Islamic political movements by what happened in western Arabia in the seventh century CE, as if both are simply manifestations of an essentially unchanging entity called Islam.

Conceptions of the world

It is in any case to the ancient Greeks that we owe some of the key geographical terms which would for centuries underpin European conceptions of the world, as well as some of the connotations and images bound up with the distinction they drew between East and West. In Greek mythology Europa was a daughter of the king of Tyre (a city-state on the eastern Mediterranean coast, in what is today Lebanon) whom the god Zeus fell in love with and carried off; numerous legends developed around Europa, her siblings (including her half-sisters Asia and Libya) and her offspring. Somehow the mythological Europa came to be associated with, and gave her name to, a particular region: first the mainland of Greece (as opposed to the Aegean islands), later all of Greece including those islands, and then by extension the Greek-colonized lands to the north and west and the regions beyond, inhabited by those whom the Greeks considered barbarians.

At first the Greeks espoused a vision of the habitable world as naturally divided into two parts: Europe to the west of the Aegean Sea, the Black Sea and the Bosporus straits which connect the two, and Asia to the east of those waters. Somewhat later Greek geographers and philosophers settled on a tripartite division of the landmass that constituted what they believed to be the dry portion of the earth. Surrounding the Mediterranean Sea, which they believed was situated in the center of the landmass (hence its name: "middle of the earth"), lay Europe to the north, Asia to the east, and Libya (also called Africa, meaning the lands of northern Africa west of Egypt) to the south. These lands were in turn surrounded by a great ocean. But there continued to be disagreement over this division of the world into three zones and over the boundaries that separated these zones, and not everyone located the Greeks in Europe. For example, writing in the fourth century BCE Aristotle compared the inhabitants of the cold lands of Europe, "full of spirit but somewhat deficient in intelligence and skill" and therefore free but politically disorganized and incapable of ruling over others, with the natives of the warmer lands of Asia who were "intelligent and skillful in temperament, but lack spirit, so they are in continuous subjugation and slavery." However, Aristotle portrayed the Greeks as neither European nor Asian but rather as a distinct people who by virtue of their intermediate location between the two continents were endowed with the best qualities of both. Several centuries later the geographer and historian Strabo (c. 63 BCE–21 CE) would point out that "in giving names to the three continents, the Greeks did not take into consideration the whole habitable earth, but merely their own country, and the land exactly opposite . . . "[2]

Nonetheless, we can discern among the ancient Greeks a fairly well-developed image of the social and political character of the peoples and states of Asia, an image that much later would be drawn on by western Europeans to underpin the sharp dichotomization of East and West and that would eventually be applied to Islam. In large measure this image seems to have been a legacy of the Greeks' long conflict with the Persians, who established a powerful state based in the Iranian plateau and whose efforts to expand westward threatened the independence of the Greek city-states and their own hopes for expansion. When he died in 529 BCE Kurush (whom the Greeks called Cyrus), "great king" or "king of kings" of the Persians, ruled over a vast empire that comprised much of what is today Iran as well as Armenia, the former Babylonian empire (including Mesopotamia, Syria and Palestine), and Anatolia, home to numerous Greek settlements, and his armies were already threatening the Greek heartland. His successors would go on to conquer Egypt and invade southeastern Europe. The Greek city-states, led by Athens, fought a series of wars with the Persians, on land and at sea, over several decades. In 480 BCE a Persian army captured and burned Athens, but eventually the Persians were defeated and compelled to withdraw from Greek lands. Relations between the Persian empire and the Greek states and colonies eventually became less hostile, even relatively normal, and when in the fourth century the Greek city-states fought among themselves for hegemony, some of them would make alliances with their former enemy Persia against their fellow Greeks.

Nonetheless, the Greeks' long struggle to resist Persian domination and the ways in which they came to understand what differentiated them from the Persian enemy, coupled with their firm confidence in their cultural superiority over the "barbarians" (i.e., everyone else), left an important legacy, already evident in the passage from Aristotle quoted earlier. In the writings of philosophers, geographers and historians, and in the work of playwrights and poets, the Greeks often contrasted themselves with Asians in rather stark and essentialized terms – that is, in terms that framed the differences between Greeks and Asians as fundamental, as stemming from their entirely different natures. Asian states (like the Persian empire or Egypt of the pharaohs) were, these Greeks asserted, ruled by tyrants, despots whose power was absolute; the people were servile, virtually slaves; society was hierarchical, rigid, almost socially immobile, with an immense, indeed unbridgeable, gap between ruler and ruled; Asian despots and their courts might be immensely wealthy and powerful but they were also vulgar, corrupt and immoral. By contrast, the Greeks tended to depict themselves as a virtuous, modest people who treasured their liberty above all else; the city-state, the *polis*, was composed of free citizens mindful of their civic rights and obligations and resistant to tyranny. Roman political philosophers would later draw on some of these images of the ancient Greek city-state and of its purported opposite, the despotisms of Asia. As we will see in Chapter 2, from the fifteenth century onward many western European political theorists would do something similar, claiming for contemporary Europeans the virtues and characteristics which the Greeks attributed to themselves, in ways that still influence Western social and political thought.[3]

The images which the Greeks formulated of themselves and of their "others" – those they saw as essentially different from themselves – and the sharp polarity between Europe and Asia, between West and East, which those images buttressed, had little to do with reality. Most of the Greek city-states were far from being democracies in any sense of that term; they were monarchies or tyrannies or oligarchies, ruled by kings or strongmen or elites drawn from powerful local families, clans or factions. Even in Athens, which many later political thinkers would acclaim as the ideal democratic polity, the wealthy and powerful dominated public life, while free citizens constituted only a minority of the population; women were excluded from political life and slaves (usually of Asian origin) made up a large proportion of the city's inhabitants and produced much of its wealth. For Aristotle as for many other Greeks, Asians (and by extension all barbarians) were naturally servile and were thus well suited to serve the superior Greeks. At the same time, the societies to which the Greeks contrasted themselves so sharply – late Pharaonic Egypt, the Persia of Cyrus, Darius and Xerxes, and other states and empires of ancient Asia – were all very different from one another. Each experienced profound social, political and cultural changes over time, and none of these complex, dynamic societies conformed very neatly to the stereotype of what would much later be termed "Oriental despotism," with an all-powerful ruler lording it over an abject mass of semi-slaves. ("Oriental," derived from Latin, means "eastern," and "the Orient" would later come to refer to the Asian lands to the southeast of Europe, stretching all the way to China.)

Moreover, the East/West divide was not really as sharp as it would later appear to many European scholars and thinkers. Greece continued to be influenced by Persian and other eastern cultures after the Persian wars ended, and when the Macedonian king Alexander ("the Great," reigned 336–323 BCE) defeated and conquered the Persian empire, and much else besides, he promptly adopted the Persian style of kingship and seems to have envisioned the fusion of his own Hellenic culture with that of Persia, much of which he greatly admired. After Alexander's death his empire broke up into smaller states ruled by his generals. While the dynasties they founded promoted Hellenistic culture, whose influence in the region was considerable, they also adopted many elements of older local cultures, often in novel and creative combinations.

Roman legacies

Roman scholars generally adopted the East/West polarity developed by the Greeks, along with the division of the world into three parts, just as they borrowed so much else from the Greeks. But for the Romans that polarity does not seem to have had the same political or emotional significance that it had had for the Greeks. From their initial base in central Italy the Romans gradually expanded north and west into what they called Gaul (western Europe), Spain and Britain, as well as south across the Mediterranean to northern Africa, east into Greece and the Balkans (southeastern Europe) and on into Asia Minor and Syria, Palestine and Egypt. The empire they created thus encompassed all the lands around the Mediterranean Sea, which the Romans saw as the center of their realm, with an extension into western Europe. Political unity laid the basis for economic unity and the development of a flourishing long-distance trade, by land and by sea, across the empire as well as with India and even China.

The Romans sometimes used the terms Europe and Asia to denote western and eastern parts of the empire, and they fought a series of wars with the kingdom of the Parthians, based in the Iranian plateau. But as one scholar has put it, the Romans – unlike the Greeks – tended to use the term "Asiatic" pejoratively "only in a literary sense – bombastic and over elaborate composition could be thus described."[4] Some Roman writers and politicians decried what they regarded as the morally corrupting influence of the East, but by "East" they often meant Greece, whose culture they saw as "soft," as lacking in the manly and martial virtues which they believed had allowed the Romans to conquer and rule so vast an empire. Nonetheless, religions, ideas and customs deriving from the eastern Mediterranean lands and beyond (including Christianity) had a significant impact on Roman culture during the imperial period, and over time the empire's cultural and political center of gravity shifted eastward, toward its wealthier, more urbanized and more secure provinces at the eastern end of the Mediterranean.

This development was manifested most dramatically in the decision in 330 CE by the emperor Constantine (reigned 312–337 CE) to move the capital of his empire from Rome eastward to the city he named Constantinople, after himself – today's Istanbul, located on the Bosporus, the waterway which constituted the traditional boundary between Europe and Asia. Constantine also made Christianity, which originated as a Jewish sect in Roman-ruled Palestine but had developed into a separate religion and spread to the point where Christians constituted a numerically significant and increasingly powerful minority, the state religion of the Roman empire. Later, in 395, the empire was divided into two parts, each with its own emperor. During the fifth century the western Roman empire faded out of existence, overrun by Germanic and other peoples who established smaller kingdoms in what had been Roman-ruled Italy, Gaul, Spain and Britain.

Much later, some historians of Rome would attribute the downfall of the western Roman empire to "infection" by the vices of the East, which allegedly undermined the virtues which had once made Rome great. We can see this in Edward Gibbon's enormously popular and influential *History of the Decline and Fall of the Roman Empire*, the six volumes of which were first published between 1776 and 1788. For example, Gibbon (1737–94) asserted that "the manly pride of the Romans, content with substantial power, had left to the vanity of the East the forms and ceremonies of ostentatious greatness. But when they lost even the semblance of those virtues which were derived from their ancient freedom, the simplicity of Roman manners was insensibly corrupted by the stately affectation of the courts of Asia."[5] By framing history in this manner, by very selectively choosing which elements of Rome's culture and history to include in the "heritage" it supposedly bequeathed to Western civilization and by ignoring less pleasant aspects or blaming them (and even the decline of the western Roman empire itself) on corrupting oriental influences, Gibbon and others who helped shape European thought both built on and further buttressed the old and often highly charged dichotomy between East and West, between Europe and Asia.

In so doing they also tended to marginalize the eastern Roman empire, which scholars would call Byzantium (after the original name of Constantinople) and which would survive for another thousand years after the collapse of the western Roman empire. Though its language of administration and high culture came to be Greek rather than Latin, Byzantium saw itself as the continuation of the Roman empire. Its emperors, who ruled over a state that at its greatest extent (in the mid-sixth century) encompassed Greece, parts of the Balkans, Italy, southern Spain, Anatolia, Syria, northern Mesopotamia, Egypt and much of the North African coast, conceived of themselves not only as the heirs of Caesar and Augustus but as the lords of all Christendom, since they ruled what was for centuries the largest and most powerful Christian state in the world. Yet for westerners "Rome" eventually came to mean the western empire and its Latin culture, and when later European scholars referred to Europe's "Roman heritage" they tended to ignore or exclude Byzantium, which they often depicted as not properly Roman, as corrupted by oriental influences and culturally alien.

This tendency was exacerbated by the rivalry which developed between Rome and Constantinople, the two main Christian centers of West and East in the centuries after the fall of the western empire. The patriarchs of the eastern church in Constantinople, closely linked to the Byzantine state, rejected the claim to authority over all Christians everywhere increasingly advanced by the bishops of Rome, who became known as popes. But the spiritual primacy of the popes was eventually recognized by the rulers of the various states that emerged in western Europe following the collapse of the western Roman empire. For those rulers, men like Charles, king of the Germanic confederation of the Franks who came to be known as "Charles the Great" (Charlemagne) because he conquered and ruled much of western and central Europe, support for the papacy and the Roman church was a way of rejecting the claim of the Byzantine emperor in Constantinople to dominion over both East and West. Though the Byzantines regarded people like Charlemagne as semi-barbarian upstarts, the pope rewarded him for his support of the Latin church by proclaiming him "emperor of the Romans" in 800. Disputes over Christian doctrine also divided the western (Latin, later "Catholic") and eastern (Greek, or "Orthodox") churches. Despite many efforts at compromise and reconciliation, and despite agreement on most doctrinal questions, the differences between the western and eastern churches would harden over the centuries and in 1054 they would split into two distinct and hostile churches, amidst barrages of mutual recriminations and declarations of anathema.

Partisans of the Latin church, for whom high Roman culture and the Latin language remained exemplary, denounced Byzantium and its official Christian church not only as schismatic and deviant from true Christianity but also, from about the tenth century onward, as too "Greek" in a pejorative sense, paralleling older negative images of Asian corruption and decadence. Later scholars often implicitly or explicitly adopted the sharp distinction between Byzantium and the West, depicting the latter as the rightful heir of ancient Rome (and later of ancient Greek learning) while dismissing the former as essentially marginal to Western civilization or even denigrating it as oriental. Over time the West and Europe thus came to be associated with western, Latin Christendom and with the lands of the defunct western Roman empire and its successor states, as distinguished from the lands further to the east, even if they were (like Greece and the Balkans) actually located on the continent of Europe and also Christian (though the "wrong kind" of Christian).

This perspective also informed the work of some modern historians who sought to trace the origins of Europe, for example Henri Pirenne's influential (if controversial) *Mohammed and Charlemagne*, first published in 1937. The noted Belgian historian criticized the traditional view which saw the Germanic invasions of the fifth century and the collapse of the western Roman empire as marking a sharp break between the end of antiquity and the beginning of the medieval era. Instead Pirenne sought to show that despite political fragmentation, the cultural and economic unity of the Mediterranean basin that characterized the late Roman period remained essentially intact through the fifth and sixth centuries and well into the seventh, though with a growing "Oriental" tone owing to the pre-eminence of Constantinople and its Greek culture. It was, Pirenne argued, the Muslim conquests of the seventh century that really destroyed the unity of the Mediterranean, separated East from West, and thus definitively brought the classical era to an end and marked the beginning of the Middle Ages. Commerce across the Mediterranean, now the boundary between Christendom and Islam rather than an economic and cultural conduit linking the Christian lands surrounding it, declined sharply, the influence of Constantinople waned, and (western) Europe was for the first time compelled to live on its own cultural and economic resources, opening the way for the emergence (with Charlemagne) of a new European civilization which was a unique synthesis of Roman and Germanic elements.

Though Pirenne was right to highlight the continuity between the late Roman and early medieval periods, he did so only by positing a new and even more radical discontinuity, between the period before and the period after the Muslim conquests, which itself rested on the sharp dichotomization of Christianity and Islam. But for our purposes the accuracy of his arguments is less important than the way in which they manifest a vision of Europe (basically, Latin Christendom) as a distinct civilization and trace its origin to the crowning of Charlemagne as emperor in 800, while depicting Islam as a radically different civilization and blaming it for destroying the unity of the Roman world. This was, as Thierry Hentsch put it, a "founding myth" which had more to do with nineteenth- and twentieth-century Europeans' sense of who they were and where they came from than with what actually happened in the seventh century or with how "Europeans" of Charlemagne's time understood who they were and how they saw the world.[6]

Christian conceptions of the world

In the western European lands that had once been part of the Roman empire, the Latin church gradually suppressed both non-Christian "pagan" religions and other Christian churches and achieved hegemony, though a substantial Jewish minority endured and forms of Christianity deemed heretical by church authorities continued to surface. Early medieval church scholars – the only kind of Christian scholars there were – largely adopted the ancient Greek geographers' division of the world into three parts and the dichotomization of East and West, but they embedded this system of categorization in a conception of the world and its peoples derived from a Christian understanding of the Bible. Christian thinkers, for example the great theologian Augustine (354–430), identified each of the three continents and the peoples who settled in them after the great flood described in the biblical book of Genesis with one of Noah's sons: Japheth and his progeny with Europe, Shem (from whom the term "Semite" comes) with Asia, and Ham with Africa. But this conception also implied, for Christians, a conviction of European Christian superiority. As one scholar of European images of the world put it,

Europe was the land of Japheth, of the Gentiles, the Greeks and the Christians; Asia was the land of Semitic peoples, glorious in that they had produced the [ancient Hebrew] patriarchs and prophets, the chosen people [i.e. the Jews] and Christ himself; but – as the land of the circumcised adherents of older laws – condemned to an inferiority which was stated in the scriptures: "God shall enlarge Japheth and he shall dwell in the tents of Shem." As for Africa, the lot of the unhappy descendants of Ham, the Hamitic subjection was equally clearly laid down: Canaan was to be the servant both of Shem and Japheth: "a servant of servants shall he be unto his brethren."[7]

This hierarchical way of classifying the peoples and races of the world and fixing their place in the grand scheme of things, rooted in what Christians took to be the word of God as set forth in holy scripture, would much later be used to explain and justify the large-scale enslavement of Africans as well as European conquest and domination of non-European peoples. In secular, purportedly scientific garb it would persist well into the twentieth century and continue to influence (and legitimize) conceptions of how Europeans should treat the peoples over whom they ruled in Asia and Africa, and even how European Christians should relate to the Jewish minority living in their midst.

By the beginning of the seventh century, Christianity in its various forms had become dominant in most of the former Roman world around the Mediterranean and was slowly and unevenly spreading, by conversion or conquest, into adjacent territories in northern, eastern and southeastern Europe, Armenia, Arabia, eastern Africa and central Asia. Beyond the boundaries of Christendom, which was disunited politically but at least nominally shared the same faith, lay what Christians saw as the lands of the pagans, the idolators, by extension (drawing on Greek and Roman precedents) the barbarians. Little was known of the actual extent or contours of those lands, especially in Asia, or of the nature of those pagan peoples; myth and fantasy were freely mixed with what little had been salvaged from the writings of the geographers, historians and travelers of antiquity, and all had been recast in a biblical mold, with scholars linking various real or imagined pagan peoples to peoples mentioned in the Bible and fancifully tracing the lineages of Germanic tribal chieftains back to Japheth.[8] Yet given the slow but nonetheless perceptible spread of Christianity in East and West, it was possible for Christians to imagine that eventually the whole world would be converted to what they were convinced was the one true faith.

The coming of Islam

The eruption of Islam onto the scene did not immediately disrupt that vision. For European Christians, raids and invasions by those they deemed pagans were a common (if much feared) occurrence, and the Muslims were for a long time understood to be just another pagan horde assaulting Christendom, not the bearers of a new monotheistic faith which was in many ways similar to Christianity and Judaism and therefore an ideological as well as a military-political challenge. Before discussing early European Christian views of Islam and Muslims, however, it may be worth recapitulating, very briefly and schematically, the early history of Islam.

The new faith emerged in the Hijaz region of western Arabia, in the towns of Mecca and nearby Medina (originally known as Yathrib), located on trade routes which linked the richer, more fertile and more densely settled Syrian lands to the north with today's Yemen to the south, as well as with Egypt, Ethiopia and other lands across the Red Sea, and eastward into the interior of the Arabian peninsula, largely desert and inhabited by nomadic or semi-nomadic tribes, known as Beduin ("the desert people"). Mecca was also the site of a religious sanctuary which housed shrines of some of the deities worshipped by many Arabs before the coming of Islam.

Arabia was relatively remote from the centers of power and high culture in the Mediterranean region and the adjacent Asian lands, but it was by no means isolated, politically, culturally or economically. Arab merchants traveled into the domains of both the Byzantines and their main rival for domination in western Asia, the Sasanians, who ruled a great empire based in Persia. The Arabs were in contact with, and influenced by, the Hellenistic and Aramaic cultures of the lands to their north, and there were significant numbers of Jews and Christians in parts of Arabia, especially among the townspeople and settled farmers in the fertile oases. Moreover, both the Sasanians and the Byzantines had Arab client-states on the fringes of Arabia, and their respective allies in southern Arabia fought bitterly for control of the lucrative trade routes to east Africa and India.

This was the world into which Muhammad, prophet of Islam, was born in Mecca around 571 CE, into a clan of the locally powerful tribe of Quraysh. His parents died while he was still young and he was raised by his uncle. When he was around twenty-five he married the somewhat older widow for whom he worked, a woman who had become wealthy from the caravan trade with Syria. But a happy marriage and prosperity did not bring Muhammad spiritual contentment. He began devoting time to meditation and prayer, often retreating to a cave in the hills near Mecca, and Muslims believe that it was on one such retreat, in about 610, that the archangel Gabriel spoke to Muhammad and began to convey to him, and through him to all humanity, God's message. That message, revealed to Muhammad in segments over many years, was eventually compiled into the Qur'an ("recitation"), believed by Muslims to be the literal word of God as transmitted by his prophet Muhammad.

The content of the revelation Muhammad received has a great deal in common with Judaism and Christianity, both of which Muhammad was at least somewhat familiar with and which Muslims would come to see as earlier, less complete and distorted versions of Islam. Muslims therefore venerate Abraham, Moses, Jesus and others as earlier prophets or messengers chosen by God to convey his word to humanity, though for Muslims Muhammad enjoys special distinction as the last in the line of prophets sent by God to carry his message, and the Qur'an revealed through him is regarded as the most pure and most complete revelation, correcting and superseding the Hebrew Bible and the Christian Gospels.

Muhammad preached belief in the one true god, called Allah in Arabic – the very same all-powerful, all-knowing, omnipresent god worshipped by Jews and Christians and central to the Bible and the Gospels – and warned his fellow Meccans of God's judgment if they failed to repent of their idol-worship and immorality. Muhammad's following grew to the point where it threatened the Meccan elite, who began to harass and persecute Muhammad and his followers, who would come to call themselves Muslims, i.e. those who submit to God's will, and their faith Islam, submission to God's will. In 622 Muhammad and the Meccan Muslims left their home town for the nearby oasis town of Yathrib/Medina, where he also had followers, and this "emigration" (*hijra*) would be taken to mark the beginning of the Muslim era, the first year of the Muslim calendar. Muhammad now became the political as well as spiritual leader of a substantial and growing community of believers, and in the years that followed he became the ruler of an increasingly powerful state which defeated the neighboring Jewish tribes, compelled the Meccans to submit, and began to expand rapidly by mobilizing the Arabs of the towns, the oases and the desert who embraced the new faith into a highly effective fighting force. By the time Muhammad died, in 632, the Arabs bearing the new faith of Islam had already conquered a large part of western and central Arabia (see Map 1).

But the Muslim conquests were only beginning. After Muhammad's death leadership of the Muslim community passed to a series of caliphs (from the Arabic word *khalifa*, "successor" of God's messenger Muhammad), drawn first from the prophet's closest associates and family and then (after a civil war among the Muslims) from a leading Meccan family which established a hereditary dynasty. Within two decades of Muhammad's death the Muslim Arabs had created a vast new empire, defeating the Sasanian dynasty and conquering the empire it had ruled for centuries in Persia and adjacent lands while also conquering much of the territory which had long been part of the Roman and then Byzantine empires, including Syria, Mesopotamia and Egypt, as well as the rest of the Arabian peninsula. After these astonishingly rapid conquests the pace of expansion slowed somewhat, but it did not stop. In the west the Muslims gradually conquered the remainder of North Africa and in 711 a Muslim army landed in Spain; almost the entire Iberian peninsula was soon brought under Muslim control and Muslim forces began raiding into southern France and Italy. In the east, Muslim forces reached all the way to what is today Pakistan by the mid-eighth century. Very gradually, over the following centuries, most of the Christian, Zoroastrian, Jewish and other inhabitants of the lands conquered by the Muslims adopted Islam, though significant non-Muslim minorities remained. At the same time, what began as very much an empire dominated by Arab Muslims gradually became less Arab and more cosmopolitan as non-Arab Muslim converts and their descendants (including Persians, and later Turks and many others) came to play important roles in the rich social, political and cultural life of the growing Muslim community.

The "age of ignorance"

The astonishingly rapid emergence and expansion of the Muslim empire might at first thought seem to have been an unmitigated disaster for all Christians everywhere. But here we must differentiate among Christians. For those eastern Christians who rejected the version of Christian belief and practice imposed by the Byzantine state – for example, the many Christians in Egypt and Syria who despite pressure from Byzantine governors and bishops held fast to their own forms of Christianity and their autonomous churches – the coming of the Muslims and the end of Byzantine rule may not have been such a terrible thing. The new Muslim rulers generally did not care what their Christian subjects believed as long as they were docile and paid their taxes, and as a result scholars have suggested that Christian communities in Egypt and Syria, which the Byzantine state and its official church had harassed as heretical, actually welcomed their Arab conquerors, or at least quickly accepted Muslim rule. As a ninth-century patriarch of the Jacobite church of Syria, whose understanding of the nature of Christ differed from that of the mainstream in both Constantinople and Rome, put it looking back two centuries to the Muslim conquest of Syria and Egypt: "If, as is true, we have suffered some harm . . . nonetheless it was no slight advantage for us to be delivered from the cruelty of the Romans [i.e. the Byzantines]."[9]

That the Muslim conquests were a catastrophe for the Byzantine empire, still the bulwark of mainstream Christianity, is more obvious: having already lost most of its possessions in western Europe to Germanic invaders, it now lost Syria and Egypt to the Arabs and was thus suddenly reduced to Anatolia, Greece and small parts of the Balkans and Italy, and had to live in fear of further Arab assaults. That Christians in western Europe – or at least that very small minority of rulers, officials and churchmen who in an age of almost universal illiteracy, poor communications and general ignorance of the world could form any more or less accurate picture of what was going on – perceived these developments as disastrous is also clear. Palestine, the "holy land" in which Christianity had been born, had been lost, along with vast territories in Asia and Africa in which Christianity had long been the dominant faith; and with the Muslim invasion of Spain the threat reached western Europe itself, with the Pyrenees eventually marking the unstable border between Christian and Muslim domains and an apparently high likelihood of further Muslim advances into the heartlands of western Christendom.

In the formerly Christian lands now ruled by the Muslims, in the east and somewhat later in Spain, a few educated churchmen came to understand that these conquerors were not idolatrous or polytheistic pagans but had brought a new faith which bore considerable resemblance to Christianity and Judaism. Writing in Armenia (subject to indirect Arab rule) in the 660s, the bishop and chronicler Sebeos reportedly could explain that "there was an Ishmaelite [i.e. Arab] called Mahmet [i.e. Muhammad], a merchant; he presented himself to them as though at God's command, as a preacher, as the way of truth, and taught them to know the God of Abraham, for he was very well informed and very well acquainted with the story of Moses. Since the command came from on high, they all came together, at a single order, in unity of religion, and, abandoning vain cults, returned to the living God who had revealed himself to their father Abraham."[10] Sebeos thus apparently understood that the Muslims were monotheists and adherents of an Abrahamic religion akin to Judaism and Christianity, rather than pagan idolators.

In the following century the theologian John of Damascus, who knew Arabic as well as Greek and who, like his father and grandfather before him, served as an official in the caliph's administration, discussed Islam in some detail and with considerable accuracy in order to demonstrate to his fellow Christians that it was just one more heresy that had to be fought. Obviously, direct and prolonged interaction gave Christians living under Muslim rule the opportunity to gain a more accurate understanding of Islam, as well as a motive to do so: local church leaders needed to refute Islam and "prove" that Christianity was the true faith in order to keep their flock from converting to Islam. In fact, most of the Christians, Jews and Zoroastrians in the Muslim-ruled lands of western Asia and northern Africa did eventually convert to Islam, whether from religious conviction, to escape the disabilities to which non-Muslims were subject, or because of the material advantages and enhanced status which membership in the Muslim community brought.

In western Europe, contemporary chroniclers had very little access to accurate knowledge of the Muslim conquests or of the character of this new threat to Christendom. They had to rely largely, often exclusively, on accounts of what was happening in the East (and even in nearby Spain) that were transmitted orally, relayed from person to person over long distances and across many cultural boundaries, and that often reached the West long after the events they related had taken place. The usual result was a great deal of distortion, misinformation and even fantasy mixed with accurate tidbits. But the very real difficulty in obtaining accurate knowledge was perhaps less important in shaping the early European understanding of Islam than the availability of conceptual categories, derived from antiquity and from the Bible, through which European Christians could filter and make a certain kind of sense of the appearance and rapid spread of Islam.

It is worth noting that despite this topic's obvious importance, it received little scholarly attention until the early 1960s, when two British scholars published studies that would help lay the groundwork for subsequent efforts to question and rethink the foundations of Orientalism – the term which, as we will see in Chapter 2, would much later come to denote the scholarly study of the Orient and Islam. In 1960 Norman Daniel (1919–92), who was trained at the universities of Oxford and Edinburgh and worked for many years with the British Council, a government agency whose mission it is to promote British culture abroad, published *Islam and the West: The Making of an Image*. Two years later Richard W. Southern (1912–2001), a distinguished Oxford historian of medieval Europe, published *Western Views of Islam in the Middle Ages*, which originated as a series of lectures delivered at Harvard University the previous year.[11]

As Daniel, Southern and other scholars pointed out, early medieval European writers tended to see the Muslims in ethnic rather than religious terms and usually called them "Saracens," from the Greek and Latin term for Arabs, derived from a Greek word for tent (i.e., the tent-dwellers). Late Roman and early medieval Christian observers had regarded the Saracens/Arabs as a particularly rapacious bunch of pagans even before the emergence of Islam, and what was happening now seemed to confirm that view. Thus Fredegar, a Frankish chronicler writing in the 650s, told of the Saracens, "a circumcised people who . . . had now grown so numerous that at last they took up arms and threw themselves upon the provinces of the [Byzantine] emperor Heraclius, who despatched an army to hold them . . . [After their victory over Heraclius] the Saracens proceeded, as was their habit, to lay waste the provinces of the empire that had fallen to them."[12]

The Saracens were thus depicted as a plague upon Christendom, spreading devastation wherever they went, but in principle no different from the other pagan peoples whom God had sent to scourge and test his faithful. As Southern put it, western chroniclers "knew virtually nothing of Islam as a religion. For them Islam was only one of a large number of enemies threatening Christendom from every direction, and they had no interest in distinguishing the primitive idolatries of Northmen, Slavs, and Magyars from the monotheism of Islam, or the Manichean heresy from that of Mahomet [which is how medieval Europeans usually rendered Muhammad's name]. There is no sign that anyone in northern Europe had even heard the name of Mahomet." Latin Christian scholars thus knew nothing of how the Muslim Arabs absorbed elements of the Persian, Hellenistic and Aramaic cultures of the peoples they had conquered and brought into being a new Islamic high culture, expressed mainly in the Arabic language. Nor did they have anything but the vaguest inkling that, especially during the heyday of the 'Abbasid dynasty from the mid-eighth century into the tenth, the vast Islamic empire was experiencing a period of cultural and economic efflorescence whose magnificence is only heightened by comparison with the material and cultural impoverishment that characterized western Europe in what later historians would call "the dark ages." Southern accurately summed up the state of western knowledge of Islam in the entire period from the seventh century until about 1100 as the "age of ignorance."

But, Southern also pointed out, "despite their ignorance, Latin writers were not left entirely without a clue to the place of the Saracens in the general scheme of world history. This clue was provided by the Bible."[13] The Bible provided Latin Christians with a framework of interpretation within which Christians could make sense of the onslaught of the Saracens. Church scholars like the monk and Bible scholar Bede (673–735), writing in northern England, expressed the dominant view when he asserted that the Saracens were descendants of Hagar, one of Abraham's wives and the mother of his son Ishmael, brother of Isaac who was the forefather of the Jews (and thus, spiritually, of the Christians). As a result the Arab Muslims were sometimes called Hagarenes or Ishmaelites, though Saracen seems to have been the most widely used term; rather illogically, some scholars claimed that "Saracen" came from Sarah, Abraham's senior wife and mother of Isaac. The Muslims of North Africa and Spain were often called "Moors," and many European observers did not quite grasp that the "Saracens" in the East and the "Moors" in Spain were all Muslims.

Early medieval European observers thus generally failed to see what was clear to many Christians in the East: that these "Saracens" adhered to a monotheistic religion related to (and obviously influenced by) Judaism and Christianity. Direct observation does not always seem to have helped: for example, Arculf, a bishop from western Europe who actually visited

Muslim-ruled Jerusalem and Damascus (at the time the capital of the Muslim empire) in the 670s and whose account was recorded not long after, learned almost nothing about what the "Saracens" in whose domain he traveled actually believed. For him as for most European Christians over the next few centuries, they were simply unbelievers, pagans, and therefore in religious terms not worthy of special or close attention.[14] At the same time, all sorts of bizarre and derogatory myths about the Saracens circulated in Europe, among the educated as well as the masses, reflecting the fear and hostility which Christians felt toward this threatening enemy about whom they knew so little.

In Muslim-ruled Spain things were somewhat different. Sporadic warfare continued in the border zone along the Pyrenees, though Muslim efforts to expand into France were blocked. But in most of the Iberian peninsula Christians lived under Muslim rule for centuries, subordinated and isolated from their coreligionists elsewhere but (like the Jews) tolerated as a "people of the book," i.e. a people who espoused an earlier version of the message God sent to humanity through Muhammad. But proximity did not necessarily lead to understanding: the writings of most Spanish Christian churchmen do not consistently demonstrate much more interest in, or accurate knowledge about, Islam than the writings of Christians elsewhere in Europe. Nonetheless the intermingling of Muslim, Christian and Jewish influences in Muslim-ruled Spain gave birth to a flourishing high culture unparalleled anywhere else in Europe, as well as a great deal of cultural mixing at the popular level. Writing in Cordoba in the mid-ninth century, Paul Alvarus lamented the powerful attraction which Arab culture exerted on his fellow Spanish Christians:

The Christians love to read the poems and romances of the Arabs; they study the Arab theologians and philosophers, not to refute them but to form a correct and elegant Arabic. Where is the layman who now reads the Latin commentaries on the Holy Scriptures, or who studies the Gospels, prophets or apostles? Alas! all talented young Christians read and study with enthusiasm the Arab books; they gather immense libraries at great expense; they despise the Christian literature as unworthy of attention. They have forgotten their language. For every one who can write a letter in Latin to a friend, there are a thousand who can express themselves in Arabic with elegance, and write better poems in this language than the Arabs themselves.[15]

Alvarus saw Muslim rule as portending the arrival of the Antichrist and the imminence of the Second Coming and hoped to arouse Spanish Christians to resist what he saw as the decline of their faith. But only a few responded, openly denigrated Islam and achieved the martyrdom they sought; most Spanish Christians, churchmen and lay people alike, acquiesced in Muslim rule, and some were active participants (along with many Jews) in the cultural efflorescence that would later be characterized as Muslim-ruled Spain's "golden age."

The Crusades

As the French scholar of Islam Maxime Rodinson put it in his study of European views of Islam, "the Western image of the Muslim world came into sharper focus in the eleventh century."[16] This was a period in which, though western Europe was politically fragmented, the papacy had succeeded in asserting its spiritual and even to some extent political primacy. A measure of security and stability returned as the pagan peoples who had repeatedly raided western and central Europe in the ninth and tenth centuries (the Normans, the Magyars and others) converted to Christianity and were integrated politically and culturally. Western Europe's population began to grow and there was a quickening of economic life and an expansion of local, regional and transregional trade. In Spain, the kings of the small Christian states in the north which had survived the Muslim conquest took advantage of the disintegration of Muslim-ruled Spain into numerous feuding principalities to launch the Reconquista, the gradual "reconquest" of Spain for Christianity. At around the same time a Norman adventurer began to conquer Sicily from the Muslims.

In the East, however, it was the Muslims who seemed to be on the offensive. In 1071 the Byzantines suffered a catastrophic defeat at the hands of the Muslim Seljuq Turks, who were carving out their own empire in western Asia, and lost almost all of Anatolia. The Muslims now seemed poised to capture Constantinople, extinguish the Byzantine empire and perhaps move on into southeastern Europe. The Seljuq seizure of Palestine from another Muslim state based in Egypt also disrupted Christian pilgrimage to Jerusalem and the Holy Land, long tolerated by Muslim rulers, as well as trade in the eastern Mediterranean.

These developments helped make western Christians more responsive when the desperate Byzantine emperor appealed for help, an appeal which Pope Urban II answered in 1095 with a call to Christians everywhere to unite, mobilize and attack the "enemies of God." Urban reportedly reminded a church council held at Clermont in France that the Saracens had centuries earlier seized (western) Asia, where Christianity had been born, as well as (northern) Africa which had also once been Christian; now they were stepping up their attacks on the "third continent," Europe.

You are a people sprung from the more temperate regions of the world, and you lack neither martial prowess nor discretion: you are a people both disciplined in camp and skilful in the field of battle. Thus endowed with wisdom and courage, you are embarking on a memorable enterprise. Your deeds will be sung down the ages if you rescue your brothers from this danger . . . May those who go forth as champions of Christendom mark their clothes with the sign of the Cross . . . Rid the sanctuary of God of the unbelievers, expel the thieves and lead back the faithful.[17]

Pope Urban's call elicited a strong response among western European Christians. Some joined the ensuing "crusade" (derived from the word "cross") because of religious fervor and the promise of salvation; others hoped for adventure or personal gain. The Crusade offered an outlet for knights who lacked land of their own and was backed by Italian mercantile city-states like Venice and Genoa who hoped to win control of the lucrative trade with the East. For the pope the Crusade was a way to enhance the political and spiritual power of the church he led. Whatever the motivations of the participants, within a year of Urban's call forces of crusading knights, mainly from France, began converging on Constantinople, not infrequently massacring the European Jewish communities they encountered along the way. By 1097 the Crusader armies were advancing into Seljuq-controlled territory, winning a series of victories over Turkish Muslim forces, and in 1099 the Crusaders captured Jerusalem and established several principalities ruled by Latin Christian noblemen in Syria and Palestine.

This First Crusade succeeded in large part owing to disunity and lack of preparedness among the Muslims. But eventually the Muslims recovered and launched their own campaign to expel those whom they perceived as alien invaders who had seized lands which had been under Muslim rule for centuries, especially Jerusalem and Palestine which Muslims (like Jews and Christians) regarded as sacred. In response to Muslim victories against one of the Crusader states in Syria, the Latin church called for a Second Crusade in 1145, but it was a military failure. The Muslims now took the offensive, and by 1187 Salah al-Din, known in the West as Saladin and sultan (ruler) of a state that stretched from Egypt to Iraq, had retaken Jerusalem and all but destroyed the Crusader kingdoms. This led the pope to call for yet another crusade, the Third, led by the kings of France and England and the "Holy Roman Emperor," who ruled the German lands and northern Italy. But though the Third Crusade did conquer a strip of territory along the coast of Syria and Palestine, it failed to regain Jerusalem for the Christians, and in its wake Saladin signed a treaty with King Richard of England allowing Christian pilgrims to visit Jerusalem.

The response in western Europe to papal calls for subsequent crusades grew increasingly feeble and the crusades themselves proved unsuccessful. During the Fourth Crusade (1202–04) the Latin Christian forces accomplished little against the Muslims but did seize and sack Constantinople, putting in place a Latin-dominated regime which lasted for some decades. In 1229 the Holy Roman Emperor Frederick II actually won control of Jerusalem through negotiations with the Muslim ruler of Egypt and Syria, much to the anger of the pope who promptly excommunicated Frederick for being overly friendly with the Muslims, but by 1244 the city was again in Muslim hands. In 1291 the Mamluks, a military caste of freed Muslim slaves who now ruled Syria and Egypt, captured the last Crusader stronghold on the coast, and the Holy Land was to remain under Muslim rule until it was conquered by British forces in 1917.

From the eleventh century onward, then, through increased trade and pilgrimage, through the conquests which brought many Muslims under Christian rule in Spain and Sicily and renewed the links between Christians who had lived under Muslim rule and their Latin coreligionists, and then in the course of the Crusades, western European Christians began to develop better defined images of Islam. But better defined did not necessarily mean more accurate, for even as a handful of scholars began to try to acquire a less distorted understanding of Islam, other scholars, chroniclers, poets and story-tellers were generating and spreading the most bizarre notions about Islam and Muhammad, notions which would persist for centuries and which sometimes still surface in western popular culture today.

Knowing the enemy

The first efforts by western church scholars to acquire a more precise understanding of Islam were largely motivated by the kind of "know your enemy" attitude that often informed the field of Soviet studies in the United States during the Cold War: one had to understand the enemy's ideology if one was to combat it effectively. Peter the Venerable (c. 1094–1156), abbot of the monastery of Cluny in central France, played a key role in this endeavor. Like some earlier church scholars, Peter saw Islam as a Christian heresy and argued that it could not be destroyed unless its errors were understood. He therefore set a team of translators to work in Spain rendering Arabic texts into Latin; this project's high point was the first translation of the Qur'an into Latin, completed in 1143 by the Englishman Robert of Ketton.

Somewhat earlier a few individuals, like the Spanish Jewish convert to Christianity Pedro de Alfonso, had begun to publish the first more or less accurate accounts of the life of Muhammad, the teachings of Islam and Arab history, and others were to follow. There thus developed, very slowly and unevenly, a small body of literature which offered those few who were interested a fuller and more serious understanding of Islam as a faith and of Islamic history. It thereby became possible, by the middle of the twelfth century, for the chronicler Otto of Freising to dismiss as fanciful the claim that an archbishop had been martyred in Cairo for smashing the Muslims' idols because, as Otto put it, "it is known that the whole body of Saracens worship one God and receive the Old Testament law and the rite of circumcision. Nor do they attack Christ or the Apostles. In this one thing alone they are far from salvation – in denying that Jesus Christ is God or the Son of God, and in venerating the seducer Mahomet as a great prophet of the supreme God."[18]

Through their study of translations of the Qur'an, of biographies of Muhammad and of other Arabic-language texts, European Christian scholars and theologians began to produce what would eventually be an extensive polemical literature designed to refute Islam as false, heretical and incompatible with Christian doctrine. They hoped that such works would prevent Christians in Muslim-ruled lands from converting to Islam while opening the way for the eventual conversion of the Muslims to Christianity. The effort to prove that the Qur'an was not an authentic revelation from God and that Muhammad could not have been an authentic prophet often involved, especially early on, a great deal of distortion of what Muslims actually believed and did. Over time some Christian scholars achieved a greater degree of accuracy, but nothing they said would have been likely to convince Muslims that their faith was invalid: their critique of Islam was thoroughly grounded in Christian theology and thus irrelevant to Muslims.

In his 1975 book *The Arabs and Medieval Europe,* Norman Daniel suggested that such polemics were in any case primarily directed not externally, against Muslims, but rather internally, against the threat of heresy among Christians. "Condemnations of Islam," Daniel argued, "are only an aspect of other condemnations, of the oriental [i.e. non-Catholic] churches, as well as of the great heresies which sprang up in, or invaded, Europe, and even of each individual intellectual eccentricity. It is in the context of [the] European thirst for orthodoxy that we must see the passion for identifying the heresies that Islam resembled (or might be supposed to derive from), and for specifying minutely each separate count on which Islam must be detested."[19] In other words, the church's attacks on Islam were in part a way of enforcing ideological conformity among Christians – much as, during the Cold War, denunciations and hostile depictions of the capitalist West (the external enemy) facilitated the efforts of the communist regimes in the Soviet Union and its client-states to suppress opposition and silence real and potential dissidents at home (the internal enemy), while in the United States vociferous right-wing forces used the threat allegedly posed by "international communism" and its nefarious secret agents to isolate, discredit and defeat their domestic enemies on the left.

Europe's Arab-Muslim heritage

In addition to seeking, and in part achieving, a more accurate understanding of Islam, European scholars began in this period to grasp that the Muslim world (including its Jewish communities) possessed great intellectual riches from which their own comparatively impoverished culture might benefit. In Toledo, a great center of learning in Muslim Spain and since 1085 in Christian hands, as well as elsewhere in Spain, Christian scholars, aided by Spanish Muslims, Christians and Jews, began to translate, study and disseminate the voluminous Arabic-language writings on medicine, astronomy, mathematics and philosophy they found in the libraries of Spanish mosques and courts. This was a treasure-trove of knowledge, well in advance of anything available in Europe at the time. It was by this means that western Europeans first gained access to many works of Greek antiquity which had been lost in the West but were preserved in Arabic translations; but in the process they also encountered the Arabic-language writings of Muslim and Jewish thinkers who had absorbed the work of the Greeks but had gone well beyond them to blaze new paths in medicine, philosophy, the sciences, mathematics and literature.

Engagement with these texts had a profound impact on many arenas of western European intellectual life. Translated Arabic writings on medicine, mathematics, astronomy and other sciences were for centuries used as textbooks in medieval Europe, while the writings of Muslim philosophers like Ibn Sina' (980–1037, known in the West as Avicenna) and Ibn Rushd (1126–98, known as Averroes), and Jewish philosophers who wrote mainly in Arabic like Maimonides (Rabbi Moses ben Maimon, 1135–1204), were eagerly read and discussed and influenced several generations of medieval Christian philosophers and theologians. Southern noted that "it would be difficult to exaggerate the extent to which these influences changed the outlook of learned Europeans in the half century after 1230. It is as if modern economists in the tradition of Alfred Marshall and Keynes were suddenly to start using the language of Karl Marx, or liberal statesmen to start expressing themselves in the idiom of Lenin."[20] The powerful impact of Arabic learning is suggested by the large number of scientific and mathematical terms in western languages which derive from Arabic terms or names, including *alchemy* (from which *chemistry* comes), *alcohol*, *algebra*, *algorithm* and *alkali*, as well as the names of many stars.

The Latin church would ultimately reject Avicenna's philosophical views and embrace the synthesis developed by Thomas Aquinas (1225–74), greatest of the medieval Catholic theologians; but Aquinas himself drew on concepts and language taken from Islamic philosophy, particularly Averroes, and he was strongly influenced by Maimonides. The English philosopher Roger Bacon (*c.* 1214–1292) would go so far as to say that "philosophy was revived chiefly by Aristotle in Greek and then chiefly by Avicenna in Arabic,"[21] while many of his educated contemporaries who vehemently rejected Islam as a religion nonetheless admired the Arabs as a people who had produced great philosophers and scientists from whose writings Christians could learn much.

Curiously, the one major Muslim figure who won widespread popular (as opposed to scholarly) admiration in western Europe was not a philosopher or a scientist but a military man, indeed the most effective foe of the Crusaders and the man who had driven them from Jerusalem in 1187. This was Saladin (1138–1193), who came to be depicted in many popular stories and epic poems of the medieval period as chivalrous, humane, just and wise. Rodinson noted, however, that "surely such a perfect knight could not be excluded from the Christian experience," and so fanciful stories circulated that his mother had actually been a Christian princess and that he had converted to Christianity on his deathbed.[22] While in his *Inferno* the poet Dante (1265–1321) would place Muhammad in one of the worst circles of hell, subject to endless torment, Saladin was depicted as enjoying a relatively pleasant afterlife, along with Avicenna and Averroes among near-contemporaries and various other virtuous non-Christians of antiquity like Socrates, Plato and Aristotle.

The extent to which medieval Latin philosophy and science borrowed from Arab learning (which for our purposes also encompasses writings in the Arabic language by non-Muslims) has generally been recognized by scholars, but the Arab influence on medieval western European popular and high culture more broadly has been less fully explored or acknowledged. In Spain and Sicily, where Muslims, Christians and Jews lived side by side for centuries, and through contact between Europe (especially southern Europe) and the Muslim lands of western Asia and northern Africa by means of trade and pilgrimage, there was, despite the Crusades and continuing religious hostility, a great deal of cultural interaction and borrowing, especially around the Mediterranean basin. The extent to which, at a crucial stage in its development, western Europe drew heavily on Arab-Muslim culture would be largely forgotten or obscured when, during the Renaissance and after, European thinkers and scholars began to denigrate medieval learning and culture and instead claimed a more or less unbroken cultural continuity between ancient Greece (now seen as the source of the quasi-secular humanism which many Renaissance thinkers espoused) and their own times. Yet as the author of a pioneering 1977 study on the influence of "Araby" on medieval English literature put it, "the migration of literary works, as well as concepts, images, themes, and motifs, was a natural by-product" of the process whereby "the Arabs did not only transmit and interpret the knowledge and ideas of classical antiquity, but became the teachers and inspirers of the West at the very heart of its cultural life: its attitude to reason and faith . . . " This literary material "brought Islamic modes of thought within the reach of a far wider circle of readers than the intellectual élite, for it was widely translated into the vernacular."[23]

A decade later Maria Rosa Menocal would develop this argument much further and advance it much more vigorously. In her 1987 book *The Arabic Role in Medieval Literary History: A Forgotten Heritage*, which was clearly influenced by Edward W. Said's 1978 book *Orientalism*, she argued that "Westerners – Europeans – have great difficulty in considering the possibility that they are in some way seriously indebted to the Arab world, or that the Arabs were central to the making of medieval Europe." Broadening the argument, she pointed out that

The most general, and in many ways the most influential and pervasive, image or construct we have is that of ourselves and our culture, an entity we have dubbed "Western," a clearly comparative title. Whether it is spoken or unspoken, named or unnamed, we are governed by the notion that there is a distinctive cultural history that can be characterized as Western, and that it is in distinctive, necessary, and fundamental opposition to non-Western culture and cultural history.

European literary scholarship, Menocal went on, "has an a priori view of, and set of assumptions about, its medieval past that is far from conducive to viewing its Semitic [i.e. Arab] components as formative and central." How, she asked, would our interpretation of medieval European culture change if we included the *Thousand and One Nights* and the work of Spanish and Sicilian poets who wrote in Arabic in the canon of medieval European literature? Menocal argued that a fuller and more accurate understanding of Europe's cultural past required a critical re-examination of what she termed the "myth of Westernness" which has informed most literary scholarship, as well as a readiness to investigate the West's "mixed ancestry" with an open mind.[24]

Images of Islam

The late eleventh and especially the twelfth centuries thus witnessed the first efforts by scholars to achieve a more accurate understanding of Islam, as well as western Europe's initial encounter with the great cultural and intellectual riches of the Muslim world. But this same period, the period of the Crusades, also witnessed the elaboration and diffusion of a great deal of "knowledge" about Islam, among literate and educated people but also among the largely illiterate masses, that was more sophisticated and detailed but also more distorted than anything that had come before. As R. W. Southern put it, "from about the year 1120 everyone in the West had some picture of what Islam meant, and who Mahomet was. The picture was brilliantly clear, but it was not knowledge, and its details were only accidentally true. Its authors luxuriated in the ignorance of triumphant imagination."[25]

Alongside (and in spite of) the efforts of the handful of scholars who sought to acquire some accurate understanding of what Muslims actually believed and the origins of their faith, there simultaneously emerged a much more widespread and thoroughly inaccurate portrait of Islam and its founder Muhammad. This portrait derived from the work of church scholars who drew on distorted readings of the Qur'an in translation, biographies of Muhammad and dubious secondary sources, from the often fanciful writings of Muslim or Jewish converts to Christianity, from the fantastic tales told by returning Crusaders, merchants and travelers, and from the fertile (and sometimes feverish) imaginations of poets and story-tellers. Somehow, as Norman Daniel put it, the "Arabs" who were so admired as the source of great philosophical and scientific wisdom were completely disassociated from the "Saracens," i.e. the adherents of Islam, whose religious beliefs were depicted not as merely exotic but as bizarre, even monstrous, and of course utterly false and deluded. "That they represented one continuous culture," Daniel wrote, "would be incredible to someone who knew nothing at all of the subject, except through the medieval sources."[26]

Christians could of course not accept that Muhammad had received an authentic revelation from God, and at both the scholarly and popular levels the man and his message therefore came in for a great deal of denigration. The form which that denigration took was often shaped by Christians' difficulty in perceiving Islam except as a distorted mirror image of their own faith. If Christians worshipped Jesus Christ as the son of God, the Muslims must worship Muhammad as a god; and so, in popular songs and poems of the time, and especially those which told of battles between Christians and Muslims in northern Spain and then in the Holy Land during the First Crusade, the Saracens were often depicted as idolators who worshipped, in the most depraved manner imaginable, their pagan god "Mahomet." Other accounts, popular as well as scholarly, insisted that the Saracens actually worshipped three idols, Mahomet, Apollo and Tervagant, an imitation of the Christian trinity; or else they prayed to these three plus a great many more.

But even those who understood that the Muslims were strict monotheists who vehemently rejected idolatry and regarded Muhammad as a man, albeit a man worthy of having been chosen by God to convey his final revelation to humanity, produced countless venomous stories about him. Muhammad was said to be a magician, a sorcerer who used his evil powers to produce fake miracles and thereby seduce men into embracing his false doctrines; he was a renegade Christian priest, perhaps even a cardinal, whose frustrated lust for power led him to seek revenge on the church by propagating his own pernicious teachings; he was sexually promiscuous, an adulterer, and promoted licentiousness in order to ensnare men into depravity; his death was as disgusting and shameful as his life, for he was devoured by dogs, or suffocated by pigs during an epileptic fit. These stories and many others, embellished with a wealth of utterly fantastic and lurid details, appeared in popular song, poetry and folklore but also in the writings of scholars. Nothing was so outrageous or so completely unsupported by evidence that it could not be said about Muhammad. As Guibert of Nogent (*c.* 1053–1124), author of one of the earliest biographies of the prophet outside Spain, explained, whether or not the awful things he relates about Muhammad are true "it is safe to speak evil of one whose malignity exceeds whatever ill can be spoken."[27] Islam was depicted as a religion of violence, bloody and cruel, its adherents fanatics who offered those they conquered the grim choice of conversion or death.

It is thus not possible to trace the development of Latin Christian views of Islam as a simple progression from ignorance to knowledge. Instead, the profound ignorance and lack of interest that characterized the period before 1100 was followed by the production of a small body of more accurate knowledge about the tenets of Islam and the life of its prophet, largely for polemical or missionary purposes, but also by the emergence of a set of distorted and usually derogatory images and notions that were widespread at all levels of society. These different kinds of knowledge emerged and evolved side by side, often drawing on the same sources and interacting in complex ways, so that the same scholarly or popular medieval text might contain some accurate information about Islam or Muhammad alongside crude distortions and derogatory assertions. It is clear, however, that in terms of their social and cultural significance and diffusion, the negative images of Islam and Muslims generated in this period far outweighed efforts to achieve a relatively nuanced and balanced understanding of Islam, one which could, despite a firm conviction of Christianity's superiority, nonetheless recognize how much Christianity and Islam had in common and accept at least the sincerity of Muslim belief.

It might be suggested that hostile and disparaging medieval European Christian attitudes toward Islam were simply one more manifestation of the unfortunate human propensity not only to perceive people who are deemed to belong to another group (clan, village, tribe, ethnicity, religion, race, nation, etc.) as essentially different from "us" but also to believe that "we" are superior to "them." Scholars have come to use the terms "self" and "other" to denote the distinction individuals and groups draw between those deemed basically like themselves and those deemed essentially different. From this perspective, there is nothing all that special about medieval Europeans' negative perceptions of Islam and Muslims.

It is certainly true that in this same period Europeans generated all sorts of bizarre images of, and "knowledge" about, China and India and many other exotic peoples and places; in fact one does not even have to go so far afield to see this process at work, for most medieval European Christians regarded the Jews who had for centuries been their neighbors as fundamentally alien, accepted as true all sorts of bizarre assertions about Jewish beliefs and practices, and often subjected Jews to hostility, discrimination, harassment and episodes of massacre. Moreover, Christians showed little hesitation about attacking and killing fellow Christians who were deemed to be heretics or who were defined as enemies for whatever reason.

Yet it can be argued that Islam occupied a unique (though never simple) place in the imaginations of western Europeans from at least the eleventh or twelfth century onward – that it was Europe's "other" in a special sense. The Jews were close at hand, but they were a subordinated and sometimes segregated minority; and though they were sometimes regarded as an ideological problem as a result of their steadfast refusal to accept that Jesus was the messiah and the son of God, they never constituted a political or military threat to the hegemony of Christianity in Europe. China and India and all those other strange peoples and places were very far away and also constituted no direct threat to Europeans; they could therefore for a long time simply be exotic objects of curiosity, wonderment and fantasizing.

In stark contrast, the domain of Islam bordered Christendom, and many Christians were in more or less direct contact with Muslims, whether in Spain or in Sicily, or in Palestine and Syria during the

Crusades, or through trade and travel. Muslim states and societies were medieval Christian western Europe's nearest non-Christian neighbors, and Islam constituted the closest cultural alternative to Latin Christendom. Moreover, Islam was a *powerful* political and cultural alternative, one with which European Christians were for centuries engaged in military and ideological conflict. Islam was perceived as the dangerous enemy right next door, the usurper which had seized the Holy Land as well as many other lands in which Christianity had once flourished, and which continued to constitute a serious threat to Christendom.

Islam was thus Europe's "other" in a way that China or India or (after 1492) the indigenous states of the New World could never be. Despite its geographic proximity – or perhaps because of it – Islam was generally perceived as more alien and certainly as more threatening. Islam usually evoked revulsion, fear and hostility; for a brief period there was admiration, not of Islam but of the wisdom of the Arabs, but soon that largely faded into indifference and routine denigration. Like other peoples throughout history, Europeans (and, much later, Americans) had and still have all sorts of images of other peoples, cultures and religions in their heads, not a few of them derogatory; but it is only the image of Islam which has historically evoked both a profound sense of cultural difference and a deep sense of threat, today associated with the image of the fanatical Muslim terrorist mindlessly attacking Westerners.[28]

For centuries, though never in a simple or unconflicted way, Islam was a screen onto which Europeans could and did project their anxieties and conflicts about who and what they were or were not, a mirror in which Europeans could discern the traits that seemed to make them unique by highlighting how different, defective and inferior Islam was. As we will see in subsequent chapters, it was in part by differentiating themselves from Islam (and the various characteristics they saw as part of Islam's essential and unchanging nature) that European Christians, and later their nominally secular descendants, defined their own identity. These representations persisted for centuries in popular and high culture and in scholarship, and some of them continue to circulate today. In movies, in television programs, in newspaper and magazine articles and in books, in children's comic books, indeed across the popular imagination of western Europe and the United States, images of the Muslim as other, as profoundly different from ourselves, as fanatical, violent, lusty and threatening – images that as we have seen have very old roots – still have emotional resonance for many people and can be drawn on and deployed for political purposes.

2   Islam, the West and the rest

By the end of the thirteenth century the era of the Crusades was essentially over: there was little interest or energy among western European Christians for further campaigns to regain the Holy Land. In Spain, however, the Reconquista continued until only Granada in the far south remained under Muslim rule, though many Muslims (and Jews) continued to live in the Christian kingdoms of Castile and Aragon. In the 1220s western Europeans first received reports that a powerful new invader had come out of central Asia and was attacking the heartlands of Islam. At first some believed that these defeats for Islam had been inflicted by the armies of the legendary Prester John, great king of a fabled long-lost Christian land somewhere in the East. It soon became evident that these invaders were not fellow Christians but the very same pagan, thoroughly terrifying and seemingly invincible Mongols (sometimes called Tatars) who overran much of Russia in the 1230s and by 1241 were attacking Poland and Hungary. The sudden death of the Mongol Khan (chieftain) in 1242 brought expansion into central Europe to a halt, but the Mongol conquest of Persia continued and in 1258 a Mongol army seized Baghdad and extinguished the 'Abbasid caliphate.

These developments allowed Latin Christians to hope that the Mongols had been sent by God to destroy Islam once and for all, and efforts were made to secure an alliance with them. Popes and European kings sent emissaries to the Mongol court to ascertain their intentions and if possible convert them to Christianity, and in the period 1285–90 the Mongols sent several embassies to western Europe, led by Christians who belonged to the Nestorian church, deemed heretical by Rome and Constantinople alike. But the advance of Mongol forces into Syria and Palestine had already been stopped by the Mamluks in 1260, and by the end of the century it was becoming clear that the Mongols had opted for Islam rather than Christianity, quashing hope for the imminent destruction of Islam.

The failure of the last Crusades and the disappointment of the hopes placed in the Mongols helped some educated Christians in the West realize that Islam was unlikely to be destroyed by military force. At the same time, the reports of papal emissaries to the Mongol court, and later of merchants like Marco Polo, a Venetian who between 1271 and 1295 claimed to have journeyed as far as China, began to lead Europeans to the understanding that the world was very much larger, more populous and more diverse than they had hitherto thought, with Christians constituting a small proportion of its inhabitants. As a result it became increasingly evident that the Christianization of the world would be a much more difficult and protracted undertaking than had once been imagined. This led some church scholars, Roger Bacon among them, to argue that the church should pursue a patient, consistent and long-term effort to peacefully convert the Muslims and other unbelievers. To achieve this they urged the church to foster the study of Islam and the Arabic language in order to arm Christians with the tools they would need to convince Muslims that their faith was false and Christianity true, and thus make effective missionary work possible. In 1312 a church council held at Vienne seemed to endorse this approach by calling for the establishment of chairs in Arabic, Greek, Hebrew and Syriac at the universities of Paris, Oxford, Bologna, Avignon and Salamanca. But this decision was not implemented and over time interest in this enterprise faded away.

In the fourteenth and early fifteenth centuries the sense that Islam posed an imminent military and ideological threat receded somewhat. The religious fervor that the Crusades had evoked dissipated, more or less peaceable relations were established with many of the Muslim states of western Asia and northern Africa, and trade across the Mediterranean flourished, dominated by the great Italian commercial city-states, above all Venice. What later historians would call the Renaissance – the "rebirth" of western European culture from the fifteenth century onward, contrasted to the purported stagnation of the "Middle Ages" that were said to have begun with the fall of Rome a thousand years earlier – brought with it a weakening of the authority of the church and a decline in the religious fervor that had helped fuel hostility to Islam. Gradually, "Christendom" as a unifying principle and form of identity became less powerful, and the more geographic and nominally more secular notion of "Europe" gradually came to the fore. Yet distorted and pernicious depictions of Islam and Muslims continued to be generated and spread. As Norman Daniel put it, "The themes of hostile mediaeval misinterpretation of Islam were constantly reiterated with the total assurance with which one would teach the alphabet or multiplication tables, and by major writers using old information, often without direct reference to such sources as were available . . . Many who traveled in Islamic countries . . . preferred the ideas that they had brought with them to what they might observe."[1]

The Ottomans in Europe

In the fifteenth century this attitude of disdainful indifference became more difficult to sustain as a new Muslim dynasty began to conquer large portions of southeastern and central Europe. The Ottomans (named after the founder of the dynasty, Osman, who died in 1326) began their long career as warrior chieftains of a confederation of Muslim Turkish tribes who had carved out a small principality for themselves in Anatolia, along the borders of what little still remained of the once mighty Byzantine empire. As Osman and his successors expanded the territory under their control they became major players in Byzantine and regional politics. By the 1350s Osman's son Orhan was not only the Byzantine emperor's son-in-law but effectively his overlord, and the Ottoman sultans who followed took advantage of conflicts among the kings and princes of the Christian states in the Balkans to win control over much of what is today Bulgaria, Serbia, northern Greece and southern Romania. Desperate Balkan rulers and Byzantine emperors (whose domain by this time consisted only of the city of Constantinople and bits of Greece) repeatedly appealed to the pope and the kings of western Europe for help, but little was forthcoming. Latin Christians were not much inclined to go out of their way to assist adherents of what they regarded as the deviant and schismatic Orthodox church, and anyway they were preoccupied with concerns closer to home.

The Ottoman advance into Europe was temporarily halted early in the fifteenth century when they were defeated by a Tatar conqueror from Central Asia, known in the west as Tamerlane, but after a decade of disorder the Ottoman state was restored and began to expand once again. In 1453 Sultan Mehmed II ("the Conqueror") finally extinguished the thousand-year-old Byzantine empire by capturing Constantinople, which he made the capital of the Ottoman empire and which would come to be known as Istanbul. The fall of Constantinople was a psychological shock to western Christians: however shrunken and decrepit the Byzantine empire had become, in the Christian popular imagination Constantinople had remained a great bastion of the faith. But no concerted and sustained military response to Ottoman expansion was forthcoming from the rulers of western Europe. Venice, whose wealth and power depended on the trade routes across the eastern Mediterranean, challenged the Ottomans in a series of inconclusive wars at sea, but on land the Ottomans continued to expand into southeastern Europe and western Asia. Sultan Selim (reigned 1512–20) defeated Persia and conquered

Syria, Egypt, northern Iraq and western Arabia; his son Suleiman ("the Magnificent," reigned 1520–1566) conquered most of Hungary and in 1529 laid siege to Vienna, capital of the so-called Holy Roman Empire in central Europe and Spain, ruled by the Habsburg dynasty. Though that siege was unsuccessful, the Ottomans remained in control of great stretches of southeastern and central Europe as well as of most of the Arab lands of what is today called the Middle East, as well as the North African coast up to Morocco. This made the Ottomans the dominant power in the Mediterranean as well as the Red Sea and gave them control of the most lucrative trade routes between Europe and Asia (see Map 2).

In the later fifteenth and sixteenth centuries, and even beyond, western Europeans thus had good reason to perceive the Ottomans (whom they usually called "Turks," which now often came to be used as a synonym for "Muslims") as a grave threat: there were long periods during which it seemed as if no European army or state could stand up to the apparently invincible Ottoman forces. But although the Ottoman state was officially Muslim, the threat it posed to Europe was not perceived as primarily religious or ideological, even if the coalitions that formed to fight the Ottomans often did so in the name of Christianity and were backed by the papacy. The crusading spirit had in fact long since dissipated in Europe, replaced by the power politics of an emerging state system in which, despite being perceived as culturally alien, the Ottomans were deeply involved. The Ottoman empire was obviously one of the great states of Europe, in fact it was the single most powerful state in Europe, and the relations of European Christian states with the Ottomans were largely governed not by religion but by political expediency, by *raison d'état*, in ways that would have been shocking to medieval Latin Christians.

In the 1490s, for example, Mehmed the Conqueror's younger son Jem, who had fled into exile in Europe after his older brother Bayezid seized the sultanate, was a pawn in the intrigues of various European Christian princes who hoped to use him to undermine the Ottomans even as they were taking money from Bayezid to keep Jem a prisoner. That same decade witnessed Pope Alexander VI secretly assuring Sultan Bayezid that he opposed the Habsburg emperor's plans for a crusade against the Ottomans, and a number of Italian city-states conspiring with the Ottomans to jointly attack their common enemy Venice. In 1535 King Francis I of France concluded a treaty of friendship and alliance with Sultan Suleiman, directed at their common enemy the Habsburgs, while later in the century the pope sought an alliance with Muslim (but Shi'i) Persia, historic enemy of the Ottomans, in order to confront the latter with enemies on both its western and eastern frontiers.

On other levels, too, relations were complicated. Conversion to Islam could open the highest positions in the Ottoman state and army to ambitious and talented European Christians, and not a few took advantage of the opportunity and "turned Turk." Many Balkan Christian noblemen became loyal vassals of the Ottomans and even fought fellow Christians as part of the Ottoman army. The Ottoman empire, which like most Muslim states generally tolerated Christians and Jews and left them in peace as long as they did not make trouble and paid their taxes, welcomed refugees and outcasts from a much less tolerant Christian Europe. This was true for many of the Jews expelled from Spain in 1492, when Muslim-ruled Granada fell and the Reconquista was completed, but also for Protestant refugees from Catholic persecution and other dissident Christians.

The zenith of Ottoman power in the first half of the sixteenth century coincided with the era of the Reformation in Europe, which witnessed the disintegration of a nominally unified western Christendom into mutually hostile Catholic and Protestant churches, amidst much bloodshed. Islam was no longer such a burning issue in and of itself; it was, rather, something which one group of Christians used to attack other Christians. Like his medieval predecessors, the Protestant reformer Martin Luther had plenty of unpleasant things to say about Islam, but for him it was not the real Antichrist, the main enemy; rather, the arch-enemy of Christ and his true church was the corrupt Roman Catholic church headed by the pope. Luther insisted that Christendom would never defeat Islam unless it first confronted and destroyed the enemy within and restored the true faith. Other Protestants saw Catholicism as fundamentally similar to Islam and denounced what they termed "Turkopapism." In a similar vein, defenders of Catholicism denounced Protestantism as akin to Islam, although (as one Catholic polemicist put it in 1597) "the fundamental principles of Muhammadanism are far better than those of Calvinism. Both seek to destroy the Christian faith, both deny the Divinity of Christ, not only is the pseudo-Gospel of [the Protestant leader John] Calvin no better than the Qur'an of Muhammad, but in many respects it is wickeder and more repulsive."[2] For their part the Ottomans soon became involved in the wars of the Reformation, indirectly supporting the Protestant cause (in alliance with France and some of the German states) since their common enemy was the empire ruled by the Habsburgs, the bulwark of Catholicism.

The Ottoman image and the emergence of Orientalism

For an entire historic period the Ottomans were the great bogeyman of Christian Europe: they evoked considerable fear and in popular literature were often depicted as cruel, violent and fanatical, in ways that drew on long-prevalent caricatures of Islam. There were also many lurid and titillating stories in circulation about the purported sexual vices of the Turks and what allegedly went on in the sultan's "harem" (the private quarters of the imperial palace). But some Europeans, while continuing to reject Islam and insist on the truth of Christianity, were able to adopt a more objective attitude toward the Ottomans. In fact, in the sixteenth century many educated European observers were awed by the immense power and wealth of the Ottoman state – it was they who gave Sultan Suleiman the epithet "magnificent," not the Ottomans, who called him "the lawgiver" – and sought to grasp the secret of the empire's success, often contrasting Ottoman virtues with the defects of their own societies.

Ogier Ghiselin de Busbecq, who served as the Habsburg emperor's ambassador to the Ottoman court in 1554–1562, praised the Ottoman civil and military elite as a meritocracy: "no single man owed his dignity to anything but his personal merits and bravery; no one is distinguished from the rest by his birth, and honour is paid to each man according to the nature of the duty and offices which he discharges . . . Thus, among the Turks, dignities, offices, and administrative posts are the rewards of ability and merit; those who are dishonest, lazy, and slothful never attain to distinction, but remain in obscurity and contempt. This is why the Turks succeed in all that they attempt and are a dominating race and daily extend the bounds of their rule." By contrast, Busbecq noted with apparent disgust, "our method is very different; there is no room for merit, but everything depends on birth; considerations of which alone open the way to high official position."[3]

Writing around the same time, the French jurist and historian Jean Bodin (1529/30–96) rejected the claim of the Habsburgs to the title of emperor and insisted that "if anywhere there exists an authority worthy of the name of empire or of authentic monarchy, it is surely the [Ottoman] sultan who wields it."

He occupies the richest lands of Asia, Africa, and Europe; his dominion extends throughout the Mediterranean, with the exception of a few islands. His military might rivals that of all the other princes combined: he has driven the Persian and the Muscovite troops far beyond his borders, he has conquered Christian kingdoms and the Byzantine empire and has even laid waste the German provinces . . . It would be far more just to regard the Osmanli [i.e. Ottoman] sultan as the inheritor of the Roman Empire . . .[4]

The great political theorist Niccolò Machiavelli (1469–1527) saw the Ottoman empire as exemplifying one of the two main types of states. Unlike states such as France, ruled by both a king and a hereditary aristocracy, states such as the Ottoman empire were ruled by "a prince and his servants, who help in the administration of the territory by his grace and favor" but (unlike European noblemen) had no hereditary privileges or independent power base. Yet although Machiavelli argued that the Ottoman type of state gave the ruler greater personal power, he did not classify the Ottoman empire as tyrannical and felt that it possessed many of the virtues associated with the great empires of antiquity, including Rome.[5]

The same period that witnessed such relatively dispassionate, objective and sometimes even admiring evaluations of Ottoman state and society also saw the earliest stages of the emergence of a distinct branch of the humanities whose focus was the study of the Orient – which initially meant virtually all of Asia, from the lands along the eastern shores of the Mediterranean (which Europeans often called "the Levant," derived from the French term for "land where the sun rises") all the way to India and China. Much later, in the nineteenth century, the specialized field of scholarly learning which studied the languages, religions, histories and cultures of that Orient would come to be called "Orientalism." Islam was obviously central to this emerging new field of knowledge, since much of the region between Europe and China was predominantly Muslim, and Renaissance proto-Orientalists saw themselves as developing a fuller and more accurate understanding of that religion by studying a wide range of texts in the actual languages of the Orient, rather than relying on the poor translations and flawed commentaries produced by medieval scholars for polemical or missionary purposes.

Political and commercial considerations also sometimes helped stimulate the development of Orientalism as a scholarly field in this period. For example, the creation of chairs of Arabic at the universities of Oxford and Cambridge in the mid-seventeenth century was supported by English officials and merchants anxious to expand English trade in the Mediterranean; there was also widespread concern about the many Britons who had been captured and held for ransom by Muslim raiders (the "Barbary pirates") based along the North African coast. But a changing cultural and intellectual climate also contributed: the spirit of Renaissance humanism, the growing pluralism of thought made possible by the collapse of the medieval church's ideological monopoly, and a spreading scholarly commitment (not always achieved) to objectivity enabled scholars to begin to study Islam, the Ottoman empire and related subjects in what they took to be a much less prejudicial manner and to share their work with others across Europe.

In 1539 Guillaume Postel became the first holder of a newly created chair in Arabic at the Collège de France in Paris, and gradually other

European institutions and universities, including the Vatican, began creating positions for scholars and teachers of the languages, cultures and religions of Asia. Postel, his colleagues and their successors over the succeeding two centuries published translations from Arabic, Persian and Turkish, including literary classics like the *Thousand and One Nights*, as well as numerous studies of Islam and of the customs and histories of the peoples of the Orient. While many of these translations and studies were a great improvement on what had come before, they were in many cases still imbued with – or at least influenced by – derogatory attitudes toward Islam inherited from the medieval period. Thus Postel, while emphasizing that he had studied the Qur'an in the original Arabic rather than in translation and dreaming of somehow integrating Christianity and Islam, felt obliged to point out what he saw as the Qur'an's "perverse arguments" and Muhammad's "stratagems" for obtaining acceptance of his (false) doctrines and to emphasize how unfortunate it was that so many people had succumbed to his "disastrous dogmas."[6]

As we will see, derogatory attitudes toward Islam and the Orient were to persist in Orientalist scholarship for a very long time, even as the fruits of that scholarship multiplied and eventually reached a much wider public than ever before. Beyond the world of scholarship, translations and a great outpouring of books by European travelers in the Ottoman domains and beyond, some relatively accurate and fair-minded and others much less so, fed (and further stimulated) popular interest in an Islamic Orient often perceived as exotic and mysterious but (by the eighteenth century, at least) no longer very threatening.

Ottoman decline and Oriental despotism

Toward the end of the sixteenth century, favorable attitudes toward the Ottomans began to be replaced among educated western Europeans by much less positive views which emphasized how profoundly different and defective the Ottoman empire was. As the French historian Lucette Valensi put it in *The Birth of the Despot*, her 1987 study of how members of the ruling elite of Venice saw the Ottoman empire in whose giant shadow they lived, "from now on the Ottoman Empire belongs to a different horizon. All of the reports emphasize the empire's fundamental incompatibility with the Venetian system . . . their basic premise is that the two orders are absolutely at variance with each other."[7] Many of the same things that had earlier been highlighted as signs of Ottoman virtue and superiority now began to be interpreted as defects, as signs of inferiority and degeneracy. As the seventeenth century wore on, Venetian and other European observers found little or nothing to admire or respect in Ottoman society, nothing from which they could learn; instead, the "Turks" were increasingly depicted as boorish, ignorant, dishonorable, immoral, ineffectual, corrupt and irrational. The older image of the Ottoman state as an efficient, just, virtuous and tolerant meritocracy faded away, to be replaced by a depiction of that state as corrupt, oppressive and brutal.

This changing perception of the Ottomans certainly had something to do with developments in the Ottoman empire in the late sixteenth and seventeenth centuries. In that period the Ottoman empire reached the limits of territorial expansion in Europe and gradually lost the military superiority it had long enjoyed over European Christian states. Although an Ottoman army was able to lay siege to Vienna, the Habsburg capital, as late as 1683, the campaign ended disastrously for the Ottomans and with the Treaty of Karlowitz in 1699 the Ottomans were for the first time compelled to surrender territory they had long held in central Europe. By then Europeans were coming to perceive the Ottoman empire not as a serious military threat but as weak and on the defensive. In the eighteenth century aggressive European states, primarily Russia and Austria, began encroaching successfully on Ottoman-ruled territory, and for the first time it became possible to imagine the empire's disintegration or dismemberment.

Contemporary Ottoman officials and chroniclers themselves noted – and lamented – what they saw as the contrast between the military success, political stability and economic prosperity which the Ottomans had enjoyed down through the reign of Sultan Suleiman, and the political and financial crises, breakdown of internal order, widespread corruption and military defeats that seemed to characterize the reigns of most of Suleiman's successors, few of whom were deemed as capable as their forebears. They decried what they saw as the deterioration of the institutions which had made the Ottoman state great and sought ways to restore its fortunes.

However, as Lucette Valensi and others have argued, changing European perceptions of the Ottoman empire and explanations of its difficulties had as much to do with western Europe's evolving self-image as they did with what was actually happening in that empire itself. In the later sixteenth and seventeenth centuries, under the impact of the Reformation, numerous protracted and bloody wars, and profound social and economic changes, leading European states became more centralized, more bureaucratized and more powerful. This led western European statesmen and political philosophers to search for ways to make sense of the rapidly changing world around them by formulating new conceptions of political order and legitimacy that met the needs of the emerging state system and its new kinds of internal and interstate politics. Rejecting what they had come to see as medieval stagnation, ignorance and obscurantism, Renaissance and early modern European thinkers instead often turned for inspiration to the ancient Greeks and Romans. They reread and reinterpreted Aristotle and other classical political philosophers and found in the Greek *polis* and the Roman republic models for emulation. Along the way they adopted the contrast which many writers of ancient Greece had drawn between Greek freedom and Asian despotism, identifying themselves with the former and the Ottomans with the latter.

European political thinkers came to see their own societies as based on freedom and on law, which limited (or should limit) the power even of kings and the aristocracy. In contrast, the Ottoman empire now came to be seen as the prime contemporary example of despotism, a state characterized by the concentration of arbitrary, lawless and absolute power in the hands of the all-powerful sovereign (the sultan) and the reduction of all his subjects to virtual slavery. That this image had little to do with the actual dynamics of Ottoman society, law, statecraft or politics was irrelevant: this was the lens through which the Ottomans came to be perceived in Europe, and as a result much that had seemed admirable about the Ottomans in the fifteenth and early sixteenth centuries came to seem abominable in the late sixteenth and seventeenth centuries. When they looked at the Ottoman empire, Europeans now perceived an extreme case of tendencies they feared and condemned in their own societies, the triumph of despotism and of the moral corruption and social degeneration it inevitably produced.

The Ottomans thus became a prime example of what European political thinkers came to call Oriental despotism, a concept which was most fully developed by the great French writer and jurist Montesquieu (1689–1755). In his enormously popular *Persian Letters* (first published in 1721), purportedly written by two Persian travelers in France, Montesquieu satirized and criticized many aspects of contemporary French society and politics. In *The Spirit of the Laws* (1748), which had a great influence on political thought in Europe and in the British colonies in North America, Montesquieu analyzed what he saw as the three main types of government – republic, monarchy and despotism – and argued for separating and balancing the various powers of government in order to protect individual rights. Like Aristotle and many others since, Montesquieu thought that human temperament, and thus social and political systems, were largely determined by geography and climate. People in colder climates, like Europe, were naturally active, virile and brave and could therefore preserve and extend their liberty, while those who lived in hot climates were naturally effeminate and servile; this was why power in Asia was always despotic.

As with earlier depictions of the Ottoman empire as tyrannical and profoundly alien, Montesquieu's denunciation of Ottoman despotism had more to do with anxieties and debates within Europe itself than with Ottoman realities. The odious example of the Ottomans gave Montesquieu and others a safe way to criticize and resist what they saw as the despotic tendencies of European monarchs and to delineate, by means of a sharp contrast, their emerging vision of a new kind of rational and moral political order. Not all European political thinkers accepted Montesquieu's assertions about Oriental despotism, but as we will see the concept would live on and flourish, in a variety of forms, through the nineteenth and twentieth centuries. Karl Marx, Max Weber and many other European thinkers would accept and deploy the fundamental premises of the concept of Oriental despotism in order to help explain why a socially, economically and culturally dynamic "West" had come to dominate the world, including many parts of Asia and Africa inhabited largely by Muslims, and why that domination was necessary and good.

The beginnings of European global hegemony

Changing European perceptions of the Ottomans, and the growing relative weakness of the Ottoman empire, must be set in their broader historical context: the profound transformation of (western) Europe's relations with other regions of the world that began at the very end of the fifteenth century and eventually produced a new structure of global political and economic power, the one within which we still live today. To gauge the significance of these transformations, one must remember that compared to China, India or parts of what is today called the Middle East, western Europe was until about 1500 relatively poor, underpopulated and technologically unremarkable, off on the periphery of the "Old World" (i.e. Asia, Europe and northern Africa) and rather remote from what had long been its economic and political centers of gravity. In Roman times and then again on a much larger scale between 1250 and 1350, there was substantial trade between western Europe and east Asia, via what by the latter period were the largely Muslim lands of western and central Asia. But it is an indication of Asia's economic primacy that its exports – spices from today's Indonesia and India, silk and porcelain from China, and other luxury items – were in much greater demand in Europe than European products (mainly textiles) were in Asian lands. Europe's gold and silver thus tended to drain eastward, to pay for the luxury imports

wealthy Europeans so desperately desired and for which they had little
to offer in exchange except bullion.[8]

In this transregional trade across the Old World, Middle Eastern merchants (Muslim, Jewish and Christian), cities and states played a key
role: they dominated many of the land and sea routes, trading centers
and networks which connected western Europe with Iran, the Red Sea
and Indian Ocean regions (including the east coast of Africa), central
Asia, India, southeast Asia and China. The merchants of the great Italian
commercial city-states, especially Venice and Genoa, who traveled across
the Mediterranean seeking Asian products for resale in western Europe
were thus confronted with a monopoly they could not evade or break: if
they wanted the pepper, nutmeg, ginger, cloves, cinnamon, sugar, silk,
gold, coffee and other commodities for sale in the markets of Egypt and
the Levant, they had to pay the high prices demanded by local merchants
and states, including the Ottomans, who were well aware of the wealth
that control of these trade routes brought them. They faced a similar
problem in northern Africa, where Muslim states and merchants in the
cities and towns along the Mediterranean coast controlled the trade in
gold, slaves and spices originating in the lands south of the Sahara desert.

European merchants and states had long dreamed of finding some way
to gain direct access to India, the "Spice Islands" of southeast Asia, China
and Africa and thereby cut out the middlemen who were pocketing the
lion's share of the enormous profits to be made from transregional trade.
This dream finally began to be realized in the second half of the fifteenth
century, when Portuguese expeditions started pushing their way down
the western coast of Africa, eventually reaching lands beyond the sphere
of Muslim control and inaugurating direct trade in spices, slaves and
gold. Over a period of decades Portuguese expeditions voyaged further
and further south along the African coast and eventually reached the
Cape of Good Hope at the southern tip of Africa. In 1498 Vasco da
Gama led an expedition which went all the way around Africa, crossed
the Indian Ocean and for the first time reached India itself.

Portugal followed up the opening of this new route to India by establishing trading posts, forts and then colonies along the east African coast,
in India and among the Spice Islands. Direct access to, and eventually
control of, the lucrative spice trade, and later trade in other commodities as well, brought the Portuguese and their European partners vast
new wealth. The Ottomans and some local rulers understood the threat
which the arrival of the Portuguese in the Indian Ocean posed and did
their best to drive them out, but their efforts failed. Within a few decades
the Spanish would follow in the footsteps of the Portuguese, seeking to
establish a trading empire of their own in southeast Asia, and later still

the Dutch, the English and the French would arrive to challenge the Portuguese and the Spanish for hegemony in the region and carve out their own spheres of economic and political influence.

A few years before da Gama reached India, Portugal's neighbor Spain had sponsored an expedition led by a Genoese named Christopher Columbus, who planned to reach Asia by sailing west across the Atlantic. In 1492 Columbus reached what turned out to be not Asia but a "New World" hitherto unknown to Europeans and others in the Old World – a hemisphere which soon came to be called the Americas. (In that same year Granada, the last Muslim stronghold in the Iberian peninsula, fell to the Christians, and the king and queen of a fully "reconquered" Spain ordered the expulsion of all of that country's Jews; Spain's remaining Muslims would be expelled or forcibly baptized a little later.) The subsequent conquest of vast territories in Central and South America and the exploitation of their rich mineral, agricultural and human resources brought Spain great wealth and power; later other European states – Portugal, the Netherlands, England and France – began seizing territory and establishing colonies of their own in the Americas, amidst rivalry and considerable warfare among them.

Initially situated in something of a backwater, then, western European countries began from the early sixteenth century onward to establish new global trading networks and eventually empires. These were made possible by new technologies of seafaring, warfare and communications that enabled European states to conquer and effectively control far-flung territories and exploit them with a relatively high degree of efficiency for the benefit of the colonizing power. In the sixteenth century European states conquered vast stretches of territory in the Americas, destroying indigenous states and subjugating their populations; at about the same time they began to seize control of strategic trading centers and routes and eventually came to dominate substantial territories in India and the islands of southeast Asia as well as along the coasts of Africa. The creation of empires by means of military conquest was of course not a new phenomenon in human history; in a sense the Portuguese, the Spanish and the other European states were simply following in the footsteps of earlier conquerors and empire-builders in all parts of the world. What was new and different about the global system that began to emerge in the sixteenth century was above all its scale and its structure.

The global empires which western European states began to carve out for themselves from the sixteenth century onward consisted not of adjacent territories in Europe itself, the kinds of empires which the Romans or Habsburgs or Ottomans had created by conquering neighboring principalities. Rather, the new colonial empires consisted of diverse territories in very different parts of the world, often separated from one another and from the colonizing power by thousands of miles of ocean. Thus the Portuguese empire eventually came to encompass Brazil in the Americas, Angola and Mozambique in Africa, and key sites in southern and southeast Asia; the Spanish ruled most of South and Central America as well as parts of North America, various Caribbean islands (including Cuba and Puerto Rico), and what became known as the Philippines in southeast Asia. The Dutch gradually seized the vast archipelago of islands that would later constitute Indonesia as well as territories in South America, the Caribbean and North America (New Amsterdam, later renamed New York), and sponsored colonial settlement in southern Africa. The English, having conquered Ireland and absorbed Scotland and Wales, established extensive colonies in North America and the Caribbean, came to rule vast chunks of Africa and southeast Asia (as well as parts of the Middle East), and beat out European rivals to become the dominant power in India, the "jewel in the crown" of the British empire; by the mid-nineteenth century the British empire encompassed nearly one-fourth of the world's population. France's empire ultimately included huge swathes of Africa, parts of the Middle East and much of southeast Asia (later Vietnam, Cambodia and Laos) along with a number of Caribbean and Pacific Ocean islands. In the late nineteenth and early twentieth centuries Germany, Italy, Belgium, the United States and Japan also sought to acquire colonies.

Having said this, it should be kept in mind that the division of the globe among the European imperialist powers was a process that unfolded very unevenly and gradually over three or four centuries. As one scholar of relations between Europe and Asia put it, "from 1500 to 1800 relations between East and West were ordinarily conducted within a framework and on terms established by the Asian nations. Except for those who lived in a few colonial strongholds, the Europeans in the East were all there on sufferance . . . And, in the sixteenth century, they were never in a position to force their will upon the imperial rulers of India or China."[9] In fact, some scholars have argued that until 1800 or so China and Britain were not that different from one another in economic terms and that it was only during the nineteenth century that (thanks largely to Britain's natural resources and its overseas empire) their economic paths diverged so sharply.[10] In any case, it was not until the middle of the nineteenth century that China and Japan began to be directly threatened by foreign encroachment and that all of India fell under more or less effective British control, and not until late in that century that new military and medical technologies allowed European states to expand beyond the coastal regions of East and West Africa and conquer, "pacify" and effectively administer the vast interior of the African continent. A number of the colonies originally settled by Europeans – the British colonies that became the United States, the Spanish colonies in South and Central America, Canada, Australia, New Zealand and South Africa – eventually came to form independent or autonomous states. Nonetheless, by the end of the First World War, the old European colonial powers, joined by European latecomers like Italy, Germany and Belgium as well as by the United States and Japan, had effectively divided much of the planet outside Europe and the Americas amongst themselves.

The gradual carving up of the non-European world into formal or informal empires ruled from Europe was from the start propelled by the development of new dynamics and networks of trade, production and the provision of labor. Vast new wealth flowed into Europe as European merchants and states used diplomacy, cunning and violence to gain access to, and then monopolize, the sources of commodities which they had previously been able to obtain only in small quantities and at high prices from Middle Eastern and other middlemen. But European business interests, backed by their governments, quickly moved to realize even greater profits by controlling and expanding the actual *production* of profitable commodities. This presented them with new problems, and the solutions they developed to those problems transformed political, economic and eventually cultural relations among the various regions of the globe as well as social, economic and political life within many of those regions, including Europe itself, shaping the contours of the modern world and establishing hierarchies of wealth and power that persist into the present.

For example, to take maximum advantage of the vast mineral and agricultural potential of their new colonies in the Americas, the Portuguese and the Spanish, and later other European powers, needed an abundant supply of labor with which to work the mines and cultivate valuable export crops. Enslaving the indigenous inhabitants (the "Indians") proved unsatisfactory, since they died off too quickly as a result of exposure to Old World diseases and of overwork. To solve this problem European states, merchants and planters turned to Africa, where they could tap a new source of labor – slave labor. Over the course of three centuries, Portuguese, Spanish, British, Dutch, French and later United States businessmen, backed by their governments, acquired millions of Africans, transported them to the New World under unspeakable conditions, and implanted them there as a servile labor force. Thus the European conquest of the Americas led to the development of what eventually became key (and immensely profitable) components of the new global economy, the transatlantic slave trade and the new societies in the Americas that relied heavily on African slave labor.

A complex system developed in which Africans (initially captured largely by fellow Africans) were sold to European slave dealers and shipped to the Americas, where they were usually put to work cultivating and processing crops in the colonies, for example sugar cane in Brazil and on the islands of the Caribbean, supplying the apparently insatiable European demand for sugar, previously a luxury only the wealthy could afford. This system provided a great many European plantation owners, merchants, shipbuilders and ship owners, slave traders, bankers, investors and producers of provisions for the slaves with large profits. Later, slave labor would also be used to cultivate crops intended for use in manufacturing, for example the cotton grown in parts of the southern United States which British textile factories turned into cloth and which was then sold around the world. Slavery in various forms had been a feature of many human societies for thousands of years; but with the discovery of the New World and the vast new opportunities for profit it opened up, the trade in enslaved human beings and their exploitation in agricultural production (and to a lesser extent in other arenas) expanded on an unprecedented scale.

Elsewhere Europeans used other labor systems, coerced or free, to produce commodities for export to the growing European market and to new markets in other parts of the world. Coffee is a case in point: initially grown in the highlands of Ethiopia and largely monopolized by the Muslim coffee merchants of Cairo, it was by the eighteenth century being cultivated on a huge scale on plantations at opposite ends of the earth, in Dutch-ruled Java (hence "java" as a nickname for coffee) and in Spanish and English colonies in the Americas (including the countries today known as Colombia and Jamaica). By late in that century people in the Middle East were often drinking coffee imported from Asia and the Americas, which was now cheaper than coffee from local sources. Dutch merchants expanded the production of cotton textiles in India and exported them worldwide, while the English imported vast quantities of tea from China and later from new plantations elsewhere in Asia. New World food plants like the potato and maize (corn) spread rapidly to become a staple of life in many other regions, including much of Europe.

As a result of these developments, which radically expanded the volume of world trade and dramatically transformed patterns of production and consumption, western Europe gradually became the center of a new global economy, the region into which the lion's share of the vast profits of transregional trade and production flowed. This brought unprecedented wealth to some Europeans (though many others remained or became poor) and enhanced the power of European states, or at least those states which managed to utilize their wealth effectively. Portugal and Spain, the first to create vast empires outside of Europe, lost out in the seventeenth century to aggressive rivals, first the Dutch and then the leading colonial powers of the eighteenth, nineteenth and twentieth centuries, Britain and France. By contrast, other parts of the world, once fabled for their wealth and refinement, were gradually incorporated into this emerging economic and political order as subordinate and dependent players, a vast periphery of colonies and of independent but weak states whose foreign trade was dominated by European merchants and whose course of development was increasingly influenced by the requirements of the economies of the system's core in western Europe.

The Industrial Revolution, which began to transform the economies of Britain and subsequently other western European countries from the later eighteenth century and which the wealth brought by empire and slavery helped stimulate and finance, sharply deepened the disparities between the European center and the non-European periphery of the emerging new global system. The workings of the world market, policy decisions by hegemonic European states and their superior military power led to partial deindustrialization in other parts of the world as machine-made European goods undermined or destroyed local production. Increasingly (though never entirely), the new system of political and economic power tended to assign two roles to much of the non-European world: they supplied agricultural and mineral raw materials for use or processing in western Europe, and they consumed the finished goods that Europe exported.

By the later nineteenth century Europeans dominated trade among various regions of the world, but also in some places a great deal of regional and even local trade. They also controlled key markets and sources of capital and enjoyed supremacy in manufacturing. European economic power was backed up by the might of European warships, armies and colonial administrations; as a result the great bulk of the wealth this new world system produced flowed into the hands of European companies, investors and states, with local rulers, landowners and traders as lesser beneficiaries. Everywhere, including in Europe itself, the knitting together of this modern global system was a complex, disruptive, often violent and sometimes catastrophically painful process. The outcome over the centuries was a growing chasm between western Europe and the large portions of Asia, Africa and the Americas subject to its control, with the latter experiencing deepening poverty and backwardness, sometimes in absolute terms but certainly relative to a western Europe which was attaining unprecedented wealth and new heights of scientific, technological and cultural achievement.[11]

The Ottoman empire offers a good example of the deleterious impact which incorporation into this emerging global system of trade, production and consumption could have even on a state that would remain formally independent of European rule into the twentieth century. From the sixteenth century onward the key trade routes linking Europe with Asia no longer ran through the Middle East and the region very gradually became something of an economic backwater. The Ottoman state's ability to expand, to maintain internal order and eventually even to defend itself against its enemies was weakened by inflation and recurring fiscal crises.[12] European merchants, backed by their governments, exploited the commercial privileges which the Ottomans had granted them much earlier and, often working with local non-Muslim partners, secured a dominant role in foreign trade. Eventually the empire's economy became more oriented than it had been earlier to exporting agricultural products and raw materials to Europe and importing European manufactured goods, for example textiles, which hurt local craftsmen. In the late nineteenth century heavy borrowing from European banks led to bankruptcy and the imposition of European financial supervision. The empire's growing political and military weakness was thus accompanied by, and was in part attributable to, important shifts in its economic life and a deepening dependency.

The West versus the rest?

We saw in Chapter 1 how "Europe" began as a geographical term denoting one of the segments of the earth's landmass as it was then known to (or imagined by) Europeans – though they did not yet think of themselves as such. We also saw how, early in the Christian era, the term came to be associated with a biblical genealogy ("the sons of Japheth") which seemed to promise Latin Christians dominion over the descendants of Noah's other sons in Asia and Africa. Similarly, the idea of a "West" (successor to the western Roman empire, Latinate in culture, Catholic in religion) developed in the medieval period, in opposition to a Byzantine "East" whose high culture was Greek and in which the dominant form of Christianity came to be seen as deviant, but also in opposition to the world of Islam, perceived as a grave threat and as a deeply alien and repellent culture, and finally to the largely unknown lands further east, fabled India and China. Later, from the Renaissance of the fifteenth century onward, the medieval western church's dream of a unified Christian commonwealth faded away, to be replaced by a somewhat more secular and geographic conception of a West which included more than one kind of Christian (as well as a Jewish minority) and consisted increasingly of (often warring) independent states whose bases of legitimacy were no longer predominantly religious.

In the course of this shift in how the world was conceived and how people identified themselves, many thinkers in Europe moved away from the traditional Christian view which looked back to the birth of Jesus as having marked a radical break with all that came before, the beginning of a new era, and forward to Christ's "second coming," which would mark the end of historical time and usher in the kingdom of heaven on earth. Instead they reached back into the pre-Christian era and traced the ancestry of "the West" to the great (albeit pagan) civilizations of classical antiquity, Greece and Rome. As they saw it, with the Renaissance that began in the fifteenth century Europeans had finally begun to move beyond centuries of medieval stagnation and ignorance, ushering in a new age, the modern era, in which they had not only recovered the authentic wisdom of the ancients but were building on it to achieve unprecedented advances in many fields of human endeavor.

This emerging conception of the West as a distinct civilization was based on the assertion of an essential continuity and coherence across vast stretches of time and space, from the purported birth of that civilization in ancient Greece through almost twenty centuries to its re-emergence and flowering in the modern age, in the very different setting of fifteenth- and sixteenth-century western Europe. To claim this kind of unbroken cultural continuity required presuming that the West as a civilization had some essence, some core, which had always remained basically unchanged, intact and unsullied by contamination from "outside" sources. It also required assuming that as a civilization the West was unique and essentially different from all other cultures. Accepting these premises had the effect of defining the West and framing its history in such a way as to render invisible many of the cultural, economic and political interactions, linkages and processes which had helped shape what would later come to be called the West – for example, what the ancient Greeks and Romans had borrowed from other peoples and the powerful impact which (as we have seen) Arab culture had had on medieval Europe. It also meant ignoring the many aspects of European history, society and culture that could not be made to fit with the new story Europeans began to tell themselves about the West and its transcendent values. At the same time – and most crucially for our purposes here – it also made it difficult for early modern Europeans (and their successors) to grasp how it was they had come to see themselves as inhabitants of a distinct and superior West.[13]

This is a crucial point because this reconceptualization of European identity began to take place just as Europeans' geographical and cultural horizons were expanding enormously as a result of the late fifteenth- and early sixteenth-century "voyages of discovery," and just as the new European global empires and a new world economic order increasingly dominated by Europeans were coming into being. Inevitably, emerging new conceptions of what Europe and the West meant were profoundly influenced by the fact that western European states were simultaneously moving toward a position of global hegemony, exercising political and economic power over non-Western states and peoples.

Like people everywhere, the inhabitants of western Europe tended to define who they *were* in relation to who and what they thought they *were not*. The process by which people in the West came to define what made their own civilization distinctive among the civilizations of the world therefore entailed drawing a series of sharp contrasts between what they now began to see as Western and what they began to see as non-Western. These contrasts delineated those characteristics and virtues which Europeans were coming to see as unique to Western civilization, especially in its modern form, and which they thought accounted for its increasing power, wealth and knowledge. Conversely, it was other societies' lack of these characteristics, these core values and traits, that made them weak and backward and that thus both facilitated and justified Western domination. In the course of defining who they were not and who their "others" were, Europeans simultaneously defined and consolidated their own identity.

We have already seen a good example of this process at work in the way in which, in the early modern period, western European thinkers appropriated the contrast which the ancient Greeks had drawn between Greek freedom and Asian despotism, a contrast the Greeks had used to highlight their self-perceived uniqueness and superiority and denigrate their enemies. Europeans now deployed that contrast to explain what they were coming to see as a profound difference which distinguished their own societies from those of their neighbor the Ottoman empire, other Muslim states and more broadly all Asian and African societies. In this conception the West, or Europe, came to see itself as the domain of freedom and of law, as opposed to the Ottomans and other "Oriental" societies which were despotisms and suffered from all the social and political perversions which despotic government invariably produced. The freedom and commitment to the rule of law which allegedly characterized the West not only explained the West's superiority, it also tended to justify Western rule over non-Western societies, since only Western tutelage could terminate the despotism endemic in those societies and replace it with the order and the rule of law necessary for real progress and modern civilization.

In reality, of course, European or Western culture has been no more uniform and monolithic than any other culture: people in the West, like people elsewhere, have never really ceased to struggle (often very violently) amongst themselves over differing definitions of who they are and who they should be. Yet although there were always dissenting schools of thought which offered alternative visions of what the West was and was not and how it should relate to the rest of the world, over the last few centuries a powerful view emerged that became deeply ingrained in many domains of society and culture in the West, so ingrained that it has been very hard for people to even recognize its pervasive influence. By delineating and positing a series of qualities which the modern West seemed to possess and which differentiated it from other civilizations which lacked those qualities, western Europeans gradually defined what they believed were the special and exclusive hallmarks of their civilization: freedom, law, rationality, science, progress, intellectual curiosity, and the spirit of invention, adventure and enterprise.

These were what Westerners came to see as the core values of Western civilization. Their origins could supposedly be traced back to the ancient Greeks, and they were what enabled Westerners, uniquely among the peoples of the earth, to develop the attitudes, the ideas, the technologies and the institutions necessary to bring the modern world into being and dominate it politically, economically and culturally. As a result the West came to be conceived of as the driving force in world history: while other civilizations may have contributed to the store of human knowledge and culture in the past, it was the West alone which was now truly dynamic, forging ahead in the vanguard of modernity. And as people in the West came to define themselves and their age as modern, separated from their own ancient and medieval ancestors by a great and ever-widening gulf, they increasingly transposed that same division between premodern and modern onto the contemporary world. The West was envisioned as modern, while the non-West was premodern, traditional, backward, even primitive. Non-Western societies thus seemed to face a stark but inescapable choice: they could either emulate the West and become truly modern or they were doomed to stagnate and increasingly fall behind in the march of civilization.

Explaining the "rise of the West"

Over the centuries European thinkers have explained the "rise of the West" – the unquestionable fact that from about 1500 onward (some)

Europeans began to forge ahead in science, technology and many other fields of human endeavor and came to dominate the world politically, economically and culturally – in a variety of ways. Many early modern people simply saw Europe's success as a manifestation of God's favor: God was bestowing the blessings of superior knowledge and power on those who adhered to the one true faith and was enabling them to bring Christianity to the whole world. Moreover, had not the Bible foretold that the descendants of Japheth were ordained to rule over the descendants of Ham (i.e. Africans) and of Shem (Asians)? Later, as we will see in Chapter 3, especially in the latter part of the nineteenth century and on into the twentieth, many people, including many eminently respectable scientists, would come to believe that there were clear and profound biological differences among the races, with the "white" (or "Aryan" or "Caucasian") race deemed to be naturally superior and therefore uniquely suited to be the prime creator of civilization and to rule over the other inferior races. Such theories helped justify the enslavement of black Africans and the subjugation of nonwhite peoples in the colonies, who were deemed to be not fully human or inherently inferior to "Caucasians" and therefore not entitled to the rights and liberties Europeans would come to see as their birthright. These same theories would also be used to define European Jews as subhuman and therefore deserving of segregation, persecution and even extermination.

Beyond appeals to God or to myths of racial superiority, which are today not deemed intellectually or socially respectable and always had their opponents, the great majority of those who have sought to explain what the author of a 1981 book called "the European miracle" have pointed to specific cultural traits, patterns of social organization or historical forces which they regard as having been unique to Europe well before 1492 and which enabled it to achieve unprecedented worldly success and power thereafter.[14] For example, some scholars have argued that unlike people in other cultures, late medieval Europeans were well endowed with such traits as intellectual curiosity, rationality, openness to innovation, a belief in progress, and a spirit of adventure and enterprise. Echoing the environmental determinism of Aristotle and Montesquieu, others have suggested that Europe's temperate climate and relatively benign environment facilitated its rise to global pre-eminence.

Still others have argued that late medieval European societies had unique features – the role of the church, the fragmented and decentralized character of state power, the structure of European families, a distinctive European personality type, and so on – which laid the basis for Europe's leap into modernity a bit later on. Scholars influenced by Marxism, while strongly critical of the evils of colonial rule, have tended to argue that the feudal social and economic order that characterized premodern western Europe was uniquely suited to give rise to the social forces and dynamics that brought capitalism, and with it the modern world, into being. By contrast, Asian societies and states hindered or blocked the indigenous development of capitalism, which therefore had to be introduced by European conquerors, traders, planters and financiers from the outside.[15]

Over the last few decades, however, a growing number of scholars have begun to criticize the work of those who explained Europe's rise largely or exclusively in terms of some factor supposedly internal to Europe and already operative before 1492. Such an approach, they argue, is profoundly "Eurocentric," because it unjustifiably locates Europe (or more broadly, the West) at the center of world history and assumes that historical developments in the West have been the motor force of most, if not all, human progress, from the ancient Greeks until the present. Critics of Eurocentrism often start from the premise that while the various societies, cultures and economies of premodern Asia, Africa and Europe certainly had their differences from one another, Europe was not at all unique in ways that can adequately account for its subsequent rise to power. Therefore, rather than accepting that Western civilization possessed some special "genius" or innate superiority or trying to identify which feature of European culture or society was responsible for catapulting Europe into world leadership, they instead focus on examining the change in Europe's structural relationships with other parts of the world *after* 1492, especially the consequences of the "discovery" and conquest of the Americas.

Scholars who belong to this school of thought often argue, for example, that European states reached the Americas first not because Europeans were uniquely venturesome – in the fifteenth century Arab, Indian, African and Chinese merchants also engaged in a great deal of long-distance sea trade – but simply because the western hemisphere was much closer and more accessible to northwestern Europe than it was to the developed regions of Asia or Africa, and because Europeans had a pressing need to find a direct route to the East which would bypass the mainly Muslim middlemen with whom they had to deal. The rapid conquest and settlement of the Americas, facilitated by the catastrophic decline of the indigenous population caused by the introduction of Old World diseases and by the Europeans' superior military technology, caused vast new wealth to flow into Europe, from mines and plantations worked largely by unfree local and African labor and from the flourishing trans-Atlantic trade (in goods and slaves) which the exploitation of the Americas opened up. The influx of wealth from Europe's New World empire, along with the profits from European-controlled trade and production in Asia, greatly stimulated the European economy during the sixteenth and seventeenth centuries, speeding up and intensifying the development of capitalism there and laying the basis for a new global economic and political order centered in Europe and incorporating, on a subordinate basis, much of Asia, Africa and the Americas.[16]

It is certainly possible to combine elements of the "internalist" account of the West's rise to global supremacy (which focuses on factors internal to Europe) and the "externalist" account (which focuses on Europe's changing relations with the rest of the world); they are not necessarily mutually exclusive. Nor should one ignore or belittle the very real and very important scientific, technological, cultural and intellectual advances which Europeans achieved over the centuries. At the same time, it will clearly not do to treat the emergence of the modern West – or the birth of the modern world, or the rise of capitalism, or whatever we choose to call it – as if it was the product of factors entirely internal and unique to Europe and basically unconnected with Europe's changing relations with other parts of the world. The concepts of Europe and of the West in their modern senses emerged just as a new global order centered on Europe was coming into being, and the two processes were intimately and inextricably interwoven. Europe and the rest of the world, "the West" and "the rest," therefore cannot be usefully depicted as two utterly distinct or monolithic entities; on the contrary, they have created, molded and defined each other, and mixed with each other, through many complex interactions over the last five centuries (and well before, too).

Indeed, scholars have begun to explore how those very interactions helped *produce* the idea of a distinctive West and the dualistic division of the world between West and non-West on which it is based. From their work we can begin to see how much of what we are accustomed to thinking of as quintessentially modern, European and/or Western actually originated in interactions between those who, as an outcome of those very same interactions, would come to be categorized as either Westerners or non-Westerners. For example, scholars have argued that many modern capitalist methods of industrial production, transport and labor discipline were actually first developed not in England during the eighteenth-century Industrial Revolution, as historians have conventionally argued, but in the plantations, refineries and shipping enterprises involved in the production of sugar in the Americas of the sixteenth and seventeenth centuries. As a result, they argue, the rise of capitalism cannot be understood as essentially the product of some factor inherent in European society or culture; rather, it was the result of complex sets of forces and relations operating on a global scale and is therefore as much about slavery as it is about free wage labor, as much about plantations and shipyards as it is about factories, and as much about the Caribbean and Brazil as it is about England.

Other scholars have sought to show how various modern conceptions of race, nationhood and cultural identity first developed in non-European, especially colonial, settings, through interactions between European colonists and indigenous peoples and among the colonists themselves, and were subsequently adopted and reformulated by Europeans to become key elements of what would later come to be seen as a distinctively Western culture, their "external" origins forgotten.[17] Nonetheless, exploration of how the modern West has in crucial ways been shaped, if not constituted, by its interactions with other societies is still at an early stage and remains vastly outweighed by the huge scholarly and popular literature that takes for granted the West's self-conception as a distinct and self-generated civilization and then focuses on the West's impact on the rest of the world.

Islam and Enlightenment

As we have seen, Islam had a long history of being cast as Christianity's great "other." Now, in a somewhat more secular age, with the idea of a modern West replacing the idea of Christendom, Islam was often cast as the West's polar opposite, a distinct civilization in its own right but sharply differentiated from the West and located on an entirely different historical trajectory. Among Orientalist scholars, among writers and in the popular imagination, Islam was often portrayed as lacking those very qualities which had made the West great: if the West valued freedom, rationality, progress and enterprise, Islam was now perceived as fostering servility, superstition, stagnation and indolence.

Many European observers from the later sixteenth century onward were coming to see just these things as characteristic of Islamic societies, including the Ottoman empire. And while the West was ascending to global supremacy, the course of Ottoman history from the mid-sixteenth century onward was interpreted as a story of decline, from the glory days of the reign of Suleiman to the political, military, cultural and moral decrepitude that they saw as prevalent a century or so later. This view fits in well with older ideas which drew a parallel between the historical trajectory of states and empires and the human life cycle: after a vigorous youth in which they expanded rapidly, states and empires reached the height of their power and territorial extent and then, undermined by bad rulers, tyranny and corruption, they became feeble and vulnerable to disintegration, whether by civil war or by conquest and incorporation into some younger and more vigorous empire.

As we will see in later chapters, notions of Ottoman decline (and the broader conception of Islam as a declining or defective civilization essentially different from the West, indeed in many crucial ways its polar opposite) would eventually come in for a great deal of criticism; in fact, critiques of these views would be central to debates within Middle East studies from the 1960s onward. But for centuries this perspective was often accepted as simple common sense and underpinned both popular and Orientalist scholarly views of the world. It had become central to the story western Europeans had come to tell themselves about who they were, where they had come from and how they had risen to such prominence and power in the world from the sixteenth century onward. It was never the *only* story, among Europeans or among non-Europeans; but it was (and remains) an extremely powerful story which in many crucial ways still shapes how many Westerners and non-Westerners see the world and which has only just begun to be questioned.

We can see both the power of what was coming to be the dominant Eurocentric approach as well as the persistence of alternatives in European writing on Islam and the Orient in the eighteenth century, especially those decades which would come to be known as the period of the Enlightenment. To promote humanity's emergence from what they saw as centuries of ignorance and oppression into an enlightened modern age of reason and liberty, Enlightenment thinkers (mainly but not exclusively in France) powerfully criticized the church's obscurantism and intellectual tyranny as well as the fetters which repressive states imposed on free thought. Believing that the use of human reason could open the door to scientific progress and a better world, they questioned established ideas and institutions and developed new conceptions of humanity and of social organization. Universalistic and optimistic, Enlightenment thought tended to emphasize what all peoples and cultures had in common rather than what made them different from one another.

This opened the way for a much more objective approach to Islam in Orientalist scholarship, for which Paris was now the major European center, and sympathetic portrayals by some Enlightenment writers, who saw Islam as a relatively rational and tolerant faith and often depicted Muhammad as a just and wise lawgiver. If Muslim societies suffered from moral and social defects, they were more or less the same defects which afflicted Christian societies and could be remedied in just the same way: by exposure to the cleansing light of reason. Yet negative stereotypes persisted: Voltaire had many disparaging things to say about Islam, Muhammad and the Arabs (as well as some positive things), and as we have seen it was Montesquieu who in this same period elaborated his theory of Oriental despotism, though it is also important to recall that for him the degeneracy of Muslim societies was not inherent in Islam but was caused by geographic and climatic conditions. Broadly speaking, Enlightenment views of Islam were significantly less hostile, and certainly less fearful, than earlier views.

Alongside the works of Orientalist scholars and Enlightenment thinkers, a large popular literature on the Orient was available in Europe by the eighteenth century, satisfying and further stimulating a widespread fascination with the "exotic" lands of the Muslim East. In 1704 a translation of the *Thousand and One Nights* appeared in France. As one scholar put it, "it was an immediate success and continued to go through retranslation and re-edition for two centuries and more. Its impact was powerful and lasting. The tales were appreciated for the magic element which (since the bawdy was left out) dominated the collection, and for the picture of oriental ways which they conveyed. In the highest degree exotic, this work has been in the minds of almost every European visitor to the Muslim world from that date until this."[18]

European audiences could also read an ever-growing number of accounts by travelers to Muslim lands. Many of these accounts were highly fanciful and emphasized what their authors (very few of whom actually knew the language of the people among whom they traveled) depicted as the strange and bizarre customs and beliefs of Muslims. Other travelers were so preoccupied with their own narrow interests, for example visiting the places in Palestine where the events described in the Christian Gospels were believed to have taken place almost two thousand years earlier, that they paid very little attention to the people who were currently living in those places, or perceived them only as part of the picturesque background.

However, some travelers' accounts were more perceptive and fair-minded. For example, Lady Mary Wortley Montagu (1689–1762), wife of Britain's ambassador to the Ottoman empire in 1717–1718, wrote letters to friends in England which were widely circulated and later published to much acclaim. Said to be the first Englishwoman to travel in, and publish her observations of, the Ottoman lands, she took the trouble to study Turkish and had access to (and befriended) not only the male members of the Ottoman elite but also – unlike European men – the female members of their households. She derided earlier travel writers and Orientalist scholars whose descriptions of Ottoman society (and especially of Ottoman women) were, she insisted, based on ignorance or gross distortion. "They never fail," she wrote, "giving you an account of the Women, which 'tis certain they never saw, and talking very wisely of the Genius of the men, into whose company they were never admitted," and offered a much more nuanced and balanced perspective. Countering widespread Western images of veiled Ottoman women as oppressed and miserable, she argued that "['t]is very easy to see they have more Liberty than we have . . . there is no distinguishing the great Lady from her Slave, and 'tis impossible for the most jealous Husband to know his Wife when he meets her, and no Man dare either touch or follow a Woman in the Street. This perpetual Masquerade gives them entire Liberty of following their Inclinations without danger of Discovery . . . I think I never saw a country where women may enjoy so much liberty, and free from all reproach as in Turkey."[19]

Whether or not everything Lady Mary wrote about Ottoman society was entirely accurate, it is clear that her writings offered literate Europeans a different perspective on the Orient than had previously been available to them and influenced many writers, artists and thinkers during the Enlightenment era and well beyond. Nonetheless, while succeeding periods would witness major advances in the Western study of Islam and the Middle East, historical developments – including the changing power relations between Europe and the Middle East – would also foster new sources and forms of misunderstanding and distortion.

3   Orientalism and empire

Over the course of the nineteenth century, Europeans and Americans would increasingly come to see the Orient as divided into two distinct units: a "Near East" comprising southeastern Europe, the Levant (as I mentioned in Chapter 2, the lands along the eastern shores of the Mediterranean and their hinterlands) and other parts of western Asia nearer to Europe, and a "Far East" encompassing India, southeast Asia, China and Japan. By the latter part of the nineteenth century, the term "Oriental" had in popular usage in the United States come to refer largely to people from East Asia, especially the Chinese whose arrival as immigrants was often met by considerable hostility.

Nonetheless, the Orient remained a powerful category in nineteenth-century European popular and scholarly culture. It was in this period that the term Orientalism actually entered French, English and other European languages as (among other things) the special name for the scholarly field which focused on the Orient, including the predominantly Muslim lands of Asia, reflecting the dramatic expansion and institutionalization of scholarship in the field over the course of the nineteenth century. Over the previous century or two the study in Europe of the languages, histories, religions and cultures of the Orient had been sustained by a scattered handful of scholars. But a revival took place in the nineteenth century which would for a time feed into what a French scholar called "the Oriental renaissance," with a powerful impact on several arenas of European thought and culture.[1]

However, the nineteenth century also witnessed a new stage in the lengthy and uneven process of extending European hegemony over most of the planet that had begun three centuries earlier. As we have seen, European states had begun to carve out economic and political spheres of influence, and then colonial empires, in Asia, Africa and the Americas from about 1500 onward. Along the way, those states (particularly Britain, the Netherlands, and France) had begun to exercise direct or indirect rule over growing numbers of Muslims, mainly in India and southeast Asia (especially today's Indonesia); by the 1700s Russia was also vigorously expanding into Central Asia, inhabited mainly by Muslims. But it was only after 1800 that the European colonial powers were able to secure more or less effective and direct political dominion over significant portions of the predominantly Muslim lands of Asia and Africa. Through the eighteenth century, the major Muslim states closest to Europe – including the Ottoman empire, Morocco, Tunisia, Algeria and Persia (today's Iran) – had been able to preserve their independence, though they were often relatively weak and had in some cases already lost significant territory to expanding European powers (mainly Russia and Austria). In the nineteenth century, however, the expansion of European power into every other corner of the globe, the proximity of the Middle East and North Africa to Europe, and the potential value of these lands in the power struggles among the European powers made it all but inevitable that European states (including such latecomers to imperialist expansion as Germany and Italy) would seek to extend their economic and political influence (and if possible control) into this region as well.

As we have seen, from the medieval period onward European perceptions of Islam and of Muslims, particularly those in the lands of western Asia and northern Africa, had been influenced by, and had helped shape, the power relations between Europeans and their Muslim neighbors. This was true of the nineteenth century as well: the growth and dissemination of Western knowledge about the Orient and the generation of certain images of the Orient in Western culture in this period were linked, in complex ways which we will be exploring through the remainder of this book, with the simultaneous growth of European (and later American) power over Muslim lands and peoples.

The Oriental(ist) Renaissance

In the late eighteenth century French and British scholars (some of the latter served in the administration of British-ruled India) began learning Sanskrit, largely from Indian scholars for whom it was still the living language of the sacred texts of what would become known as Hinduism, and introducing Western audiences to the ancient learning of India, of which they had previously had little or no knowledge. Not long after, new translations of parts of the classical literature of Persia began to appear. In the 1820s, Jean-Francois Champollion (1790–1832) and other scholars began to decipher the hieroglyphs in which ancient Egyptian was written and thereby unlocked the door to the scientific study of that civilization. These developments contributed to the rapid growth in western and central Europe of both scholarly and popular interest in the Orient.

In the nineteenth century Orientalism as a scholarly discipline came to be embodied in new institutions and career paths as well as in numerous translations and scholarly publications. France was one important center of this emerging field. A School of Living Oriental Languages was established in Paris in 1795, at the height of the French Revolution. Silvestre de Sacy (1758–1838), who taught Arabic at the new school early in his career, would go on to help lay the foundations of modern Orientalism: he published numerous scholarly works and translations from Arabic, Persian and Turkish, he trained several generations of scholars and translators, he advised the French government on Muslim affairs, and he served as the first president of the Société Asiatique (the "Asiatic Society"), founded in 1821 to bring together scholars, officials and others interested in the lands of Asia (including the Muslim Near East). The formation of such national organizations dedicated to the study of Asia and Islam and sponsoring scholarly meetings and publications – including the American Oriental Society, established in the 1840s – was eventually followed by the emergence of international networks linking scholars in different countries. The first international congress of Orientalists convened in 1873, and such gatherings took place more or less regularly from then on.

For Sacy as for many of the new breed of modern Orientalist scholars who came after him, the key to scholarly understanding of the Orient (as of other civilizations) was philology, the historical analysis and comparison of languages, pursued largely through the study of written texts which, it was believed, could yield unique insights into the timeless essence of a civilization. The training of scholars specializing in Islam gave pride of place to the acquisition of Arabic, Persian, Turkish and other languages of the region, and to the techniques required for the retrieval, reconstruction, analysis, translation and publication of texts in those languages. Indeed, philological training was often deemed all that was necessary to achieve a profound understanding of what this subset of Orientalists regarded as their object of study: Islamic civilization. As a result, the methods and approaches forged by emerging new disciplines from the mid-nineteenth century onward, including anthropology, sociology, economics and "scientific" history, were often deemed irrelevant, even misleading, when applied to this segment of humanity.

The expansion of scholarly Orientalism, manifested in a growing number of translations from ancient and modern languages, the proliferation of scholarly studies on Oriental (including Islamic) history and culture, and new scholarly institutions and networks coincided with, and contributed to, a growing interest in – sometimes even an obsession with – the Orient among many of the thinkers, writers and artists identified with the

Romantic movement in European literature and art in the early decades of the nineteenth century. Rejecting the rationalism of the Enlightenment and instead stressing emotion, imagination and intuition, some of the Romantic poets, novelists, dramatists and philosophers saw the Orient as the repository of a hitherto inaccessible source of wisdom on which they might draw in order to revive and redeem a spiritually exhausted and increasingly materialistic West. For some of them the work of the Orientalist and Egyptologist scholars indicated, as one enthusiastic French writer put it in 1841, that "an antiquity more profound, more philosophical, and more poetical than that of Greece and Rome was emerging from the depths of Asia," heralding "a new Reformation of the religious and secular world." In 1820 Victor Hugo asserted that "in the century of Louis XIV one was a Hellenist; today one is an Orientalist . . . the Orient – as an image or as an idea – has become for the intellect as well as for the imagination a sort of general preoccupation . . . "[2]

It was in this context that, for example, the great German poet, novelist and dramatist Johann Wolfgang von Goethe (1749–1832) produced work that drew heavily on Muslim imagery and themes and emulated Arabic and Persian literary styles. European architects and designers developed styles that utilized ancient Egyptian stylistic elements.[3] In the 1820s this strain of Romantic Orientalist exoticism emerged strongly in the work of a number of artists, most of them French; as Maxime Rodinson put it, their work would "capture the European imagination and fascinate such a widespread audience for years." The images used in this Orientalist genre of painting were "characterized by fierce and lavish scenes in a wild array of colors; harems and seraglios; decapitated bodies; women hurled into the Bosporus in sacks; feluccas and brigantines displaying the Crescent flag; round, turquoise domes and white minarets soaring to the heavens; viziers, eunuchs, and odalisques [female slaves or concubines]; refreshing springs under palm trees; *giaours* [captive Christians] with their lustful captors."[4] Some of these themes can also be found in the work of poets and writers, including the authors of influential accounts of travel in the Levant, notably Nerval, Flaubert and Chateaubriand.

The images that writers and painters influenced by this cultural Orientalism evoked were sometimes eroticized and titillating, drawing on and further developing much older European depictions of Muslims as violent, lusty and sexually perverse. Muslim women played a particularly crucial role in European perceptions of Islam in the nineteenth century; in fact, one scholar went so far as to say that "[t]here is no subject connected with Islam which Europeans have thought more important than the condition of Muslim women."[5] As we have seen, some European observers, like Lady Mary Wortley Montagu, depicted upper-class Ottoman women as relatively free and socially empowered even though veiled and kept from contact with men who were not relatives or servants. But it was much more common to portray Muslim women as terribly oppressed and subjugated, indeed as little more than slaves, constantly available for the erotic gratification of oversexed Muslim men. Just as Ottoman sultans and other Muslim rulers were said to tyrannize their subjects, so Muslim men were said to tyrannize their wives and daughters. Not surprisingly, the degraded status of Muslim women would later be cited as a justification for European intervention and colonial rule.

European writers and artists were particularly fascinated by what they imagined went on in the "harem," the private quarters of upper-class households, and by the institution of polygamy. To satisfy this curiosity Orientalist artists produced highly suggestive paintings of nude or semi-nude Muslim women in the harem, even though, with rare exceptions, they had little or no contact with Muslim women and had never been inside the family quarters of a Muslim home. Later, photography made possible the dissemination of lurid images of women on a much larger scale, including quasipornographic postcards which were widely circu-lated; the photographers who produced them generally used prostitutes as their models, since no respectable woman would pose for them. Such depictions of Muslim women, as well as suggestive depictions of boys, gave Europeans a socially acceptable way to express their own fantasies while simultaneously reaffirming the moral superiority of the West.

But even when images of Middle Easterners were not explicitly sex-ualized, they were often still exoticized. Nineteenth-century European artists, photographers and writers tended to portray Muslim women and men and the lands in which they lived either as alien and mysterious, or as picturesque backdrops for the things that really interested European visitors and audiences, for example Palestine as the land of the Bible.[6] Popular images of these peoples and lands also continued to be shaped by such classics as the *Thousand and One Nights*, refracted through a multitude of travelers' accounts, literary works, and adventure stories for adults and children set in an Orient that was strange, exotic and sometimes threatening. There was, by contrast, relatively little interest in how the indigenous inhabitants of these lands actually lived, what they thought, or how they saw the world.[7]

The age of European encroachment

In the summer of 1798, as the revival of scholarly Orientalism was just getting under way, a French army commanded by an ambitious young general named Napoleon Bonaparte landed near Alexandria, in Egypt.

At the time, Egypt was nominally a province of the Ottoman empire, but in reality it had long been dominated by a Turkish-speaking military caste known as the Mamluks. Revolutionary France was at war with Britain and most of the monarchies of Europe, and by invading Egypt the French government hoped to acquire a potentially valuable new colony, undermine British naval control of the eastern Mediterranean, and perhaps even secure a springboard for an eventual invasion of British-ruled India.

Before invading Egypt Napoleon had sought to learn all he could about the country; among his most valuable sources were the Comte de Volney's 1787 account of his travels in Egypt and Syria, and another book by Volney on the current state of the Ottoman empire. Though in his books Volney had discussed the prospects for French colonial expansion in the Levant, he had expressed pessimism about such a project. Yet the fact that he could even entertain the idea, and that just a few years later his careful study of Egypt and Syria would be used to help make that project a reality, suggests the close connection between what contemporary Europeans were thinking and writing about the Levant and the imminent exertion of European power over it.

Napoleon's army quickly defeated the Mamluks, proceeded to conquer most of Egypt and tried to conquer Syria as well. The French saw themselves as bringing science and civilization to the benighted Orient, and so a team of scholars and scientists accompanied Napoleon's forces to Egypt, where they conducted comprehensive studies of the country's geography, population, archeological remains, economy and technology, later published in many volumes as the *Description de l'Egypte*. It was French soldiers in Napoleon's army in Egypt who in 1799 found a stone bearing inscriptions (the "Rosetta stone") which would later allow Champollion and others to begin to decipher the written language of ancient Egypt. But the French expedition to Egypt was short-lived and ended in failure: by 1801 the British and their ally the Ottomans had compelled the French forces occupying Egypt to surrender and withdraw. Napoleon himself had long since returned to France, where he used his initial victories in Egypt as a springboard for seizing power and eventually making himself dictator and later emperor. Nonetheless, the French invasion of Egypt inaugurated a new era in which the lands of the Middle East and North Africa would be increasingly subject to European economic and political encroachment, and finally European colonial rule (see Map 3).

In 1830 France invaded Algeria, which the French had come to see as a prime site for colonial expansion. Algerians resisted the French conquest by force of arms, and decades would pass before indigenous resistance was completely crushed, with great brutality. France eventually came to regard Algeria as a territory in which colonists from France and other European countries could be settled, on land seized from Algerians. The European settlers in Algeria (which the French came to treat not as a colony but as a part of France that happened to be situated on the other side of the Mediterranean) became a privileged elite, endowed with all the rights of French citizens, while the Muslim majority was disenfranchised, dispossessed and largely impoverished. In 1881–83, the French seized Algeria's neighbor Tunisia and made it into a protectorate, nominally autonomous under a local dynasty but in reality completely under French control. In 1912, after extensive maneuvering among the European powers, most of Morocco fell under French control, with a portion placed under Spanish rule. By that time the French had also carved out a vast empire to Morocco's south, in Saharan and sub-Saharan Africa, while Italy had invaded Libya, the last Ottoman province in North Africa. The Ottomans were in no position to block the Italian invasion, but Libyan resistance to Italian conquest continued for twenty years.

Britain's imperial interests lay further east, in Egypt, the Persian Gulf and Persia itself. After the withdrawal of the French in 1801, Egypt came to be ruled by Mehmet Ali (known in Arabic as Muhammad Ali), an Albanian Muslim who had arrived in Egypt as an officer with the Ottoman forces. Muhammad Ali won autonomy from the Ottomans and rapidly restructured Egypt's finances, economy, military and administration in order to secure the country and its resources for himself and his family and create a state which could withstand not only Ottoman claims but also the very real threat of European encroachment. But some of the measures he and his successors implemented had a paradoxical effect: for example, the large-scale planting of cotton, which Muhammad Ali envisioned as a lucrative export crop, eventually bound Egypt ever more tightly to the Europe-centered world economy. Similarly, the opening of the Suez Canal in 1869 dramatically enhanced Egypt's geostrategic as well as economic importance, especially to Britain, which wanted to control this vital link in the fast route to its most important colony, India.

Muhammad Ali's successors borrowed heavily from European banks in order to bolster their grip on Egypt and develop its infrastructure, and by the mid-1870s the country was bankrupt. European financial control was imposed to ensure that European banks and investors who held Egyptian bonds were repaid, which provoked demands from nationalist Egyptian army officers and civilians for an end to European interference in Egypt's affairs and constitutional government. In 1882 British forces occupied Egypt to overthrow a nationalist government which seemed to threaten European financial and political influence. Britain would remain in full control of Egypt until 1922, when the country was granted limited self-rule, and a greater measure of independence would be achieved in 1936. But the last British soldiers would not be withdrawn from Egypt until 1956, and they would be back just a few months later when Britain, France and Israel jointly attacked Egypt in the ill-fated "Suez campaign."

The British also made themselves the dominant power on the southern and eastern fringes of the Arabian peninsula during the nineteenth century, seizing the port of Aden in 1839 for use as a coaling station on the route to India and establishing de facto protectorates over many of the small Arab principalities along the west coast of the Persian Gulf. Britain and Russia came to dominate Persia's foreign trade and a growing proportion of its economy and together exerted powerful political influence over that country, though it remained nominally independent.

In a series of wars in the eighteenth and nineteenth centuries Russia seized extensive lands which had once been under direct or indirect Ottoman control around the Black Sea, and additional territories in the Caucasus which had previously been ruled by or subject to Persia. Tsarist Russia expanded by conquering and annexing adjacent lands rather than by seizing overseas territories, as Britain and France had done; but all three empires (along with the Dutch in what is today Indonesia) had by the end of the nineteenth century come to encompass large numbers of Muslim subjects.

The Ottoman empire, once the most powerful and feared state in Europe, managed to survive through the nineteenth century – but only barely. With the support of Russia and/or Austria, and sometimes of other European powers, many of the largely Christian provinces the Ottomans had long ruled in southeastern Europe revolted and broke away to form more or less independent states (Serbia, Greece, Romania, Bulgaria and Montenegro), while Austria took control of the heavily Muslim provinces of Bosnia and Herzegovina. To preserve what was left of the empire and prevent its complete dismemberment, the Ottoman ruling elite desperately sought to modernize its military and administrative institutions, with limited success. The Ottoman empire thus remained weak and on the defensive, and the "Eastern Question" – the fate of the Ottoman empire and disputes among the European states which coveted its territories – preoccupied European statesmen and caused a series of diplomatic crises down to the outbreak of the First World War in 1914.

The rise of *homo islamicus*

As I suggested earlier, in the nineteenth century the ways in which European scholars, writers and artists analyzed, imagined and depicted the Orient were often intertwined, in complex ways, with the reality of growing European power over those peoples and lands. This is not to suggest that every Orientalist was a conscious agent of imperialism or that every scholarly or artistic product of Orientalism served to justify or legitimate colonialism; as we will see, there was never an entirely monolithic European stance toward Islam, Muslims, the Orient or colonialism. At the same time, however, the dramatic expansion in this period of European power over vast stretches of the Muslim world served to bolster certain premises and assumptions, certain ways of understanding and defining Islam and the Orient (as well as the West) rather than others. This in turn made it more likely that scholars would define what they were studying, and the questions they were asking, in certain ways rather than others, yielding interpretations which in turn served to bolster largely taken-for-granted assumptions about the sources and character of Western superiority and of Islam's inferiority and decadence.

One key (but never uncontested) element of mainstream nineteenth-century European (and later American) thought about the Orient was a particular conception of the difference between East and West. Alongside the fascination with the Orient characteristic of segments of the Romantic movement, there developed a widespread (but of course never universal) sense that Westerners were fundamentally different from, and culturally superior to, Muslims and everyone else now defined as non-Western. Maxime Rodinson effectively summarized the shift in European attitudes:

The Oriental may always have been characterized as a savage enemy, but during the Middle Ages, he was at least considered on the same level as his European counterpart. And, to the men of the Enlightenment, the ideologues of the French revolution, the Oriental was, for all his foreignness in appearance and dress, above all a man like anyone else. In the nineteenth century, however, he became something quite separate, sealed off in his own specificity, yet worthy of a kind of grudging admiration. This is the origin of the *homo islamicus*, a notion widely accepted even today.[8]

For Rodinson the term *homo islamicus* (Latin for "Islamic man") referred to the perception that the Muslim constituted a distinct type of human being, essentially different from "Western man." As I have already discussed, western Europeans were coming to see themselves as belonging to a distinct and unique civilization, the West, which was fundamentally different from all other civilizations, including Islam. Underpinning this view of the world was the premise that the key entities into which humankind was divided were not states or empires but civilizations, each with its own distinctive essence and its unique core values which powerfully shaped the consciousness and actions of those subject to it. Human history was thus essentially the story of the rise and decline of civilizations.

The view of history as a succession of civilizations (and of Islam as a once-great civilization now in decay) was widely accepted in the nineteenth century and remains powerful even today. The idea was central to the thinking of the enormously influential German philosopher Georg Wilhelm Friedrich Hegel (1770–1831). Hegel portrayed the history of humanity as the story of the successive rise and fall of civilizations, each of which contributed something from its own unique spirit or "genius" and then faded away. For Hegel this manifested the process whereby what he called the "Absolute Spirit" – his term for the totality of all that is real, actually a sort of philosophical reconceptualization of God – moved dialectically toward self-consciousness. As Hegel saw it, the historical trajectory of the Absolute Spirit ran from east to west, from its infancy in the Orient via Greece and Rome to adulthood with the rise of the Germanic peoples. Along the way the Jews had contributed monotheism, the belief in one all-powerful and all-knowing god rather than many, while the relatively minor role of Islam had been to preserve and hand on to Europe the heritage of Greek and Roman civilization, after which it had faded into senescence. Now, in the nineteenth century, all the older civilizations had disappeared or decayed, but the Absolute Spirit could finally achieve full self-knowledge in the modern West – more precisely, in Hegel's native Germany.

But even many of those less inclined to grandiose philosophical-historical schemes accepted the civilization as the basic unit of historical analysis and traced the roots of the civilization they termed the West back to ancient Greece, where they believed that many of the core values and beliefs which they saw as the distinguishing characteristics of Western civilization – including liberty, democracy, philosophy, science and rationalism – first surfaced in human history. It was this conviction that would allow the English philosopher and economist John Stuart Mill (1806–73) to assert that "the Battle of Marathon [where the Greeks defeated the Persians in 490 BCE], even as an event in English history, is more important than the battle of Hastings [where the invading Normans defeated the Anglo-Saxons in 1066 CE]."[9] This assertion could make sense to Mill (and others) because they saw Athens in the fifth century BCE as the direct and necessary progenitor of nineteenth-century

English culture and liberty, a perspective which had the effect of dismissing much of what had happened over the course of the intervening twenty centuries and rendering invisible or unimportant many other factors and processes which had shaped England's historical development.

Well into the twentieth century, many historians and philosophers advanced similar views. The philosopher Oswald Spengler (1880–1936), whose influential book *The Decline of the West* was published after the First World War, traced what he saw as the growth and decay of successive civilizations, culminating in the contemporary West, which he argued had now entered its final stage of development. Arnold Toynbee (1889–1975), a prominent British historian who was influenced by Spengler and who had a significant impact on several generations of historians, including some who wrote about Islam and the Middle East, also accepted the premise that civilizations, which he saw as large, coherent and relatively stable cultural entities, were the proper unit of analysis for historians. In his monumental twelve-volume work *A Study of History*, published between 1934 and 1961, he undertook a comparative study of twenty-one civilizations (including Islam) in recorded history, tracing their origins and development and attributing their ultimate decline to an inability to respond adequately to moral and religious challenges. Though many scholars criticized Toynbee's tendency to make sweeping historical generalizations and his reading of history along Christian teleological lines, we will see later on that aspects of the approach he adopted remain influential to this day.

Orientalists and others who took this view of human history for granted regarded Islamic civilization as having arisen, young and vigorous, in the seventh century, reached the height of its political and military might and cultural glory (its "golden age") in the eighth, ninth and tenth centuries under the 'Abbasid dynasty whose capital was Baghdad, and then gradually lost its vigor, its powers of cultural creativity, its ability to absorb and be enriched by new ideas and cultural influences. The Ottomans constituted something of a last gasp, a final burst of territorial expansion and perhaps cultural flowering, before the inexorable decline of Islamic civilization resumed. In this view Islam grew increasingly rigid, inflexible, tyrannical, intolerant, and hostile to outside influences, and thus proved unable to absorb and keep up with dynamic new ideas and techniques first developed elsewhere, in the West. As the West surged ahead, Islam slipped into social and cultural stasis and political despotism.

In keeping with this interpretation of history, nineteenth-century European Orientalist scholarship tended to focus on what scholars saw as Islam's "classical" period, from its rise to the period in which it had supposedly reached its zenith and attained its purest form; everything thereafter was regarded as largely a story of decline and degeneration, or at least cultural and social rigidity and stasis. Moreover, a view of Islam as a coherent and distinctive civilization with an essentially unitary culture led many Orientalists to assume that the dominant ideas and institutions of all Muslim societies, and the ways in which Muslims behaved and interacted in all places and times, were at bottom expressions of Islam's unchanging cultural essence, its core values and ideas, which could best be understood by studying texts from its classical period. As a result Orientalist scholars tended to be less interested in the ways in which the thinking and behavior of Muslim communities varied from place to place or changed over time – that is, in the persistent diversity and complexity of Muslim belief and practice – or in what contemporary Muslims actually did and thought and how they lived.

In other words, the implicit or explicit premise of much of nineteenth-century Orientalist scholarship was that there was indeed a *homo islamicus*, a distinctive "Islamic man" with a more or less fixed mindset that was fundamentally different from, indeed absolutely opposed to, the mindset of "Western man." The essential characteristics of the members of this subspecies could be identified by the use of philological methods to study certain key texts which were regarded as embodying the core principles of Islamic civilization. The Qur'an was naturally deemed to rank first among these, followed by a relatively limited set of religious, moral, philosophical and legal writings generated by the learned elite before Islam's decline set in. Through the study of these key texts scholars believed that they could deduce the characteristics of "the Muslim mind," on the assumption that all Muslims, from the rise of Islam until the present, were constrained to think and believe and act within the rigid limits set by the essential character of the civilization to which they belonged. The upshot of the prevalence of this paradigm, and of the philological methods which underpinned it, was that, despite the enormous erudition of the best of the nineteenth-century Orientalist scholars and the very important contributions they made to scholarship on Islam, over time the field would become rather isolated and introverted, unwilling or unable to change in order to make better sense of a changing world and of new intellectual perspectives.

Orientalism thus took shape within the context of a retreat from Enlightenment universalism on the part of many in Europe and a new (or renewed) insistence on the differences among peoples and civilizations, with the modern West set at the pinnacle of a new hierarchy of human evolution. By the end of the nineteenth century this perspective was supplemented by a much more pernicious notion of how humanity was divided up, mentioned briefly in Chapter 2. Influenced by certain (mis)interpretations of Charles Darwin's theory of evolution as the product of natural selection and by the triumphal march of European imperialism, some European and American thinkers began to argue that the cultural and political superiority of the West was the result not simply of that civilization's superior values and institutions – which non-Western peoples might with proper tutelage eventually assimilate – but rather of the superior innate biological characteristics of the "white" race – often referred to as "Aryan" or "Caucasian." In this view, which came to be widely accepted among respectable scientists and intellectuals and shaped much of academic scholarship, humanity was naturally divided into distinct biological groups, with a clear hierarchy of superior and inferior races.

Not surprisingly, most of the inhabitants of Africa and Asia were deemed to belong to biologically inferior races which were by nature less intelligent and less capable of achieving civilization than was the white race – a system of classification which of course made European colonial rule seem natural and inevitable. As the popular American journalist Lothrop Stoddard put it in his 1921 book *The Rising Tide of Color Against White World-Supremacy*:

Out of the prehistoric shadows the white races pressed to the front and proved in a myriad of ways their fitness for the hegemony of mankind. Gradually they forged a common civilization; then, when vouchsafed their unique opportunity of oceanic mastery four centuries ago, they spread over the earth, filling its empty spaces with their superior breeds and assuring to themselves an unparalleled paramountcy of numbers and dominion . . . [A]t last the planet was integrated under the hegemony of a single race with a common civilization.[10]

Though there were always many scholars and others who denounced biological racism as unscientific and pernicious, much of late nineteenth- and early twentieth-century Euro-American discourse about the world – including the Muslim Orient – was to varying degrees infected by racial ideology. And most of those who rejected an explicitly biological racism nonetheless accepted the widespread and extremely durable assumption that one could best characterize and categorize different ethnic groups, races, peoples and civilizations in terms of more or less fixed cultural essences, an assumption which remains influential down to the present day.

Ernest Renan and and his interlocutors

For a better understanding of this assumption, which some have argued was central to nineteenth-century Orientalism, and for a sense of some of the ideas about Islam widespread in the West, we can turn to Ernest Renan (1823–92). In the latter part of the nineteenth century Renan was widely regarded as France's pre-eminent philologist and scholar of religion. Though he wrote mainly on Christianity and Judaism and was not trained or regarded as an Orientalist, Renan's perspective on Islam and the contemporary Muslim world – expressed quite clearly and forcefully in a widely circulated 1883 Sorbonne lecture titled "Islam and Science" – can give us some insight into how many Orientalists (and other intellectuals but also government officials and the educated public) understood Islam and the contemporary Muslim world at this time.[11]

Although Renan began his lecture by criticizing those who spoke of races and nations as if they were unchanging and monolithic categories, his discussion of what he called "the actual inferiority of Mohammedan countries, the decadence of states governed by Islam, and the intellectual nullity of the races that hold, from that religion alone, their culture and their education" was clearly essentialist, in the sense of relying on a vision of Islam as a monolithic, unitary entity with an unchanging essence or character that, furthermore, totally controlled the mental life and social behavior of all Muslims everywhere.

All those who have been in the East, or in Africa, are struck by the way in which the mind of a true believer is fatally limited, by the species of iron circle that surrounds his head, rendering it absolutely closed to knowledge, incapable of either learning anything, or of being open to any new idea. From his religious initiation at the age of ten or twelve years, the Mohammedan child, who occasionally may be, up to that time, of some intelligence, at a blow becomes a fanatic, full of a stupid pride in the possession of what he believes to be the absolute truth, happy as with a privilege, with what makes his inferiority... The [Muslim] has the most profound disdain for instruction, for science, for everything that constitutes the European spirit. This bent of mind inculcated by the Mohammedan faith is so strong, that all differences of race and nationality disappear by the fact of conversion to Islam.

It is worth noting that here and throughout this essay, Renan spoke confidently of "the Mohammedan" in the singular, because for him all Muslims everywhere were essentially the same. Once someone became a Muslim, they apparently immediately lost whatever powers of reasoning they might have been born with (though for Renan Muslim children were only "occasionally" born with "some intelligence") and became narrow-minded fanatics, robots who were entirely subservient to the prescriptions of their faith, which Renan believed could be deduced from Islam's key texts. Islam was, for Renan, inherently and eternally antirational and antiscientific; that was built into its very core, its essence, and could never change.

But how, Renan went on to ask, can we then explain the brilliance of Islamic science and philosophy in the Middle Ages, when Islamic civilization was "the mistress of the Christian West?" Renan dealt with this problem by asserting that Islam was initially a product of nomadic Arabs who, like other "Semites," were utterly devoid of any interest in philosophy or science. Later, during the 'Abbasid period, ancient Persian civilization and the ancient Greek learning preserved by local Christians asserted themselves beneath an Islamic veneer and produced a flowering of philosophy, science and culture. The caliphs who patronized this cultural and intellectual efflorescence could, Renan argued, hardly be called Muslims, and though this civilization used the Arabic language it was not really Arab, it was essentially Greek and Persian – that is, "Aryan."

But then the "torch of humanity" which had for a moment blazed so brightly in the Orient expired and passed into other hands: "this West of ours was fully awakening out of its slumber . . . Europe had found her genius, and was commencing upon that extraordinary evolution, the last term of which will be the complete emancipation of the human mind." Soon the "Turkish race" came to dominate in most Muslim lands and "caused the universal prevalence of its total lack of philosophical and scientific spirit," plunging them into intellectual decadence. For Renan as for many other contemporary European social and historical thinkers, race thus played a key explanatory role: the Arab race was deemed to be inherently incapable of – even hostile to – philosophical or scientific thought; the Turks were similarly defective; but among the (Aryan) Persians intellectual curiosity and creativity continued to flourish even after they became Muslims. It therefore did not matter to Renan what the great medieval Muslim philosophers and scientists may have thought about who they were or about the relationship between their faith and the use of reason: Islam was by definition everywhere and always implacably opposed to the free use of human reason, and if these people contributed to human thought it must have been because their innate racial characteristics triumphed over the strictures of the faith they professed.

Today, Renan went on, Islam "oppresses vast portions of our globe, and in them maintains the idea most opposed to progress, – the state founded on a pseudo-Revelation, theology governing society. The liberals who defend Islam do not know its real nature. Islam is the close union of the spiritual and the temporal; it is the reign of a dogma, it is the heaviest chain that humanity has ever borne . . . What is, in fact, essentially distinctive of the Moslem is his hatred of science, his persuasion that research is useless, frivolous, almost impious . . . " Unlike the "liberals" he attacked, Renan claimed to understand Islam's true nature: it must everywhere and always be a hindrance to progress and an enemy to reason. Here Renan's characterization of Islam as a "pseudo-Revelation" echoes medieval Christian polemics, while the tone of his language hints at an animosity toward Islam that does not sit well with his claim to speak as a disinterested scholar.

Renan concluded with an endorsement of the use of European military might to contain or suppress anticolonial resistance. He praised science as the very soul of civilized society and expressed pleasure that "it gives force for the service of reason." "In Asia," Renan warned, "there are elements of barbarism analogous to those that formed the early Moslem armies, and the great cyclones of Attila and Genghis Khan. But science bars the way. If [the early Muslim caliph] Omar or Genghis Khan had found good artillery confronting them, they would never have passed the borders of their desert . . . What was not said at the beginning against fire-arms, which nevertheless have contributed much to the victory of civilisation?"

That Renan was as disparaging about Jews and Judaism as he was about Arabs, Turks, Muslims and Islam, and that his writings on Christianity scandalized devout Catholics, is no great consolation: he was in his day a very influential scholar and intellectual and his opinions were widely shared across Europe and beyond, helping to foster a derogatory attitude toward Islam and a sense of Western superiority which in turn legitimized European colonialism. Yet Renan's views were by no means universally shared, even among contemporary students of Islam. For example, Ignaz Goldziher (1850–1921), a scholar of Hungarian Jewish extraction who was one of the pre-eminent founders of modern Arabic and Islamic studies, strongly criticized what he regarded as Renan's overblown and unsupported pronouncements on the moral, cultural and intellectual inferiority of the "Semitic" peoples (Jews as well as Arabs) and rejected his claim that every ethnic or racial group possessed a unique spirit and mind-set to which its cultural achievements (or alleged lack thereof) could be attributed.[12] Instead, Goldziher argued that the origins and development of Islamic civilization should be studied by means of a close and historically contextualized reading of key sources. Those who adopted this approach, among them many Central European scholars but also others, would constitute an influential strand within European Orientalism into the twentieth century.

But Renan's views also faced criticism from other directions. When Renan derisively referred to naive "liberals who defend Islam" in his lecture at the Sorbonne, one of those he probably had in mind was Wilfred

Scawen Blunt (1840–1922), an Englishman who became interested in Islam and vigorously opposed the British occupation of Egypt in 1882, as well as British colonialism in Ireland and India. Blunt argued that Islam was compatible with human reason and could be re-interpreted so as to serve the needs of modern Muslims.[13] The ideas Blunt expressed were largely those of the Muslim intellectuals with whom he was in close contact, for by the late nineteenth century there were lively debates across the Muslim world about how to resist European colonial encroachment and about what Muslims might utilize from Western science and technology, as well as from the Islamic tradition, to enable them to address the challenges faced by their societies.

Educated Muslims were also increasingly aware of what Europeans were saying about them and about Islam, and some were trying to have their own perspectives taken into account. In fact, Renan's pronouncements on Islam and science did not go unanswered. A few weeks after Renan's lecture at the Sorbonne a French newspaper published a letter from a leading Muslim activist who was then living in Paris and who had met Renan through a mutual acquaintance. Jamal al-Din al-Afghani (1838/9–97) was born and raised a Shi'i Muslim in Iran and was trained as a Shi'i man of religion, but because he wanted to have an impact in the wider Sunni Muslim world he concealed his origins and claimed instead to be of Afghan Sunni origin. Al-Afghani (whom Ignaz Goldziher also got to know during a stay in Egypt in the early 1870s) was a sort of professional agitator and propagandist: he traveled across the Muslim world, from India to Afghanistan to Iran to the Ottoman empire to Egypt, as well as through Europe, urging Muslims to work together to reform their societies and resist the imminent threat of colonial domination.

In his letter al-Afghani praised Renan's erudition and insight but rejected his argument that the greatness of Islamic civilization owed nothing to the Arabs. Al-Afghani agreed that Islam had tried to stifle science; indeed, among Muslims as among Christians, "so long as humanity exists the struggle will not cease between dogma and free investigation, between religion and philosophy." But, al-Afghani went on, "I cannot keep from hoping that Muhammadan society will succeed someday in breaking its bonds and marching resolutely in the path of civilization after the manner of Western society, for which the Christian faith, despite its rigors and intolerance, was not at all an invincible obstacle."[14]

Renan began his response to Jamal al-Din al-Afghani's letter by situating him within a familiar system of racial categories. "The Sheik Gemmal Eddin is an Afghan," Renan explained, "entirely emancipated from the prejudices of Islam; he belongs to those energetic races of the Upper Iran bordering upon India, in which the Aryan spirit still flourishes so strongly, under the superficial garb of Islam. He is the best proof of that great axiom, which we have often proclaimed, that the worth of religions is to be determined by the worth of the races that profess them . . . The Sheik Gemmal Eddin is the finest case of racial protest against religious conquest that could be cited." Renan claimed that he had not asserted that all Muslims must always be sunk in ignorance; but he insisted that the regeneration of Muslim lands could not come about through the reform of Islam but only through its enfeeblement, through the emancipation of the Muslim from his own religion, primarily by means of education, just as enlightened Europeans had abandoned orthodox Christianity and embraced reason and science instead.

We do not know what else Jamal al-Din al-Afghani might have had to say to Ernest Renan, who will therefore have the last word in this exchange. And indeed, despite sporadic criticism from Muslims and from dissident Europeans, views like those expressed by Renan remained very influential well into the twentieth century, among scholars but also among the European public at large, including those most directly concerned with governing European colonies with substantial Muslim populations.

Karl Marx and Oriental despotism

The image of the Orient as essentially different from the West, and the accompanying sense that Western rule was necessary to bring civilization and progress to the Orient, were pervasive in the broader intellectual arena, to the extent that we can find variants of them in what may initially seem surprising places. By way of illustration let us look at what one of the most radical social thinkers of the nineteenth century had to say about the character of Asian societies and about what differentiated them from the West.

Karl Marx (1818–83), the great critic and theorist of capitalism and the founder of what he termed "scientific socialism," devoted most of his life to analyzing the workings of capitalism, in order (as he saw it) to equip the working class with the understanding it needed to overthrow that oppressive and exploitative social order and create a more just and egalitarian mode of human social life. While he was well aware that colonial pillage, coercion and slavery in the Americas and elsewhere had helped jump-start capitalist development in Europe, he was primarily interested in how capitalism operated as a socioeconomic system in Europe itself, and particularly in Britain, which he saw as the world's most advanced capitalist society and thus a model for the rest of the world. But along the way he did briefly address the question of why capitalism had developed first in western Europe and not in the initially much richer and more populous lands of Asia. The answer he gave to this question illustrates how what we today might see as Eurocentric premises informed the work of even as vigorous a critic of capitalism and of the costs of European colonialism as Karl Marx.

In 1853 Marx published two short articles on British rule in India in the *New York Daily Tribune*, to which he contributed regularly for a while.[15] As he saw it, Indian society, like other Asian societies, had been essentially static and unchanging for thousands of years: "All the civil wars, invasions, revolutions, conquests, famines, strangely complex, rapid and destructive as the successive action in [India] may appear, did not go deeper than the surface." The real reason for this, Marx argued, had to do with climate, geography and social structure. Arid climatic conditions made artificial irrigation necessary across much of Asia, from Egypt to Mesopotamia to Persia to India, and this meant that a strong central government was needed to build and maintain the irrigation systems on which agriculture depended. This was, Marx suggested, the economic basis for the despotism so characteristic of Asian societies, where rapacious and all-powerful governments owned the land and collected taxes from the great bulk of the population living since time immemorial in their largely self-sufficient village communities.

Marx's sparse and scattered remarks on the character of Asian societies would later be developed into the concept of an "Asiatic mode of production," distinct from the other major modes of production delineated by Marx: the "primitive communism" of early human societies, slavery, feudalism and capitalism. The basic elements of this Asiatic mode of production stand out most starkly when contrasted with the feudal system which Marx saw as characteristic of medieval Europe. In European feudal societies the king was relatively weak and the land (and its revenues) were largely controlled by a hierarchy of hereditary nobles; the dispersion of power this created allowed for the emergence of an increasingly wealthy and ambitious city-based mercantile class, the bourgeoisie, the bearer of a new social order, capitalism, which eventually undermined, destroyed and replaced the old feudal order. In Asian societies, on the other hand, power was concentrated in the hands of the absolute ruler, the despot, who also controlled almost all land; there was no independent hereditary aristocracy, only a mass of peasants working the land and paying taxes to the state, i.e. the ruler. With no opportunity for a vigorous bourgeoisie to emerge, these societies were essentially stationary and capitalism could not develop in them until it was introduced from the outside by European traders, investors and colonists.

Marx fully recognized the disruption and suffering which British rule had brought to India, but he urged his readers to remember that Oriental despotism had imprisoned the human mind and condemned those who lived under it to an "undignified, stagnatory, and vegetative life." "Indian society has no history at all," Marx went on, "at least no known history. What we call its history, is but the history of the successive intruders who founded their empires on the passive basis of that unresisting and unchanging society." But unlike previous conquerors, who never dreamed of interfering with the existing social order, the British were driven by rapacious greed and the capitalist drive for profit to undermine the village communities, the very basis of Indian society, and destroy native industry. This amounted, Marx argued, to the beginnings of a fundamental social revolution in India, one which was destroying the old order and laying "the material foundations of Western society in Asia." As Marx and his collaborator Friedrich Engels had written fifteen years earlier in the *Manifesto of the Communist Party*,

the bourgeoisie, by the rapid improvement of all instruments of production, by the immensely facilitated means of communication, draws all, even the most barbarian, nations into civilization. The cheap prices of its commodities are the heavy artillery with which it batters down all Chinese walls, with which it forces the barbarians' intensely obstinate hatred of foreigners to capitulate. It compels all nations, on pain of extinction, to adopt the bourgeois mode of production; it compels them to introduce what it calls civilization into their midst, i.e. to become bourgeois themselves. In a word, it creates a world after its own image.[16]

Thus the British had introduced private ownership of agricultural land in India, enriching a handful of Indian landowners while dispossessing and impoverishing many millions of peasants; British capitalists were building railways in India, not to benefit the Indian people but to increase their profits; factories would soon follow, bringing a working class into being; and so on. Though the human costs of these profound transformations would certainly be terrible, a capitalist society would emerge in India as it had emerged elsewhere. The people of India would, however, not reap the potential benefits of this disruptive and painful development unless there was social revolution in Britain or until the Indians succeeded in freeing themselves from British colonial rule.

It is clear that Marx embraced an image of Asian societies which was in reality based on crude generalizations and a very faulty understanding of their (quite diverse) histories and social structures. Moreover, like many of his contemporaries, if for very different reasons, Marx saw colonialism as a necessary and progressive factor in human history: despite its brutalities, it enabled capitalism to realize its "historic mission" of transforming the entire globe, thus creating the conditions which would foster the eventual emergence of another, more equitable social order.

As Engels put it in 1848, commenting on a particularly brutal episode of colonial expansion, "the [French] conquest of Algeria is an important and fortunate fact for the progress of civilization . . . All these nations of free barbarians look very proud, noble, and glorious at a distance, but only come near them and you will find that they, as well as the more civilized nations, are ruled by the lust of gain, and only employ ruder and more cruel means. And after all, the modern *bourgeois*, with civilization, industry, order, and at least relative enlightenment following him, is preferable to the feudal lord or to the marauding robber, with the barbarian state of society to which they belong."[17]

However, it should also be kept in mind that unlike many of his contemporaries, Marx did not believe that Asians were racially inferior to Europeans or inherently incapable of achieving modern civilization. Nor did he downplay the horrendous price which Asian peoples would have to pay as a result of colonial rule and the development of capitalism. Moreover, Marx insisted that the static character of Asian societies had an essentially economic basis – the alleged absence of private property in land in these societies and thus the absence of class conflict – rather than being the result of defects in their psyches, cultures or religions, and he could envision the day when Asian peoples would overthrow their colonial masters.

Marx's portrayal of the character and historical trajectory of the non-Western world has engendered considerable debate down to the present day. Marx's analysis of precapitalist Asian societies and their history was obviously rooted in the Oriental despotism model. On the other hand, as I will discuss in Chapters 5 and 6, scholars using Marxian modes of social and historical analysis would from the 1960s onward play a leading role in criticizing that same model, the related portrayal of Islam as a stagnant civilization, and the broader claim that it was only the impact of the West which led to change in these essentially static societies, and in elaborating powerful alternatives. In effect, those scholars would use Marx's methods to challenge some of Marx's own pronouncements.

Max Weber and the sociology of Islam

The central (if often unacknowledged) role which the elaboration of a sharp distinction between the West and the rest of the world played in shaping modern European social thought can also be discerned in the work of Max Weber (1864–1920), widely regarded as one of the founders of modern historical sociology. Weber's influential (if often disputed) analysis of how the "Protestant ethic" had helped foster the "spirit of capitalism" in Europe has frequently been regarded as an attempt to refute Marx's insistence on the primacy of material forces, and the class conflict they produced, in driving social change. Yet as a British sociologist who studied what both men had to say about Islam put it, "the outline, assumptions and implications of their perspectives on Asian–European contrasts are very similar."[18]

For Weber – who drew on contemporary Orientalist scholarship, for which Germany had become a major center by the late nineteenth century – as for Marx and for many other observers down to our own day, Muslim societies were weak and backward because they lacked many of the key institutions which enabled Western societies to become wealthy and powerful. In feudal Europe property rights were protected by law and autonomous cities could emerge, opening the way for the flourishing of a bourgeoisie and the development of capitalism. In Muslim lands, however, powerful "patrimonial" states dependent largely on the military and the bureaucracy dominated all of social and economic life and most of society's resources, including land. Weber used the term "sultanism" to characterize the political systems of these patrimonial states, whose rulers he saw as rapacious and arbitrary despots unencumbered by any effective limits on their power over their subjects. As a result Islamic societies failed to develop institutions and centers of power independent of the state, including a vigorous urban middle class, autonomous cities or a system of rational formal law (as opposed to the sacred law of Islam), leading to stagnation and social decay.

Weber's views on Islam, like those of Marx on Asian societies in general, drew on the powerful tradition in European thought I discussed in Chapter 2, from Renaissance political thinkers to Montesquieu to Hegel to James Mill and John Stuart Mill and beyond. In this tradition, which as we have seen also drew on contemporary Orientalist understandings of the essential characteristics of Islamic civilization, Muslim and other Asian societies were classified as Oriental despotisms, the very antithesis of modern Western political and social systems. Moreover, in much of nineteenth- and twentieth-century sociological thought those societies were judged deficient because they allegedly lacked many of the features and institutions which modern European societies seemed to possess and which had supposedly enabled Europeans to achieve progress, knowledge, wealth and power. This way of contrasting Islamic societies to an idealized model of European history and society provided a basis for depicting the former as culturally or racially defective and fatally mired in tradition and backwardness.

As I will discuss in more detail in subsequent chapters, the sharp dichotomies on which these contrasts are based – between Western freedom and Oriental servitude, between Western law and Oriental arbitrariness, between Western modernity and Oriental tradition, between private property in land in the West and its absence in the Orient, and so on – have been subjected to intense challenge in recent decades. Scholars of both Europe and the Middle East have argued that neither European nor Middle Eastern societies actually conformed to the patterns of historical development which the nineteenth-century model and its twentieth-century successors ascribed to them. On the European side it has become increasingly obvious that these models generalize very crudely from a highly questionable interpretation of English and to a lesser extent French history; on the Middle Eastern side research has shown that it is based on a very faulty understanding of those societies and their histories. For example, it turns out that although Middle Eastern states like the Ottoman empire generally did claim formal legal ownership of most agricultural land, in many places peasants and local power-holders were nonetheless able to buy, sell and mortgage land well before the nineteenth century, thereby undermining one of the key pillars of the Oriental despotism model and its explanation of those societies' alleged stagnation. To criticize these dichotomies is not, of course, to suggest that there are no significant differences among societies and their patterns of historical development. It is simply to insist that we resist overarching generalizations based on unexamined premises and meager empirical data, and be wary of approaches to history and modes of social analysis that deem one society's path of development "normal" and then judge all others by how they measure up to that impossible and inevitably misleading standard.

Orientalist knowledge and colonial power

Most nineteenth-century Orientalist scholars saw themselves as simply and wholly devoted to the disinterested pursuit of objective knowledge and had no direct or indirect involvement in policymaking; and in fact many of them produced scholarly work of lasting value, laying the foundations of modern Arabic and Islamic studies on which future generations of scholars would build. Moreover, not all European scholars of Islam and the Orient shared the same views: some expressed admiration for Islam while others disparaged it, some enthusiastically supported colonial expansion while others opposed it. Nonetheless, as we will see in more detail later, scholars in the 1970s and beyond would argue forcefully that Orientalism as an intellectual enterprise was in significant ways linked to contemporary European colonialism and that the kind of knowledge Orientalism as a discipline tended to produce was often used to justify and further the exertion of European power over the Muslim world.

At the most general level, if one assumed that the West and Islam were fundamentally different civilizations which operated on essentially incompatible principles, it was only natural to accept that there was indeed a distinct *homo islamicus* who in his beliefs, attitudes toward life and social habits was the polar opposite of modern Western man. Given the decline into which Islam had seemingly fallen and the assumed superiority of Western civilization, it seemed reasonable to conclude that to achieve progress the Orient must emulate the West. Western influence could therefore easily be seen as a wholly positive force which would bring the blessings of modern civilization to an exhausted, stagnant and defective Muslim world unable to revive itself by its own efforts. In the late nineteenth and early twentieth centuries, the zenith of European colonialism, Western influence increasingly meant Western rule. It was thus no great leap to endorse the exercise of Western tutelage over non-Westerners – in a word, colonialism – or at least to take for granted the reality and morality of Western hegemony.

At the same time, a substantial number of individual Orientalists and the institutions with which they were connected were ready and willing to put their expertise at the service of their countries' colonial ambitions. Silvestre de Sacy, the foremost Orientalist scholar of his generation, advised the French government on Islam and the Orient and among many other services translated into Arabic the proclamation which that government issued when it invaded Algeria in 1830. Later in the century, the prominent Dutch Orientalist scholar Snouck Hurgronje (1857–1936), who studied mystical tendencies in Islam, helped the Dutch government formulate and implement policy toward the Muslim population of its colonies in Indonesia. Russian Orientalists helped the Tsarist government formulate policies designed to pacify, control and assimilate the empire's Muslim subjects, and if possible even convert them to Christianity.[19]

Scholarly institutions were also often deeply involved in the colonial enterprise. The Société Asiatique which Sacy had helped found, and the other new learned societies and academic disciplines which sprang up in France and elsewhere in Europe around the same time to foster the study of non-Western peoples and cultures, generally took colonialism for granted. Western rule over non-Western lands was the reality that to a large extent shaped their intellectual horizons and framed the questions in which they took an interest. And Islam was often seen as a threat or a challenge to European colonial power, or at least a real or potential problem for it.

Even German scholars of Islam, citizens of a country which had relatively few Muslim subjects and which toward the end of the nineteenth century established an alliance with the Ottoman empire and portrayed itself as Islam's protector against British and French encroachment, were sometimes engaged with colonial questions. The eminent German Orientalist Carl Becker (1876–1933), founding editor of *Der Islam*, Germany's first journal devoted to the contemporary Muslim world, is a case in point. In 1910, the same year in which *Der Islam* began publication, Becker addressed the National Colonial Conference in Berlin to oppose the demands of Christian missionaries that the colonial authorities support their work in German-ruled Tanganyika. "The [German] Government," Becker argued, "in its policy should not be led by religious, but by national points of view . . . [Islam] must be regarded – at least in East Africa – though hostile to Christianity, as thoroughly capable of development in the direction of modern civilisation, if it be brought under the strong influence of European culture."[20]

It should come as no great surprise that many Orientalists took for granted the superiority of Western civilization and the right of Europeans to rule over Asians and Africans: these assumptions were pervasive in nineteenth-century European culture. Though there were always those who rejected them and opposed colonialism and imperialism, most Europeans (and later Americans) sincerely embraced the notion of the "white man's burden" – the idea that the civilized white Europeans had a duty to exercise a firm but beneficent tutelage over what they regarded as the less advanced, child-like, dark-skinned races and guide them toward civilization. The French often spoke of their country's unique *mission civilisatrice*, its "civilizing mission" through which the blessings of French culture and the Enlightenment would be instilled in the inhabitants of the colonies. As one French colonial official put, "Our natives need to be governed. They are big children, incapable of going alone. We should guide them firmly, stand no nonsense from them, and crush intriguers and agents of sedition. At the same time we should protect them, direct them paternally, and especially obtain influence over them by the constant example of our moral superiority. Above all: no vain humanitarian illusions, both in the interest of France and of the natives themselves."[21]

We can see an example of the sometimes close relationship between "knowledge" *about* the Orient and colonial power *over* the Orient – as well as the growing influence of racial theories – in the way many French scholars and colonial officials categorized the inhabitants of Algeria in the nineteenth century and on into the twentieth. Just a few years before the launching of the French conquest of Algeria in 1830, a French scholar had advanced the theory that the inhabitants of that country's Kabyle region, who like a substantial portion of Algeria's population spoke a dialect of the Berber language rather than Arabic, were not only linguistically but also racially distinct from Arab Algerians. Unlike the "Semitic" Arabs, the Kabyles were, he claimed, a "Nordic people, descending directly from the [Germanic] Vandals, handsome with their blue eyes and blond hair." And whereas the Arabs were by nature servile, authoritarian and fanatical, the Kabyle Berbers were said to be egalitarian, free-spirited and rational. In subsequent decades some (though not all) French military men and colonial officials in Algeria embraced this view, which had no basis in reality, and went on to claim (just as fancifully) that the Kabyles were actually descendants of the Christians who had lived in North Africa before the Muslim conquest and had retained their distinctive characteristics.

The propagation of what one scholar has called the "Kabyle myth," with its insistence on drawing a sharp distinction between Arabs and Kabyles (or Berbers in general), was not an idle exercise in ethnic or racial classification: it had concrete consequences. In keeping with the classic colonial strategy of divide and rule, some French officials sought to make the inhabitants of the Kabyle region into allies of French colonialism in Algeria and therefore implemented policies which favored the Kabyles in employment, education, taxation and representation. Moreover, the French tried to insist that the Kabyles be judged in accordance with their customary law instead of Islamic law while fostering Berber and suppressing Arabic in Kabyle schools. These policies, based on a highly tendentious and obviously racialized classification of Algeria's population, helped transform what had long been fluid and contingent forms of identity into fixed, officially sanctioned and officially enforced categories. French officials in Morocco implemented similar policies after the establishment of French rule there in 1912, hoping to separate that country's large Berber-speaking minority from its Arabic-speaking majority and thereby weaken Moroccan opposition to colonial domination.[22]

Colonialism and Islam

The linkage between Orientalist knowledge and colonial policymaking is clearly manifested in an inquiry which a leading French journal devoted to colonial and foreign policy – *Questions diplomatiques et coloniales* – conducted in 1901. Asserting that France had become "a great Muslim power," the editors of the journal asked leading Orientalists to offer their views on the evolution of Islam in the twentieth century just begun.[23] Behind this inquiry lay a widespread European anxiety about "pan-Islam," the term (literally meaning "encompassing all Muslims," on the model of "pan-German" or "pan-American") which European colonial officials and experts on Islam used to denote the persistent feelings of solidarity among Muslims across national boundaries which, they feared, might be mobilized against colonial rule. At the very zenith of European global hegemony, Europeans conjured up vague but threatening notions of secretive cabals of cruel and fanatical Muslims plotting to overthrow colonial rule everywhere across the Muslim world in an orgy of bloodshed. At the beginning of the twentieth century, fear of the threat which pan-Islam allegedly posed to colonial domination was as widespread (and as exaggerated) as was Americans' fear of an "international communist conspiracy" run from the Kremlin during the 1950s.

One of those who contributed a response, a French specialist on the medieval Muslim philosopher Ibn Sina' (mentioned in Chapter 2), asserted that though Islam as a religion was basically finished, the colonial powers still faced a serious threat from pan-Islam, which might foster anticolonial revolts in a number of Muslim lands at the same time. Therefore the goal must be "to weaken Islam . . . to render it forever incapable of great awakenings." "I believe," this scholar wrote, "that we should endeavour to split the Muslim world, to break its moral unity, using to this effect the ethnic and political divisions . . . In one word, let us *segment Islam*, and make use, moreover, of Muslim heresies and the Sufi orders." Other participants argued that the spread of Western ideas and institutions would lead to the emergence of new educated Muslim elites which in the lands under European colonial rule would accept Western tutelage as beneficial to their societies and elsewhere would promote gradual reform and modernization.

Perhaps not surprisingly, the two Muslims whose views appeared in this forum approached the question from a very different angle. One, an Algerian named Muhammad Ben Rahal, insisted that Islam promulgated positive and progressive moral and social values and castigated what he saw as Europe's hostility to Islam: "if the Muslim defends his home, religion, or nation, he is not seen as a patriot but as a savage; if he displays courage or heroism, he is called a fanatic; if after defeat he shows resignation, he is called a fatalist." In short, he argued, Islam is "ostracized, systematically denigrated, and ridiculed without ever being known." He went on to denounce colonialism: "Dreaming to annex half a continent and to reduce the native – even by legal means – to misery is no policy, charging him with all kinds of crimes is no justification and no solution."

Ben Rahal's response was echoed by that of Edward Browne, a prominent British scholar in the field of Persian studies. "To my mind," Browne wrote, "Asia is right to be wary of Western civilization, of the rapacity and materialism, which are direct and necessary consequences of the blind attachment to the natural sciences...It is more the future of Europe than that of Asia which preoccupies me, which provokes my anxiety. How can one construct a pure and disinterested ethic on the basis of a theory which clearly declares that it is the strongest and the most rapacious that have the right to survive; a theory that lacks compassion for the weak. Such a theory can only lead to unending war between nations." A few years later Browne would express sympathy for Iran's constitutional revolution and criticize his own government's efforts to dominate that country.

From the attempts by Ben Rahal, Browne, Jamal al-Din al-Afghani, Goldziher, Wilfred Blunt and others to offer alternative perspectives, we can see that the mainstream view of Islam was never entirely hegemonic, that it was never impossible for dissident voices to make themselves heard when Europeans discussed Islam and European rule over Muslims. But it is also true that those dissenting voices usually remained marginal: it was the current represented by Renan which was accepted as common sense not only among the public at large but also among those most directly involved in colonial policymaking and administration, and even by many scholars of Islam. We can find further evidence of this in the writings of one of the leading colonial administrators of the late nineteenth and early twentieth centuries, the man who for a quarter of a century ruled Egypt on Britain's behalf.

Evelyn Baring (1841–1917) was born into a wealthy and prominent English banking family. While still in his thirties he served as private secretary to the British viceroy of India; then, in 1877, he was posted to Egypt to help straighten out that bankrupt country's finances and make sure that the European banks and investors who held Egyptian bonds got their money back. After a few years he was back in India, in charge of that colony's finances, but in 1883, shortly after British troops occupied Egypt, he returned to Cairo, where he would remain until 1907. Baring (who was created Earl of Cromer in 1892) was officially just Britain's "consul-general and agent" in Egypt; but Egypt was now a British protectorate and it was Cromer who really ran the country. In 1908, a year after leaving Egypt and retiring from government service, Cromer published *Modern Egypt*, in whose two large volumes he offered a detailed narrative of events in Egypt over the previous three decades as well as his evaluation of the results of the British occupation.[24] Though Cromer never learned Arabic (he did know some Turkish), he was by that time widely regarded as a leading authority on Egypt and the Orient in general, and his views can fairly be taken as representative of much of British (and European) elite and popular opinion.

Cromer began by establishing what he saw as the unbridgeable gap between the "logical" West and the "illogical and picturesque" East, between the European mind and the Oriental mind, and this theme was central to the entire book.

The European is a close reasoner; his statements of facts are devoid of ambiguity; he is a natural logician, albeit he may not have studied logic; he loves symmetry in all things; he is by nature sceptical and requires proof before he can accept the truth of any proposition; his trained intelligence works like a piece of mechanism. The mind of the Oriental, on the other hand, like his picturesque streets, is eminently wanting in symmetry. His reasoning is of the most slipshod description. Although the ancient Arabs acquired in somewhat high degree the science of dialectics, their descendants are singularly deficient in the logical faculty . . . The Egyptian is also eminently unsceptical.

. . . Look, again, to the high powers of organisation displayed by the European, to his constant endeavour to bend circumstances, to suit his will, and to his tendency to question the acts of his superiors unless he happens to agree with them, a tendency which is only kept in subjection by the trained and intelligent discipline resulting from education. Compare these attributes with the feeble organising powers of the Oriental, with his fatalism which accepts the inevitable, and with his submissiveness to all constituted authority.

. . . A European would think that, where a road and a paved side-walk existed, it required no great effort of the reasoning faculty to perceive that human beings were intended to pass along the side-walk, and animals along the road. The point is not always so clear to the Egyptian. He will not unfrequently walk in the middle of the road, and will send his donkey along the side-path. Instances of this sort might be multiplied. Compare the habits of thought which can lead to actions of this nature with the promptitude with which the European seizes on an idea when it is presented to him, and acts as occasion may demand.

Cromer's depiction of "Orientals" as fundamentally irrational was widely accepted. As Rudyard Kipling, the bard of British imperialism, put it at around the same time:

You'll never plumb the Oriental mind
And even if you do, it won't be worth the toil.

As for Islam, Cromer quoted the English Orientalist Stanley Lane-Pool: "As a religion, Islam is great; it has taught men to worship one God with a pure worship who formerly worshipped many gods impurely. As a social system, it is a complete failure." Islam, Cromer declared, keeps women subjugated, it subordinates all of social life to an inflexible religious law, it tolerates slavery, it is intolerant toward non-believers. "Islam cannot be reformed," Cromer wrote, echoing Renan; "that is to say, reformed Islam is Islam no longer; it is something else."

Given the mental and social defects of Orientals, and particularly of Muslim Orientals who were especially burdened by their retrograde and oppressive religion, it was only fitting that they be subjected to the tutelage of Europeans – if possible, of Anglo-Saxons, an "imperial race" whose "sterling national qualities" and selfless Christian morality made it particularly well suited to assume responsibility for raising the dark-skinned races from their abject state and guiding them toward civilization. Such tutelage, in the form of direct or indirect colonial rule, was all the more necessary since, Cromer argued, the "subject races" generally did not constitute distinct nations. Egyptian nationalists and their European sympathizers like Wilfred Blunt might demand "Egypt for the Egyptians," but in reality the inhabitants of Egypt were a hodge-podge of races who were utterly incapable of governing themselves in a civilized manner.[25] Cromer's views were not at all untypical; on the contrary, while there were always people in Europe who condemned what we today term racism and opposed the more brutal aspects of colonialism, most people regarded the cultural and moral superiority of Western civilization as simple common sense and saw European rule over non-Westerners as both necessary and right.

It is certainly true that in the nineteenth century many Europeans also perceived other Europeans who belonged to different nationalities, ethnic groups or religions as very different from themselves, and sometimes as almost as alien and uncivilized as the inhabitants of India or China or Africa. As one noted British historian of colonialism put it,

Europeans of superior countries thought of inferior Europeans and non-Europeans in not very different terms. Travelers described their journeys through Spain, before the railways, as if Madrid were somewhere near Timbuctoo. Stereotypes such as the Englishman's image of Paddy the Irishman, a feckless nimble-tongued fellow at whom one felt a mixture of amusement and impatience – or of the Italian as an organ-grinder with a monkey – provided ready-made categories for Burmese or Malays to be fitted into. And if the "native" on occasion reminded the Englishman of his familiar Paddy, Paddy might sometimes remind him of the native. Lord Salisbury, the Conservative leader, supporting coercion in Ireland, said that Irishmen were as unfit for self-government as Hottentots. Ireland was subject politically and economically to England, Italy through much of the nineteenth century to Austria. Down to 1918 a large proportion of Europeans occupied a more or less colonial status, differing only in degree from that of the Asian or African countries that were being annexed . . . Treatment of these subject minorities was not always gentler than in colonies outside, and must have been roughened by the habits formed by Europe's ruling classes in dictating to the other continents.[26]

It is also the case, one might add, that eighteenth- and nineteenth-century European elites often regarded the lower classes of their own countries, peasants and urban working people, as ignorant, benighted semi-savages and responded to popular demands for social justice and democracy with brutal repression.

Nonetheless, for a very long time colonial subjects in Asia and Africa were deemed to be in a rather different category than subordinated Europeans. European ruling classes were ultimately compelled to grant concessions to their own lower classes and accept them as fellow citizens and at least nominal equals. Moreover, Italians, Poles, Czechs, Slovaks, Hungarians, and other disunited or subordinated European peoples often advanced their claims to independence from Habsburg or Russian or German rule, or from domination by other European states, on the ground that they were in fact *not* like those uncivilized dark-skinned natives in the colonies (those "Hottentots") but rather Europeans, white people, who were therefore entitled to equality, self-rule and a free national life. In the course of the nineteenth and early twentieth centuries most of these claims would be recognized, leading to the creation of new nation-states that won acceptance as legitimate members of the European "family." Even Europe's Jewish minority, subjected in the middle of the twentieth century to a systematic (and largely successful) campaign of extermination by what had been regarded as one of the most culturally advanced countries in Europe, would subsequently come (despite persistent antisemitism) to be widely accepted as authentically European, as part of Western civilization, now frequently rebranded as "Judeo-Christian civilization."

It took much longer for Europeans to accept the notion that Asian, African and American subjects of the British, French, Dutch, Portuguese and other European empires were entitled to the same human rights as Europeans, including the right of self-determination and self-government. The elaboration of the idea of Western civilization in the nineteenth century involved the drawing of sharp lines between what was deemed Western and what was deemed non-Western. So the same process of categorization which enabled Europeans to demand liberty and equality as the birthright of all Westerners also defined non-Westerners as not inherently entitled to those things, or at least not yet ready for them. The subjugation of most Asian and African peoples to colonial rule thus persisted long after the right of European peoples to independence was widely recognized, and in many lands European colonial domination was brought to an end only after protracted and often violent struggles. And even after formal independence was largely won in the two decades following the end of the Second World War, the categories of West and non-West continued to exercise a powerful influence on how people all over the globe perceived who and what they were – as well as who and what they were not.

As we saw at the beginning of this chapter, in the nineteenth century many Europeans (and Americans) had come to regard "the Orient" as too broad a category and began to break it down into a "Near East" and a "Far East." In the early twentieth century a new term for the lands of southwestern Asia emerged in the United States which would first complement and then largely supplant "Near East." The term "Middle East" was coined in 1902 by the noted American military historian, Alfred Thayer Mahan (1840–1914). Mahan's insistence on the crucial importance of sea power influenced strategic thinking in the United States and Europe at the turn of the century and helped induce the United States to build up its ocean-going naval forces, which soon enabled it to take control of Hawaii, Cuba, Puerto Rico and the Philippines and effectively dominate the Caribbean and Central America. In his writings and lectures on global strategy Mahan demarcated a Middle East which he regarded as stretching from Arabia all the way across Persia and Afghanistan to the borders of today's Pakistan; by contrast, he defined the Near East as encompassing the Balkans (parts of which were then still within the Ottoman empire), western Anatolia, which at the time still had a large Greek-speaking population, and the lands of the eastern Mediterranean.

Valentine Chirol (1852–1929), then the Tehran correspondent of the *Times* of London, picked up Mahan's new term and used it in his 1903 book *The Middle Eastern Question; or, Some Political Problems of Indian Defence* to denote "those regions of Asia which extend to the borders of India or command the approaches to India."[27] The new term spread quickly and was initially used more or less as Mahan had defined it, so that to cover the whole region between the eastern Mediterranean and British-ruled India observers now spoke of "the Near and Middle East." But in the longer run the distinction Mahan drew between the Near East and the Middle East did not really catch on. The Balkans, which western Europeans had long regarded as rather uncivilized or even "oriental" in character, were eventually incorporated (though not without some ambivalence) into a reformulated and expanded conception of Europe, while in the 1920s Anatolia lost nearly all of its Greek population and became part of the new, almost entirely Muslim Turkish Republic. Over time, Near East and Middle East came to be used more or less interchangeably to refer to the same geographical space, usually encompassing the present-day states of Turkey, Iran, Syria, Lebanon, Iraq, Jordan, Israel and the Palestinian territories it occupies, Saudi Arabia, Yemen, Oman, the smaller Arab principalities along the Persian Gulf, and Egypt, though the vast majority of that country is actually located on the continent of Africa. Sometimes the predominantly Arab countries of North Africa west of Egypt, and even the Sudan to its south, are also loosely included in the Middle East. Afghanistan, which Mahan had included within his Middle East, was often relegated to a sort of geographical limbo (see Map 6).

After the Second World War the term "Middle East" came to predominate (in the United States the journalese term "Mideast" is also used); it now has a more contemporary ring to it, while "Near East" has come to sound a bit old-fashioned, just as "the Levant" and "the Orient" had become antiquated somewhat earlier. Of course, denominating this portion of the earth's surface as the Middle East is just as arbitrary as depicting it as part of the Orient. It encompasses a vast area of great ecological diversity, from snowbound mountains to barren deserts to fertile river valleys and rain-watered coastal plains, includes huge cities as well as myriad towns and villages, and is inhabited by many different peoples with their own distinct languages, cultures and ways of life. The majority of its population is Muslim (though of different kinds), but it includes many non-Muslims as well, and the majority of the world's Muslims live elsewhere, in non-Middle Eastern lands like Indonesia, India, Pakistan and Bangladesh, so religion does not work as the key criterion for defining this region. At the same time, calling this region the Middle East obviously manifests a Eurocentric perspective: it is "middle" and "eastern" only in relation to western Europe.

Yet the term Middle East has caught on, not only in the West but even in the languages of the region itself, where it is widely used. Other ways of defining all or parts of the same territory persist as well, however. In journalism and official parlance, for example, Arabs often use "the Arab world" or "the Arab homeland" to denote the predominantly Arabic-speaking lands of the Middle East and North Africa, from Iraq to Morocco. Arab geographers traditionally divided those lands into two parts, *al-mashriq* ("the east") to denote the eastern half of the Arab world and *al-maghrib* ("the west") to denote the western half, and Arabic speakers continue to use these terms. The Maghreb is also used in French (and to a lesser extent in English) to refer to Morocco, Algeria, Tunisia and

Libya. In an effort to avoid Eurocentrism, the United Nations and other international bodies sometimes officially refer to the region as "Southwestern Asia and North Africa," but this more neutral designation has not really caught on. It would seem that the Middle East as a designation for this region will be with us for the foreseeable future, however recent its origins, however arbitrary its definition and however arguable its utility.

4   The American century

In the summer of 1914 the First World War broke out, pitting Germany, Austria-Hungary and (a few months later) the Ottoman empire against Britain, France and Russia, joined the following year by Italy and in 1917 by the United States. The war, which cost some ten million lives, resulted in the defeat and dismemberment of the Ottoman empire. After the war the victorious Allies, particularly Britain and France, proceeded to redraw the map of the Middle East and carve a number of new states – Iraq, Syria, Lebanon, Transjordan (later renamed Jordan) and Palestine – out of what had been the predominantly Arab provinces of the defunct Ottoman empire. Most of Palestine would become part of the new State of Israel in 1948, with the remainder falling under Jordanian or Egyptian control. But otherwise the states which Britain and France established in 1920–21 remain in existence today, their borders little changed. The war also helped set the stage for the conquest by the Sa'ud family and its allies of much of the Arabian peninsula and the creation in 1932 of the new Kingdom of Saudi Arabia, which a decade or so later would begin to develop strong ties with the United States (see Maps 4 and 5).

In Europe, the Allies largely fulfilled their wartime commitment to the right of subject peoples to national self-determination, and a number of newly independent nation-states – including Poland, Czechoslovakia, Hungary, Latvia, Lithuania and Estonia – came into being on territory that had previously been ruled by the Austro-Hungarian, Russian or German empires. But the British reneged on their wartime promise to support Arab independence. Instead, Britain retained control of the new states of Iraq, Palestine and Jordan which it had just helped create, while France became master of Syria and Lebanon. And although Britain and France were formally "mandatory powers" – trustees of a sort, responsible for guiding these new states toward eventual self-rule and supposedly subject to League of Nations supervision – the mandate system was in essence a new form of colonial rule. Anatolia, the predominantly Turkish heartland of the defunct Ottoman empire, was initially slated for dismemberment, but there Allied plans were thwarted by nationalist resistance which brought into being the new nation-state of Turkey. Allied promises to grant autonomy in parts of Anatolia to Kurds and Armenians were never fulfilled.

During the First World War, many Orientalist scholars had naturally put their expertise at the service of the war effort. For example, the noted Oxford Orientalist and archeologist D. G. Hogarth was stationed in British-ruled Egypt during the war, where he oversaw the effort to make contact with dissident Arabs within the Ottoman empire and induce them to revolt. His student Thomas Edward Lawrence was sent by British military intelligence to Arabia in 1916 to work with the Arab insurrectionary forces. After the war, Lawrence's writings (which sometimes exaggerated or distorted his own role in the Arab revolt) and his glorification by enterprising journalists made him a celebrity, hailed in Britain and the United States as "Lawrence of Arabia." Other British operatives in the wartime and postwar Middle East, including St. John Philby (Britain's contact with the Sa'ud family) and Gertrude Bell (who helped engineer Britain's creation of Iraq), picked up local languages as they went along and (like Lawrence) sometimes developed a romantic identification with the Arabs.

Early twentieth-century Orientalism

In the aftermath of the First World War, contemporary observers sought to make sense of the dramatic redrawing of the map of the Middle East by Britain and France and of what they saw going on in that region and in the wider Muslim world. Journalists like the prolific American Lothrop Stoddard – who as we have seen in Chapter 3 was an avowed white supremacist – argued in his 1921 book *The New World of Islam* that people like Renan and Cromer had been dead wrong when they asserted that Islam was inert and unchangeable. Islam could change, Stoddard insisted; in fact the Muslim world was undergoing significant political, social, economic and cultural transformations, with uncertain consequences. "The [Islamic] Orient is to-day in full transition, flux, ferment, more sudden and profound than any it has hitherto known. The world of Islam, mentally and spiritually quiescent for almost a thousand years, is once more astir, once more on the march."[1]

While Stoddard was wrong to assert that "the world of Islam" had been stagnant for a millennium, he was certainly right about the contemporary scene: things *were* changing in the Muslim world, including the predominantly Muslim lands of the Middle East and North Africa. In the decades that followed the First World War, the pace of social, economic and cultural change in this region accelerated and its scope widened.

Moreover, here as elsewhere in the colonial world, the aftermath of that war witnessed anticolonial agitation on an unprecedented scale, including large-scale uprisings from Iraq to Egypt to Morocco. And although Britain and France had the military might to suppress these uprisings and retain control, nationalist movements persisted and gained strength, eventually mobilizing large sections of the population to demand independence and making colonial rule increasingly costly. In the end, as we will see, Britain and France would be compelled to give up all their colonial domains in the Arab world.[2]

In the decades before the Second World War, however, these developments were largely deemed outside the purview of university-based Orientalist scholarship as it was practiced in Europe and the United States. As Maxime Rodinson put it, "The modern development of Muslim nations was not considered an important subject of scholarly inquiry and was disdainfully relegated to people such as economists, journalists, diplomats, military men, and amateurs. Moreover, there was a tendency to reduce any examination of the modern Muslim world to a narrow focus on whatever remained from the past."[3]

This is not to say that there were no institutions or journals specializing in the contemporary Muslim world. In 1906, for example, the French Scientific Mission in Morocco – created two years earlier in order to study that society, soon to fall under French colonial rule – began to publish the influential *Revue du Monde Musulman*, which surveyed contemporary developments across the Muslim world. As I mentioned in Chapter 3, in 1910 Germany followed suit with *Der Islam*, edited by the Orientalist Carl Becker, who sought to influence German colonial policy. The following year the United States acquired its first journal devoted to the contemporary Muslim world. The journal's publisher, the Hartford Theological Seminary in Connecticut, and its full title, *The Moslem World: A Quarterly Review of Current Events, Literature, and Thought Among Mohammedans, and the Progress of Christian Missions in Moslem Lands*, indicate the Protestant missionary impulse behind its launching. The new journal's editor hailed the *Revue du Monde Musulman* as "invaluable," particularly for its "careful review of the Moslem press," but noted with apparent regret that its standpoint was "purely scientific and wholly neutral as regards the Christian faith." And he (disdainfully?) depicted the new German journal *Der Islam* as devoted to "the scientific study of Islam, but especially to its art, literature, and civilisation as they relate to the expansion of German commerce and empire."[4] Yet while the launching of *The Moslem World* was clearly part of an effort to reinvigorate and accelerate Protestant missionary work among Muslims, it did give interested Americans greater access to what was going on in the Muslim world than they had previously enjoyed.

Nonetheless, to a considerable extent Orientalism as a branch of the humanities continued much as it had in the nineteenth century: still bearing the imprint of men like Sacy and of the German scholars who pioneered modern Islamic studies in Europe, it was imbued with a strong philological orientation and a vision of Islam as a distinct civilization now in crisis as a result of its confrontation with the more advanced and powerful modern West. A scholar with mastery of the main languages and classical texts of Islamic high civilization was still presumed to be able to pronounce on almost anything related to Islam, across vast stretches of time and space.[5]

For the most part, university-based scholars who studied Islam in Europe and the United States came to be situated in departments or institutes of "Oriental studies" or "Near Eastern studies" or "Near Eastern languages and civilizations" or some variant thereof, though others might work in departments or institutes focusing on art history or even anthropology. Over time, academic Orientalism tended to subdivide institutionally, into separate Near Eastern and East Asian departments and programs at universities, with the latter focused mainly on China and Japan; the Indian subcontinent, Afghanistan and Central Asia were often relegated to a sort of scholarly limbo in between the Near East and the Far East. Scholars who studied aspects of Islamic civilization thus often worked and taught alongside scholars who specialized in the languages, histories, religions and cultures of ancient Egypt and Mesopotamia, and sometimes even the history and religion of ancient Israel and the Jews.[6] This division of academic labor reflected and perpetuated classical Orientalism's vision of itself and of its object of inquiry: Orientalism remained that branch of the humanities which studied something called the Orient from the beginning of recorded history until the present, including the predominantly Muslim lands of Asia usually conceived of as components of a distinctly Islamic civilization.

Unlike their colleagues who studied (for example) the history of Britain or France or the United States or Russia, were trained as historians and were situated in university or college departments of history, scholars who studied the rise of Islam or the 'Abbasid dynasty or the Ottoman empire or some other aspect or period of Islamic history were usually philologists by training, and they tended to interact largely with fellow Orientalists whose training was also heavily philological. As Hamilton Gibb, in his day probably the leading Orientalist scholar in the English-speaking world, put it as late as 1956, "In England and Europe there are at most some three or four orientalist scholars who are professional historians; the difference this makes can be easily seen when their production is compared with the usual orientalist works on Middle Eastern history. In the United States it would be hard to find as many."[7] Nor did many Orientalist scholars have much training (or interest) in the new methods and interpretive approaches being developed and debated in sociology, anthropology or other disciplines. As a result much of even the best Orientalist scholarship – and many scholars steeped in the Orientalist tradition continued to produce important work on which later generations of scholars would build – was isolated from what was going on in other fields, and some of the most widely acclaimed scholarly work was rooted in the same problematic premises that had underpinned a great deal of the earlier work in the field.[8]

Ottoman despotism and decline revisited

To see how some of the key themes of nineteenth-century Orientalist scholarship persisted into the twentieth century, we can begin with Albert Howe Lybyer's 1913 study *The Government of the Ottoman Empire in the Time of Suleiman the Magnificent.* Lybyer's analysis of the character and evolution of the Ottoman state remained widely accepted and widely taught into the 1960s. Lybyer, who spent most of his academic career at Oberlin College in Ohio, was unable to read manuscripts in the Ottoman Turkish language and therefore based his work on translated materials, sources in European languages and the work of other historians. Today this shortcoming would render his interpretation highly questionable, to say the least, and even in 1913 it is hard to imagine that, for example, a book on medieval French history written by someone who had not made extensive use of original source materials in the relevant languages would be taken very seriously by scholars. Yet most of the scholars who reviewed Lybyer's book acclaimed it as a major scholarly advance. They seemed to assume that the Ottoman sources were of little real value and that Lybyer's failure to engage directly with the voluminous Turkish-language material relevant to his topic in archives and libraries in Istanbul and elsewhere was no great problem.

As a result, several generations of scholars accepted and passed on to their students Lybyer's assertion that the Ottoman state could be neatly divided into two distinct components, which he called "the Ruling Institution" and "the Moslem Institution" – roughly equivalent to the dichotomy between church and state widely used by historians of medieval Europe. Lybyer claimed that in the heyday of the Ottoman empire in the fifteenth and early sixteenth centuries, the members of the

Ruling Institution – the sultan's household staff, the top officials and military officers, the bureaucracy, the standing army – consisted almost entirely of men who had been born to Christian parents in the Balkans or the Caucasus, enslaved (or otherwise acquired) by the Ottoman state while still boys, converted to Islam and rigorously trained for government service. By contrast, the Moslem Institution, which comprised all those involved with Islam, Islamic jurisprudence and the judicial system, and religious education, was said to have been made up almost exclusively of men born of free Muslim parents.

For Lybyer as for Renan, what was most important about a people was not the religion it nominally professed but its racial characteristics and the unchanging "spirit" associated with that race. Thus for Lybyer the Ottoman Ruling Institution was until the later sixteenth century essentially "Turkish-Aryan" in spirit, reflecting the racial origins of its members. And just as Renan had insisted in "Islam and Science" that the "golden age" of Islamic civilization had nothing to do with the Arabs or Islam but was really the product of the "Aryan" racial genius of the Persians and the Greeks, so Lybyer suggested that the rise and expansion of the Ottoman empire, and its ability to adapt to changing circumstances, were due largely to what he claimed was the fact that its civil and military elites were almost entirely composed of people who had been born Christian and Aryan. In contrast, Lybyer depicted the Moslem Institution as "Semitic" in spirit and therefore conservative and inflexible in character.

Over time, Lybyer asserted, and especially after the Ottoman conquest of the eastern Arab lands in 1516–17 increased the proportion of Muslims in the empire's population, Islam came to play a more central role in state and society, and free-born Muslims gained access to positions of power in the administration and military formerly held exclusively by men of Christian birth. As a result the Ottoman civil and military elites, and what had been the most effective Ottoman fighting force, became increasingly inflexible, ineffective, corrupt and disloyal. In other words, the Ottoman empire began to decline because it became actually (rather than just nominally) Muslim and Semitic in character. "It is true," Lybyer wrote, "that as a nation the Ottoman Turks remained Mohammedans; this has constituted the real 'tragedy of the Turk'" because it meant that the largely Aryan Ottoman Turkish elite was "bound hand and foot by that scholastic Mohammedanism which was reaching rigid perfection at the time when the Turks first became prominent in the Saracen [i.e. Arab] empire..."[9]

Lybyer's thesis was incorporated more or less wholesale into what was in the 1950s and 1960s widely regarded as the standard scholarly work on the Ottoman empire in the period just before what its authors saw as the beginning of the fateful encounter between the modern West and Islamic civilization. This was *Islamic Society and the West: A Study of the Impact of Western Civilization on Moslem Culture in the Near East*, by Sir Hamilton Alexander Rosskeen Gibb and Harold Bowen, published in two parts in 1950 and 1957. As I mentioned earlier, Gibb (1895–1971) was probably the pre-eminent English-speaking Orientalist of his day; he was also a central figure in several of the most important developments in the field after the Second World War. Over a period of four decades Gibb published books, articles and encyclopedia entries on early Islamic history, medieval Islamic political thought, modern Arabic literature, modern trends in Islamic thought, and modern Middle Eastern history, as well as numerous book reviews and several translations.[10] He also served as editor of the *Encyclopedia of Islam*, a compendium of the state of Orientalist knowledge on all things Islamic. His intellectual and personal trajectory may thus serve to illustrate essential features of what might be called "late Orientalism."

It was not merely Gibb's great erudition that made such a range feasible; it was also his conviction – and that of many, perhaps most, other Orientalists – that Islam was a coherent civilization whose historical dynamics, institutions, thought, and way of life were expressions of a basically unitary and stable set of core values and beliefs, such that (as I will discuss shortly) Gibb could regard medieval Islamic thought as directly relevant to the problems which Muslims everywhere faced in the middle of the twentieth century. This way of categorizing and conceptualizing knowledge was, as we have seen, not uncommon in the late nineteenth and early twentieth centuries; but a scholar today would be much less likely to define the scope of his or her expertise so broadly or feel confident about writing with authority on such a wide range of topics and periods.

Gibb was born in Egypt, of Scottish parents. He studied Semitic languages – the rubric under which Hebrew, Arabic, and other related tongues were grouped – at Edinburgh University, and after military service in the First World War he continued his studies at the School of Oriental Studies (later renamed the School of Oriental and African Studies, SOAS) at the University of London. This institution had been established during the war, with the strong support of colonial officials like Cromer and Lord Curzon, former viceroy of India, to more effectively train those who would go on to serve the empire in Asia and Africa. Gibb rose through the ranks and eventually became a professor at SOAS, but in 1937 he was appointed to the Laudian Chair of Arabic at Oxford, where he remained until the mid-1950s. He was much influenced by Arnold Toynbee's conception of history as the story of the rise and fall of civilizations, briefly discussed in Chapter 3. It was Toynbee, then director of studies at the Royal Institute of International Affairs, a sort of "think tank" which brought together scholars and government officials, who asked Gibb and his colleague Harold Bowen to contribute a volume on Islam to a series of studies on the impact of the modern West on the civilizations of Asia.

Gibb and Bowen did most of the research for their *Islamic Society and the West* during the 1930s and 1940s. They had initially planned a massive study of almost every aspect of the transformations which Ottoman state and society experienced under Western influence since the beginning of the nineteenth century. But the only parts actually published constituted a sort of introductory survey, covering the period "before the process [of transformation] in question began." As the title of their book indicates, Gibb and Bowen accepted without question the central premise of nineteenth-century Orientalism: the basic object of their analysis was an Islamic civilization (or "Islamic society," as they termed it) which, they believed, had until quite recently (around the middle of the eighteenth century) remained essentially intact and unaffected by that other, fundamentally different civilization which would later transform it, the modern West. *Islamic Society and the West* sought to delineate the main features of this pristine Islamic society as it existed before it first felt the transformative impact of the West.

In the first part of the volume, therefore, Gibb and Bowen drew on a broad range of sources in a variety of languages to offer a detailed portrait of the Ottoman "Ruling Institution," as well as descriptions of the peasantry, land tenure and agriculture, and urban life. In so doing they adopted not only Lybyer's terminology but also much of his explanation of Ottoman decline, asserting that the "capture" by free-born Muslims of positions once held exclusively by Christian-born "slaves of the sultan" had had "disastrous results."[11] But when they came to the second part of their study, on the (again following Lybyer) "Religious Institution," a serious question arose. "The term 'Islamic Society' applied to the social organization which we are analysing," Gibb and Bowen wrote,

implies that its distinguishing features are related in some way or another to the religion of Islam. Yet in those groups and activities which have been considered up to this point there is little that can be considered as specifically Islamic; on the contrary, the organization of village and industrial life belongs rather to a stage of social evolution which finds close parallels in many non-Islamic regions of Europe and Asia; and that of the Court and the army, though of a more peculiar type, is based upon principles to which such Islamic elements as they display appears to be purely incidental.

In what useful sense, then, could this be called an *Islamic* society?

To resolve this dilemma, on which the credibility of their intellectual enterprise (and that of much of Orientalist scholarship) rested, Gibb and Bowen drew on the venerable concept of Oriental despotism, though they did not explicitly acknowledge their debt. As we saw in Chapters 2 and 3, there was a well-established tradition in European thought, running from certain Renaissance and early modern thinkers through Montesquieu to Mill to Marx and Weber and on into the twentieth century (with such once influential but now largely forgotten figures as Karl Wittfogel), which depicted Asian societies as typically ruled by tiny, rapacious and often ethnically alien elites despotically dominating the mass of society, with a vast gap between rulers and ruled. Moreover, Oriental societies were seen as lacking the organic unity and coherence characteristic of Western societies; they were instead a hodgepodge, or more politely a "mosaic," of largely self-governing, disconnected and often feuding religious, ethnic, clan, tribal, occupational and racial groups.

This was just the image of late Ottoman society which Gibb and Bowen evoked: "It has already been pointed out," they wrote, "that that society was composed of a vast number of small social groups, almost self-governing, with a wide gap interposed between the governing class of soldiers and officials and the governed class of merchants, artisans, and cultivators." What then held this society together? What kept its disparate components from flying apart, resulting in social disintegration and chaos? This is where, for Gibb and Bowen, Islam came into the picture, and why this could be characterized as an Islamic society. Islam and the "Religious Institution" functioned as a sort of social glue which prevented Islamic society from disintegrating into a myriad of small autonomous units by bridging the great gulf which divided ruler from ruled and by linking together all ranks and elements of society in a common framework of belief and social organization, mainly the Sufi brotherhoods. As they put it, "The religious institution was thus charged with a double task: on the one hand, to fill the major gap [between rulers and ruled], and, on the other, to knit the separate small groups together by supplying a common ideal and a common organization superimposed upon the group loyalties and if need be overriding them in a wider common loyalty."[12]

H. A. R. Gibb and modern Islam

In Chapter 5 I will discuss some of the critiques advanced from the late 1950s, and then more comprehensively in the 1970s, of the premises and arguments of *Islamic Society and the West*, and by extension of the intellectual premises of classical Orientalism as a scholarly enterprise. As we will see, these critiques would mark a significant turning-point in the development of what by then had come to be called "Middle East studies" in the United States. But for now, in order to get a somewhat fuller picture of mainstream Anglo-American Orientalism in the post-Second World War period, I will continue to discuss the work and career of H. A. R. Gibb.

In 1945, some years before *Islamic Society and the West* appeared, Gibb delivered a series of lectures at the University of Chicago which were published two years later as *Modern Trends in Islam*. In this book Gibb sought to analyze the "present religious attitudes and movements of the Muslim peoples," especially Arab and Indian Muslims. As Gibb correctly noted, modern Islamic thought had received little scholarly attention, and Gibb's own knowledge of Islamic history and thought was certainly both wide and deep. However, the categories he used to organize that knowledge and to interpret Islam and the history of the Muslim peoples are illustrative of what many critics would eventually argue were the grave shortcomings of the Orientalist tradition.

Like many earlier Orientalists, Gibb started from the assumption that there was an unchanging and distinctive "Arab mind" or "Muslim mind" (both derived from an even more primordial "Semitic mind") whose essential nature he could deduce from his knowledge of the classical texts of Islamic civilization and which could be implicitly or explicitly contrasted with an equally unitary and essentialized "Western mind." As we have seen, this concept had its roots in the division of humanity into distinct civilizations and in the notion of "the West" whose origins I discussed in Chapter 3. On this basis it was possible for Gibb to offer sweeping generalizations about the character of the thought processes of all Arabs and Muslims, from the rise of Islam to the present and from Morocco to Indonesia.

"We know something of the effect of the spoken and written word upon ourselves," Gibb wrote – as if what that effect was and who exactly "ourselves" referred to were self-evident. "But," he went on, "upon the Arab mind the impact of artistic speech is immediate; the words, passing through no filter of logic or reflection which might weaken or deaden their effect, go straight to the head." This was, for Gibb, an innate characteristic of the Semitic mind, which furthermore had a special affinity for the "unseen world." The Arab mind, Gibb continued,

cannot throw off its intense feeling for the separateness and individuality of the concrete events. This is, I believe, one of the main factors lying behind that "lack of a sense of law" which Professor Macdonald regarded as the characteristic difference in the oriental.

It is this, too, which explains – what is so difficult for the Western student to grasp – the aversion of the Muslims from the thought-processes of rationalism.

[The defeat of rationalist schools of thought in the early centuries of Islam] not only conditioned the formulation of the traditional Muslim theology but set a permanent stamp upon Islamic culture; and they still lie behind the conflicts arising in more recent years out of direct contact with modern Western thought. The rejection of rationalist modes of thought and of the utilitarian ethic which is inseparable from them has its roots, therefore, not in the so-called "obscurantism" of the Muslim theologians but in the atomism and discreteness of the Arab imagination.[13]

Gibb's analysis of contemporary trends in Islamic thought was some-times insightful, and Gibb insisted that, contrary to the claims of some denigrators, "Islam is a living and vital religion, appealing to the hearts, minds, and consciences of tens and hundreds of millions, setting them a standard by which to live honest, sober, and god-fearing lives."[14] But Gibb's analysis, and especially his conclusions about the prospects for Islam in the modern world, were at the same time deeply colored by a conception of Islam as possessing an unchanging essence, fixed many centuries ago, which continued to determine both the minds of its believers and its historical trajectory.

Islam might be a living faith, Gibb asserted, but Islam's "orthodox formulations, its systematic theology, its social apologetic" were inflexible and moribund. Yet Gibb was dismissive of modern Muslim thinkers who were seeking to draw on Islamic tradition in order to renovate their faith so that it could better serve Muslim societies struggling to come to grips with the social, cultural and political problems they faced in the modern world. The modernists were, he felt, inconsistent, intellectually shallow, romantic and overly attracted to some of the worst elements of Western thought. Ignorant of and alienated from what Gibb saw as the essence of their faith, they were unlikely to achieve the Islamic renaissance they were striving for. Moreover, Gibb went on, in the Middle East nationalism was confined to Westernized intellectuals and was in any case inherently contradictory to Islam; and "as the nationalist idea penetrated into the popular mind, it was transformed, and could not avoid being transformed, by the pressure of the age-long instincts and impulses of the Muslim masses," who remained faithful to the essence of traditional Islam. So secular nationalism was unlikely to provide Muslims with a way out of their crisis.

For Gibb the real problem with Islam was that it had taken a disas-trously wrong turn a thousand years earlier, when the innate character of the Semitic or Arab mind had led Muslim theologians to reject Greek rationalist thought. As a result Muslims today were still imbued with a fundamentally antirational mind-set which rendered them unable to come to terms with modernity. To repair this grievous and deeply rooted flaw in Islamic civilization and allow Islam to survive in the modern world, Gibb insisted, the Muslim mind would have to fundamentally reshape itself by embracing the rationalism which the West had embraced much earlier and on which the power of its science, philosophy and technology rested. I will discuss criticisms of Gibb's understanding of Islam in Chapter 5; in the meantime his reliance on such concepts as "the Muslim mind" and his treatment of Islam as a unitary entity governed by its purported core characteristics should be kept in mind.

In 1955, at the age of sixty, Hamilton Gibb left Oxford to take up a position at Harvard University. Gibb had grown frustrated with Oxford, where his efforts to develop Islamic studies in the direction he favored had been stymied. Harvard seemed to offer the opportunity for a fresh start and access to much greater resources, not merely as a Harvard professor but also as director of a newly established center devoted to the study of the Middle East. Gibb's decision to leave Oxford for Harvard was of course his own, but his move across the Atlantic can nonetheless be taken as emblematic of several major developments in the field.

For one, it signaled the growing weight of US-based scholars and academic institutions focusing on the Middle East relative to those based in Europe. It also coincided with the emergence and rapid growth of "area studies" in American (and to a much lesser extent European) academia, including the rise of the new field of "Middle East studies." This new field, supported by government and private funding on an unprecedentedly lavish scale, created a set of new institutions within and outside of the university in whose framework traditionally trained Orientalists could interact with scholars in other humanities and social science disciplines. These developments were accompanied, and intellectually underpinned, by the elaboration of a new theoretical framework that sought to explain the character and historical trajectory of Middle Eastern societies. This framework reformulated some of the key assumptions of Orientalism in contemporary social-science language and provided an influential research agenda for scholars of the Middle East across a range of disciplines.

To understand what these institutional and intellectual shifts meant for the study of the Middle East and of Islam, and the critiques they eventually engendered, we must first locate them in their larger historical contexts, especially the rise of the United States to global pre-eminence, the decline of the colonial empires and the acceleration of decolonization around the world, and rapid social change accompanied by political instability in the Middle East itself. A brief review of these historical developments may seem like a digression; but as we will see, they profoundly influenced the form and content of the academic study of the

Middle East in the United States during the 1950s and 1960s. For just as the evolution of nineteenth-century academic Orientalism was linked with the extension of European power into Muslim lands, so too was the development of Middle East studies as an academic field closely connected with the emergence of the United States as a global superpower and its deepening involvement in the Middle East.

The United States becomes a global superpower

By the time the Second World War came to an end in 1945, the United States had emerged as the world's leading military, economic and political power. Wartime hopes that the coalition which had defeated Germany and Japan could hold together and reach agreement on the contours of the postwar world soon collapsed, and by 1948 what would be called the Cold War was under way. This conflict pitted the United States and its allies and clients (often referred to as "the West" or "the Free World," though it included quite a few brutal and corrupt but pro-American dictators) against the Soviet Union and its allies and clients ("the Soviet bloc," "the communist bloc," or "the East").

The protracted struggle for global hegemony between these two blocs was central to international, regional and (in many countries) even national politics down to the collapse of the communist regimes in Eastern Europe, and then of the Soviet Union itself, in the late 1980s and early 1990s. It was termed a "cold" war because the two main protagonists never actually went to war against each other, a good thing given that within a few years both were armed to the teeth with nuclear bombs and other weapons of mass destruction whose use might well have led to the extermination of most life on the planet. But the Cold War did involve a sometimes tense military stand-off in Europe, and it engendered or aggravated many very bloody "hot" wars in other parts of the world. It also enabled regimes on both sides to justify repression and even violence against their own citizens on grounds of national security, and on the same pretext led to the diversion for military use of vast resources that might otherwise have been used to improve people's lives.

Europe, which was soon divided between a US-led bloc of Western European states and a Soviet-dominated bloc of Eastern European states, was one key arena of the Cold War. As the Soviet Union gradually installed communist regimes in the countries of Eastern Europe, the United States sought to "contain" the further spread of communism by whatever means necessary. In 1947, with an exhausted Britain no longer able to prop up a pro-Western right-wing monarchist regime in Greece challenged by a communist-led insurgency, President Truman announced that the United States would step in and provide military and economic aid to the Greek government; aid would also be provided to Turkey, a staunch US ally. In so doing the Truman administration claimed that a communist victory in Greece might threaten Western dominance in the nearby Middle East.

The Truman Doctrine, as this policy came to be called, quickly expanded into an open-ended and global American commitment to come to the aid of any state deemed to be under threat from what was termed "Soviet expansionism," which in Washington's eyes came to encompass any real or imagined left-wing or radical nationalist threat to Western economic or political interests or to regimes friendly to the West, however unpopular, tyrannical or reactionary they might be. The United States went on to pour billions of dollars into Western Europe to rebuild its allies' shattered economies (the Marshall Plan), constituted West Germany as a separate (and rearmed) state, and in 1949 established the North Atlantic Treaty Organization (NATO), a military alliance linking many Western European countries with the United States. The US also assumed a leading role in combating efforts to challenge pro-Western regimes in Europe, for example by secretly funneling money to sympathetic parties and trade unions in Italy and France in order to undermine those countries' popular communist parties.

Over time, however, it was not Europe but Asia, Africa and Latin America which became the main battlegrounds of the Cold War. In large part this was due to the fact that the first half of the Cold War witnessed the dismantling of the colonial empires in Asia and Africa which the European powers had begun to carve out for themselves four centuries earlier, a process known as decolonization. The Second World War had left Britain, France and the Netherlands economically weakened and less able to suppress nationalist challenges to colonial rule in places that just a few years earlier they had expected to rule for many decades to come. In 1947 Britain was compelled to grant independence to India (which was partitioned into India and Pakistan) and to announce its intention to withdraw from Palestine; two years later the Dutch had to accept Indonesia's independence, and by 1954 France had to admit defeat in its war to retain control of Vietnam and the rest of Indochina and found itself fighting to hold on to Algeria. For its part, in 1946 the United States granted independence to the Philippines, which it had seized from Spain in 1898. The pace of decolonization accelerated in the later 1950s and 1960s as virtually all of the British, French, Dutch and Belgian colonies in Asia, Africa and the Americas became independent nation-states, sometimes peaceably and sometimes after much violence. Portugal resisted decolonization a bit longer, but by the mid-1970s its remaining possessions in Africa had won independence as well, leaving only a few scattered remnants of the once vast European colonial empires. As I will discuss shortly, many of the Arab states also achieved, or were struggling for, full political independence in this same period.

The host of newly independent nation-states in Asia and Africa had to confront the economic, political and cultural legacies of colonialism, including widespread poverty and underdevelopment, even as they struggled to achieve unity and forge viable new national identities. Moreover, the postwar period witnessed rapid social and economic change across Asia and Africa as well as in Latin America, as older ways of life were disrupted or transformed by a variety of global and local economic, social and cultural forces. In both newly independent and long-established states new social movements and political parties, many of which demanded a fuller measure of political and economic independence and far-reaching social transformation, emerged to challenge ruling elites, making for a great deal of political instability.

In this context of rapid change and widespread instability, US government officials became convinced that the United States had to use its influence to shape the postwar world, particularly what were seen as weak and vulnerable new nation-states in Asia and Africa but also Latin American states which had a long history of formal independence. In the 1950s and especially the 1960s, many scholars and activists would come to refer to these relatively poor and largely agricultural states as constituting a "Third World," as opposed to the capitalist "First World" of Western Europe and the United States and the communist "Second World." In the Third World as elsewhere, the avowed goals of US policy were to preserve political order and stability, protect and extend the capitalist system (which the United States promoted as the only route to economic development), and prevent the spread of communism, which the US depicted as an international criminal conspiracy run by Moscow.

The United States therefore began to assert its political, economic and military power around the globe, whether to ensure its strategic superiority, to reduce or eliminate Soviet influence, to fend off radical challenges to friendly regimes, to get rid of governments viewed as inimical to US interests, or to protect investments and access to resources and markets. Whereas the Soviet Union (and later communist-ruled China), anxious to undermine Western influence and in keeping with communist ideology, tended to support movements and regimes fighting against colonialism and seeking radical social transformation, the United States came in many cases to assume the mantle discarded by Britain and France as the dominant outside power, the chief guarantor of an (often unjust and oppressive) political and socioeconomic status quo. Ultimately, when it came down to it, the United States usually opted for order, stability and the protection of friendly local oligarchies, even if that meant blocking much-needed social, economic and political reform.

I will discuss the post-1945 role of the United States in the Middle East shortly, but to provide some context it may be worthwhile recalling two instances of US intervention in other regions of the Third World. In 1954 the Central Intelligence Agency, set up in 1947 to pursue the Cold War by covert means and (as I will explain below) fresh from successful coup-making in Iran, engineered a military coup in Guatemala which overthrew that country's elected (and noncommunist) government because it had dared to nationalize property belonging to the US-owned United Fruit Company, in order to effect a modest land reform which might benefit the country's impoverished peasants. For the next four decades brutal military-dominated regimes, armed with US support and weapons, protected US economic interests in Guatemala and the wealth and power of the local elite by viciously crushing every effort to achieve some measure of social and political reform.

In another case the United States took up where the former European colonial power had left off. After the French were defeated and withdrew from Vietnam in 1954, the United States put an unpopular regime in place in the southern half of the country and tried to crush an insurgency backed by the communist government which had come to rule the northern half. Ultimately, convinced that the spread of communism must be stopped in Vietnam or all of Asia might be lost (the "domino theory"), the United States dispatched half a million soldiers to Vietnam and dropped more bombs on the country than had been dropped in the entire Second World War. In the long run, however, tenacious Vietnamese resistance, high US casualties and the war's growing unpopularity in the United States forced a change in policy. In the early 1970s the United States gradually withdrew its forces and its allies in the south were defeated, leading to the unification of Vietnam under communist rule in 1975. Some two million Vietnamese – the proportional equivalent of 27 million Americans – and other peoples of Indochina were killed in the long conflict, most of them civilians, along with 58,000 American soldiers.

The United States in the Middle East

As elsewhere in Asia and Africa, the Cold War era witnessed heightened US interest and involvement in the Middle East and North Africa. Until the Second World War, the American political and economic presence in the region had been relatively modest. There were a number of US educational institutions – for example, the Syrian Protestant College in Beirut,

founded by American Protestant missionaries in the mid-nineteenth century and later renamed the American University of Beirut, and Robert
College in Istanbul, later renamed Bosphorus University – which exerted
a significant cultural influence. After the First World War American oil
companies (with the backing of the US government) sought to buy or
muscle their way into the region's burgeoning oil industry. Naturally,
British and French oil companies dominated production in those Middle Eastern countries under British or French control, as well as in Iran
where British interests were predominant, so US oil companies usually
remained junior partners.

In the early 1930s some US oil men turned their attention to Saudi
Arabia, then a poor country whose king was desperate for additional rev-
enue. Happily for him and for the consortium of US companies which
would later form the Arabian-American Oil Company (ARAMCO),
Saudi Arabia turned out to have the biggest oil reserves in the region
and US companies played the leading role in developing that country's
oil industry, reaping vast profits in the process. Nonetheless, before the
Second World War the Middle East and North Africa were of relatively
minor importance to those who made US foreign policy. They generally perceived America's vital political and economic interests as lying
elsewhere, in western Europe, in Central and South America, in the
Philippines and in the Pacific region and Asia. As a result they were
largely content to let Britain and France run the show in the Arab lands
and Iran.

After the Second World War that was no longer possible. In the Middle East as elsewhere, decolonization and newly independent countries'
growing insistence on reducing the political and economic influence of
their former colonial masters and achieving more rapid economic development were high on the historical agenda. Egypt had won limited independence in 1922 and a fuller measure in 1936, but after the Second
World War many Egyptians wanted the British military bases that still
remained on Egyptian soil to be removed and increasingly resented European political and economic power. The British and Soviet forces which
had occupied Iran during the Second World War to secure it for the Allies
withdrew after the war ended, but there was widespread resentment over
the fact that it was a British-owned oil company which garnered most of
the profits from Iran's oil. Iraq achieved formal independence in 1932,
but after the war there was growing discontent about the British-backed
monarchy's failure to use the country's oil wealth to benefit its people.
The French withdrew from Syria and Lebanon in 1945; Libya gained
independence in 1951, and Tunisia and Morocco five years later. By
the later 1950s the only large Arab country still under colonial rule was

Algeria, which the French insisted was part of France and could never be given up. It took years of bloody fighting before France came to terms with reality and, in 1962, accepted Algeria's independence. And once independence was won, governments in the Middle East faced the very difficult tasks of uniting new nation-states and meeting growing popular demands for more rapid economic development and social policies that would benefit the great majority of their citizenry who were poor peasants or urban working people.

Across the Middle East, new social and political forces emerged after 1945 to challenge the old elites and demand reform. Among them were pro-Soviet communist parties, but much more important and popular were radical nationalist movements and independent groups of young army officers determined to free their countries from lingering foreign control and chart a new course toward development and greater social justice. In some cases, as in Egypt where in 1952 a corrupt monarchy was overthrown by a group of reformist army officers led by Colonel Jamal 'Abd al-Nasir (in the West his name was usually rendered Gamal Abdul Nasser), the challengers succeeded in attaining power and setting their countries on a new course. In other places old ruling elites were severely challenged by opposition forces but (with Western support) managed to hold on, for example in Jordan, Saudi Arabia and the small Arab principalities along the Persian Gulf. But everywhere in the region, the 1950s and 1960s were a period of great social ferment and change, which inevitably meant considerable political instability.

With Britain and France no longer in a position to maintain control of the Middle East, the United States deemed it necessary to step in and assume the mantle of the former colonial powers as the guarantor of stability. For one, the Middle East contained a very substantial proportion of the world's oil reserves, and while the United States did not itself depend heavily on this oil, its allies in Western Europe and Japan did. A 1945 State Department analysis had described oil-rich Saudi Arabia as "a stupendous source of strategic power, and one of the greatest material prizes in world history."[15] As President Eisenhower put it in 1956, "The oil of the Arab world has grown increasingly important to all of Europe. The economy of Europe would collapse if those oil supplies were cut off. If the economy of Europe would collapse, the United States would be in a situation of which the difficulty could scarcely be exaggerated."[16] The United States was thus determined to keep as much of the region as possible – and above all the oil-rich Arab states and Iran – under the control of friendly governments; this would keep cheap oil flowing on terms advantageous to both the United States and its allies while giving the former considerable leverage over the latter.

The Palestine issue, and then the Arab–Israeli conflict, also contributed to growing US involvement in the region. After 1945 Britain proved unable to maintain control in Palestine or find a political solution which would reconcile the demands of the country's Arab majority with those of its Jewish minority, led by the Zionist movement. The Arabs sought the independence of Palestine as an Arab state, while the Zionists fought for unrestricted Jewish immigration and land purchases and the creation of a Jewish state in as much of Palestine as possible. The Truman administration pressed Britain to accept some Zionist demands, and when an exhausted Britain turned the Palestine issue over to the new United Nations the US (along with the Soviet Union) endorsed the UN plan to divide Palestine into separate Arab and Jewish states. In 1948 a Jewish state, Israel, was established in most of Palestine, amidst warfare between Palestinians and Jews and then between Israel and the neighboring Arab states. After that war ended, the Arab states refused to discuss peace with Israel unless Israel agreed to allow the hundreds of thousands of Palestinian Arab refugees who had fled or been expelled from their homes during the fighting to return; this Israel refused to do. The Arab–Israeli conflict remained a major source of tension in the Middle East, compelling the United States to try to reconcile its support for Israel with its close ties to Arab states which, while friendly to the US, regarded Israel as a colonial-settler enclave illegitimately established on Arab land by violent means.

In this same period, the late 1940s and early 1950s, the United States increasingly came to see the Middle East through the lens of the Cold War. Presidents Truman and Eisenhower, and their successors, knew that there was little prospect of the Soviet army invading the region and seizing its oil fields. They also understood that growing unrest and instability in the Middle East were caused not by communist agitation on Moscow's orders but by widespread poverty and social inequality and by resentment over continued Western political and economic domination. Many US officials even felt that moderate social and political reform was necessary if communist-led revolutions were to be prevented. "We should seek to use the social and economic tools available to us," recommended a 1952 National Security Council analysis of US goals in the Middle East, "in ways that will reduce the explosive power of forces pressing for revolutionary change to the point where necessary changes can be accomplished without uncontrollable instability. This may often mean that we should work with and through the present ruling groups and, while bolstering their hold on power, use our influence to induce them to accommodate themselves as necessary to the forces that are emerging."[17]

Despite talk of pressing friendly regimes to accommodate political and social change, however, US policymakers gave priority to maintaining the paramount position of the US in the region, keeping the Soviet Union out and protecting local clients, however tyrannical or opposed to social and political reform. To achieve these goals the United States used a variety of means. For a number of years it maintained military bases in several Arab countries; it kept powerful naval forces permanently stationed nearby (the Sixth Fleet in the Mediterranean and what is now designated as the Fifth Fleet in the Persian Gulf, the Red Sea and the adjacent Indian Ocean); it funded, armed and trained the military and internal security forces of friendly governments; it sought to draw Middle Eastern countries into anti-Soviet military alliances; and it intervened in the internal affairs of Middle Eastern countries by covert means (starting in the late 1940s with support for *coups d'état* which installed pro-US military dictators in Syria) and on several occasions with military force.[18] The United States also began to provide economic aid to Middle Eastern countries on an increasingly large scale, first under the rubric of President Truman's "Point Four" program and then through a variety of other programs.

Although the United States and its allies enjoyed a dominant military, economic and political position in the Middle East and North Africa at the beginning of the 1950s, US officials grew increasingly unhappy that even strongly anticommunist nationalists in the Middle East were opposed to letting their countries be dragged into the Cold War and instead wanted to chart their own independent course, maintaining friendly ties with (and accepting aid from) both the West and the Soviet bloc. Such a stance, Washington argued, played into the hands of the Soviets, and so US officials demanded that Middle Eastern governments toe the US line in the Cold War. As a result, by the mid-1950s US officials increasingly regarded as anti-Western and pro-Soviet any Middle Eastern government or movement which rejected US hegemony in the region, insisted on non-alignment or seemed to threaten the stability or legitimacy of America's allies in the Middle East – the monarchies of the oil-rich Arab states and Iran as well as other conservative governments. Such governments and movements were to be isolated and, if possible, gotten rid of.

So it was that, after an initial honeymoon with Washington when he first came to power, President Nasser of Egypt came to be the major bogeyman of US Middle Eastern policy. US–Egyptian relations cooled when Nasser rejected US demands that Egypt join a Middle Eastern counterpart of NATO, encouraged other Arab states to do the same, and began to promote Arab unity, which undermined the legitimacy of some of the Arab governments friendly to the US and Britain. In 1955

Nasser dealt a major blow to Western power in the region (and made the Eisenhower administration even angrier) by buying weapons for his army from the Soviet bloc, which broke the Western monopoly on arms sales to the region.

The US saw this as a great victory for the Soviets, though Egypt argued it was simply exercising its right as a sovereign state to buy weapons wherever it saw fit. The US sought to punish Egypt for its defiance by withdrawing the funding it had promised for the construction of a huge new dam on the Nile at Aswan, the centerpiece of Nasser's development program. But instead of knuckling under to what he and most fellow Arabs perceived as American bullying, Nasser responded with a unanticipated master-stroke: in July 1956 Egypt nationalized the British-owned company which owned and operated the Suez Canal, promising to use the waterway's revenues to replace the funding the US had withdrawn. In an effort to reverse the nationalization of the canal and overthrow Nasser, Britain, France (which hated Nasser for aiding the Algerian revolt against French colonial rule) and Israel (which had escalating border conflicts with Egypt) colluded in a military attack on Egypt in October 1956. But this scheme, reminiscent of the old days when colonial powers could use their superior military might to enforce their will, failed owing to US and Soviet opposition. Nasser was thus able to snatch political victory from the jaws of military defeat, and that victory transformed him into the pre-eminent Arab leader of his day, the man who had stood up to the West (and Israel) and emerged triumphant.

Despite its refusal to endorse the British-French-Israeli attack on Egypt in 1956, the US government remained concerned about Nasser. In the later 1950s he became one of the pre-eminent leaders of an emerging bloc of Asian and African states, many of them newly independent, which refused to take sides in the Cold War and instead sought to remain non-aligned, pursuing their own interests as they themselves defined them. With regard to the Middle East he was regarded in Washington as a major threat to America's friends and allies in the region and beyond. Among those friends and allies were the conservative monarchies in Saudi Arabia and Jordan, but also Lebanon, which by the mid-1950s was seen as a beleaguered pro-Western (and heavily Christian) island in an increasingly turbulent and radicalized Arab (and largely Muslim) sea. The CIA funneled cash to the conservative president of Lebanon, which he used to get his allies elected to parliament, ensure a pro-US (and anti-Nasser) majority and try to change the constitution so that he could secure an unprecedented (and hitherto unconstitutional) second term in office. This led to the outbreak of a civil war in Lebanon in 1958 and then, when the pro-Western monarchy in Iraq was overthrown by nationalist army officers, the dispatch of US troops to Lebanon.

US military intervention in Lebanon was justified in terms of the Eisenhower Doctrine, announced in 1957, by which the United States authorized itself to intervene "to secure and protect the territorial integrity and political independence of such nations, requesting such aid, against overt armed aggression from any nation controlled by International Communism." Eisenhower and his advisors knew very well that the pro-American president of Lebanon was not the innocent victim of "overt armed aggression" instigated by "International Communism." Rather, he was being challenged by fellow Lebanese who wanted political reform, backed by other Arabs who wanted Lebanon to align itself with what they saw as Arab interests and not the Cold War interests of the United States. And Washington realized that the Iraqi monarchy had fallen because it was increasingly perceived by many Iraqis as corrupt, reactionary and overly subservient to foreign powers, perhaps especially Britain, Iraq's former colonial master. Nonetheless, the United States had come to define almost any threat to the political and economic status quo in the region as a threat to its interests, putting stability and control ahead of all other considerations.

Iran provides an even more dramatic case in point. In the early 1950s that country was the world's fourth largest petroleum exporter and supplied western Europe with much of its oil, but the great bulk of the profits from Iran's oil went to the Anglo-Iranian Oil Company, a majority of whose shares were owned by the British government. In 1951 Iran's parliament voted to nationalize the AIOC in order to secure more of the country's oil wealth for its people. Although the nationalization was perfectly in accordance with international law, Britain was outraged and sought to overturn it, and the United States supported Britain by participating in a Western boycott of Iran's oil designed to force that country's government to capitulate. When that failed, and even though the Iranian government at the time was democratically elected and dominated by rather conservative nationalists, the CIA helped organize a military coup in Iran which in 1953 overthrew the government and installed the shah (Iran's king) as absolute ruler.

Soon thereafter the shah gave a consortium of European and US oil companies access to Iran's oil on advantageous terms. Over the following decade the United States gave Iran more than a billion dollars in military and economic aid, enabling the shah to crush all opposition and bolster his power. Few Americans knew of or remembered this episode in Iranian history. But the fact that the United States had helped to overthrow their elected government and impose the brutal dictatorship of the shah in order to keep cheap oil flowing abroad left an indelible imprint on several generations of Iranians and would come back to haunt the United States when that same shah was finally overthrown by his people in 1979.[19]

The rise of area studies

After the Second World War, then, US officials as well as academics involved with foreign policy issues came to regard the Middle East and North Africa as a region of great strategic importance and a key arena of the Cold War. But the deepening involvement of the United States in the region only heightened their concern that so few Americans knew much about the Middle East and its history, cultures, peoples and languages. This, they felt, put the United States at a grave disadvantage in the struggle with the Soviet Union and its allies for power and influence in the region. In this respect the Middle East was not at all unique: from the Second World War onward, propelled by the war itself, the subsequent emergence of the United States as a global superpower, decolonization and, of course, the exigencies of the Cold War, government and foundation officials in the United States argued forcefully that the United States needed to develop a much larger pool of expertise on the rest of the world, and especially those parts of the former colonial world where the US was becoming deeply involved but about which very few Americans had much knowledge.

Before that war, only a handful of US universities offered degree programs that focused, in some comprehensive and coherent fashion, on a defined area of the modern world, and teaching and research on the history, politics, economics and cultures of Asia, Africa and Latin America in the modern and contemporary periods were very underdeveloped. Nor did many colleges and universities offer instruction in the written or spoken languages used by hundreds of millions of people living in places the US government was now coming to define as of crucial strategic importance. For example, as we have seen, few Orientalists had much interest in contemporary developments in the Middle East, while Arabic, Persian, Turkish and other languages of the region were taught in only a few institutions in the United States, often with antiquated methods, as if they were dead languages useful only for gaining access to the kinds of texts philologically oriented scholars typically focused on.

"The Near East is almost completely neglected," one observer noted in 1947, "and there are few scholars in the country who know anything about the area except in the field of languages."[20] As a result, when the United States government sought to beef up its expertise on the Arab world and fill positions in the foreign and intelligence services during and immediately after the Second World War, it drew heavily on the small number of young men who had grown up in the region, often as children of Protestant missionaries or of faculty at institutions like the American University of Beirut. These men, joined by others who encountered the Middle East and North Africa for the first time during the war, would constitute key components of the State Department's cadre of "Arabists" – experts on the Arab world who filled key diplomatic and policymaking posts – into the 1970s, when they were largely shunted aside by Henry Kissinger and the new foreign policy team he put in place.

The Second World War brought about a dramatic expansion of international studies in the United States. As one historian of the field put it, "With the possible exception of those physicists engaged in the Manhattan Project [to develop the atomic bomb], no academics were so dramatically affected by the national mobilization following Pearl Harbor as were those in international studies."

Those in Japanese studies, whether specialists in Japanese poetry or the history of the Tokugawa period, suddenly became experts on "the Enemy." Similarly, those in Russian or Chinese studies became experts on important if problematic allies. Those familiar with North Africa, the eastern Mediterranean, Southeast Asia, or the Pacific islands became valued sources of information about prospective theaters of military action. Even those specializing in the Middle East and Latin America, areas removed from the combat zone, were assumed to possess language skills and insight into alien cultures sufficiently above those of most other Americans to put their services in demand among those responsible for staffing the war effort.[21]

During the war, universities hurriedly created intensive language training programs and crash courses designed to acquaint military personnel with the countries they might soon be fighting in and the peoples they might be administering. A great many US and British scholars with some knowledge of "exotic" countries and their languages entered government or military service, often in intelligence or in a research department of the foreign service or the military. There they met, and worked together with, other scholars who might have been trained in different disciplines (history, anthropology, political science, economics, and so on) but shared their interest in a particular region of the world, about which they sought to gather and process information and offer analyses that would serve the war effort. In this sense, while what quickly came to be called "area studies" certainly had some older roots, it is nonetheless plausible to regard the Second World War as the midwife of this approach to producing policy-relevant knowledge. As one prominent US government official would later put it, "the first great center of area studies . . . [was] in the Office of Strategic Services" – the wartime forerunner of the Central Intelligence Agency.[22]

But if the Second World War was the midwife of area studies, it was the Cold War and decolonization which enabled area studies to get off the ground and flourish in the United States. As the United States began to act like a global superpower, with political, economic and military interests and commitments around the globe, and the Cold War got under way, government officials and academic leaders became ever more concerned about the shortage of people who were trained in foreign languages and had some expertise on parts of the world which were now regarded as key fronts in the Cold War and crucial arenas of instability. The author of a 1947 report on area studies commissioned by the Social Science Research Council, a nongovernmental body founded in 1924 to advance the social sciences, put it this way: "National welfare in the postwar period more than ever before requires a citizenry well informed as to other peoples, and the creation of a vast body of knowledge about them . . . [A]rea studies are essential if our universities are to meet their obligations to the nation. Two ghastly wars within a generation have proved beyond reasonable doubt that we must know more of the other nations of the earth."[23]

Area studies portrayed itself as a new and better way of conducting academic research and teaching. Instead of scholars being confined and separated by the narrow boundaries of their disciplines, each with its own limited perspective, advocates of area studies argued that all those interested in a particular region of the world, whatever their disciplinary training, should work together to produce useful – that is, policy-relevant – knowledge. "Teamwork is absolutely necessary in area study, as in medicine," the author of a 1948 Social Science Research Council report explained. "No single person, or even science or discipline, is capable of dealing with the complexities of the culture and environment of an area. The geographic limits of an area induce the specialists to pool their knowledge and prevent them from ignoring the relevance of factors which are outside the domains habitually considered by any one of them."[24] Moreover, whereas traditional fields like Orientalism had tended to regard the civilizations they studied as static and incapable of change, the grounding of area studies in the social sciences was supposed to shift the focus of research to the dynamics of political, social and cultural change in the contemporary world and give rise to interdisciplinary and multidimensional expertise that would be of use to policymakers.

From the late 1940s and through the 1960s, the Social Science Research Council played a key role in developing and promoting area studies, including Middle East studies. As early as 1946 the SSRC established a Committee on World Area Research whose mission was (as one key figure in the early development of Middle East studies would later put it) to "identify foreign regions of growing American national concern, to evaluate the state of the art in American universities and to administer a program of area fellowships and travel grants . . . "[25] This committee commissioned reports and sponsored conferences intended to spread the gospel of area studies among social scientists and overcome lingering opposition to this still vague new conception of how to organize the production of knowledge and allocate academic resources. In 1951 the SSRC created a Near and Middle East Committee to promote the development of social science research and training on the Middle East, just as it created committees to promote the study of other world regions. Four years later the committee was reorganized (in collaboration with the American Council of Learned Societies, which had earlier established its own – apparently not very effective – committee on the Middle East) to encompass the humanities disciplines as well. With funding from the Ford Foundation, the resulting SSRC–ACLS Joint Committee on the Near and Middle East sought to develop an agenda for the field and strengthen it by funding what it saw as promising research projects and conferences. Among the committee's members was Hamilton Gibb, just arrived from Oxford to assume the directorship of Harvard's new Center for Middle Eastern Studies.

Meanwhile, leading American universities, anxious to preserve and expand the programs they had launched during the war, scrambled in the early postwar years to develop area studies, creating a number of new area studies centers and offering new master's degree programs in (for example) Latin American studies and Southeast Asian studies, as well as new doctoral-level programs that sought to combine training in a particular discipline with a focus on a specific region and mastery of one or more of its languages. But to establish and maintain such programs cost a great deal of money, money even the wealthiest private universities found it difficult to come up with. Since the federal government was at the time not involved in funding education or supporting university-based research in the humanities and social sciences, private donors and foundations stepped into the breach, building on links they had already begun to establish as far back as the 1920s.

The Rockefeller Foundation, whose original endowment came from the Rockefeller family's vast holdings in the petroleum industry, had begun to get involved in funding international studies even before the war, albeit on a relatively modest scale. During the war it began to make more substantial grants to a number of universities to support programs in Far Eastern and Russian studies, and by 1951 it had given US universities a total of $6 million for the development of international studies. The Carnegie Foundation (established by steel magnate Andrew Carnegie) also got into the act, funding centers for research on Japan (at the University of Michigan) and on Russia (at Harvard). Carnegie, and later other foundations, also gave money to the Social Science Research Council to fund graduate student fellowships in area studies.

But area studies really took off when the enormously wealthy Ford Foundation got involved. In the early 1950s the Ford Foundation redefined its mission to embrace the promotion of peace and progress in the newly independent countries of Asia and Africa through economic development, which it hoped would help stop the spread of communism – a sort of privately funded Marshall Plan for the world outside Europe. Ford began spending millions of dollars on overseas development projects, mainly in South Asia and the Middle East, but it also began to fund area studies programs at US universities and fellowships for foreign study and research. Within a few years, under public and congressional pressure to give away more of its huge endowment, the foundation was making multimillion dollar grants to major universities for international studies and funding fellowships for research overseas. By 1962 the Ford Foundation's International Training and Research program had appropriated more than $100 million and by 1968 the total had exceeded $250 million. Not all of this money went to universities in the United States, but the substantial part that did made relatively vast new resources available for the academic study of Asia, Africa and Latin America.[26]

In the late 1950s the federal government also began to fund area studies. Many conservatives, including powerful members of Congress representing southern states, had long opposed federal funding for education, in part because they feared that a larger federal role would undermine racial segregation in public schools, and they had made effective common cause with diehard isolationists who rejected the globally engaged foreign policies of Presidents Roosevelt, Truman and Eisenhower. But in 1957 the Soviet Union launched Sputnik, the first artificial satellite, setting off a panic among Americans who feared that the US was falling behind the communist enemy in science and technology. These fears engendered widespread concern about the purportedly poor state of education in America and helped build public support for federal spending on education.

In 1958 Congress passed the National Defense Education Act, which for the first time provided large-scale government funding for colleges and universities. To foster the study of foreign languages deemed critical to the national security of the United States – including Arabic, Turkish and Persian – and of regions of the world deemed to be of strategic importance, Title VI of this law appropriated funding for university-based area-studies centers (designated "national resource centers") and for graduate student fellowships. By 1965 Title VI funding had reached

$13 million a year, of which centers for Middle East studies received their share. Later, an amendment to a foreign aid bill (Public Law 480) allowed the use of proceeds from the sale of US agricultural products to Middle Eastern countries for the purchase of books for US libraries, and eventually to help fund American research centers in the Middle East and the research fellowships they offered. Federal funding for area studies would continue to rise into the late 1960s, after which it began a gradual and uneven decline to lower levels. For example, in 1967 some 2,344 Title VI-funded National Defense Foreign Language (NDFL) fellowships were awarded by area studies programs to promising graduate students for language and area studies training; the total had dropped to 1,640 by 2003.

Universities rushed to secure foundation and later government funding, establish or expand centers for Middle East studies, and recruit faculty and students. By 1951 there were already five such centers, at Columbia, Dropsie College, the University of Michigan, Princeton and the School of Advanced International Studies of Johns Hopkins University. In 1955 Harvard would establish its own Center for Middle East Studies, and the University of California at Los Angeles joined the roster three years later. A number of other universities, including the University of Pennsylvania, the State University of New York at Binghamton, Indiana University at Bloomington, the University of Chicago, the University of Utah and the University of Washington (in Seattle) followed in their footsteps in the 1960s, when funding was still abundant and easy to secure.

As senior American-trained scholars who could launch and run these new centers were in short supply, a number of them were initially led by senior scholars imported from the Middle East or Europe. For example, in 1944 the Lebanese historian Philip Hitti became chair of what was then called Princeton's Department of Oriental Languages and Literatures; three years later he created a Program in Near Eastern Studies at Princeton, the country's first, which served as a model for similar centers at other universities. As mentioned earlier, H. A. R. Gibb came to Harvard to head its new Center for Middle Eastern Studies, and soon thereafter the Viennese Orientalist Gustave von Grunebaum (1909–72) would arrive in the United States to run UCLA's new Center for Near Eastern Studies. Eventually they would be succeeded by scholars educated in the United States.

In short, from the 1950s onward concern in elite circles about the dearth of expertise necessary to maintain US global power and the resulting flood of new funding got Middle East studies up and running in the United States. The field took institutional form through a new network of university-based programs and centers, funded by foundations and later by the federal government, charged with fostering language training, interdisciplinary research and teaching on the Middle East, and public education through community outreach and teacher-training programs. In addition to NDFL fellowships for language and area studies training in the United States, students could also take advantage of other new government fellowship programs that funded study and research in the Middle East itself, including Fulbright and Fulbright–Hays (named after the senator and congressman who sponsored the legislation creating them), as well as fellowships funded by the Ford Foundation and from the early 1960s administered by the SSRC–ACLS Joint Committee on the Near and Middle East. A great deal of new money also became available from a variety of sources, including the Joint Committee, for postdoctoral research in the region.

By the late 1960s this massive injection of funding had led to a dramatic increase in the number of Ph.D.s awarded in Middle East studies broadly defined, some of them by relatively traditional Near Eastern studies departments which still usually focused on language, literature and Islamic studies but others by disciplinary departments like history, political science and anthropology. As a rough gauge of the expansion of the field in the United States, one scholar calculated the number of doctorates awarded annually for dissertations on Middle East-related topics by a sample of sixteen universities at the forefront of area studies. The number rose from thirteen a year in 1940 (most of them probably in philology or religion) to twenty-four in 1951, forty in 1966 and a high of eighty-six in 1979.[27]

Until the mid-1960s, however, Middle East studies in the United States and Canada still lacked a scholarly association of its own. In this respect it lagged well behind most other area studies fields: the Far Eastern Association (later renamed the Association for Asian Studies) had been founded in 1943, and associations for Slavic and African studies had been established by the late 1950s. As I mentioned in Chapter 3, the American Oriental Society had been in existence since the 1840s, but it was small, traditionally Orientalist, and played only a minor role in Middle East studies as it had developed after the war. In 1946 the Middle East Institute had been founded in Washington DC and began publishing the quarterly *Middle East Journal* a year later. However, funded largely by foundations and by corporations with business interests in the Middle East, it focused primarily on contemporary politics and international relations (particularly the growing role of the United States in the region) rather than academic scholarship, and it sought to reach (and influence) a wide audience that included policymakers, journalists, businessmen and the general public. An ineffectual American Association for Middle East Studies, established in the 1950s, had ceased to function by the following decade.

Under the chairmanship of Princeton sociologist Morroe Berger, the SSRC–ACLS Joint Committee on the Near and Middle East resolved to fill this gap. In 1966, with funding from the Ford Foundation, it laid the foundations of the Middle East Studies Association (MESA) as the organization which would embrace all those interested in the scholarly study of the Middle East, regardless of their disciplinary affiliations. With Berger as its first president, MESA held its inaugural annual meeting in 1967, attended by a few dozen people, and soon began publishing its own scholarly journal, the *International Journal of Middle East Studies*, as well as various newsletters and bulletins for members. MESA would expand quickly over the years that followed to become the largest and most influential organization in the field of Middle East studies in the United States, with a membership of about 2,500 by the early twenty-first century.

Middle East studies followed a somewhat similar trajectory in Britain, if more slowly and with much less lavish funding. As a colonial power Britain had long had a need for people with a command of local languages and some ability to function in exotic cultures and climes, for positions in the diplomatic and colonial services and in the military. While some of those who filled these posts were trained at traditional Oriental studies faculties or at more modern institutions like the School of Oriental and African Studies in London, many acquired what they needed to know of local languages, politics and cultures on the job – or not at all. In Britain as in the United States, many scholars with expertise on other parts of the world entered government service during the Second World War. Hamilton Gibb, for example, served as head of the Middle East section of the Royal Institute of International Affairs, which worked closely with the Foreign Office.

As in the United States, the British government came to feel during the war that a more vigorous and systematic approach to producing expertise on Asia and Africa was needed. In 1947 a government commission appointed to explore ways of strengthening Oriental, Slavic, East European and African studies in Britain recommended the expansion of teaching and research on these areas, though with a rather traditional emphasis on philology, religion and literature rather than on the social sciences. Fourteen years later another committee appointed to survey area studies in Britain visited the United States and returned to recommend that Britain emulate the American system by creating new institutions which would be run by historians and social scientists who could bypass the old-fashioned Oriental studies faculties. In the aftermath of this report the British government provided funding for centers for Middle East studies (and new teaching positions) at Oxford, the School of Oriental and African Studies, and Durham University.[28]

Orientalism and the Cold War

The postwar years thus witnessed the dramatic expansion of area studies in the United States, an expansion closely linked to Cold War policymakers' heightened need for reliable knowledge about critical regions of the world. This was the historical context in which Hamilton Gibb left the faculty of Oriental Studies at Oxford in 1955 and moved to Harvard University in Cambridge, Massachusetts. There he took up not only a distinguished professorship but also the post of director of Harvard's new Center for Middle Eastern Studies. As we have seen, Gibb also joined the new SSRC–ACLS Joint Committee on the Near and Middle East, which sought to promote and guide the development of Middle East studies in the United States. He wanted traditional Orientalism to overcome its intellectual isolation and introversion and reposition itself at the center of the emerging field of Middle East studies, dominated by social scientists many of whom had scant respect for what they regarded as Orientalism's old-fashioned concepts and methods and its irrelevance to urgent contemporary policy concerns. In arguing for the expansion of programs of Oriental studies in the United States and Britain a few years earlier, Gibb had explained that "the whole situation of the Western countries in regard to the countries of Asia and Africa has changed. We can no longer rely on that factor of prestige which seemed to play a large part in prewar thinking, neither can we any longer expect the peoples of Asia and Africa or of Eastern Europe to come to us and learn from us, while we sit back. We have to learn about them so that we can learn to work with them in a relationship that is closer to terms of mutuality."[29]

In a lecture delivered in 1963, Gibb elaborated on his vision of area studies and Orientalism's relationship with it. He acknowledged the limitations of classical Orientalism, with its focus on "the 'great culture,' the universal norms expressed or predicated in literature, religion and law, recognised as authoritative and paradigmatic by all its adherents, but rarely more than loosely approximated in their diverse local groups, at grips with the actualities of their existential situation . . . Rather suddenly the orientalist has come to realise that diversity is not just a modern phenomenon – on the contrary, it has always been there, a permanent feature of social life and organisation under the overarching unity of the 'great culture.'" The Orient, Gibb argued, was now much too important to be left to the Orientalists alone; it had become necessary to have Orientalists and social scientists work together to produce knowledge about the Middle East and Islam that was not only more comprehensive but also of more use to policymakers.

Yet, Gibb insisted, only the Orientalist really understood the essential characteristics of Islamic civilization, and possession of this special knowledge meant that Orientalists retained a unique and necessary role in Middle East studies. It was the Orientalist's function, he explained,

> to bring together and correlate the findings of the separate social studies . . . The orientalist's function is to furnish that [central] core out of his knowledge and understanding of the invisibles – the values, attitudes and mental processes characteristic of the "great culture" that underlie the application even today of the social and economic data – to explain the why, rather than the what and the how, and this precisely because he is or should be able to see the data not simply as isolated facts, explicable in and by themselves, but in the broad context and long perspective of cultural habit and tradition.[30]

In 1964 ill health ended Gibb's involvement in realizing this vision, and as we will see developments would soon take the field in a different direction. But his insistence that Orientalists' deep understanding of Islamic civilization rendered them uniquely capable of shedding light on Cold War foreign policy concerns persisted. This conviction can be clearly traced through much of the scholarly work of Bernard Lewis who, like Gibb, would leave Britain to take up a new position in the United States, at Princeton University, and who by the 1970s had stepped into Gibb's shoes as the doyen of Anglo-American Orientalism.

Lewis was born in 1916. Trained at the University of London, he began teaching Islamic history at its School of Oriental and African Studies in 1938. His early scholarly work focused mainly on medieval Arab history and he served for a period as editor of the *Encyclopedia of Islam*. He was also one of the first Western scholars to be permitted to do research in the vast Ottoman archives, on which he drew for his influential book *The Emergence of Modern Turkey*, published in 1961.

In 1953 Lewis, still a professor at the School of Oriental and African Studies, delivered a lecture on "Communism and Islam" at Chatham House, the headquarters of the Royal Institute of International Affairs, which was soon published as an article in the Institute's journal.[31] Lewis' analysis of the relation between communism and Islam was motivated by an urgent Cold War policy-related concern: to assess, "in the present competition between the Western democracies and Soviet Communism for the support of the Islamic world . . . what factors or qualities are there in Islamic tradition, or in the present state of Islamic society and opinion, which might prepare the intellectually and politically active groups to embrace Communist principles and methods of government, and the rest to accept them?" Lewis set himself the task of delineating "what qualities or tendencies exist in Islam, in Islamic civilization and society, which might either facilitate or impede the advance of Communism."

To do this, Lewis asserted, one had to distinguish between the "accidental" factors which might favor the success of communism, that is, factors which were part of the current historical situation, and the "essentials," those factors "which are innate or inherent in the very quality of Islamic institutions and ideas." Lewis' distinction between accidental and essential factors was clearly rooted in his conception of Islam as a civilization with a distinct, unique and basically unchanging essence. It was this framing of the problem which made it possible for Lewis to largely ignore local contexts and histories as well as the very different ways in which contemporary Muslims might perceive the world and act in it – the very things that a decade later Gibb would argue Orientalists had failed to take into account. Instead, Lewis deemed it possible to compare an allegedly monolithic communism to an equally monolithic Islam whose essential characteristics could be deduced from medieval texts and presumed to govern the minds of all Muslims everywhere and at all times.

After recounting the accidental factors which might lead Muslims to embrace communism – growing resentment of Western power and privilege and the abject poverty of the Muslim masses – Lewis turned to what he saw as the more important essential factors. Citing a fourteenth-century Muslim jurist, Lewis argued that the Islamic political tradition had always been, and remained, essentially autocratic: the sovereign was owed "complete and unwavering obedience as a religious duty imposed by Holy Law." "A community brought up on such doctrines," Lewis asserted, "will not be shocked by Communist disregard of political liberty or human rights; it may even be attracted by a régime which offers ruthless strength and efficiency in the service of a cause . . . " Moreover, Lewis argued, there were uncomfortable similarities between the communist party and the 'ulama (clergy) of Islam: "Both profess a totalitarian doctrine, with complete and final answers to all questions on heaven and earth"; both offer their followers a sense of belonging and of mission. Like communism, Islam was also collectivistic. Yet, Lewis concluded, most Muslims were deeply pious and would not tolerate communism's atheism. "The present revolt of the Muslims against the immorality and opportunism of their own and of some Western leaders may temporarily favour the Communists, with their appearance of selfless devotion to an ideal, but will work against Communism when Muslims come to see the realities behind the propaganda. Let us hope that they will not take too long over it."

An essay written by Lewis some years later and published in 1972, in a volume edited by P. J. Vatikiotis entitled *Revolution in the Middle East, and Other Case Studies,* provides yet another illustration both of the assumptions which framed his understanding of Islam and of the concern with contemporary political issues which informed much of his work.[32] "Islamic Concepts of Revolution" strongly manifested traditional Orientalism's grounding in philology: Lewis devoted most of the essay to discussing the meaning of a number of Arabic terms associated with revolution found in classical texts, and only at the end did he briefly turn to what such terms and various newer terms might actually mean to contemporary Muslims. From his reading of a number of medieval Arabic political and legal treatises, Lewis concluded that while Islam accepted in principle the duty of believers to resist impious government, "the Western doctrine of the right to resist bad government is alien to Islamic thought." The contrast he suggested was clear: Islam fosters subservience to authority, while the spirit of resistance to tyranny and misrule is inherent in the core values of Western civilization.

This was just the kind of overarching and monolithic "great culture" perspective that Gibb had ultimately seemed to come to question. By deducing from a limited selection of classical texts the key principles which are presumed to govern the minds of all Muslims everywhere, this approach rendered unnecessary careful investigation of the many different ways in which, over the centuries and in various places, Muslims actually understood authority, legitimacy and the right to rebel, and what they actually did when confronted with impious or tyrannical rule. No serious scholar would today try to deduce what all Christians everywhere must believe about legitimate authority and the right to rebel by looking only at the Gospels (for example, Romans 13, which enjoins Christians to obey the powers that be) and a few medieval texts. Rather, she or he would feel it necessary to investigate how, at different times and in different places, different Christians read different meanings into those texts and behaved in a wide variety of ways. Yet, as we will see, the approach Lewis used to delineate what he saw as timeless and uniform "Islamic concepts" of revolution and (more broadly) to demonstrate how the behavior even of contemporary Muslims could best be explained in terms of what were deemed to be Islam's essential characteristics remained influential and would continue to surface in his work and that of others into the twenty-first century.

Of course, not all of Lewis' contemporaries shared either his perspective on Islam or his political views: while there may well have been a powerful mainstream tradition in Anglo-American Orientalism, that "discipline" was never entirely monolithic. By way of example one might mention the work of Marshall Hodgson (1921–68), who taught Islamic history at the University of Chicago. Strongly influenced by the French Orientalist Louis Massignon, Hodgson's writings – particularly his posthumously published three-volume masterwork *The Venture of Islam* – are distinguished by a strong rejection of the Eurocentrism that he believed pervaded the writings of many scholars of Islam and by a determination to set Islamic history within the broader framework of world history. Though Hodgson was trained in the Orientalist tradition and continued to use "civilization" as a key category, he regarded what he termed "Islamicate" culture – one of several neologisms he coined – as more dynamic, flexible and open than had many Orientalist scholars. His work was also implicitly critical of the way most US social scientists had by the 1950s come to conceptualize and explain social change in the modern and contemporary Middle East – the issue to which I will now turn.[33]

Modernizing the world

Orientalists with an interest in current affairs and a desire to influence policymakers, like Gibb and Lewis, insisted that it was they who were best suited to interpret what was going on in the Middle East. But the social scientists who played the leading role in Middle East studies as it emerged in the United States during the 1950s and 1960s were in general not overly impressed with such claims. Instead, most of them embraced what they came to see as a new and intellectually powerful way of thinking about social, political and cultural change which, they believed, offered a better way of understanding what the Middle East (as well as most of Asia, Africa and Latin America) was undergoing and where it might be heading. This paradigm came to be known as "modernization theory," though it was not so much a coherent theory as a collection of approaches which differed in some key respects but were rooted in a common set of assumptions about the character and trajectory of historical change. From the early 1950s into the 1970s, modernization theory was the dominant paradigm in US area studies in general and Middle East studies in particular, informing a mass of research and writing on political change, economic development and social transformation, and interacting with Orientalism in complex ways. Its impact varied widely across the disciplines, exerting considerably less of an influence on, say, anthropologists than on political scientists; but overall it certainly functioned as the "big idea" underpinning a good chunk of US social science research about the world in this period.

Modernization theory's intellectual roots can be traced back to Max Weber, the great turn-of-the-century German sociologist. Weber had distinguished between "traditional" societies and "modern" societies. Traditional societies were, he asserted, largely rural and agricultural, and social change and economic growth were slow and gradual. In such societies, Weber argued, relationships among people were based largely on such things as kinship, religious affiliation and occupation, so that an individual's status and role in life were normally determined by the status and social role of the family into which he or she was born. Religion and other forms of supernatural belief were culturally dominant, while political power was hierarchical and authoritarian, exercised by monarchs or the nobility. By contrast, modern societies were largely urban and industrial; rapid social change and economic growth were the norm rather than the exception. The status of an individual in a modern society and the opportunities open to him or her were determined mainly by his or her own abilities and achievements, and people were primarily classified not in terms of their family or kinship group or tribe or religion but by more general criteria, such as nationality and citizenship. Modern societies were rational, scientifically oriented, democratic and relatively egalitarian.

After the Second World War, this sharp dichotomy between tradition and modernity, defined as polar opposites, was taken up and reworked by leading sociologists, political scientists and other social scientists in the United States who used it to make sense of the dynamics of social, political and cultural change in Asia, Africa and Latin America. These social scientists used the term "modernization" to denote the process of transition from a traditional society to a modern society. They saw this process as both universal and unilinear. It was universal because every society on earth had to undergo more or less the same, often painful, disruptive and destabilizing process of transition if it was to escape tradition and reach the promised land of modernity. Modernization was a unilinear process in the sense that each contemporary society could be located somewhere along the fixed trajectory of historical development that led from tradition to authentic modernity. By definition, the advanced industrial countries of North America and Western Europe, and a few others, were deemed to have already achieved modernity; straggling behind them at various points along the road to modernity were all the rest, all those societies (especially in the Third World) which were still in transition, still struggling to overcome the debilitating legacies of tradition and achieve modernity. There was only one possible path to becoming modern – that is, like the United States and Western Europe of the 1950s – and that was the destination of all societies, unless they took a wrong turn during the transition and got stuck or sidetracked.

Some social scientists operating within the modernization paradigm identified specific personality or cultural traits which they believed were characteristic of tradition or modernity. For example, David McClelland asserted that people in traditional societies lacked a strong orientation toward "achievement," which he saw as a key feature of the psyche of modern people and the product of modern modes of socialization in childhood. Sociologist Bert Hoselitz blamed underdevelopment and poverty in traditional societies on such outmoded and debilitating cultural traits as particularism, the distribution of power and rewards on the basis of status rather than achievement, and the diffuseness of social roles – the precise opposite of what he believed prevailed in modern societies, where people were rewarded for achievement and had well-defined social roles. Others, like the Israeli sociologist S. N. Eisenstadt, argued that modern societies could be distinguished from traditional societies by how they responded to change and the specific form change took.

However, other theorists of modernization rejected psychological and cultural explanations of backwardness and instead emphasized economic factors. Among them was the economic historian Walt Whitman Rostow (1916–2003), whose influential 1960 book *The Stages of Economic Growth: A Non-Communist Manifesto* helped him secure key foreign policy advisory positions in the Kennedy and Johnson administrations, eventually serving as national security advisor. In government service he focused on economic development and counterinsurgency – that is, how to defeat communist-led guerrilla struggles in the Third World – and was a leading booster and architect of escalating US military intervention in Vietnam. As the subtitle of Rostow's book suggests, his goal was to provide a plausible and coherent alternative to Marxist explanations of underdevelopment and show that, with assistance and investment from the wealthy capitalist countries, poor countries could achieve economic development without embracing communism or any other form of radical social change. Rostow argued that all societies had to undergo the same five distinct stages of economic growth and social change, beginning with traditional society, passing through what he called the "take-off" to rapid and self-sustaining economic growth, and culminating in the type of high mass-consumption society characteristic of the modern West. If poor countries did not succumb to communism, which Rostow saw as a "disease" of the transition to modernity, they could follow the same path to development which the United States and Western Europe had followed some centuries earlier.

Whatever the differences among them, adherents of modernization theory tended to see traditional societies as essentially static. Unlike the early modern West, they were said to lack the institutions and internal dynamics which might lead to fundamental social transformation from within. As a result, change had to come from outside, which meant largely from the political, cultural and economic influence of the West. Modernization theory therefore saw local elites as playing a crucial role in introducing change into their societies: modernizing rulers and the handful of Western-educated people who initially came into contact with Western ideas and institutions would disseminate them in their own societies, often in the face of resistance from entrenched traditional forces and the great mass of the population which saw those ideas and institutions as a threat to their way of life, interests and customary beliefs. Modernization theory thus fitted nicely with, and tended to justify, US policymakers' inclination to support pro-Western political and economic elites in Asia, Africa and Latin America on the grounds that this would not only preserve US influence and access and ward off the threat of communist revolution and Soviet penetration but also support those local forces crucial to proper modernization.

As it happened, the Middle East was the focus of one of the most influential studies of modernization, a book widely acclaimed by social scientists as modern social science's alternative to old-fashioned Orientalist notions about the region. This was Daniel Lerner's *The Passing of Traditional Society: Modernizing the Middle East*, first published in 1958, which nicely illustrates how the premises underpinning modernization theory's way of looking at the world helped shape Middle East studies as it emerged and flourished in the 1950s and 1960s. Lerner had previously published an analysis of psychological warfare during the Second World War and had written (or co-authored) several other studies which sought to bring the behavioral sciences to bear on foreign policy issues. With sponsorship from the United States Information Agency, which wanted to make US radio broadcasting (seen as a weapon in the Cold War) to Asia, Africa and Latin America more effective, Lerner had in 1950 begun to conduct interviews and surveys of public opinion to gauge the impact of modern media in a number of Middle Eastern countries. It was on the basis of this research that he developed his understanding of modernization in the Middle East. The fact that Lerner's research was based in part on quantitative (and therefore seemingly objective) data helped give *The Passing of Traditional Society* an air of authority.

For Lerner as for many of his colleagues, modernity was a coherent system, a package deal, with a well-defined set of attributes which could be sharply distinguished from the set of attributes typical of traditional societies. Whereas the latter were essentially rural, agricultural, nonliterate, authoritarian and based on personal and oral modes of communication, modern societies were urban, industrial, literate, participatory and based on communications through various mass media, first print and later radio and television. Moreover, while traditional societies were static, modern societies were typified by physical and social mobility and the fostering of a "mobile personality." By this Lerner meant that modern people were in psychological terms fundamentally different from traditional people because they possessed a "personal style" characterized by "empathy," which he defined as "the capacity to see oneself in the other fellow's situation."[34] The social, economic and cultural changes which Middle Easterners were experiencing – urbanization, greater physical mobility, the spread of mass media, and so on – all helped foster the ability of individuals to shed their traditional styles of life and adopt the mobile and empathetic personality characteristic of people in modern societies like the United States.

Lerner saw modernization as a universal process initiated by the West: "From the West came the stimuli which undermined traditional society in the Middle East; for reconstruction of a modern society that will operate efficiently in the world today, the West is still a useful model. What the West is, in this sense, the Middle East seeks to become."[35] But the path from tradition via a "transitional" stage to modernity was rocky and full of pitfalls. Those pitfalls, as Lerner saw it, had little to do with the legacies of colonialism, continuing foreign domination or economic underdevelopment; indeed, his analysis hardly mentioned these factors. Rather, certain Middle Eastern societies had run into trouble because many of their "newly-mobile men and women, liberated by their imagination of better things from reverence toward what *is*, become frustrated and depressed, or antagonistic and aggressive, when their social institutions provide inadequate opportunities for mobility. They move toward the extremes of political action, attracted toward the instruments of propaganda, agitation and violence, by which they hope to disrupt the settled order and to speed their way toward a more satisfying way of life."[36] In other words, instead of becoming properly modern people who saw the United States as the model of what they wanted their own societies to become and accepted its guidance, they had become disoriented, even pathological, and headed off down the wrong track toward ultranationalism and radicalism.

In fact, as Irene Gendzier pointed out in her 1985 book *Managing Political Change: Social Scientists and the Third World*, what really mattered to Lerner was not whether Middle Eastern leaders and political activists displayed such attributes of modernity as empathy and an orientation toward change but rather the specific character and goals of their policies and activism – at bottom, whether they were on the side of the United States in the Cold War.[37] Thus for Lerner Arab nationalism, resentment of continuing Western influence in the Middle East, and demands for political and social transformation that challenged pro-US elites were not only illegitimate but pathological. They were, in fact, manifestations of irrational psychic disturbances, magnified by the power of the new mass media. Lerner therefore vehemently denounced Nasser's Egypt for broadcasting Arab nationalist and anticolonial messages that, he claimed, stimulated a "chain reaction of assassination and mob violence" across the Arab world, incited murder and terrorism and promoted "Islamic World Power" as far away as Pakistan and Indonesia. Lerner went on to quote approvingly from "psychological warfare specialist" Edmond Taylor, who claimed that Nasser was a hero only to the "gutter-barbarians of the teeming Near Eastern or African slums" and "the uprooted, muddle-minded, inferiority-obsessed young Arab intellectuals who are torn between East and West . . ."[38]

Given this, it is not surprising that when Lerner ranked the countries he studied in terms of their progress along the path to modernity, it was pro-Western Turkey and Lebanon which did best, while Egypt and Syria, whose leaders were often in conflict with the United States government, performed badly. Lerner's premises and model, and their roots in Cold War thinking, become even clearer in his discussion of Iran where, it will be remembered, the United States had just a few years earlier helped overthrow an elected government which had nationalized the Anglo-Iranian Oil Company. Lerner claimed that his data demonstrated that in Iran psychological and political moderation – a desirable modern trait – was associated with pro-Americanism, while psychological and political extremism – characteristic of an out-of-kilter transition to modernity – was associated with a pro-Soviet orientation. Of course, the savage reign of terror which the shah of Iran had unleashed against democratic, nationalist and leftist forces in that country after regaining the throne in 1953 with the help of the CIA went entirely unmentioned in Lerner's study; that episode certainly did not fit neatly with his claims about moderation and modernity.

Only a small proportion of the social scientists influenced by one or another variant of modernization theory focused on the Middle East or knew much about the Orientalist scholarly tradition. And while Orientalism tended to see its primary object of study as Islamic civilization during its "classical age," i.e. before its long decline set in, social scientists who embraced the modernization paradigm focused on the processes of change going on before their very eyes as societies outside Europe and the United States struggled to achieve the transition to modernity. Nonetheless, there was something similar in how modernization theory and classical Orientalism approached the world, in the sense that both assumed that it could be neatly and usefully divided into distinct parts. That is, both approaches can be seen as premised upon the drawing of sharp distinctions between "us" (Westerners living as modern people in modern societies) and "them" (non-Westerners, especially Muslims, traditional people living in tradition-bound societies), even if the adherents of modernization theory focused on the processes whereby "they" would (or at least could) eventually become like "us."

Of course, Orientalism and modernization theory divided up the world in different ways. Orientalism tended to draw a sharp distinction between Islam and the West, depicted as two essentially different civilizations, while modernization theory tended to posit an equally sharp distinction between tradition and modernity, conceptualized as two completely different stages along the one and only path of human social evolution. Yet both Orientalism and modernization theory shared a bipolar, dichotomizing vision of the world with much older roots, a vision which modernization theory recast in the language of contemporary social science and deployed to explain a mid-twentieth-century world scene marked by rapid social change, decolonization and the Cold War. So while many Orientalist scholars regarded social scientists as undereducated dabblers overly inclined to grandiose theories and lacking any profound understanding of Islam (and perhaps anything else), and while many social scientists with an interest in the Muslim world disdained Orientalists as ivory-tower scholars preoccupied with their moldering texts, there was at this very basic level some significant common ground.

Nadav Safran's 1961 book *Egypt in Search of Political Community* provides a good illustration of how modernization theory and Orientalism could overlap and reinforce one another.[39] Safran (1925–2003) was born in Egypt and lived briefly in Israel but was trained as a political scientist in the United States; he taught at Harvard University for over four decades. Safran's central argument in this book was that the "belief-system" to which modern Egypt was heir – a belief-system based on "Islamic doctrine" – had crystallized by 1517, when the Ottomans conquered Egypt, and over the following three centuries neither that belief-system nor the country's material conditions underwent any significant change. In the early twentieth century, however, the character of Egypt's government, as well as its economy and society, began to undergo rapid change under the impact of contact with Europe; unfortunately, Egypt's belief-system (i.e., Islam) remained frozen, resulting in "an increasingly widening gap ... between reality and ideology which undermined the existing political community and threatened to condemn Egypt to a permanent state of instability and tension, unless the gap were bridged by means of a readjustment of the traditional belief-system or the formulation of a new one capable of serving as a foundation for a new political community."[40]

Safran's explication of the belief-system dominant in premodern Egypt was very much in keeping with the tenets of the classical Orientalist mainstream. His delineation of what he saw as the main characteristics of "the Muslim attitude to life" and "the Islamic theory of history" were derived from his reading of the Qur'an and a number of medieval legal and philosophical texts, rather than from engagement with the wide range of what Muslims in Egypt and elsewhere had thought and done across the centuries and the continents. Indeed, by failing to evince interest in anything that Muslims – whether rulers, thinkers, jurists or anyone else – might have had to say between the sixteenth and late nineteenth centuries, Safran's approach essentially assumed the total stasis it purported to demonstrate. At the same time, his analysis of modern Egypt's "intellectual evolution" – more precisely, the ideas of a small number of elite Egyptian political and social thinkers – was shaped by the stark dichotomization of tradition and modernity which was central to modernization theory. Safran argued that by the 1930s liberal Egyptian intellectuals had failed in their attempt to "replace an obsolescent belief-system founded on a conception of truth as something that is objectively defined in revelation, with a world view, more applicable to a new reality, that would be based on a conception of truth as something that is ascertained by the human faculties."[41] The result of Egypt's purported failure to escape the stranglehold of Islamic tradition and embrace modernity was, Safran insisted, stagnation and crisis.

In the trenches

Like Hamilton Gibb and many others, Safran hoped that his scholarly work would enhance policymakers' efforts to understand and manage the contemporary Middle East. They saw it as their responsibility to use their expertise to further what they genuinely believed were the interests not only of their own country and its allies but of those of the people whom they studied. This intersection of scholarship and policymaking was of course neither new nor unique to Middle East studies. As we have seen, from the time of Sacy, if not earlier, academic knowledge about Muslims and Islam had often been used to justify and implement European rule in the Middle East, North Africa and elsewhere. During the Second World War most US, British and other Western academics saw the development of policy-relevant knowledge as a worthy contribution to the war effort, and it was largely out of that conjuncture that area studies emerged. This attitude persisted as the Cold War got under way, so that for a long time many scholars, convinced that the United States was engaged in a life-and-death struggle around the globe to defend the cause of freedom against an implacable, immoral, totalitarian enemy, were more than willing to do their part by using their skills and expertise to produce policy-relevant knowledge. Given the strong and widespread belief in the virtue and righteousness of the West and of its standard-bearer, the United States, few scholars were overly concerned that those in power might use their research in ways that might have pernicious consequences for people in the societies they were studying and whose interests they saw themselves as defending.

One important service which scholars rendered the state during the era of the Cold War was to provide intellectual frameworks which policy-makers could use to make sense of what was going on in the world and formulate policy accordingly. One of the key goals of social scientists engaged in elaborating modernization theory (particularly political scientists working on theories of "political development") was to formulate a plausible alternative to Marxist and Marxist-influenced explanations of imperialism and economic underdevelopment. Such explanations, which were popular in the Third World (as well as western Europe and of course the communist-ruled countries), attributed poverty and underdevelopment largely to the legacies of colonialism and to contemporary global and local structures of power that were unequal and exploitative and blocked social and economic development. Activists, leaders and intellectuals on the left, in the Third World and elsewhere, therefore argued that far-reaching social and political transformations (including land reform, state-led economic development and a fuller measure of economic independence) were necessary to overcome underdevelopment and set the poorer countries on the road to self-sustaining economic growth and a better life for the masses.

In contrast, mainstream social scientists in the United States believed that social change in the Third World was producing potentially dangerous instability, which might in turn open the way for communist-led revolution. Their goal was therefore to manage social and political change in ways that avoided instability, prevented the spread of communism, and served US strategic and economic interests. It was this challenge that led scholars like W. W. Rostow to formulate his "non-communist manifesto," an attempt to provide an alternative way of explaining and remedying Third World poverty and instability. As one prominent US political scientist put it in 1956, stopping communism in Asia required "finding some other auspices under which the transition from the traditional form of social relationships can be effected."[42] I have already noted the influence which Rostow's model of modernization had on policymakers during the Kennedy and Johnson administrations, in which Rostow himself served. Rostow's model, and others informed by modernization theory, argued that the problems of Third World countries stemmed not from colonialism and capitalism but from those countries' own social and cultural defects. The way to fix these problems and achieve modernity was therefore not social reform and economic independence, as the left argued, but proper modernization, which meant adopting the political guidance of the United States (along with US products and investment) and policies that fostered capitalism and stability and, in the long run, democracy.

It was this vision which underpinned the policies which Rostow and others advocated with regard to Vietnam in the 1960s. Communism was a disease that could surface as societies made the difficult transition from tradition to modernity, and it was not only the right but the duty of the United States – the beacon of freedom and modernity in the world – to use whatever means were necessary to eradicate this pathology and save the Vietnamese. Hence Rostow's key role in searching for effective ways to defeat the communist-led insurgency in South Vietnam, first by escalating involvement in the counterinsurgency campaigns of a series of unpopular regimes there and then, when that strategy failed, by direct US military intervention, in the form of a massive bombing campaign against both North and South Vietnam and the dispatch of hundreds of thousands of American soldiers.

Writing in the prestigious journal *Foreign Affairs* in 1968, the Harvard political scientist Samuel Huntington drew on modernization theory to develop an intellectual rationale for the massive bombing of the South Vietnamese countryside and the creation of "free-fire zones" there – zones in which US and South Vietnamese forces were authorized to shoot at and bomb anything that moved, which usually meant the Vietnamese peasants who lived there.[43] The authoritative character and impact of Huntington's pronouncements on Vietnam were enhanced not only by his status within his discipline but also by his position as chair of the Council on Vietnamese Studies of the US Agency for International Development's South-East Asia Advisory Group from 1966 to 1969. Indeed, this *Foreign Affairs* article had its origins in a classified report produced for the State Department.

"In an absent-minded way," Huntington wrote, "the United States in Viet Nam may well have stumbled upon the answer to [communist-led] 'wars of national liberation.'" By using military force in the countryside "on such a massive scale as to produce a massive migration from countryside to city, the basic assumptions underlying the Maoist doctrine of revolutionary war no longer operate. The Maoist-inspired rural revolution is undercut by the American-sponsored urban revolution." In keeping with modernization theory's premise that societies "are susceptible to revolution only at particular stages in their development," Huntington argued that "forced-draft urbanization and modernization" – the product of massive bombing which uprooted millions of peasants and forced them into (purportedly more modern) urban areas controlled by the US and its allies – would rapidly bring South Vietnam "out of the phase in which a rural revolutionary movement can hope to generate sufficient strength to come to power."[43] This justification of the use of massive military force against civilians, a policy that had catastrophic consequences for the Vietnamese, led antiwar activists at Harvard and elsewhere to denounce Huntington as complicitous in war crimes.

During the Cold War era (and beyond) there were a substantial number of academics who were willing, indeed eager, to put their skills to use in even more direct ways, accepting (even soliciting) open or secret funding from the military or intelligence agencies to conduct research that had a clear bearing on US policy in the Third World. One of the most notorious examples was Project Camelot, launched in the early 1960s by the Special Operations Research Office, a contractor funded by the US Army. With a total cost estimated at $44 million, Project Camelot recruited numerous US and foreign scholars in order to foster social science research that would not only allow policymakers to anticipate "social breakdown" in vulnerable Third World countries and the opportunities it presented for communist "penetration" and "takeover" but also provide them with better strategies for preventing or countering the growth of communism.

Project Camelot provoked widespread controversy: when its military funding and close links with US policy goals became known, many academics and others denounced it on the grounds that it (and many similar government-funded projects) compromised the principle that scholars should set their own research agendas and not allow the state to so obviously exploit their expertise for its own (possibly pernicious) purposes. Senator J. William Fulbright (1905–1995), a leading critic of US intervention overseas, saw Camelot and the many similar (if less grandiose) government-funded research projects and institutions as symptoms of how the Cold War and interventionism had transformed American campuses. They were now, he argued, "inhabited by proliferating institutes and centers with awe-inspiring names that use vast government and contract funds to produce ponderous studies of 'insurgency' and 'counterinsurgency' – studies which, behind their opaque language, look very much like efforts to develop 'scientific' techniques for the anticipation and prevention of revolution, without regard for the possibility that some revolutions may be justified or even desirable."[44]

Project Camelot was ultimately canceled. But this was something of an aberration: US social scientists had been serving as paid consultants for government agencies and working on government-funded policy-oriented research projects since the early 1950s, if not before, and this practice continued long after the controversy about Project Camelot faded away. There were strong links between the world of scholarship and the world of policy in Middle East studies as well, where (as in other fields) a substantial number of scholars sincerely believed that tailoring their research agendas to suit policymakers' needs (and having their research well funded in return) did not compromise their independence or integrity as scholars or in any way undermine their avowed commitment to the truth. A few examples will suffice.

Born in Germany in 1924, Manfred Halpern worked as a researcher at the State Department in the mid-1950s and then became a consultant for the RAND Corporation. RAND's origins went back to 1945, when the Air Force created a separate entity to conduct scientific and technological research and development – "r and d," hence RAND – for military purposes. In 1948, with financial support from the Ford Foundation, RAND became an independent nonprofit corporation, though through the 1960s the great bulk of its research contracts came from military, intelligence and other government agencies concerned with foreign policy. While at RAND and with funding from the Air Force, Halpern researched and wrote his 1963 book *The Politics of Social Change in the Middle East and North Africa*.[45] The book's opening lines explained its purpose: "The area from Morocco to Pakistan is in the midst of a profound revolution. This book attempts to explain the causes and character of that revolution; examine the forces, groups, ideas, and institutions now in motion; and estimate the direction which politics may take in the future in the Middle East and North Africa." It concluded with a section discussing the "limitations and opportunities for Western policy" in the Middle East. Halpern taught political science at Princeton University for many years.

J. C. Hurewitz served during the Second World War as a research analyst for the Office of Strategic Services, the forerunner of the CIA. After stints at the State Department and the United Nations he began teaching at Columbia University, where he spent the remainder of his career. During the 1950s he served as a member of the SSRC (and then joint SSRC–ACLS) Committee on the Near and Middle East, where he played a key role in launching Middle East studies as an organized field in the United States. He received many fellowships and served as a consultant for the RAND Corporation and the State Department during the 1960s. Research for Hurewitz's 1969 book *Middle East Politics: The Military Dimension* – a topic of obvious importance to policymakers and the military – was funded by the Council on Foreign Relations and apparently by the Defense Department as well, and was facilitated by access to top-secret government reports and records. Because it relied on classified material (and because it seems to have been partially government-funded), Hurewitz's book had to be reviewed and approved by both the Pentagon and the State Department before it could be published.[46]

Leonard Binder, one of the leading political scientists working on the Middle East during the 1960s and 1970s, at the University of Chicago and then at the University of California, Los Angeles, provides another example of how policy and scholarship often intersected. In the mid-1960s Binder received $60,000 from the Air Force for a study of political development and modernization in a number of Islamic countries. A description of his research project noted that "one of the principal products will be the provision of a tested scheme for the analysis of development that can be applied in other developing areas. These studies bear directly on the role of the US Military in providing military advice, assistance and training in US Military Schools for the indigenous military leaders, and to the problems of long-range military planning." Binder later led a RAND Corporation study of "Factors Influencing Iran's International Role."[47]

In the late 1960s and early 1970s, alarmed by developments in the Middle East, the Defense Department and other agencies (including the CIA) continued to fund research projects with strong policy implications, directly or through such entities as RAND. A bit later, as Chapter 5 will discuss, the emergence of Islamist movements in many predominantly Muslim countries, and then the revolution which led to the overthrow the shah of Iran in 1979, would arouse considerable concern in official circles and lead to further efforts to draw on scholars' expertise. As we will see in Chapter 7, Nadav Safran, whose 1961 account of Egypt's failed encounter with modernity I discussed a bit earlier, would himself become embroiled in controversy in the mid-1980s over covert CIA funding of some of his academic projects.

During the Cold War era and beyond, the pool of undergraduate and graduate students studying the Middle East at American universities, sometimes with government or foundation funding for language training and research abroad, was an obvious source of recruits for service in various government agencies, including the State Department but also the CIA, the less well-known (but much larger) National Security Agency, the FBI, and so on. It is impossible to know how many students who had specialized in some aspect of the study of the Middle East or Islam eventually went into government service. But it is not hard to see why the opportunity might have been tempting for some, perhaps especially the prospect of being able to influence policy that government service seemed to offer. There was a considerable time lag before any substantial number of scholars of the Middle East came to share the sentiment growing among scholars of Asia and Latin America and other area studies fields in the later 1960s that accepting research funding from, or sharing research data with, the military or intelligence agencies compromised the integrity of the scholarly enterprise and might well have pernicious consequences for Third World societies at the receiving end of American global power. Before that time there were certainly US-based scholars of the Middle East who disagreed with aspects of US policy toward the region, but few doubted (publicly, at least) that policymakers had basically good intentions (whatever mistakes they made along the way) or that the United States was at bottom justified in its efforts to preserve order and stability there. More radical critiques of US policy would gain little currency in the field until the 1970s.

Of course, the intellectual quality of a scholar's research on some aspect of the politics, economics, history or culture of the Middle East cannot be judged solely by whether or not it was funded, directly or indirectly, by the CIA, the Defense Department, RAND, or some other governmental or quasigovernmental agency. Some of the books, articles and studies produced by scholars working on government-funded research projects were of little intellectual import or lasting value, while others were more intellectually significant and insightful. It should also be kept in mind that most US scholars of the Middle East and Islam had no direct connection with, or interest in, policymaking, and even among those who did there were no doubt differences of opinions and ongoing disagreements about both intellectual and policy issues.

Nonetheless, it remains true that in a range of disciplines and fields – perhaps most notably political science and those area studies fields which, like Middle East studies, focused on key arenas of the Cold War – scholarly agendas were often influenced by the needs of the "national security state" to which the Cold War had given birth. More broadly, beyond the question of (overt or covert) official funding for research and the shaping of scholarly agendas by the needs of the state, there remains the larger issue of the framework of interpretation within which most scholars studying the contemporary or modern Middle East worked in this period and how that framework shaped their analyses and conclusions. There were certainly always scholars whose research on the past, present or future of the predominantly Muslim lands was rooted in other approaches. Yet it remains the case that into the 1970s a good part of academic writing on this region, and on Islam more generally, was produced by scholars who still took for granted either a heavily philological Orientalism and an essentialized conception of Islam as a unitary, largely unchanging civilization, or modernization theory with its sharp dichotomy between the traditional and the modern, or some (often uneasy) combination of the two. The intellectual and political issues which these approaches raised had hardly begun to attract attention, much less generate serious controversy, among scholars in the field of Middle East studies as it was practiced in the United States and western Europe.

The field of Middle East studies had burgeoned in the later 1950s and especially the 1960s, largely because of the availability of unprecedented levels of foundation, government and university funding. The rapid growth and maturation of the field were manifested in, among other things, the proliferation of the new centers and departments of Middle East studies at an increasing number of universities, the expansion of existing programs, and the formation of a professional organization for the field, the Middle East Studies Association. While leading scholars in the field had their complaints – largely about what they saw as inadequate funding, the failure of officials to heed their advice, and the field's perceived status as less intellectually advanced and innovative than some other area studies fields – there was nonetheless a sense into the late 1960s that Middle East studies in the United States was well launched and on more or less the right track, if not always as intellectually productive or successful as its founders might have hoped.

As the next chapter will discuss, the later 1960s and especially the 1970s would witness a rising tide of challenges both to the intellectual paradigms which had long dominated the field and to what many people would come to see as its complicity with Western power in the Middle East. These challenges had complex origins, including important developments in the region itself whose reverberations ultimately affected how scholars in the United States and western Europe understood their own enterprise and how to go about it. Over the decades that followed the field would be transformed in important ways, even as it would continue to be marked by legacies of the past.

5   Turmoil in the field

The winter 1963 issue of the humanities journal *Diogenes* included an article (originally published somewhat earlier in French) entitled "Orientalism in Crisis," by Anouar Abdel-Malek. A veteran of the Egyptian communist movement, which the Nasser regime had ruthlessly suppressed, Abdel-Malek now lived in exile in France. His 1962 book on Nasser's Egypt, later published in English as *Egypt: Military Society*, was a trenchant critique of Nasserism in theory and practice. But in "Orientalism in Crisis" Abdel-Malek had a different purpose: he sought to convince his readers of the urgent need to "undertake a revision, a critical reevaluation of the general conception, the methods, and implements for the understanding of the Orient that have been used by the West, notably from the beginning of the last century, on all levels and in all fields."[1]

Abdel-Malek argued that the arduous labors of even the best Orientalist scholars had often been undermined by defective, if not pernicious, "postulates, methodological habits and historico-philosophical concepts." These included the treatment of "the Orient and Orientals as an 'object' of study, stamped with an otherness... customary, passive, non-participating... non-active, non-autonomous... understood, defined – and acted [upon] – by others." This was in turn linked to what Abdel-Malek saw as "an essentialist conception of the countries, nations and peoples of the Orient under study" which reduced them to ethnic stereotypes, ultimately tending toward racism. Orientalism had too often operated as if the human race were divided into fundamentally distinct types ("Chinese man," "Arab man," "African man," and so on), all of whom were implicitly or explicitly measured against "normal man" – "the European man of the historical period, that is, since Greek antiquity." Moreover, traditional Orientalism was focused on the past, largely ignoring the dramatic social, cultural and political transformations which the countries and peoples of the contemporary Middle East were experiencing, and had thereby isolated itself from current debates and advances in the humanities and social sciences.

To remedy this situation, Abdel-Malek called for a thorough and rigorous critique of "europeocentrism" – what we today call Eurocentrism – whose "fundamental error" (here Abdel-Malek quoted Joseph Needham, the great historian of Chinese science) was to assume that because much of modern science and technology had its origin in Western Europe, "everything that is European is equally universal." He went on to echo Needham's call for "disorientalizing" the study of Asia, which by extension entailed abandoning the essentialist assumption that "Islam" was a distinct and utterly different "world" unto itself and instead insisting that similar concepts and methods should guide the study of all parts of the world.

Abdel-Malek's article reflected, and contributed to, debates in French intellectual circles in the 1950s and early 1960s, especially on the left. In this period Marxist scholars like Maxime Rodinson and others were pioneering approaches to the study of the Middle East past and present that sought to move beyond traditional Orientalism's philological orientation. He and other French scholars were in active dialogue with students, intellectuals and anticolonial activists from various Arab and Muslim lands who were then living in France and who had also begun to produce innovative work. Among them was the young Egyptian economist Samir Amin, who in this period was formulating a theoretical framework for understanding global development and underdevelopment that challenged the core assumptions of modernization theory, as well as the Moroccan Abdallah Laroui, who was grappling with questions of tradition, modernity and cultural change and would somewhat later produce an important critique of Orientalism as well as widely discussed essays on contemporary Arab culture.[2]

There were also scholars in the English-speaking world in this period who were explicitly or implicitly critical of the study of Islam and the Middle East as conventionally practiced. As I noted in Chapter 1, Norman Daniel's *Islam and the West* was first published in 1960, and though he focused on medieval Latin Christian views of Islam he was also critical of what he saw as the enduring legacies of those views to be found in later Orientalist work. In a second book published in 1966, *Islam, Europe and Empire*, Daniel offered a wide-ranging essay on the "new ideas of the Islamic world which took shape in Western Europe during the period of colonial expansion."[3]

In 1958 Norman Itzkowitz, who had just joined the faculty of Princeton University, published an article titled "Eighteenth Century Ottoman Realities" which demolished A. H. Lybyer's assertions about the character of Ottoman state and society and criticized Gibb and Bowen's uncritical acceptance of those assertions in their widely acclaimed and cited *Islamic Society and the West*, published in two parts in 1950 and 1957 (see Chapter 4). Itzkowitz castigated "the attitude that knowledge of Near Eastern languages was unnecessary – anything worth knowing could be found in European sources" and described what he called the "Lybyer, Gibb and Bowen thesis" as "comforting to the Christian West's deep-seated sense of superiority" but grossly inaccurate.[4]

In the mid-1960s the Oxford historian Albert Hourani (1915–93) published several essays assessing the place of Islam in European historiography and the problematic use which philosophers like Hegel (and historians influenced by him) had made of Islam in their interpretations of history. Several of Hourani's other essays from the late 1950s and 1960s played an important role in encouraging greater scholarly attention to the modern Arab world's Ottoman legacy. Scholars influenced by modernization theory, Arab nationalism, or both had tended to see the late Ottoman period as one of unmitigated decline or at best stagnation, a "dark age" preceding the era of modernization and "westernization" (the two were often treated as if they were synonymous) that followed upon Napoleon's invasion of Egypt in 1798. Hourani called attention to understudied but important changes which the Arab East was already undergoing in the eighteenth century, and specifically to what he called the "politics of notables" in the cities of the Ottoman Arab lands. This helped lay the groundwork for a surge of scholarship on the Arab provinces of the Ottoman empire which made innovative use of a much wider range of local and imperial archival and other materials than ever before and yielded a much more detailed, complex and nuanced portrait of this period.[5]

There were certainly other scholars in Europe and the United States who expressed or felt criticism of, or at least unhappiness with, part or all of the period's two dominant approaches to the study of the Middle East, Orientalism of the Hamilton Gibb or Bernard Lewis variety and modernization theory. And there were certainly other factors and milieux that could help produce or sustain disaffection with those approaches, including embrace of an Arab or other Middle Eastern nationalist perspective or the empathy sometimes gained from long interaction with the Middle East. In any case, throughout this period as earlier, alongside work informed by the dominant approaches, important scholarship on the Middle East and Islam was being produced in a variety of disciplines which sought to offer an alternative perspective or open up new avenues for research.

Until the 1970s, however, there was not yet evident a significant degree of theoretical and methodological self-criticism, or even self-awareness, in Middle East studies as practiced in the United States and Britain.

Nonetheless, the political, social and intellectual developments which would lead to the emergence of vigorous challenges and alternatives to the dominant paradigms can, at least in retrospect, already be discerned in the latter part of the previous decade. In the following section I focus on developments in the United States, not only because I am more familiar with that case but because in the remainder of this book my main concern will be the contention and transformations experienced by Middle East studies in the United States. But it is worth keeping in mind that much of western Europe underwent similar political and intellectual upheavals in this period and that, as I will discuss later in this chapter, some of the first comprehensive critiques of Anglo-American Orientalism and Middle East studies from the left would come out of Europe, especially Britain, in the early 1970s.

The 1960s and the rise of a "New Left"

The 1960s witnessed profound changes in American society and culture, changes which had significant political but also intellectual consequences. The civil rights movement that arose in the mid-1950s to demand equality and justice for African-Americans and gathered additional momentum in the early 1960s highlighted the deep fissures of race and class in American society. The example of the civil rights movement, and later its mid-1960s offshoot the "black power" movement, helped bring to birth a new women's movement and a new gay rights movement later in the 1960s. These movements were also bound up, if in different and complex ways, with the youth culture of "the sixties," featuring that famous trinity "sex, drugs and rock 'n' roll," and the whole tumultuous mix was further politicized – and often radicalized – by the fact that for much of the decade the United States was waging an increasingly bloody, futile and unpopular war in Vietnam, which sparked the emergence of a growing antiwar movement.

College students often spearheaded the antiwar movement, but it eventually spread to encompass much broader segments of the population, including even sections of the policymaking and corporate elites. Disgusted and disillusioned by the lies which officials told to justify the war and subdue protest, many people came in the 1960s to adopt a much more cynical attitude toward politicians and the government. This helped undermine the Cold War consensus on foreign policy that had prevailed through the 1950s and into the early 1960s and made it much more difficult for the Johnson and Nixon administrations to sell their policies to the American public than it had been for earlier administrations. A great many people across the political spectrum came to see the Vietnam war as a mistake, the wrong war in the wrong place at the wrong time, though they did not necessarily challenge the underlying assumption that the United States was essentially a force for good which sought to preserve freedom around the globe against communist subversion and aggression while selflessly promoting development and progress, nor did they necessarily extend their criticism of US policy in Vietnam to other aspects of US foreign policy.

For a good many others, however, the experience of Vietnam had a more radicalizing effect, leading them toward the conclusion that US military intervention there was in fact not a well-intentioned mistake on the part of policymakers but only one instance of a consistent effort to preserve American political, economic and military domination of as much as the globe as possible, largely in the service of corporate profits. From this perspective, embraced by adherents of what became known as the "New Left" – as opposed to the old-line socialist and communist groups which had been marginalized by the early 1950s – official talk of freedom, democracy and progress was mere lip service, easily refuted by the fact that in many parts of the world the United States supported reactionary and authoritarian regimes and stood ready to intervene militarily (as it had in Vietnam) or by covert means (as in Iran) when the oppressive and unjust status quo upheld by the US and its local allies was threatened by radical and/or nationalist governments or movements. This radical critique of the US role in the world was usually linked to a critique of a social structure and political system which also sustained glaring inequalities of wealth and power at home, especially for racial minorities.

The centrality of racial issues to US politics in the 1960s, the growth of opposition to the war in Vietnam, the politicization and radicalization of many, especially on college campuses, and in general a much more critical attitude toward established authority, whether political, academic or cultural, had their effects on intellectual life as well, especially at the leading private and public universities in the United States. These factors helped undermine the image, central to the dominant theoretical approaches in many of the social science and humanities disciplines, of the United States as an essentially consensual, conflict-free and classless society which played a benign role in the world as it promoted freedom and progress and fought communism. This in turn helped open up space for the emergence within academia of alternative ways of understanding the modern and contemporary world, ways that took conflict and change rather than consensus and stability as the normal state of affairs, focused on the structural sources of persistent economic and social inequality and oppression rather than on the purported character defects of the oppressed, highlighted race, class and later gender as key categories for social analysis, and pointed to the links between particular kinds of knowledge and their (generally unacknowledged and sometimes pernicious) political assumptions and consequences.

Those who used class – broadly speaking, a social group's relative location within hierarchies of wealth and power – as a key category for the analysis of politics and society often described their approach as "political economy," but many of their methods, and the social theory on which those methods rested, were derived from some variant of Marxism. Scholars who took Marx seriously as a social theorist had largely been eliminated or excluded from US institutions of higher education during the anticommunist ("Red Scare" or "McCarthy") purges of the late 1940s and early 1950s and had exerted little intellectual influence for some two decades, so the resurgence of interest in the late 1960s in Marx as a thinker and in Marxism as a way of understanding both historical change and the workings of contemporary societies constituted a significant challenge to both conservative and "Cold War liberal" modes of analysis in many disciplines and fields.

Across the disciplines, dissident scholars – usually but not exclusively young – struggled to develop and deploy alternative methods and theories which challenged the thinking and authority of their elders. They sought to show how the theories the latter espoused not only failed to adequately account for reality but often played a pernicious role in justifying and buttressing oppressive, undemocratic and unequal structures of power and wealth at home and abroad. So, for example, in these years dissident historians pioneered a "history from below" movement that called for greater attention to groups often left out of elite-focused narratives – working people, racial, ethnic and later sexual minorities, women and so on – which fed into a broader revival of "social history" and from the 1970s the flowering of women's history. Similar trends emerged in other disciplines as well, often cross-fertilizing one another – for example, the work of the anthropologist Clifford Geertz, whose focus on the interpretation of cultures as systems of meaning not only challenged structural-functionalist approaches in his own field but was drawn on by historians developing new approaches to cultural history. The 1960s and 1970s were thus a time of intellectual (and political) ferment, if not turmoil, in many disciplines and fields, and it is therefore not surprising that modernization theory also came under fire. After all, as I discussed in Chapter 4, this framework of interpretation had to a large extent underpinned post-1945 area studies (including Middle East studies), and it was very much bound up with the global engagements of the United States in the Cold War.

"Dependency theory" as critique and alternative

Some of the most influential early challenges to modernization theory came from dissident scholars in the field of Latin American studies, in which modernization theory had long held sway just as it had in Middle East studies and various other area studies fields. That Latin American studies should have engendered some of the first powerful critiques of modernization theory is not surprising. The question of why the countries of Latin America were poor, despite great natural and human resources, and how they could achieve genuine economic and social development, as well as a greater degree of democracy in a period when many of them were ruled by brutal US-backed military dictatorships, was high on the agenda of intellectuals and academics across Latin America as well as in the United States. The question was clearly not just a scholarly one; it was inevitably political as well. This linkage was highlighted by the example of Cuba, where a revolution led by Fidel Castro had in 1959 overthrown a US-backed dictatorship and installed a left-wing authoritarian-populist regime which (with Soviet support) pursued an anticapitalist development strategy at home and sought to foster socialist revolution across Latin America and the Third World, despite US efforts to destroy it and kill its leader. Here as elsewhere, New Left activists and academics argued, politics and scholarly knowledge could not easily be separated.

That very linkage was central to a seminal article, "Sociology of Development and Underdevelopment of Sociology," published in 1967 by the sociologist André Gunder Frank.[6] Gunder Frank, who had been educated in the United States and taught at a number of universities in that country and in Latin America, began by charging that the "sociology of development" produced in the United States was "empirically invalid when confronted with reality, theoretically inadequate in terms of its own classical social scientific standards, and policy wise inadequate for pursuing its supposed intentions of promoting development of the underdeveloped countries."

Gunder Frank went on to attack proponents of modernization theory for their claim that Latin American societies were underdeveloped and undemocratic essentially because of their "traditional" cultures and social structures, which lacked the "modern" personalities and social relations which allegedly characterized the United States and other developed countries. He also vigorously criticized W. W. Rostow's model of the "stages of economic growth" through which all countries supposedly had to pass in order to achieve proper economic development, discussed in Chapter 4. He argued that that model, and most other mainstream social-science approaches, assumed that today's underdeveloped countries were where today's developed countries had been one or two or three centuries ago, and that to achieve development and modernity they had to pass through the same stages and undergo the same social, economic, cultural and/or psychological changes.

This conception was a core premise of modernization theory, but Gunder Frank argued that it was fundamentally wrong. To understand historical change one could not treat societies in isolation and focus on their cultures, social structures and political institutions as if they were entirely self-contained and internally generated; one had to look at how they had long been, and continued to be, part of a global system that had profoundly shaped their course of development. The fact that today the United States and Britain were wealthy while India and Brazil were poor was, Gunder Frank insisted, *not* because India and Brazil had not yet gone through the transition to modernity which the United States and Britain had undergone over the past centuries. Rather, the very same historical transformations – stretching back some four or five centuries to the beginnings of Europe's encounter with the Americas and its achievement of direct access to East Asia – that had resulted in the United States and Britain eventually becoming wealthy had *simultaneously* set India and Brazil on a course toward impoverishment.

In other words, these lands were poor today, Gunder Frank (and others) argued, because back in the sixteenth century they had begun to be incorporated into a newly emerging global economic system that was structured in such a way as to drain resources from certain countries and regions – that is, the Third World of Asia, Africa and Latin America – and channel them to other countries and regions – the developed countries of western Europe and later the United States. These countries were not underdeveloped today because they were at an early stage of the transition from tradition to modernity so dear to modernization theory. In reality, Britain and the United States had *never* been like India or Brazil were today; the poverty of today's underdeveloped lands was actually the *outcome* of a long history, not a result of their being stuck in some original "traditional" stage.

Underdevelopment, Gunder Frank insisted, should therefore be regarded not as a state of being or a stage but as a *process*: the same historical forces, global systems and structural inequities of wealth and power that over the past few centuries had *developed* certain countries had *underdeveloped* other countries and were continuing to do so today, producing and sustaining the huge disparities of wealth and power between and within countries all too visible in today's world. The very same processes that over the centuries produced development for today's wealthy countries had produced underdevelopment for today's poor countries.

India and Brazil were thus just as "modern" as the United States and Britain, in the sense that all four were products of the same global processes, though their very different structural locations in the global system of wealth and power had obviously produced very different outcomes.

In numerous other writings André Gunder Frank would go on to argue that the only way that underdeveloped countries in Latin America (or elsewhere) could achieve real economic development and a better life for their people was to break out of the global capitalist system, whose structural relations of investment and trade benefited the wealthy capitalist countries and their local clients while blocking authentic development.[7] This perspective directly contradicted mainstream US economic theory, which argued that the capitalist system market was inherently rational and that free trade and investment in the long run benefited everyone, and it also flew in the face of modernization theory's insistence that today's underdeveloped countries could be just like the developed West if only they assimilated proper modern character traits and social institutions, including the free market. For Gunder Frank and others on the left in Latin America, real development required social revolution, for only through revolution could the local oligarchies closely associated with US corporate interests be removed from power and the way opened for economic development that would be guided by national needs and not by the requirements of bankers, investors and transnational corporations based in the United States and western Europe.

Gunder Frank's understanding of the causes of, and the solution to, economic underdevelopment also constituted an intervention in ongoing debates about strategy and tactics within the Latin American left. Many of those who shared the Marxist perspective underpinning Gunder Frank's analysis nonetheless argued that left-wing Latin American parties and movements should seek to ally themselves with potentially progressive local "national capitalists" in order to oppose the domination of US multinational capital as well as to defeat the reactionary, quasifeudal landowning classes that were so powerful in many Latin American countries and effect genuine land reform and other vital social reforms. In contrast, for Gunder Frank and those who shared his views, there was no "national capitalist" class of any significance: the ruling oligarchies in most or all of Latin America, whether industrial or commercial or landowning, were so closely bound to foreign capital and integrated into the global capitalist system that left-wing parties and movements had no choice but to emulate the Cuban example by mobilizing the masses, winning power and opting out of that system altogether.

But one did not have to be a Marxist or Marxist-influenced, or even a leftist, in order to embrace something like Gunder Frank's understanding of the causes of, and remedy for, underdevelopment. In fact, Gunder Frank and others like him borrowed from, built on, and gave a Marxist inflection to an approach that had been developing among non-Marxist development economists and others in Latin America and elsewhere since the 1950s, if not earlier. Inspired by a desire to achieve greater economic development and independence for their countries as well as to alleviate widespread poverty, the so-called *dependencia* ("dependency") school of economic thought rejected the assertion of mainstream economists that foreign investment and unfettered trade would allow each country to maximize its own "comparative advantage" and inevitably promote development.

Instead, dependency theory economists argued that underdeveloped countries which remained subject to disadvantageous economic relations with the wealthy industrialized countries would at best achieve "dependent development" and at worst grow even poorer, relatively and perhaps even absolutely. They argued that underdeveloped countries needed to maintain high tariff barriers on imported manufactured goods in order to protect local industries which otherwise could not hope to compete with infinitely more powerful transnational corporations – the very policy which the United States had pursued in the late nineteenth century. These countries also needed to impose controls on foreign investment and channel domestic investment in ways that would lay the foundation for sustained economic growth, rather than leave such decisions to the private sector and foreign interests which used only the criterion of their own short-term profitability. In the 1950s and 1960s many countries in the Third World, from India to Egypt to Mexico, explicitly or implicitly embraced these principles and pursued a strategy of "import-substitution industrialization" which kept out manufactured Western imports in order to promote local industries, restricted foreign investment in the name of economic nationalism, and assigned the state a central role in economic planning, which often meant state ownership of parts of the economy.

Dependency theory, whether in its non-Marxist economic-nationalist version or in one of its explicitly Marxist (or more precisely, "neo-Marxist") versions, thus constituted an important critique of, and alternative to, modernization theory, and a challenge to much of mainstream US social science.[8] It offered a way of making sense of what was going on in the Third World which focused not on those societies' purported cultural, social and/or psychological defects or their "traditionalism" but rather on questions of political economy – on the social structures of these countries, their class relations, the unequal distribution of wealth and power within them and, centrally, the character of their initial incorporation into, and ongoing role in, the global system of modern capitalism as it had emerged and developed over the past half millennium. Other scholars – for example, Samir Amin, whom I mentioned earlier, and the sociologist of Africa Immanuel Wallerstein, to whom I will return shortly – developed approaches similar to that of Gunder Frank at around the same time, and there ensued lively theoretical and political debates, within the emerging academic New Left in the United States, Europe and Third World but also well beyond it.[9]

There were, of course, many scholars who did not accept dependency theory, and work soon appeared which demonstrated its shortcomings when applied to concrete historical situations. By the mid-1970s the excitement it had initially aroused subsided, and many even of its early adherents would seek to move beyond it.[10] Nonetheless, the insights which dependency theory and other early variants of political economy approaches helped generate and disseminate continued to influence scholars. One of those insights was the importance of situating local and national histories in their regional and global contexts. Another was a vigorous critique of the presumption, central to both Orientalism and modernization theory, that a stable "tradition" or fixed "cultural values" could adequately explain what people did or how change happened.

The sociologist Barrington Moore addressed the latter issue nicely in his influential 1966 book *The Social Origins of Dictatorship and Democracy*, which focused on late medieval and early modern Europe but had much broader relevance for contemporary sociologists, historians and others:

Culture or tradition is not something that exists outside of or independently of individual human beings living together in society. Cultural values do not descend from heaven to influence the course of history. To explain behavior in terms of cultural values is to engage in circular reasoning. The assumption of inertia, that cultural and social continuity do not require explanation, obliterates the fact that both have to be recreated anew in each generation, often with great pain and suffering. To maintain and transmit a value system, human beings are punched, bullied, sent to jail, thrown into concentration camps, cajoled, bribed, made into heroes, encouraged to read newspapers, stood up against a wall and shot, and sometimes even taught sociology. To speak of cultural inertia is to overlook the concrete interests and privileges that are served by indoctrination, education, and the entire complicated process of transmitting culture from one generation to the next.[11]

Changes in the Middle East

In Latin American and East Asian studies and across the disciplines as well, contemporary political struggles (among them racial issues in the United States, the Cuban revolution, Mao Zedong's "cultural revolution" in China, and of course the war in Vietnam) helped fuel intellectual critiques of mainstream approaches as well as the emergence of dissident caucuses, networks and journals – for example, the Committee of Concerned Asian Scholars, which mobilized to oppose the war in Vietnam; the Union for Radical Political Economics; *Radical History Review*; and so on. Middle East studies lagged a bit behind, so that it was only in the early 1970s that the kinds of critiques, alternative approaches, and dissident networks and journals that were beginning to open up and transform other fields and disciplines first impinged on the academic study of the Middle East. But in this field as elsewhere, these developments owed a great deal not only to the example being set by emerging critical tendencies within American academia in general but also to developments in the Middle East itself.

In the June 1967 war Israel inflicted a rapid and humiliating military defeat on the armed forces of two of the leading pan-Arab nationalist and avowedly revolutionary regimes – that of Nasser in Egypt and that controlled by a radical faction of the Ba'th party in Syria – as well as on Jordan, led by a conservative monarchy closely linked to the United States. This defeat discredited the claims of Nasser (who died suddenly in 1970) and his ideological and political rivals in Syria that the authoritarian-populist (but strongly anticommunist) pan-Arab nationalist ideology and policies which both espoused were leading to a modernized, united Arab world which could not only achieve economic development but also successfully confront Israel and secure justice for the Palestinians. Instead, these regimes, already in economic trouble at home, had engaged in a reckless confrontation with Israel which resulted in the Israeli conquest of the remainder of Palestine (i.e., the West Bank, Gaza and East Jerusalem) as well as of Egypt's Sinai peninsula and the Golan Heights region of Syria. The war was also perceived, in the region and elsewhere, as a setback for the Soviet Union, whose two closest Arab allies had been soundly defeated, and a gain for the United States.

The defeat of the Nasserist and Ba'thist regimes, and the weakening of the Jordanian monarchy, seemed at first to have opened up space for the emergence of new and more radical political forces in the Arab world. These forces argued that the Arab states had been defeated because they were too authoritarian, bureaucratic and compromising – in short, not sufficiently revolutionary – and were therefore unable to effectively mobilize the Arab masses for a protracted struggle against imperialism, its local client regimes and Israel, still seen by many Arabs as a colonial-settler entity established on Arab land by force of arms with imperialist backing.

Foremost among these new forces was a new and independent Palestinian nationalist movement. Palestinian activists determined to remain free of control by Nasser or other Arab regimes and reverse the loss of Palestine by their own efforts had been quietly organizing for a decade, and in the mid-1960s they had even launched a number of guerrilla raids into Israel which while militarily inconsequential in and of themselves nonetheless helped touch off the sequence of events that ultimately led to the June 1967 war. But it was only after the 1967 defeat, and especially after Palestinian fighters (with some unacknowledged Jordanian support) stood up to Israeli forces at Karameh the following year, that these Palestinian activists and their organizations could emerge into the open.

The most prominent of the Palestinian organizations was FATAH (a reverse acronym for the "Palestinian Liberation Movement") led by Yasir Arafat and his colleagues, which along with a number of other Palestinian groups, some of them explicitly Marxist, seized control of the hitherto ineffective Palestine Liberation Organization and won massive popular support among Palestinians and across the Arab world. They saw themselves as the vanguard of a new, independent Palestinian nationalist movement which would put Palestinian interests first and achieve the liberation of Palestine through a protracted "people's war of liberation," on the model of the Algerian struggle against French colonial rule or the Vietnamese struggle against the United States and its local allies. The radical stance of the PLO, now led by the guerrilla organizations, soon brought it into conflict with the Hashemite monarchy that ruled Jordan, a majority of whose population was of Palestinian origin and which unsurprisingly saw the PLO in its new incarnation as a dire threat to its very existence. In the fall of 1970 the Jordanian army defeated PLO forces and forced them out of the country, whereupon Lebanon (which also had a substantial Palestinian refugee population) became the PLO's main base, exacerbating longstanding tensions among the Lebanese which in 1975 would erupt into full-scale civil war.

In the years that followed the PLO would win Arab and international recognition as the "sole legitimate representative" of the Palestinian people and sought to block any proposed resolution of the Arab–Israeli conflict that did not satisfy Palestinian nationalist aspirations. At the same time, however, the radical edge of the PLO's initial upsurge was gradually blunted as the movement's mainstream moved toward abandoning its goal of replacing Israel with an Arab or a "secular democratic" state in all of what had once been Palestine and instead endorsed the idea of an independent Palestinian state in the West Bank, Gaza and East Jerusalem – about one-quarter of pre-1948 Palestine – that would live alongside, and at peace with, the State of Israel within its 1967 borders.

More generally, despite the rise of the PLO, the establishment in formerly British-ruled South Yemen of an explicitly Marxist regime – the first and only of its kind in the Arab world – and a few short-lived radical upsurges elsewhere in the region, the post-1967 period actually witnessed the decline of the pan-Arabism and radicalism that had seemed so strong a trend over the preceding decade. The defeat of Egypt and Syria in 1967 opened the way for the growing influence of more conservative (and pro-US) regimes and forces in the Arab lands. This shift was signaled by the rise of Saudi Arabia as a political and cultural power across the region (and the wider Muslim world), thanks largely to the enormous oil wealth it could use (with US approval) to buy friends and influence as well as to export its own rather harsh and puritanical but socially and politically conservative – and pro-Western – version of Islam. It was also manifested in the decision of Anwar Sadat, Nasser's successor as president of Egypt, to abandon Nasser's commitment to "Arab socialism" and pan-Arab unity, break with the Soviets, ally his country with the United States, and eventually sign a separate peace treaty with Israel that ignored the Palestinians and the other Arab states.

Moreover, from the later 1970s and down to the present, the main challenges to the Arab regimes would come not from the secular-nationalist left but from movements which argued that (their version of) Islam was the only real and authentic solution to the profound social, economic and cultural problems facing their societies. Nonetheless, despite sometimes violent efforts by such movements to undermine or overthrow them, the Arab regimes in power at the beginning of the 1970s were still largely in place three decades later, a sharp contrast to the 1960s, when Syria and Iraq were plagued by repeated military coups and the Saudi and Jordanian monarchies seemed in imminent peril from Nasserism and other radical nationalist forces.

The emergence of the Palestinians as a central actor in the Arab–Israeli conflict, the radical upsurges of the immediate post-1967 period, and the continuing crises that many countries in the region were experiencing contributed to growing dissatisfaction among at least some American students of the Middle East with the hitherto dominant ways of understanding that region, which seemed increasingly inadequate for making sense of what was going on. At the same time the Vietnam-induced breakdown of the Cold War consensus about the role of the United States in the world also helped open the way for more critical perspectives on US policy in the Middle East, which had hitherto received little attention from the New Left (or the American public) but now began to loom larger.

In 1969, responding to growing opposition to the war in Vietnam and widespread public unwillingness to see US forces dispatched to other Third World trouble spots, President Nixon laid out what would become known as the "Nixon Doctrine." With respect to the Middle East, this new turn in US foreign policy provided that US hegemony in the region (and access to its vast oil reserves) would be preserved not through direct military intervention, which the American public would no longer readily stomach, but through local allies. The two acknowledged "pillars" of the Nixon Doctrine in the Middle East were the shah of Iran, who with US weapons and support was supposed to ensure the status quo in the Persian Gulf, and Saudi Arabia, which though militarily weak had lots of cash (and a degree of Islamic legitimacy) with which to bolster conservative and pro-US governments and political forces. Israel, which had demonstrated its military power in 1967 and with which the United States now began to develop a close "special relationship" manifested in unprecedented levels of military and economic aid and political-strategic coordination, emerged as the unacknowledged third pillar of the Nixon Doctrine. The embrace of Israel as central to the Nixon Doctrine in the Middle East also entailed US opposition to the PLO, which officials in Washington saw as a radical and destabilizing force which was to be marginalized if not destroyed – a stance Israel greatly appreciated, since in those years it adamantly rejected any recognition of Palestinian national rights and was prepared to negotiate only with Arab governments.

Elaborating a critique

One important early vehicle for critical analysis of developments in the Middle East and of US policy in the region coalesced in 1971 as the Middle East Research and Information Project (MERIP). Founded by a diverse group of young people, some of whom had been radicalized by their experiences as Peace Corps volunteers in the Middle East or as anti-Vietnam War activists, MERIP began as a sort of news service providing analysis of current events and popular struggles in the Middle East as well as of US policy to the anti-Vietnam war movement and the broader left in the United States, which was in general completely ignorant about this part of the world. Over the years the collective's bulletin, *MERIP Reports*, evolved into a regular publication, *Middle East Report*, which published analyses of contemporary politics, economics and culture in the region as well as book reviews and occasional critical essays on US Middle East studies.[12]

In 1975 a group of exiled Arab leftists and anti-Zionist Israeli Jews based in Paris began publishing the journal *Khamsin*. Its editors shared, as the introduction to an anthology of articles published in the journal noted, "a common outlook on certain crucial points, such as their radical socialist outlook, their opposition to nationalism as an ideology, their commitment to the struggle against Zionism, their rejection of foreign domination and the oppression of women."[13] *Khamsin* moved to London and began publishing in English in 1978, which gave it greater visibility among English-speaking contributors and readers.

In this same period younger scholars in Britain (where a New Left had also emerged out of elements of the old left and of the student-led movement against the US war in Vietnam) and elsewhere were beginning to publish the first systematic critiques of Orientalism and modernization theory. Among the pioneers in this endeavor was the economic historian Roger Owen, of St. Antony's College, Oxford, who had published his first book, *Cotton and the Egyptian Economy*, in 1969. In 1973 Owen reviewed the recently published two-volume *Cambridge History of Islam* – one of a great many in a series of reference works published by Cambridge University Press over the decades in order to sum up the current scholarly state of knowledge on a particular topic – edited by three of Britain's most distinguished Orientalists (P. M. Holt, A. K. S. Lambton and Bernard Lewis) and comprising chapters by many of the field's most eminent scholars.[14]

Owen's review began by noting that

Islamic studies have always been something of a mystery to those outside the discipline. Based on the knowledge of a number of difficult languages, and focused on the examination of the historical development of a complex religion, they have assumed the character of an esoteric rite in which only a few are skilled enough to take part. They proceed according to their own, often hidden, rules; each new publication is a tactful reminder to the uninitiated that his role is to listen, to wonder, but never to ask questions or to suggest that there might be an alternative way of doing things.

Owen called attention to the near-absence of social and economic history in the two volumes, such that "with one or two exceptions . . . the reader is offered little more than another breathless account of battles, murders, and the rapid rise and fall of different dynasties, with little suggestion that history is more than a chronicle of random events." He went on to depict the *Cambridge History* as a "curiously old-fashioned work, written very much in isolation from methodological advances in other fields," and also noted its focus on the first four or five centuries of Islamic history, so that most chapters "seem to be written on the assumption that nothing of significance took place after the end of their chosen period." More broadly, Owen criticized the book's unexamined adherence to the "universal assumption that Islam is a viable unit of historical study," which he saw as rooted in the nineteenth-century Hegelian vision of human history as the story of the rise and fall of civilizations, each with its own unique essence or spirit. Hence, Owen noted, the contributors' "habit of making easy, confident generalizations about large subjects" and the assumption that "everything that took places in the countries inhabited by Muslims had some essentially 'Islamic' component." Moreover, contributors tended to "see Islamic society as *sui generis* and not, in important ways, like all other non-European societies in Asia and Africa."

If the *Cambridge History of Islam* reflected the "state of the field," Owen concluded, "then 'the state of the field' is not good, and something certainly ought to be done about it." Most centrally, historians would have to question the assumptions that "the basic unit of study remains something called 'Islamic civilization'" and that scholars could "impose an artificial unity upon a world spreading from Morocco to Indonesia, thus making what it is that the societies of this area have in common far outweigh that which divides them," while failing to examine concrete similarities and differences between predominantly Muslim and predominantly non-Muslim societies. That was not to say, Owen insisted, that Islam, defined as a religion, was of no significance; it was simply to say that historians could not assume that Islamic principles shaped everything in the societies in which Islam was prevalent, or that Islam was everywhere and always the same.

The following year Owen presented a paper critiquing Gibb and Bowen's *Islamic Society and the West,* discussed in Chapter 4. Noting that it remained "one of the most important and influential books on the history of the modern Middle East," Owen suggested that it "represents a landmark in Middle Eastern historical writing in that it provides a way by which the traditional methods and presuppositions of the Orientalists can be carried over to structure an examination of the modern period." He went on to note Gibb and Bowen's adoption of the notion of Oriental despotism and their treatment of the Ottoman empire in the eighteenth century as if it were a pristine, isolated, self-contained "Islamic society" still essentially untouched by Western influence, though it was clear that that empire had long been part of, and significantly affected by, evolving transregional economic networks and had also had complex political, social and cultural interactions with other societies for centuries.

Moreover, Owen judged Gibb and Bowen's depictions of this purportedly "Islamic society" (though as noted in Chapter 4, they admitted there was nothing very Islamic about much of it) as undergoing terminal "decline" to be profoundly flawed, since it was rooted in outdated notions about the rise and fall of civilizations and was unsupported by evidence about the actual transformations which this society – like all human societies – constantly experienced. Instead of Gibb and Bowen's unself-critical reliance on the notion of a civilization in decline, which Owen saw as central to Orientalism, he proposed a turn to the methods of political economy which, he believed, could yield a much more detailed, nuanced, complex and accurate understanding of the changes which Ottoman society underwent in the course of the eighteenth and nineteenth centuries.

For critical scholars in Middle East studies as in other fields, the turn to political economy served as a way to criticize and move beyond what they saw as Orientalism's essentialist notion of culture. Instead of assuming that everything important about what Muslims believed and did was attributable to Islam, understood as a timeless essence, these scholars focused on social structures and class relations in specific historical contexts, which tended to highlight the features which predominantly Muslim societies shared with non-Muslim but similarly underdeveloped societies and opened the way for useful comparisons. The critique of Orientalism also entailed an insistence – sometimes explicit, sometimes not – on the primacy of the disciplines (history, political science, sociology, anthropology, and so on), with their specific ways of framing their object of study and their distinctive methodologies and approaches. There was a growing sense that Orientalism as a discipline, in addition to being intellectually isolated, unself-critical and lacking any methodological tools other than an antiquated philology, did not possess the kind of real intellectual foundation that underpinned the humanities and social science disciplines. It was essentially a vestige of an early modern or even medieval way of dividing up the world, and by taking "the Orient" or "Islam" (understood as a distinct and unitary civilization) as its object of study Orientalism actually made it more difficult to attain a proper understanding of the histories, societies, cultures and politics of predominantly Muslim peoples and lands.

As I discussed in Chapter 4, Hamilton Gibb had argued that classically trained Orientalists were needed to bring together and correlate the work of social scientists and others engaged in the area studies enterprise. But many of the critics of the 1970s and after rejected this vision and instead defined themselves first and foremost in terms of their disciplines – as historians, sociologists, anthropologists, political scientists and so on. They argued that as such they were better suited than those who defined themselves as Orientalists to undertake the study of the predominantly Muslim lands, past and present, using more or less the same methods and approaches as their colleagues studying other parts of the world, with due attention to specific local differences. Thus to a considerable extent the "revolt" against Orientalism took the form of an assertion of the superiority of discipline-based approaches and methods over the civilizational paradigm and philological methods now increasingly perceived as the hallmarks of Orientalism.

Roger Owen's influential critique of Gibb and Bowen was presented at a conference held at England's University of Hull in the fall of 1974 which brought together – with some funding from the Libyan government, run by the self-proclaimed revolutionary pan-Arabist Mu'ammar al-Qadhafi – a number of younger scholars to share their critiques of Orientalism and modernization theory. Many of the conference papers, along with a number of others, were published the following year as the first issue of the London-based *Review of Middle East Studies*. Introducing the new journal, Owen and the anthropologist Talal Asad noted that "some of those who write and teach about the Middle East, both in this country and abroad, have become increasingly dissatisfied with the state of Middle East studies. This is not only a reflection of concern at the politically-motivated bias which can be found in much work on the subject, but also at its profound methodological limitations so often characterised by a combination of naïve commonsense and vacuous theorising. Inappropriate concepts are regularly applied; a great deal of writing is simply irrelevant." The aim of the new journal, Asad and Owen asserted, was simply to "encourage the production of theoretically relevant work informed by a critical appreciation of the Middle East and its history."

That first issue of *Review of Middle East Studies* included a range of essays by an assortment of younger scholars and graduate students, mainly from Britain and the United States, criticizing work by some of the most senior social scientists and historians then writing on the Middle East. Two other issues of the journal, published in 1976 and 1978, featured additional sets of brief essays criticizing key works by scholars central to the study of Islam and the Middle East. The introduction of the third volume sought to clarify its mission:

in place of mere generalisations about the political bias and theoretical emptiness of Middle Eastern studies we seek precise evidence of their strengths and weaknesses. Rather than simply offering new modes of understanding Middle Eastern societies, we ask students to consider why, in what ways, and to what extent new modes are necessary. Instead of rejecting or ignoring the considerable body of discourse devoted to the Middle East (including Orientalist discourse) we urge critics to familiarise themselves with it, to question it, and to re-work it.

However, after the third volume appeared the journal went into limbo for a decade; the fourth issue did not appear until 1988 and the whole enterprise wound down in the course of the 1990s. By that time what had at the outset still been small and rather marginal nodes of intellectual dissidence had become much more mainstream, even conventional, in US and British Middle East studies – thanks in no small part to pioneers like those associated with MERIP and the *Review of Middle Eastern Studies*, whose work began to reach and influence wider circles, perhaps especially graduate students and younger scholars, in the mid-1970s.

Only a few examples of the growing body of critical work which became available in this period will be mentioned here. *Anthropology and the Colonial Encounter*, a 1973 volume edited by Talal Asad, included essays by a number of anthropologists criticizing the functionalist school of British social anthropology, particularly its links with colonialism. Among them was a discussion by Asad of two contrasting European images of non-European rule. Functionalist anthropological writings on nineteenth- and twentieth-century Africa, Asad argued, tended to depict African tribal governments as consensual and based on reciprocity while ignoring the impact of colonial domination, whereas Orientalists generally depicted the governments of Islamic states as absolutist and repressive, in keeping with the Oriental despotism model, thereby eliding the complex and changing relations between rulers and ruled.[15]

The following year the Australian sociologist Bryan S. Turner published *Weber and Islam: A Critical Study*, in which he examined Max Weber's highly influential but, he argued, flawed understanding of Muslim societies. Turner showed how (as I discussed in Chapter 3) Weber's concepts of patrimonialism and sultanism were rooted in older notions of Oriental despotism and yielded a depiction of Middle East societies as defective because they lacked the social and psychological attributes supposedly necessary for achieving modernity, including autonomous cities, an independent middle class, and something akin to the "Protestant ethic." Weber saw these attributes as key to the development of capitalism in Europe and their absence as having resulted in the persistent backwardness of Muslim societies. Turner noted the continuing influence of Weber's approach in contemporary modernization theory.[16]

In another book published four years later Turner turned his attention to Karl Marx, to whose analysis of capitalism Weber had sought to offer an alternative. Turner argued that even though much of Marx's analysis of "Asiatic" societies was also rooted in ahistorical and inaccurate notions of Oriental despotism (see Chapter 3), his focus on material forces offered a way of understanding the historical trajectories of predominantly Muslim societies that might avoid the pitfalls of both Orientalism and modernization theory. "The end of Orientalism," Turner concluded,

requires a fundamental attack on the theoretical and epistemological roots of Orientalist scholarship which creates the long tradition of Oriental Despotism, mosaic societies and the "Muslim City." Modern Marxism is fully equipped to do this work of destruction, but in this very activity Marxism displays its own internal theoretical problems and uncovers those analytical cords which tie it to Hegelianism, to nineteenth-century political economy and to Weberian sociology. The end of Orientalism, therefore, also requires the end of certain forms of Marxist thought and the creation of a new type of analysis.[17]

Abdallah Laroui's *The Crisis of the Arab Intellectual*, first published in French, appeared in English in 1976. Laroui criticized the tradition/modernity dichotomy central to modernization theory and still widely deployed in many scholarly analyses of the contemporary Arab world, but also devoted an essay to the Austrian-born Orientalist scholar Gustave von Grunebaum, who as noted in Chapter 4 assumed the directorship of UCLA's Center for Near Eastern Studies in 1957. While expressing respect for von Grunebaum's erudition, Laroui criticized his depiction of Islam as a unitary culture, a closed system whose "essential pattern... must be reproduced in space by the city, in words by the written work, in time by politics, and in eternity by theology." For von Grunebaum as for his fellow Orientalists, Laroui argued, "there is no difference between classical Islam and medieval Islam or simply Islam... There is... only one Islam: an Islam that mutates within itself when tradition takes shape on the basis of a reconstructed 'classical' period. From that time onward the actual succession of facts becomes illusory; examples can be drawn from any period or source whatever..."[18]

Our last example comes from the field of Ottoman studies, in which two young scholars – Huri Islamoglu and Çaglar Keyder – sought to intervene with a 1977 article titled "Agenda for Ottoman History," which appeared in the very first issue of the journal *Review*. This new journal was published by the Fernand Braudel Center for the Study of Economies, Historical Systems and Civilizations, founded the previous year at the State University of New York at Binghamton and named for the great French historian (1902–85) who was a central figure in the school of historical analysis which took its name from its journal, *Annales*.[19] The Braudel Center's founder and guiding spirit was Immanuel Wallerstein, whose 1974 book, best known under the title *The Modern World-System: Capitalist Agriculture and the Origins of the European World-Economy in the Sixteenth Century*, put forward an influential argument about the emergence of a new kind of global capitalist economic system and its differential impact on various regions of the world. Wallerstein's analytical framework shared a great deal with those of André Gunder Frank, Samir Amin and others, but there were also significant and much-debated differences among them. Wallerstein's approach, often referred to as "world-systems theory," had a significant intellectual impact among critical scholars in the mid-1970s, as it gave them an accessible and comprehensive way of understanding the origins and key dynamics of the structurally unequal global political and economic order that continues to prevail in most of the world down to the present day.[20]

In this seminal article, which drew heavily on the work of both Wallerstein and Gunder Frank, Islamoglu and Keyder proposed nothing less than "a new reading (and writing) of Ottoman history," deriving "from certain concepts and theoretical constructions which form the basis of an emerging paradigm in social sciences" and would, they hoped, "provide the conceptual framework in which new research problems may be defined." They began with a critique of Gibb and Bowen, along lines similar to those sketched out by Roger Owen; of Bernard Lewis' *The Emergence of Modern Turkey*, which they saw as rooted in modernization theory; and of what they saw as the prominent Turkish historian Halil Inalcik's idealist interpretation of Ottoman history. In place of these flawed approaches, Islamoglu and Keyder argued for a neo-Marxist interpretation of Ottoman history that deployed the "Asiatic mode of production" as its central analytical category. By analyzing that mode of production and the impact upon it of the Ottoman empire's incorporation into an emerging global capitalist market from the sixteenth century onward, Islamoglu and Keyder sought to highlight what they saw as the dynamics and contradictions of the Ottoman social formation, their consequences for the empire's independence, stability and viability, and the ultimate emergence and dominance of the capitalist mode of production within it.

One other nexus of critical work needs to be mentioned here, as it would soon have the same tremendous impact on Middle East studies as it had on all other area studies fields and disciplines. As mentioned earlier, the late 1960s had witnessed the birth of a new women's movement, and this in turn brought into being the new academic field of women's studies. Feminist activists and scholars – there were many who were both – argued convincingly that most scholarship, partly but by no means exclusively because it had largely been conducted by males, had ignored women as active participants in shaping the social world and proceeded as if they did not exist, except in marginal roles. They insisted that gender should be given as much weight as class and race (shorthand for identities based not only on race but also ethnicity) as an analytical category in the humanities and social sciences; without it scholars were simply ignoring an extremely important dimension of human social, political, cultural and economic life, past and present.

The 1970s thus witnessed a burgeoning of feminist scholarship which sought to put this profound insight to work, producing powerful theoretical interventions and new research in many intellectual domains. Soon enough this trend began to affect the study of the Middle East as well, as mainly younger scholars (most but not all of them women) began to delve into the history and lives of women in the Middle East and the Muslim world and to re-examine much of what had long been accepted in many disciplines as conventional wisdom.

As the critical trend within US Middle East studies gathered steam, its advocates felt the need for some more organized framework, beyond local study groups and personal or informal links. MESA, dominated by social scientists still largely loyal to modernization theory and unwilling to address the field's entanglements with US power in the Middle East and beyond, seemed an inhospitable, if not outright hostile, environment, so in 1977 a loosely-knit group of graduate students and younger scholars, some of them associated with MERIP, formed AMESS, the Alternative Middle East Studies Seminar. AMESS was envisioned less as a full-blown alternative to MESA than as a network which would connect – intellectually, politically and socially – those who saw themselves as part of an insurgent, cutting-edge minority challenging those who dominated the field. AMESS sponsored several small workshops and sporadically published a newsletter over the next few years but then faded away as many of its members and sympathizers secured academic positions and found that they were increasingly able to make a place for themselves within a changing MESA.

Many (but by no means all) of those involved with the emergence of a critical trend within Middle East studies in the United States (and probably Britain as well) saw their intellectual project as inextricably bound up with a political agenda. For them the task of challenging the dominant paradigms in Middle East studies was not understood as a purely scholarly endeavor; it was also linked to a critique of the ways in which the kinds of knowledge this field had produced over the past decades had too often been shaped by, and served, the needs of the United States government as it pursued what many perceived as imperialistic policies in the Middle East. This connection was explicit for those associated with MERIP but was also quite strongly felt by many others in this period. This is manifested quite clearly in books like Fred Halliday's *Arabia Without Sultans*, published in 1975, which argued that Western preoccupation with the 1973 oil crisis and its aftermath, yielding widespread images of filthy-rich "oil sheiks," diverted attention from deeper and potentially explosive political, social and economic tensions in Saudi Arabia, the smaller Persian Gulf states, North and South Yemen, and Iran. Halliday, who went on to a long career teaching international relations at the London School of Economics, adopted an explicitly anti-imperialist and anticapitalist stance in this book, paying particular attention to leftist guerrilla groups which he saw as the vanguard of a "Gulf revolution" challenging local autocracies propped up by Western powers anxious to keep the region's petroleum flowing cheaply.[21]

This same period also saw Arab-Americans, and perhaps especially Palestinian-Americans, becoming increasingly politicized and increasingly vocal about issues of concern to them, within as well as outside Middle East studies. This was due in part to the emergence of the PLO as the voice of Palestinian nationalism in these years, but also to the deepening US relationship with Israel, the 1973 Arab–Israeli war and the Arab oil boycott that followed it, which produced a wave of anti-Arab sentiment in the United States. In the late 1970s the Association of Arab-American University Graduates (AAUG) was formed; it soon began to speak out on controversial issues involving the Arab world and its relations with the United States and in 1979 launched a journal, *Arab Studies Quarterly*. Its editors, Northwestern University political scientist Ibrahim Abu-Lughod and the Columbia University professor of English literature Edward W. Said (about whom I will have much more to say in Chapter 6), saw the journal as "a forum for the study of the Arabs in as wide and as generous a framework as possible . . . not to push a strict ideological line, but to make it possible for the Arabs to be studied without the limitations usually imposed [by Orientalism and Western "experts"] on their actualities."[22] While the AAUG itself would cease to exist in the 1990s, the journal continues to appear.

Arab-Americans and others associated with this tendency often saw themselves as an embattled minority challenging a strongly pro-Israel establishment, in the political arena but also in academic Middle East studies. This too contributed to the increasing politicization of the field, a development that was probably inevitable as it lost its character as something of a (largely white and male) gentlemen's club with taken-for-granted links with policymakers and the government and was instead compelled to confront and somehow respond to new intellectual but also political challenges. Anyway, critics argued, the field had *always* been political: it was just that earlier a widely shared Cold War political consensus had been so pervasive as to be invisible, whereas now real intellectual and political differences, including discordant views about the Israeli–Palestinian conflict and US policy in the Middle East, were being aired (and fought out) in plain view.

The challenge of Islamism

While critical scholars, broadly defined, had by the mid-1970s begun to launch an increasingly effective and comprehensive intellectual assault on both Orientalism and modernization theory, events in the Middle East itself in that period did not always seem to bear out the alternative analyses and political prognoses they put forward any more than they did the analyses and prognoses of adherents of modernization theory. The conservative oil monarchies were able to strengthen their grip on power, thanks in part to the great wealth at their disposal after the post-1973 surge in oil prices. Lebanon, which in the 1950s and much of the 1960s had been hailed by US political scientists as a model of proper modernization, leading to political moderation, secularization and stability, imploded into a vicious and brutal civil war in 1975, with militias based in different Lebanese religious communities battling each other for power and the PLO, Syria and Israel backing different Lebanese factions. This was hardly an example of successful modernization, but it also seemed to show that even in relatively developed Lebanon religious and ethnic identities could trump class loyalties.

As noted earlier, the 1970s also witnessed the rise of Islamic political ideologies and movements in Egypt and other Arab countries, and then the leading role played by Shi'i Muslim clerics, slogans and symbols in the revolutionary coalition that overthrew the despotic regime of the shah of Iran in 1978–79. These developments seemed to manifest the continuing – indeed, growing – salience of Islam as a political ideology in the Middle East. In the West this phenomenon was often referred to as a "resurgence" or "revival" of Islam or as "Islamic fundamentalism," by analogy with the early twentieth-century movement within US Protestantism that rejected liberal theology and demanded a return to the "fundamentals," i.e. a literal interpretation of holy scripture. While the term fundamentalism came to be widely used and even entered Middle Eastern languages, many scholars have preferred a less loaded term – "Islamism" – to denote the ideologies, politics and movements regarded by their adherents as derived from Islam, and I will follow this practice here.

The rise of Islamism was not a development that either liberal modernization theorists or Marxist-influenced critical theorists brandishing political economy as an alternative tool of analysis had foreseen. We can see the influence of the modernization perspective manifested in a 1972 essay on the power of the *'ulama* (the Muslim "clergy") in modern Iran by the UCLA historian Nikki Keddie. "Given the continued growth of government power, and the expansion of the army, the bureaucracy, and of secular education, even in the villages," Keddie concluded,

> it appears probable that the political power of the ulama will continue to decline as it has in the past half century. Although the leaders of the ulama in Iran retain more independent influence on political questions than those in most Muslim countries, they now appear at most able to modify or delay certain government policies and not strongly to influence their basic thrust and direction. Despite the ulama's economic and social conservatism, however, the issues they raise continue to strike a responsive chord among many Iranians.[23]

Fred Halliday's in many ways excellent 1979 book *Iran: Dictatorship and Development* can serve as an example from the Marxist-influenced, explicitly anti-shah and anti-imperialist camp. Written shortly before the outbreak of the Iranian revolution and published before the downfall of the shah's regime and the establishment of the new Islamic Republic of Iran, dominated by Ayatollah Khomeini and his followers, Halliday's book provided a detailed, nuanced, critical analysis of Iranian politics, economy and foreign relations. It was thus a much-needed antidote to the substantial body of literature by American academics who even in the middle and late 1970s were still glossing over the less pleasant aspects of the shah's regime, failing to grasp the depth of popular opposition to it, or both.[24] But it is striking – in retrospect, of course – that even as perceptive an observer as Halliday gave little attention to the potential oppositional role of the Shi'i clergy and foresaw no prospect of their seizing power.

The spread and growing popularity of Islamism as an ideology and a politics – a development which had parallels among Christians, Jews, Hindus and others – seemed to run counter to the teleological vision of historical progress shared by both liberal modernization theory and classical Marxism and traceable back to the Enlightenment era, which posited secularization as the inexorable wave of the future. Middle East scholars would eventually develop very sophisticated ways of making sense of the rise and spread of Islamism.[25] By contrast, the growth of Islamist movements and the outcome of the Iranian revolution posed no intellectual challenge for some Orientalist scholars, since these phenomena only confirmed what they had long believed. Once again Bernard Lewis, some of whose writings on Islam from the 1950s and 1960s I discussed in Chapter 4, provides a good example of the survival, even flourishing, of a view of Islam which, as we have seen, had very old and tenacious roots.

In 1976 Lewis published an article, "The Return of Islam," in *Commentary* magazine, which had begun as a liberal Jewish journal but by the mid-1970s had become the standard-bearer of Jewish "neoconservatism." Adherents of this political camp abandoned traditional liberal-Democratic positions on social policy for more conservative positions while embracing a hard-line stance by Israel (toward the Arabs) and by the United States (toward the Soviet Union).[26] As I will discuss in Chapter 7, in the 1980s and 1990s many American Jewish neoconservatives (but also more traditionally conservative non-Jews) would come to fervently embrace the worldview of the Israeli right, which depicted Islamic fundamentalism and terrorism as the main enemy of both Israel and the West and rejected the "two-state" solution of the Israeli–Palestinian conflict which almost the entire world community (including many Israelis) had by then come to endorse. This helped lay the ideological basis for the Middle East policy pursued by the George W. Bush administration, in which a number of Jewish neoconservatives held important military and foreign policy posts.

One of a series of articles and books Lewis would publish on more or less the same topic over the next two and a half decades, "The Return of Islam" set forth his explanation for the growth of Islamist movements and ideologies in the Arab lands and the wider Muslim world. Lewis began by chiding journalists and others for their "recurring unwillingness to recognize the nature of Islam or even the fact of Islam as an independent, different, and autonomous religious phenomenon . . . " Modern Western man, now secularized, could not grasp that "an entire civilization can have religion as its primary loyalty." To remedy this, two essential points had to be grasped: "One is the universality of religion as a factor in the lives of the Muslim peoples, and the other is its centrality." From the start religion and state had been intertwined in Islam, and that remained the case today. Secular nationalist ideologies had made few real inroads among Muslims, for they never "corresponded to the deeper instincts of the Muslim masses, which found an outlet in programs and organizations of a different kind – led by religious leaders and formulated in religious language and aspiration."

As an example of this Lewis cited the Muslim Brothers, which was founded in Egypt in the late 1920s and grew into a powerful mass movement before being crushed by the Nasser regime in the 1950s. He also noted the use by Yasser Arafat's FATAH movement of Islamic terminology and the persistence of religion-based identities and political alignments elsewhere. As nationalist movements in the Arab world have become genuinely popular, Lewis asserted, so have they become "less national and more religious – in other words, less Arab and more Islamic. In moments of crisis – and these have been many in recent decades – it is the instinctive communal loyalty which outweighs all others." The key point, Lewis insisted, is that "Islam is not conceived as a religion in the limited Western sense but as a community, a loyalty, and a way of life – and that the Islamic community is still recovering from the traumatic era when Muslim governments and empires were overthrown and Muslim peoples forcibly subjected to alien, infidel rule." The "return" of Islam as a political force was thus completely unsurprising: it was for Lewis inherent in the very nature of Islam itself and in Islam's failed encounter with modernity. And as the last line of Lewis' article suggested, it constituted a serious threat to the "Judeo-Christian" West: "Both the Saturday people [i.e. the Jews] and the Sunday people [the Christians] are now suffering the consequences."

Whatever else one may say about him, Bernard Lewis showed remarkable consistency over the decades. This 1976 essay is founded upon the same conception of Islam as a unitary civilization whose basic patterns were set a millennium or more ago and which continues to shape the beliefs and behaviors of Muslims everywhere even today that was central to his 1953 essay "Communism and Islam," discussed in Chapter 4. And as we will see, Lewis would make exactly the same argument into the twenty-first century. For him Islam had always been, and remained, a civilization whose essential characteristics and historical trajectory could be deduced from the texts of the "classical" period and which did not, cannot, really change.

Lewis' assertions in this article (as in his other writings on this topic) are largely free of any serious grounding in the complex and diverse histories of predominantly Muslim lands and consist largely of vague, abstract and broad generalizations. So, for example, the fact that the prophet Muhammad was both the spiritual and the political leader of the early Muslim community is held to determine that even today, almost fifteen centuries later, Muslims cannot accept the Western notion of the separation of religion and state. At the same time, a lot gets left out: for instance, the pervasive enmeshing of Arabs and other Muslim peoples in the institutions, discourses and practices of the modern nation-state means nothing, since nationalism is for Lewis at most a thin and easily shed veneer beneath which there always remains the bedrock identity of Islam. Similarly, the ways in which modern political practices have profoundly shaped the ideologies, organizational forms and modes of collective action of modern Islamist movements are ignored, since they are really nothing new, merely another manifestation of what was always there. And the use of (often radically reinterpreted) religious language and symbols by modern Muslim states and political movements is evidence not of cynicism or ideological poverty or a striving for enhanced legitimacy or just plain old politics, but rather of the unbreakable hold of an unchanging Islam on the minds of its adherents.

In this essay as elsewhere, Lewis apparently felt no need to explain or justify or defend his premises: he simply takes it for granted that Islam and the West are distinct and fundamentally different entities, even though one could easily cite examples of Christians and Jews (whom Lewis implicitly defines as belonging to the West) doing more or less the same kinds of things which Lewis sees as characteristic of Islam. For example, a good many Christians (among them right-wing evangelical Protestants in the United States) abhor the notion of the separation of religion and state, and avowedly secular Zionist Jews vigorously appropriated (and radically reinterpreted) traditional Jewish religious symbols and language in the service of their nationalist project. For Lewis such instances (like the sectarian strife in Northern Ireland, briefly mentioned in this article) are to be explained away as unimportant exceptions to, or deviations from, the secularism and rationality that at bottom characterize Western civilization – meaning that there is a lot about that civilization which we simply have to ignore or wish away.

For Muslims, on the other hand, religious solidarity is deemed to be "instinctive," part of their nature because of the civilization to which they belong, which (among other things) requires us to ignore the fact that Muslims have (like adherents of other faiths) proven ready to fight and kill their coreligionists in the name of the nation-state and for other reasons. There is thus no need to talk about colonialism, underdevelopment, poverty, autocracy, economic dependence, foreign intervention, politics, and so on – the very factors Lewis had defined as "accidental" and largely irrelevant two decades earlier in his analysis of the relationship between communism and Islam.

Whatever their shortcomings as a serious analysis of why Islamist movements were winning widespread support in many predominantly Muslim countries, one can see why Lewis' views won him a wide audience in the United States, especially among neoconservative (and later more traditional right-wing) pundits, politicians and policymakers. Lewis' stature as a scholar lent authority to his pronouncements on contemporary conflicts in the Middle East and the Muslim world, and he knew how to write for a popular audience. His insistence that Arab (and particularly Palestinian) or Muslim claims and grievances against the United States and Israel were not to be taken seriously, because they were at bottom merely irrational expressions of a Muslim collective psyche which had been gravely damaged by its encounter with Western modernity, could be (and were) used to buttress the policy prescriptions of those who were already firmly convinced that the United States should hold fast to its policies in the Middle East, including support for Israel's rejection of Palestinian national rights, Arab opposition notwithstanding.

As I will discuss in Chapter 7, Lewis' understanding of Islamism would by no means go unchallenged. A great many scholars (and others) would seek, from many different standpoints, to study and explain the emergence, spread and significance of Islamist ideologies and movements in the Middle East and the wider Muslim world. In fact, this would be a central issue in Middle East studies in the last quarter of the twentieth century and on into the twenty-first. Debates over how to understand Islam, Islamism and such developments as the creation of an "Islamic republic" in Iran would be lively, even vociferous, as would the question of the extent and character of the challenge such movements and ideologies might pose to the interests in the region of the United States and other Western powers, and how those interests should be defined and defended.

Elaborating alternatives: political economy and gender

As we have seen, by the later 1970s a fairly extensive and well-developed critique of many of the key premises and methods of both an essentialist Orientalism and modernization theory had begun to take root in Middle East studies in the United States and Britain. Initially it was often elaborated by, and influenced, graduate students and relatively younger scholars, but over time it reached wider circles. In addition to this tendency's theoretical, generational and political dimensions, already discussed, there was also a sense that the "old guard" in the field had failed (or was unable) to engage with work by, and develop a meaningful dialogue with, scholars and other intellectuals in the Middle East and elsewhere in the Third World; as a result much of the production of knowledge about the region deemed to be authoritative was being done by Western scholars with little regard for, or interaction with, the work of scholars and intellectuals in the region itself. Critical scholars thus tended to perceive not only the power relations but also the intellectual relations between the West (especially the United States) and the Middle East as unequal and unfair.

The perception that the old order, in the region and in academia, was losing its grip added to the unease already felt by senior scholars in the field about what they perceived as its intellectual shortcomings, isolation and marginality. In his "critical reassessment" of Middle East studies, the first chapter of a volume which grew out of a 1973 conference organized by the Research and Training Committee of the Middle East Studies Association with funding from the Ford Foundation to assess "the state

of the field," the University of Chicago political scientist Leonard Binder
lamented what he saw as the fact that "Middle East studies are beset
by subjective projections, displacements of affect, ideological distortion,
romantic mystification, and religious bias, as well as by a great deal
of incompetent scholarship."[27] Some of the other senior scholars who
surveyed work on the Middle East in their own disciplines seemed to
share Binder's rather negative, or at least uneasy, assessment. And this
was before they began to come under serious fire for what younger critics were coming to see as the grave deficiencies of the theoretical and
methodological approaches their elders and seniors had championed.

As the 1970s worn on, Middle East scholars influenced by the critique
of Orientalism and modernization theory and inspired by the new intellectual currents sweeping across the disciplines and other area studies
fields began producing work that sought to put alternative approaches
into practice. Some of the earliest new work which might be understood
as challenging the dominant research agenda in the field focused on
women. The year 1977 saw the publication of *Middle Eastern Muslim
Women Speak*, an anthology edited by Elizabeth Warnock Fernea and
Basima Qattan Bezirgan which was one of the first major interventions
of its kind. In his foreword Muhsin Mahdi, Jewett Professor of Arabic at
Harvard – the same chair once held by Hamilton Gibb – praised the editors for their "valiant effort to unveil an important dimension of Middle
Eastern history and society, a dimension that has been, for the most part,
hidden from view because of the false notion that the world of Islam is a
world created by men for men rather than the joint creation of men and
women."[28]

A year later *Women in the Muslim World*, edited by Lois Beck and
Nikki Keddie, appeared. Noting that "the serious study of women in the
Third World is still in its infancy, sparked largely, in the West at least, by
movements here for the liberation of women," Beck and Keddie brought
together some of what might be called the "first wave" of scholarship
on women in the Middle East (and the wider Muslim world) by scholars
from a wide range of disciplines.[29] Over the years that followed the output
of scholarly writing on women in the Middle East past and present rose
steadily and replicated in this field the trajectory of women's studies
generally, by moving from women's history to the innovative use of gender
as a category of analysis. Work on women and gender in this region was
characterized by a high level of theoretical sophistication, a readiness to
draw on and engage with theoretical and empirical work on women and
gender in other times and places, and a strong comparative dimension.
It also acknowledged, and often sought to engage in dialogue with, the

work of such pioneering Arab feminist writers and activists as Fatima Mernissi and Nawal al-Saadawi.[30]

The burgeoning of this field led to the creation in the mid-1980s of the Association for Middle East Women's Studies as an affiliate of the Middle East Studies Association. More broadly, women's studies – and women scholars – came to enjoy an increasingly prominent place in the field. This was eventually manifested in the leadership of MESA: while a small number of women had served on its board of directors from the early 1970s onward, beginning with Nikki Keddie, the historian of Iran, in 1971–73, the percentage of female directors increased substantially in the 1980s, and the organization elected its first female president in 1979, in the person of Afaf Lutfi al-Sayyid Marsot, a historian of modern Egypt who taught for many years at the University of California, Los Angeles. But the intellectual impact of women's and gender studies on Middle East studies (as on virtually all other humanities and social science fields) from the later 1970s onward was far greater than these numbers might suggest and contributed greatly to the dramatic transformations this field underwent in this period.

There was, however, also important new work which did not focus on women or gender but was primarily informed by the turn to political economy discussed earlier and by related trends in various disciplines. One of the landmark texts in this genre was Hanna Batatu's 1978 magnum opus *The Old Social Classes and the Revolutionary Movements of Iraq*, some two decades in the making.[31] The book's subtitle effectively conveys its scope: *A Study of Iraq's Old Landed and Commercial Classes and of its Communists, Ba'thists, and Free Officers*, covering the years from the late Ottoman period into the 1970s. Unlike most earlier Western-language studies of Iraq, Batatu made explicit use of class analysis to identify the social forces that had helped shape political struggles in modern Iraq, though his broad and loose definition of class owed as much to James Madison and Max Weber as it did to Karl Marx. A second book which quickly became a classic and which also took class as a key analytical category was Ervand Abrahamian's 1982 *Iran Between Two Revolutions*, a survey of Iranian history from the nineteenth century down to the overthrow of the shah's regime in 1979.[32] The fact that both books treated communist movements in a serious, scholarly fashion also marked a break with the earlier literature on this subject, most of which was not only superficial but reflected US Cold War concerns and attitudes.

Peter Gran's 1978 book *Islamic Roots of Capitalism* can be seen as a less widely acclaimed but nonetheless significant early attempt to provide an alternative to visions of modern Middle East history informed by either modernization theory or Orientalism.[33] Gran, who had been a student of Afaf Lutfi al-Sayyid Marsot at UCLA, rejected the conventional view that Egypt had been not only unconnected to the emerging European-centered world economy before the nineteenth century but also culturally stagnant or in decline. Instead, Gran argued that a mid-eighteenth-century economic boom, fueled by Egypt's links with western Europe, had enriched Cairo's merchant class, which overlapped with segments of the *'ulama*, the men of religion, and that this boom had underpinned the flourishing of specific forms of Islamic knowledge production. Gran thus drew on the work of people like André Gunder Frank, Immanuel Wallerstein and Samir Amin, who insisted that local and regional socioeconomic transformations and structures could not be adequately understood unless they were located in their transregional and global contexts, but he also sought to link social structure and social interests with cultural change by elucidating what he saw as the eighteenth-century roots of capitalist modernity in Egypt.

Gran's book received mixed reviews. There was praise for Gran's effort to show that not all change came from the West and for his insistence on taking indigenous cultural developments (usually expressed in Islamic forms) seriously, as well as for the many important questions that he raised. But some reviewers expressed unhappiness with what they saw as claims and assertions unsupported by sufficient evidence, a heavy-handed linking of economic life and cultural-intellectual production, and alleged misconstruals of Arabic and Islamic terms and concepts. It is fair to say that the book did not have the impact its author hoped for, though in the long run others would develop and more fully substantiate aspects of Gran's research agenda, perhaps especially his commitment to moving beyond the sometimes crude economism of much early political economy work by exploring how social structure, sociopolitical conflicts and cultural production were all interrelated.[34]

Other books, along with articles and reviews, could be cited to support the argument that important changes were already well under way in US Middle East studies in the 1970s, including challenges to long-established intellectual paradigms and the elaboration of new research agendas at first rooted mainly either in feminism and in political economy (and sometimes in both), and then in other approaches as well. Even those who did not enthusiastically embrace, or even welcome, these critiques or adopt the alternative paradigms and methods they offered were nonetheless influenced by these new trends, as well as by the changing climate in their own disciplines and others, manifested in the new and very different kinds of intellectual debates and scholarly conversations that I will explore further in Chapter 6.

These intellectual shifts were also bound up with a changing political climate in the field. The debacle in Vietnam, Watergate and other political scandals, and revelations of the pernicious uses to which scholarly knowledge could be put by the government had reinforced the intellectual and political critiques offered by dissidents, all of which served to erode the once easygoing and close links between academics and policymakers. At the risk of generalizing, it may be said that during the 1970s scholars and academic institutions began to grow more wary about conducting research too closely tailored to fit the agendas of the military or intelligence agencies and about accepting funding that could be seen as compromising their independence and integrity. Over time the once powerful Cold War consensus broke down, and many scholars engaged in Middle East studies, like their counterparts in other area studies fields, came to be increasingly alienated from, or openly critical of, the policies of the United States government toward the part of the world they knew best. Of course, there continued to be some who adhered to the model of the 1950s and 1960s and saw it as their responsibility to use their expertise to serve the foreign policy interests of the United States as defined by the government. But this was less common than it had once been, signaling the emergence of a growing gap between the intellectual concerns but also the political views of many Middle East studies specialists, on the one hand, and the policymakers' vision of the world and the kinds of knowledge they wanted, on the other.

So significant changes were well under way in US Middle East studies by the later 1970s. However, much of what was going on in the field in this period would be eclipsed or subsumed by an intellectual intervention produced by someone based entirely outside of Middle East studies. This intervention – Edward W. Said's book *Orientalism*, published in 1978 – would have a very powerful effect not only on this field but on many others as well, touching off widespread (and often vociferous) debates, opening up new avenues of research, and even helping to spawn entirely new academic fields. It is to Said's book, responses to it, and its intellectual and other consequences that I turn in the next chapter.

6 Said's *Orientalism*: a book and its aftermath

Edward W. Said (pronounced "Sah-eed") was born in Jerusalem, then the capital of British-ruled Palestine, in 1935, but spent most of his childhood in Cairo, where his father ran a successful stationery and office supplies business. Said's family returned to live in Jerusalem in 1947 but, like hundreds of thousands of other Palestinians, was soon compelled to leave by the outbreak of Arab–Jewish fighting that followed the United Nations' decision to partition the country into separate Arab and Jewish states. Said went back to school in Cairo and then on to secondary school and college in the United States, graduating from Princeton University in 1957. He pursued graduate studies in English literature at Harvard University, receiving his doctorate in 1964. He had begun teaching at Columbia University the previous year, and over the decades that followed he would ascend through the academic ranks at Columbia to become University Professor of English and Comparative Literature. In September 2003, Edward W. Said finally succumbed to leukemia, the disease he had been battling for over a decade.[1]

Said's first book, on the Polish-born writer Joseph Conrad, was followed in 1975 by *Beginnings*, a literary study that also manifested Said's growing political engagement. For Said as for many Palestinians and other Arabs, the Arab defeat in 1967 and Israel's conquest of the remainder of Palestine had come as a profound shock. Said gradually moved toward a much stronger embrace of his identity as a Palestinian as well as toward political activism. He began to speak out and write on behalf of Palestinian national rights and aspirations, now articulated by the newly invigorated Palestine Liberation Organization which was in these same years winning Arab and international recognition as the only legitimate representative of the Palestinian people (see Chapter 5). In the process Said emerged as a leading advocate of the Palestinian cause in the United States and Europe. In 1977 he (like his friend and colleague Ibrahim Abu-Lughod) was elected as an independent to the PLO's parliament, the Palestine National Council. He resigned from the PNC in 1991, because of illness but also because he had grown increasingly critical of what he saw as the errors and failures of the Palestinian leadership. By that time Said had achieved global recognition as one of the pre-eminent literary scholars of his generation.

Said's deepening political engagement in the 1970s led him to criticize the ways in which Arabs and Muslims were often depicted in the Western media – for example, as filthy-rich oil sheiks or as terrorists – and then to a more scholarly analysis of the Western study and images of, as well as policies toward, Islam and the Middle East. Three major books (along with numerous articles, essays, lectures and op-ed pieces) came out of this phase of Said's work. I will discuss the first, *Orientalism*, published in 1978, in some detail. The second, *The Question of Palestine*, came out in 1979 and was a critical study of the traumatic dispossession, subordination and ongoing suppression which the Palestinians had experienced at the hands of Zionism and Israel. The third book in this series was *Covering Islam: How the Media and the Experts Determine How We See the Rest of the World*, published in 1981, which reiterated some of the key themes of *Orientalism* while addressing what Said saw as distorted and pernicious US media coverage of the Iranian revolution of 1978–1979 and its aftermath, and of the threat which Islam allegedly posed to the United States.

It would be difficult to exaggerate the intellectual impact of Said's *Orientalism*. As I discussed in Chapter 5, critiques of Orientalism were already in circulation and beginning to make a difference in US and British Middle East studies (and elsewhere as well) even before the publication of Said's *Orientalism*. But that book reached a much wider audience within and beyond academia, aroused a great deal of controversy and, translated into many languages, stimulated scholars across a range of fields and disciplines to rethink what they were doing and grapple with new intellectual problems in innovative ways. One observer who was critical of much of the book nonetheless accurately characterized its impact on both literary studies and Middle East studies as "electrifying," while a leading historian of the modern Middle East called the book a "bombshell."[2] However, as I will discuss toward the end of this chapter, *Orientalism*, and the controversies and trends it generated, tended to obscure the fact that a substantive and wide-ranging critique of Orientalism had already begun to be elaborated before its publication, largely from a political-economy perspective, which ended up being rather marginalized.

Orientalism is a long, complex and sometimes difficult book, and it is therefore not easy to summarize in a way that does it justice. It could be, and was, read in different ways by different audiences, but one important way in which it operated was as a polemic – that is, a work whose goal is to critically examine and demolish some other opinion, viewpoint or doctrine. The target of *Orientalism* was of course Orientalism, which Said began by defining very broadly as not merely an academic discipline but as "a style of thought based on an ontological and epistemological distinction between 'the Orient' and (most of the time) 'the Occident.'"[3] That is, for Said Orientalism denoted the entire way of thinking which based itself on the dichotomization of the Orient – for his purposes, the "world of Islam" – and the West as two distinct and fundamentally different civilizations or entities, and which therefore posited that to study the East one could not use the same approaches and methods one might use to study the West.

In addition to the academic and the "imaginative" meanings of Orientalism which were based on the dichotomization of East and West, Said argued that from the late eighteenth century onward one could identify a third meaning: "Orientalism can be discussed and analyzed as the corporate institution for dealing with the Orient – dealing with it by making statements about it, authorizing views of it, describing it, by teaching it, settling it, ruling over it: in short, Orientalism as a Western style for dominating, restructuring, and having authority over the Orient."[4] For Said Orientalism thus denoted all the texts, institutions, images, imaginings and attitudes through which Europeans (and later Americans) had created and perpetuated a certain image or "representation" of "the Orient," a representation that had little to do with what the parts of the world so depicted were actually like.

The Foucault connection

In defining Orientalism so broadly and in analyzing it as he did, Said drew on concepts and methods developed by the French thinker Michel Foucault (1926–1984), whose work was important in the emergence of the philosophy or mode of thought known as "poststructuralism" (sometimes also referred to as "postmodernism"), first in France and then elsewhere, in the 1960s and after.[5] Foucault's wide-ranging, complex and often elusive work focused on the relationship between knowledge and power. Foucault rejected the Enlightenment assumption that human beings, divested of the blinders of ignorance and superstition and equipped with the proper ("scientific") concepts and methods, could grasp reality as it really was, could produce objectively true knowledge of the world. Instead, he argued, what we take to be truth is in fact always really the product of a certain way of depicting or representing reality, of a certain "discourse" – a structured system of meaning which shapes what we perceive, think and do.

Put very crudely, a discourse might be likened to a pair of eyeglasses we unconsciously wear which acts as a filter that determines how what we take to be reality looks like to us, what we see (or do not see) and how we see it, foregrounding certain things and rendering other things invisible and determining what the things we do perceive mean to us. However, for Foucault there was no reality "out there" that we are perceiving through these imaginary eyeglasses, or at least none that we can gain access to, rendering moot the whole issue of how to achieve objective truth. A discourse, a particular "way of seeing," was not a *mis*representation, a false or distorted perception of reality, because no truth, no "accurate" representation of what really exists was possible in the Enlightenment sense of objective knowledge of reality. There were only alternative representations, different discourses, each of which had its own (usually implicit, unacknowledged and unexamined) premises, its own claims to truth, its own rules and conventions, and each of which in effect created the very object it purported to be studying.

For Foucault a discourse was therefore not (as with our eyeglass metaphor) something that stands between the "real world" and the knowing human subject, the purportedly autonomous, more or less rational and highly individual self we take ourselves to be. Indeed, for Foucault our own strongly held conviction that we are autonomous and rational and possess our own distinctive "self" was itself the *product* of certain modern discourses. These included the discourses which generated the new nineteenth-century sciences of psychology and psychiatry, which took as their object of study "the mind," a radically new way of conceptualizing and categorizing what people are and how they think, feel and act, along with the practices and institutions which those new disciplines generated. So even the very ways in which we conceive of ourselves come not from some sacrosanct and autonomous place deep within us which we like to think of as the very core of our personality, largely free from external influence or control. Rather, who and what we are is not only shaped or influenced but produced, *constituted*, by socially prevalent systems of meaning, that is by discourse.

Along similar lines Foucault argued that "society" is not an entity which had any "real" existence prior to or independent of the way it came to be represented in the new late nineteenth-century discipline of sociology. It was produced as an object of analysis in and by sociological discourse, which presumed that societies operate in accordance with certain regularities and rules and elaborated certain principles, approaches and methods for understanding them. And so on for a whole range of modern forms of knowledge and their associated institutions, premises and methods, which emerged out of discourses that specified certain objects of study and how they could be understood. Much of Foucault's work explored the emergence of new discourses, and the institutions to which they gave birth, in the modern era.

However, Foucault did not see specific forms of knowledge, that is discourses or "regimes of truth," as emerging out of nowhere. He insisted that their emergence and dissemination were always bound up with, indeed produced by, power. Foucault rejected the liberal Enlightenment view that power was something held or exercised by states, rulers or institutions, and thus always a repressive or negative force which could be excluded from a potentially widening sphere of human freedom or could be absent from the very core of our beings. Rather, he saw power as an inherent feature of all human social relations, and moreover as productive: it was in the matrices of the power relations that permeated social relations that discourses, practices and institutions were generated, including even our own subjective sense of ourselves, rooted in the modern notion that we are largely autonomous, self-governing, rational individuals.

Foucault used the Panopticon – a new kind of prison envisioned by the English philosopher Jeremy Bentham in which all the prisoners could be constantly observed by the guards, who could not themselves be seen – as a metaphor for the new kind of power that he saw as having structured a host of institutions, disciplines and practices from the nineteenth century onward, as well as the discourses which gave them meaning. These included the penitentiary, the hospital, the mental hospital, the school and the social sciences as well as new modes of classifying and governing populations, with their attendant technologies of control which operated not so much through the threat or infliction of physical punishment as by inculcating new notions and modes of human personality and behavior. Foucault argued that like the prisoners in the Panopticon, who must act as if they are always being observed, modern people have been "disciplined" in new ways by modern forms of knowledge and power, even in what we like to think are our basic conceptions of who we are, our most private thoughts and feelings, and our intimate relations.[6]

Orientalism as a discourse

For Said, Orientalism was very much a discourse in the sense Foucault used that term: a specific form of knowledge, with its own object of study ("the Orient"), premises, rules, conventions and claims to truth. Orientalism as a form of knowledge simultaneously was produced by, and perpetuated, certain power relations, in this case the power which Western states and authoritative individuals exercised (or sought to exercise) over the Orient. There was no objectively existing Orient; that entity, Said argued, came into being with a specific meaning for Europeans (and later other Westerners) through the very operation of the discourse of Orientalism, which defined its object in a certain way, produced widely accepted "truths" about it, and thereby made a certain representation of it appear real. Seeing Orientalism as a discourse in this sense, Said argued, enabled one to

understand the enormously systematic discipline by which European culture was able to manage – and even produce – the Orient politically, sociologically, militarily, ideologically, scientifically, and imaginatively during the post-Enlightenment era. Moreover, so authoritative a position did Orientalism have that I believe that no one writing, thinking, or acting on the Orient could do so without taking account of the limitations on thought and action inspired by Orientalism. (p. 3)

At the same time, and just as importantly, Orientalism served as a "collective notion identifying 'us' Europeans as against all 'those' non-Europeans, and indeed it can be argued that the major component in European culture is precisely what made that culture hegemonic both in and outside Europe: the idea of European identity as a superior one in comparison with all the non-European peoples and cultures" (p. 7). Orientalism for Said was thus not primarily about ignorance, prejudice, bias or racism on the part of individual scholars, officials or writers, though as he showed there was plenty of that to go around. It was fundamentally about partaking of a representation of the Orient that assumed that it was ontologically – that is, in its very being or essential nature – radically different from (and usually inferior to) "our" own Western world, a stance that could be (and was) adopted even by those who were unprejudiced or even sympathetic to Arabs, Muslims, Islam and so on, or indeed by "Orientals" or Muslims themselves.

This was not to say, Said continued, that "Orientalism unilaterally determines what can be said about the Orient, but that it is the whole network of interests inevitably brought to bear on (and therefore always involved in) any occasion when that peculiar entity 'the Orient' is in question" (p. 3). And unlike Foucault, Said insisted on the "determining imprint of individual authors upon the otherwise anonymous collective body of texts constituting a discursive formation like Orientalism" (p. 23). Nonetheless, Said argued that the linkage between European power and Orientalism as a form of knowledge could be discerned in virtually every text on the Orient produced in Europe and the United States:

For if it is true that no production of knowledge in the human sciences can ever ignore or disclaim its author's involvement as a human subject in his own circumstances, then it must also be true that for a European or American studying the Orient there can be no disclaiming the main circumstances of *his* actuality: that he comes up against the Orient as a European or American first, as an individual second. And to be a European or an American in such a situation is by no means an inert fact. It meant and means being aware, however dimly, that one belongs to a power with definite interests in the Orient, and more important, that one belongs to a part of the earth with a definite history of involvement in the Orient almost since the time of Homer. (p. 11)

In the chapters that followed Said ranged very widely, surveying European representations of the Orient from the ancient Greek playwright Aeschylus' depiction of the Persians to medieval Christian views of Islam, to the Enlightenment, to nineteenth-century thinkers like Karl Marx and Ernest Renan and colonial officials like Cromer (discussed in Chapter 3 of this book), and to Hamilton Gibb (discussed in Chapter 4). Along the way he devoted close attention to the ways in which several influential nineteenth-century French writers who had traveled in Muslim lands, among them Chateaubriand, Nerval and Flaubert, had depicted the Orient and Orientals. But for the most part Said chose to ignore nineteenth-century German Orientalist scholarship, on the ground that the main contours of Orientalist discourse could be adequately delineated from an exploration of texts produced by British, French and later American writers, scholars and officials.

As an academic tradition but also through the writings and doings of Western travelers, scientists, authors, artists, officials, pilgrims and others, Said argued, Orientalism emerged as a coherent discourse, a system of Western knowledge about the Orient that was pervasive, powerful and durable, despite having little to do with what actually went on in the part of the world designated by Westerners as the Orient. This Western representation of the Orient was predicated on the assumption that "East" and "West" were radically and irreducibly different, and (using primarily philological methods) drew on presumably authoritative texts to produce and sustain certain ideas about the Orient, among them Oriental despotism and Oriental sensuality. Moreover, Said insisted, the contours of Orientalist discourse were profoundly shaped by a Western will to dominate the Orient, finally realized with the colonial conquests of the nineteenth and twentieth centuries.

In fact the book's final section, "Orientalism Now," addressed the ways in which, from the late nineteenth century down to the present, Orientalism had been (and, Said argued, remained) a form of knowledge which authorized and justified the assertion of Western power over the predominantly Arab and Muslim lands of Western Asia and North Africa. Here too Said ranged widely, from Rudyard Kipling to T. E. Lawrence to various French and British scholars of Islam. In a final chapter, "The

Latest Phase," Said discussed the ways in which "the Arab Muslim" had recently become "a figure in American popular culture" and of particular interest to business circles and policymakers (p. 285). Since the 1973 war and the Arab oil boycott that accompanied it, Said went on, the Arab had come to appear as "something more menacing" – the leering, mustachioed oil sheik with stereotypical "semitic" features, "the disrupter of Israel's and the West's existence," and so on.[7] Said castigated what he saw as the persistence of central elements of classical Orientalism in contemporary scholarship, citing Abdallah Laroui's critique of Gustave von Grunebaum and echoing Roger Owen's critique of the *Cambridge History of Islam* (see Chapter 5), along with examples of what he saw as racist or otherwise distorted academic and popular depictions of Arabs and Muslims and of Islam. He devoted particular attention to Bernard Lewis, for his essay "The Return of Islam" (also discussed in Chapter 5) and for other work which Said deemed polemical, tendentious and grossly inaccurate – as well as constituting prime examples of the persistence of the most pernicious forms of Orientalism.

Said concluded by posing the question of whether there were any alternatives available to what he saw as a still powerful Orientalist discourse, now linked with US involvement in, and imperial designs on, the Middle East. In response he mentioned some of the critical projects of the 1970s discussed in the previous chapter and went on to insist that he continued to believe "that there is scholarship that is not as corrupt, or at least as blind to human reality, as the kind I have been mainly depicting."

Today there are many individual scholars working in such fields as Islamic history, religion, civilization, sociology, and anthropology whose production is deeply valuable as scholarship. The trouble sets in when the guild tradition of Orientalism takes over the scholar who is not vigilant, whose individual consciousness as a scholar is not on guard against *idées reçues* [received ideas] all too easily handed down in the profession . . . [Even] scholars and critics who are trained in the traditional Orientalist disciplines are perfectly capable of freeing themselves from the old ideological straitjacket. (p. 326)

Scholars had to be self-aware and self-critical, Said insisted, and begin to address the questions which he saw as central to his project in *Orientalism*:

How does one *represent* other cultures? What is *another* culture? Is the notion of a distinct culture (or race, or religion, or civilization) a useful one, or does it always get involved either in self-congratulation (when one discusses one's own) or hostility and aggression (when one discusses the "other")? . . . How do ideas acquire authority, "normality," and even the status of "natural" truth? What is the role of the intellectual? What importance must he give to an independent critical consciousness, an *oppositional* critical consciousness? (pp. 325–326)

The answer to Orientalism was not Occidentalism, Said concluded, which would be just as essentializing. "If the knowledge of Orientalism has any meaning, it is in being a reminder of the seductive degradation of knowledge, of any knowledge, anywhere, at any time. Now perhaps more than ever" (p. 328).

Bernard Lewis responds

There is much more to *Orientalism*, which many regard as one of the most influential scholarly books published in English in the humanities in the last quarter of the twentieth century. Perhaps the best way to enter into an appraisal of the book and its intellectual significance is by discussing some of the responses to it. I will begin with one of its chief targets, Bernard Lewis, who not surprisingly vehemently rejected Said's analysis of Orientalism without really engaging with the substance of Said's critique.

In an essay on the "The Question of Orientalism," published in *The New York Review of Books* in June 1982, four years after the appearance of *Orientalism*, Lewis claimed that Said and other critics of Orientalism had accused all those scholars who studied Islam and the Middle East of engaging in a "deep and evil conspiracy" in the service of Western domination.[8] Such attacks on Orientalism were not really new, according to Lewis: he rather insinuatingly mentioned an earlier "outbreak," allegedly inspired by Nazi-linked antisemitism, originating in Pakistan in the mid-1950s, as well as Anouar Abdel-Malek's critique (discussed at the beginning of Chapter 5), which Lewis deemed to have remained "within the limits of scholarly debate." Recently, however, Arabs motivated primarily by their ideological opposition to Zionism and Israel and/or by an allegiance to Marxism had initiated a series of crude and intemperate polemical assaults on Orientalism, and among these Edward Said was the leading culprit.

Lewis accused Said of launching reckless and grossly inaccurate attacks, often couched in violent language replete with sexual overtones, on respectable scholars and scholarship. Said was moreover arbitrary in his choice of targets, ignoring major scholars and studies and focusing on marginal figures and unimportant texts, and he was also guilty of neglecting or maligning Arab scholarship while treating the admittedly crude utterances of colonial officials like Cromer on a par with scholarly Orientalist writing. This was, Lewis suggested, because Said knew little or nothing about the scholars and field he presumed to criticize, which led him to ignore very important German and Soviet Orientalists and commit egregious errors of fact. More broadly, Lewis argued, the claim that "Orientalists were seeking knowledge of Oriental peoples in order to dominate them, most of them being directly or, as Abdel-Malek allows, objectively (in the Marxist sense) in the service of imperialism," was "absurdly inadequate."

Some Orientalists, Lewis acknowledged, may have "served or profited from imperial domination," but the European study of Islam and the Arabs began centuries before the age of European expansion and colonialism, and that study flourished in countries (like Germany) which never exercised domination over Arabs. "The Orientalists are not immune," Lewis asserted, to the dangers of bias, "stereotypes and facile generalizations; nor are their accusers. The former at least have the advantage of some concern for intellectual precision and discipline." Said's baseless critique had focused on the "putative attitudes, motives, and purposes" of Orientalist scholars while ignoring their actual scholarly writings; in fact, Lewis concluded, "the most rigorous and penetrating critique of Orientalist scholarship has always been and will remain that of the Orientalists themselves."

Said responded in kind in the pages of the same journal two months later – at the height, it is worth noting, of Israel's invasion of Lebanon, as its army was bombarding besieged Beirut and tempers were running very high on all sides.[9] "Insouciant, outrageous, arbitrary, false, absurd, astonishing, reckless – these are some of the words Bernard Lewis uses to characterize what he interprets me as saying in *Orientalism* (1978) . . . Lewis's verbosity scarcely conceals both the ideological underpinnings of his position and his extraordinary capacity for getting everything wrong." Said asserted that Lewis had attacked him by "suppressing or distorting the truth and by innuendo, methods to which he adds that veneer of omniscient tranquil authority which he supposes is the way scholars talk."

Said insisted that he had never said that "Orientalism is a conspiracy" or that "'the West' is evil . . . On the other hand it is rank hypocrisy to suppress the cultural, political, ideological, and institutional contexts in which people write, think, and talk about the Orient, whether they are scholars or not." Said continued:

And I believe that it is extremely important to understand the fact that the reason why Orientalism is opposed by so many thoughtful Arabs and Muslims is that its modern discourse is correctly perceived as a discourse of power. In this discourse, based mainly upon the assumption that Islam is monolithic and unchanging and therefore marketable by "experts" for powerful domestic political interests, neither Muslims nor Arabs recognize themselves as human beings or their observers as simple scholars.

Lewis' defense of Orientalism was, Said went on, "an act of breathtaking bad faith, since as I shall show, more than most Orientalists he has been [not the objective, politically disinterested scholar he presented himself as but rather] a passionate political partisan against Arab causes in such places as the US Congress, *Commentary*, and elsewhere." Lewis was, for example, a "frequent visitor to Washington where his testimony before the likes of Senator Henry Jackson mixes standard Cold War bellicosity with fervent recommendations to give Israel more, and still more, arms – presumably so that it may go on improving the lot of Muslims and Arabs who fall within the range of its artillery and airpower."

Lewis' next response to Said added little of value to the exchange. "It is difficult to argue with a scream of rage," Lewis began, and he concluded by asserting that while the question of how societies perceive each other was of profound significance, "[t]he tragedy of Mr. Said's *Orientalism* is that it takes a genuine problem of real importance, and reduces it to the level of political polemic and personal abuse." At its 1986 annual meeting, held in Boston, the Middle East Studies Association featured a debate between Said and Lewis, each of whom was (in the manner of an old-fashioned duel) accompanied by a "second." But while the event may have been good theater, it did not yield much useful elucidation of the intellectual issues at stake. Lewis was apparently never able to grasp (or cogently address) Said's treatment of Orientalism's defects as the product of its character as a systematic (and power-laden) discourse, rather than as a problem stemming from error, bias, stereotyping, racism, evil-mindedness or imperialist inclinations on the part of individual scholars. Nor could Lewis accept Said's premise that, like all human endeavors, Orientalist scholarship was at the very least partially shaped by the contexts within which it was conducted and thus that it was not hermetically sealed off from wider cultural attitudes about, and political engagements with, Islam and the Muslim world, for centuries Europe's (often threatening) "other" and an ongoing "problem" for the United States. This left the two with little or no common ground on which to conduct a useful debate, had they even wanted to.

Critical engagements

Said's critique of Orientalism generated a large number of more complex, nuanced and interesting responses, of which I will discuss only a few in order to convey something of the range of reactions to the book and of its intellectual impact.

For its review of *Orientalism*, *The New York Times Book Review* turned to J. H. Plumb, professor of history at Cambridge University and an authority on eighteenth-century England.[10] "There is a profoundly interesting concept in this book," Plumb wrote, "and underneath the self-posturing verbiage there is an acute analytical mind at work, but the book, unfortunately, is almost impossible to read." Plumb actually agreed with much of what Said had to say and asserted that "there is much in this book that is superb as well as intellectually exciting... The fundamental concept that one society's view of another's culture may be used, like an interpretation of the past, to sanctify its own institutions and political aggression is a very fruitful one that could be applied, and should be, to other constellations of nationalist or racist thought." But Plumb complained that the book was "so pretentiously written, so drenched in jargon."

It is perhaps not surprising that Plumb, an older, rather mainstream historian, was put off by Said's heavy recourse to contemporary European theory (especially Foucault) as well as by the dense, allusive and sometimes elusive mode of writing not uncommon in literary studies but often seen by historians as unnecessarily convoluted and impenetrable. More broadly, while a good many historians – especially those who studied parts of the world outside the West – saw *Orientalism* as a work of major intellectual importance and were prepared to accept much or all of its central thrust, there was also unease with what some saw as the book's sometimes extravagant language, sweeping arguments, heavy focus on literary texts, and insufficient interest in carefully situating individuals, texts and institutions in their historical contexts.[11]

One of the key reviews of *Orientalism* from within US Middle East studies was written by Malcolm H. Kerr (1931–1984) and published in 1980 in the field's leading scholarly journal, the *International Journal of Middle East Studies*.[12] Kerr's parents taught at the American University of Beirut for many years, so Kerr spent much of his childhood and youth in Lebanon. He studied international relations at Princeton under Philip Hitti and received his Ph.D. in that subject from Johns Hopkins University, though he wrote his dissertation largely under the guidance of Hamilton Gibb of Harvard (see Chapter 4). Kerr spent twenty years teaching at UCLA but returned often to the Arab world, and in 1982 he assumed the presidency of his beloved American University of Beirut. He was assassinated outside his campus office by radical Islamist gunmen two years later.

Kerr described *Orientalism* as "a book that in principle needed to be written, and for which the author possessed rich material. In the end, however, the effort misfired."

The book contains many excellent sections and scores many telling points, but it is spoiled by overzealous prosecutorial argument in which Professor Said, in his eagerness to spin too large a web, leaps at conclusions and tries to throw everything but the kitchen sink into a preconceived frame of analysis. In charging the entire tradition of European and American Oriental studies with the sins of reductionism and caricature, he commits precisely the same error.

Said had demonstrated convincingly that many French and British writers, travelers and scholars had depicted the Middle East in an essentialist and derogatory fashion; but then, Kerr went on, he "turns from an imaginative critic to a relentless polemicist," assuming what he purports to demonstrate and forgoing the opportunity to test his claims by examining the work of Orientalist scholars who were neither French nor British. Said's sample of US-based scholars was unrepresentative, Kerr argued, and had he "looked further afield he would have gotten quite different results," including a great deal of work which manifested "consistent *resistance* to the themes of denigration and caricaturization of Eastern peoples of which Said complains." Middle East studies in the United States had its shortcomings and prejudices, Kerr acknowledged; but "whether it is the Western tradition of Orientalist scholarship that is primarily to blame – in fact, whether that tradition has, in the net, really contributed to the problem – is another question." Said's claim that "whatever the individual goodwill of the scholars, they are all prisoners of the establishment" and guilty of "propagating the old racist myths of European Orientalism in order to further the cause of Western imperial domination of the East" is at best "a preconceived argument, and a highly debatable one."

Maxime Rodinson, the French Marxist scholar whom we encountered at the beginning of Chapter 5 and whom Said himself cited approvingly as a scholar who had been trained as an Orientalist but had nonetheless produced important and honest scholarly work, assessed *Orientalism* along somewhat similar lines.[13] Rodinson acknowledged that there were "many valuable ideas" in Said's book: "Its great merit, to my mind, was to shake the self-satisfaction of many Orientalists, to appeal to them (with questionable success) to consider the sources and the connections of their ideas, to cease to see them as a natural, unprejudiced conclusion of the facts, studied without any presumptions." Unlike Lewis, Rodinson understood what Said was trying to get at by examining Orientalism as a coherent, systematic discourse. But he also noted what he found problematic in Said's critique:

[Said's] militant stand leads him repeatedly to make excessive statements. This problem is accentuated because as a specialist of English and comparative literature, he is inadequately versed in the practical work of the Orientalists. It is too easy to choose, as he does, only English and French Orientalists as a target. By so doing, he takes aim only at representatives of huge colonial empires. But there was an Orientalism before the empires, and the pioneers of Orientalism were often subjects of other European countries, some without colonies. Much too often, Said falls into the same traps we old Communists fell into some forty years ago [i.e., of being excessively polemical, partisan and schematic] . . . The growth of Orientalism was linked to the colonial expansion of Europe in a much more subtle and intricate way than he imagines. Moreover, his nationalistic tendencies have prevented him from considering, among others, the studies of Chinese or Indian civilization, which are ordinarily regarded as part of the field of Orientalism . . . even Arab nations in the West receive less than their due in his interpretation.

The Oxford historian of the modern Middle East Albert Hourani, discussed at the beginning of Chapter 5, shared much of Rodinson's appraisal of *Orientalism*, as did Roger Owen, a historian of the modern Middle East who as we also saw in that chapter had been among the early critics of Orientalism and a champion of political economy as an alternative approach.[14] In an early review of the book Owen offered strong praise for Said's critique of Orientalism. But like Rodinson, Hourani and others, Owen lamented the fact that Said had ignored German and other European scholars and suggested that Said's exploration of Orientalism was sometimes overly broad and lacked nuance and subtlety. Owen also rejected Said's embrace of a Foucauldian (or poststructuralist) approach: "if we cannot make any connection between such studies [of the Middle East] and the reality they are supposed to describe, there is no way of showing how they have changed as a result of changing Middle Eastern (and not just European) circumstances. Nor is it possible to suggest how they might be improved in the future." Owen further faulted Said for a lack of interest in how the study of the Middle East could be made better. "It is not a question of first destroying the old and then rebuilding the new. The old contains material and concepts which need to be examined, to be challenged, and in some cases to be reconstructed, in terms of a science of society which transcends national boundaries and in the use of which everyone, Middle Eastern or European or American, can share." For Owen (as for the sociologist Bryan Turner somewhat earlier), that "science of society" was some variant of political economy, which left him unhappy with Said's relentless focus in *Orientalism* on how Western cultures represented the Orient, hence on images, texts, ideas and discourses, rather than on economic, social and political structures, relations, interests and conflicts.

In an important 1981 essay titled "Orientalism and Orientalism in Reverse," the noted Syrian philosopher Sadik Jalal al-ʿAzm addressed what he saw as the strengths and weaknesses of Said's *Orientalism* from a perspective that, like Rodinson's and Owen's, was influenced by Marxism.[15] Writing in the journal *Khamsin*, which as I explained in Chapter 5 had emerged in the 1970s as a forum for a group of exiled Middle Eastern left-wing intellectuals, al-'Azm suggested that Said had used Orientalism in two distinct senses: Institutional Orientalism, by which al-'Azm meant the whole set of institutions, ideologies, beliefs, images and texts linked to European expansion, and Cultural-Academic Orientalism, by which al-'Azm meant "a developing tradition of disciplined learning whose main function is to 'scientifically research' the Orient."

Al-'Azm agreed that Said had very usefully devoted the bulk of his book to deflating the latter's "self-righteous" claims to impartiality and truth, "its racist assumptions, barely camouflaged mercenary interests, reductionistic explanations and anti-human prejudices," and to demonstrating its links to Institutional Orientalism. And Said had quite accurately shown that both forms of Orientalism shared a "deep-rooted belief. . . that a fundamental ontological difference exists between the essential natures of the Orient and the Occident, to the decisive advantage of the latter. Western societies, cultures, languages and mentalities are supposed to be essentially and inherently superior to the Eastern ones."

However, al-'Azm went on, "the stylist and polemicist in Edward Said very often runs away with the systematic thinker."

In an act of retrospective historical projection we find Said tracing the origins of Orientalism all the way back to Homer, Aeschylus, Euripides and Dante. In other words, Orientalism is not really a thoroughly modern phenomenon, as we thought earlier, but is the natural product of an ancient and almost irresistible European bent of mind to misrepresent the realities of other cultures, peoples, and their languages, in favor of Occidental self-affirmation, domination and ascendancy. Here the author seems to be saying that the "European mind," from Homer to Karl Marx and H. A. R. Gibb, is inherently bent on distorting all human realities other than its own for the sake of its own aggrandisement.

This way of construing the origins of Orientalism, al-'Azm argued, drew on the same essentializing dichotomy between East and West, and the same monolithic and static conception of culture, which Said saw as central to Orientalism and set out to demolish. It made much more sense, al-'Azm argued, to treat both forms of Orientalism as modern phenomena rather than as pervasive in some timeless, monolithic and inevitably essentialized "Western culture" since its very inception. Al-'Azm also found problematic what he saw as Said's implication that it was Orientalism as a deeply rooted Western cultural tradition which was the real source of Western political interest in the Orient. As al-'Azm understood him, Said seemed to be arguing (implicitly or explicitly) that it was Cultural-Academic Orientalism which had given rise to Institutional Orientalism. "One cannot escape the impression," al-'Azm went on, "that for Said somehow the emergence of such observers, administrators and invaders of the Orient as Napoleon, Cromer and Balfour was made inevitable by [Cultural-Academic] 'Orientalism', and that the political orientations, careers and ambitions of these figures are better understood by reference to [the Enlightenment thinker] d'Herbelot and Dante than to more immediately relevant and mundane [political, strategic and economic] interests."

Al-'Azm also found troubling Said's suggestion that the Orient was essentially a representation, a projection by the West, and that all representations of one culture by another are inevitably misrepresentations. If as Said says "the Orient studied by Orientalism is no more than an image and a representation in the mind and culture of the Occident . . . then it is also true that the Occident in doing so is behaving perfectly naturally and in accordance with the general rule – as stated by Said himself – governing the [inevitably distorting] dynamics of the reception of one culture by another." Moreover, al-'Azm argued, Said's criticism of Gibb and others for making broad declarative statements about the character of the Orient, Islam, etc. was misplaced. The problem was not that all these assertions were entirely wrong, for they often contained some grain of truth; the problem was that they were overly broad, grossly ahistorical, did not allow for the possibility of change, and were often linked to ongoing European efforts to dominate the Orient.

On this same ground al-'Azm defended Karl Marx against Said's depiction of him as "no exception to all the Europeans who dealt with the East in terms of Orientalism's basic category of the inequality between East and West." Al-'Azm insisted that the contrary was true: "there is nothing specific to either Asia or the Orient in Marx's broad theoretical interpretations of the past, present and future . . . Marx, like anyone else, knew of the superiority of modern Europe over the Orient. But to accuse a radically historicist thinker like Marx of turning this contingent [i.e. temporary] fact into a necessary reality for all time [as did the Orientalists] is simply absurd."

In concluding, al-'Azm reiterated his appreciation of Said's forceful critique of the assumption – central to Orientalism – that the differences between "Islamic cultures and societies on the one hand and European ones on the other are neither a matter of complex processes in the historical evolution of humanity nor a matter of empirical facts to be acknowledged and dealt with accordingly" but rather "a matter of emanations from a certain enduring Oriental (or Islamic) cultural, psychic or racial essence, as the case may be, bearing identifiable fundamental unchanging attributes." However, al-'Azm warned, some in the Arab and Muslim lands had succumbed to what he called "Orientalism in Reverse," which accepted the basic dichotomy between East and West but insisted that it was the East (or Islam) which was superior to the corrupt, decadent, materialistic West. He had in mind (among others) Islamists who rejected secularism, nationalism, Marxism, democracy, etc. as alien Western imports and insisted that only (their interpretation of) Islam was authentic and could solve the political, economic, social and cultural problems facing their societies. For the Islamists as for Hamilton Gibb and Bernard Lewis, Islam was always Islam, an essence with a single, unchanging meaning, except that whereas the latter saw Islam as defective, inferior and in decline, the former saw it as perfect and perceived the West as spiritually and morally inferior. "Ontological Orientalism in Reverse," al-'Azm concluded, "is, in the end, no less reactionary, mystifying, ahistorical and anti-human than Ontological Orientalism proper."

A less balanced and more stridently negative assessment of *Orientalism* came from the Indian Marxist literary scholar Aijaz Ahmad. In an essay published in 1992, Ahmad acknowledged that Said was one of the most significant cultural critics writing in the English language and that his own thought had long been deeply engaged with, and influenced by, Said's.[16] He also expressed deep admiration for Said's courage in risking his standing as a scholar, and even his life in the face of death threats, by speaking out as a Palestinian critical not only of Zionism but also of various Palestinian and Arab leaders and policies. Nonetheless, Ahmad proclaimed himself in fundamental disagreement with Said. Like others, Ahmad criticized what he saw as Said's theoretical and methodological inconsistencies and eclecticism as well as his implication that there was a more or less continuous Western tradition or discourse of Orientalism stretching from the ancient Greeks down to the present, a claim that Ahmad deemed both un-Foucauldian (since Foucault rejected such long-term continuities) and ahistorical. Moreover, Ahmad complained that *Orientalism*

examines the history of Western textualities about the non-West quite in isolation from how these textualities might have been received, accepted, modified, challenged, overthrown or reproduced by the intelligentsias of the colonized countries: not as an undifferentiated mass but as situated social agents impelled by our own conflicts, contradictions, distinct social and political locations of class, gender, religious affiliation, and so on... the only voices we encounter in the book are precisely those of the very Western canonicity which, Said complains, has always silenced the Orient. Who is silencing whom, who is refusing to permit a historicized encounter between the voice of the so-called "Orientalist" and the many voices that "Orientalism" is said so utterly to suppress, is a question that is very hard to determine as we read this book.

Like al-ʿAzm, Ahmad felt that Said had not only essentialized the West but implied that the Western assertion of power over the Orient had its roots in a basically literary Orientalism, thereby ignoring other more material causes and factors. And also like al-ʿAzm, Ahmad was unhappy with Said's apparent rejection (following Foucault) of the possibility of true statements, of accurate representation. This led, Ahmad claimed, both to a form of irrationalism which had had pernicious intellectual but also political effects and to pandering to "the most sentimental, the most extreme forms of Third-Worldist nationalism." By not only jettisoning but trying to discredit Marxism as unredeemably corrupted by Orientalism, and by blaming colonialism not only for "its own cruelties but, conveniently enough, for ours too," like communalism, tribalism and the caste system, Said's critique of Orientalism had, Ahmad charged, helped "upwardly mobile professionals" from Third World countries immigrating to the West develop "narratives of oppression that would get them preferential treatment . . . " All in all, Ahmad put forward a harsh critique not only of *Orientalism* but of Said's work and intellectual stances more generally.

In a widely cited essay on *Orientalism* published in his 1988 book *The Predicament of Culture*, the anthropologist James Clifford offered a more appreciative (though by no means uncritical) appraisal of Said's book from a non-Marxist perspective.[17] Clifford began by suggesting that Said's work could usefully be seen as part of an effort to understand how "European knowledge about the rest of the planet [has] been shaped by a Western will to power," an effort he traced back to the Martinique poet Aimé Cesaire and the *négritude* movement he helped launch in the late 1930s. The "objects" of the Western gaze, the colonized peoples who had been observed and studied (and dominated) by Westerners, had begun to assert their political but also cultural independence and "write back," demanding and making room for their own perspectives, histories and visions and offering an anticolonial "alternative humanism."

Clifford went on to explore the ambivalences which he felt informed much of Said's argument: between seeing the Orient as a mental construct produced by Orientalism and treating it as a real (if misrepresented) place; between accepting and rejecting the possibility that true knowledge about the Orient, its peoples and their histories is attainable; and between a commitment to a rigorous Foucauldian discourse analysis and a humanist appreciation for individual authors and texts. Clifford pointed out that *Orientalism* was "a pioneering attempt to use Foucault systematically in an extended cultural analysis," developing it to "include ways in which a cultural order is defined externally, with respect to exotic 'others.'"

Clifford defended Said's much-criticized decision to ignore the German Orientalists. "If Said's primary aim were to write an intellectual history of Orientalism or a history of Western ideas of the Orient, his narrowing and rather obviously tendentious shaping of the field could be taken as a fatal flaw." But that was not his goal, and so even if his "genealogy" of Orientalism "sometimes appears clumsily rigged," "one need not reject the entire critical paradigm." In part, Clifford argued, the problem lay in Said's effort to derive Orientalism as a discourse, in Foucault's sense, from his inventory of Orientalism as a tradition, relying heavily on a survey of literary and scholarly texts. In so doing, and by focusing on individual authors rather than on the underlying discourse which from a Foucauldian perspective would be seen as structuring what they wrote, Said not only "relapses into traditional intellectual history" but also "gives himself too easy a target."

Nonetheless, Clifford concluded, "though Said's work frequently relapses into the essentializing modes it attacks and is ambivalently enmeshed in the totalizing habits of Western humanism, it still succeeds in questioning a number of important anthropological categories, most important, perhaps, the concept of culture." Indeed, the effect of his argument is "not so much to undermine the notion of a substantial Orient as it is to make problematic 'the Occident.'" Said's work thus contributes to, and furthers, the effort to move beyond "casual [and largely unquestioned] references to 'the West,' 'Western culture,' and so on" and examine concretely the ways in which "the West" came to be constituted as a category in relation to various "others," including Muslims, other "exotic" cultures, fictions of the primitive, and so on.

Clifford saw Said's own background as importantly related to his own "complex critical posture." "A Palestinian nationalist educated in Egypt and the United States, a scholar deeply imbued with the European humanities... Said writes as an 'oriental,' but only to dissolve the category. He writes as a Palestinian but takes no support from a specifically Palestinian culture or identity, turning to European poets for his expression of essential values and to French philosophy for his analytical tools. A radical critic of a major component of the Western cultural tradition, Said derives most of his standards from that tradition." Said's complex location is not "aberrant," Clifford insisted; the "unrestful predicament of *Orientalism*, its methodological ambivalences, are characteristic of an increasingly general global experience," and in that sense we can see Said's idealistic commitment to humanism as "a political response to the present age in which, as [Joseph] Conrad wrote, 'we are camped like bewildered travelers in a garish, unrestful hotel.' It is the virtue of *Orientalism* that it obliges its readers to confront such issues at once personally, theoretically, and politically."

Edward Said shared his own thoughts on the critical reception of *Orientalism* and on the tasks facing left-wing intellectuals in a 1985 essay titled "Orientalism Reconsidered."[18] He noted what he saw as "a remarkable unwillingness to discuss the problem of Orientalism in the political or ethical or even epistemological contexts proper to it. This is as true of professional literary critics who have written about my book as it is of course of the Orientalists themselves." Yet nothing, Said insisted, "not even a simple descriptive label, is beyond or outside the realm of interpretation," to be taken as "plain fact" or absolute truth. He went on to acknowledge earlier critiques of Orientalism, by Anouar Abdel-Malek and Talal Asad among others (see Chapter 5), who had received little attention in his book, and to attack the unregenerate Bernard Lewis as well as Daniel Pipes, a younger right-wing writer on the Middle East and Islam whom I will discuss in Chapter 7.

Said also praised recent efforts, by scholars as well as writers and activists in many parts of the world, to "dissolve" and "decenter" dominant and oppressive forms of knowledge and move beyond them to new and potentially liberatory approaches. He envisioned these disparate efforts, addressing many different issues and diverse audiences, as part of a common endeavor that was "consciously secular, marginal and oppositional" and sought "the end of dominating, coercive systems of knowledge." However, he warned against the danger of "possessive exclusivism," for example the claims that "only women can write for and about women, and only literature that treats women or Orientals well is good literature . . . [or that] only Marxists, anti-Orientalists, feminists can write about economics, Orientalism, women's literature." The emancipatory intellectual project Said envisioned called for "greater crossing of boundaries, for greater interventionism in cross-disciplinary activity, a concentrated awareness of the situation – political, methodological, social, historical – in which intellectual and cultural work is carried out . . . Lastly, a much sharpened sense of the intellectual's role both in the defining of a context and in changing it, for without that, I believe, the critique of Orientalism is simply an ephemeral pastime."

Poststructuralism and the "linguistic turn"

As James Clifford and others noted, and as I discussed earlier, one of the distinctive features of Said's *Orientalism* was the way in which it drew on the thought and methods of Michel Foucault. Foucault's own work had focused exclusively on the European origins and character of the modern Western "episteme" – the field or space within which knowledge had been constructed along certain lines. By applying elements of Foucault's approach to Western representations of a part of the "non-West" and by insisting that "the West" itself took shape in relation to what came to be defined as the "non-West," Said thus used Foucault's approach to chart very new intellectual terrain. In so doing *Orientalism* contributed significantly to the dissemination of elements of French poststructuralist thought in American academia, a development that had already been under way in literary studies but which gathered much more momentum, and affected a broader range of fields and disciplines, in the course of the 1980s.

In the years just before his death in 1984, Foucault's ideas, and perhaps even more his terminology, began to gain widespread currency among academic scholars in the humanities in the United States. Of course, a great many scholars and other intellectuals explicitly and vigorously rejected Foucault and other forms of poststructuralist thought on various grounds, political as well as intellectual, and many others displayed no interest in them. Nonetheless, the "invasion" of French theory in various forms in the 1970s and 1980s certainly stimulated vigorous intellectual debates and important developments in many fields.

For our purposes here, perhaps the most significant of these was the paradigm shift – often referred to as the "linguistic turn" – embraced by significant numbers of scholars in a broad range of disciplines and fields, a shift which drew on poststructuralism but had other sources and influences as well. It was rooted in the view that language – by which was meant any coherent and structured meaning-bearing system, from actual human languages to social customs to mainstream economics to Marxism to Orientalism to biology – provided the best metaphor for society and social relations. Language in this sense was not conceived simply, as one scholar put it, as "a medium, relatively or potentially transparent, for the representation or expression of a reality outside itself" – a form expressing an essential or "real" content outside itself. Instead, language was to be seen in more or less the same way Foucault had used the term discourse,

as a self-contained system of "signs" whose meanings are determined by their relations to each other, rather than by their relation to some "transcendental" or extralinguistic object or subject . . . Such a commitment would seem to imply that language not only shapes experienced reality but constitutes it, that different languages create different, discontinuous, and incommensurable worlds, that the creation of meaning is impersonal, operating "behind the backs" of language users whose linguistic actions can merely exemplify the rules and procedures of languages they inhabit but do not control, that all specialized language usages in a culture (scientific, poetic, philosophical, historical) are similarly determined by and constitutive of their putative objects.[19]

For those who embraced the linguistic turn most fully – and scholars engaged with it in a wide variety of ways – the task of scholarship was thus *not* to determine how these systems of meaning, these discourses, which governed what people did and how they understood who they were, did or did not accurately reflect or represent some "underlying" reality, social structure, historical process or fixed identity. In fact, poststructuralism insisted, no access was possible to reality as such, and hence philosophy's traditional quest for absolute, objective truth was a waste of time. We can only seek to understand the myriad ways in which human beings have made meaning for themselves, i.e. the systems of representation they have produced and which govern their lives, and these cannot be directly linked to, or explained as simple products or reflections of, social location or some essentialized identity or any overarching historical process or logic or social structure outside of discourse. The proper task of scholars was therefore to study those nexuses of knowledge and power in which we are all enmeshed, indeed which make us what we are, and to explore how these very systems created various representations of "reality" as they are understood and lived by human beings whose "subjectivity" was itself the product of those discourses.

This meant, among other things, abandoning the idea of "experience" as denoting what human beings purportedly learn from their encounters with the real world, since there were no such encounters that were not already and always mediated, structured, filtered by some discourse. What an individual or group "learned" from some "experience" – for example, of exploitation or oppression – depended crucially on the discourse which structured how that experience was made sense of. More broadly, a rigorous application of poststructuralism entailed rejecting all approaches to understanding the world which presume the existence of a objectively existing "real world" whose features and dynamics gave rise to the representations through which human beings make sense of who they are and what they are doing.

To put it slightly differently, poststructuralism rejected all philosophical, theoretical and historical approaches which assumed the existence of some "real" essence or foundation from which representations were derived and as reflections of which they could be adequately explained. This meant abandoning key elements of Marxist thought, most variants of which posit material factors, and the class conflict they produce, as the driving force in historical change and assume that one's relationship to ownership of the means of production, or more broadly one's location in an objectively existing social structure, will ultimately determine one's consciousness and behavior. But it also meant abandoning liberal theory, which seeks to preserve (and possibly extend) a realm of freedom purportedly outside the purview of power; modernization theory, which imputes a teleology to human social evolution; and so on. And of course any approach which posited that human beings possess a fixed or innate identity, individual or collective, was deemed essentialistic or "foundational" and was therefore to be rejected.

This is not to say that a committed poststructuralist would not scurry out of the way of a speeding car, as if she or he rejected the reality of that vehicle and its ability to hurt or kill him or her. It is rather to say that she or he would deem it a waste of time to devote a lot of attention to the philosophical question of whether the car objectively existed and whether our faculties enabled us to perceive it accurately or as it really was. The more interesting and important questions concerned the systems of meaning in which human beings were enmeshed and which structured what they took to be reality and governed their ideas, feelings, practices and institutions.[20]

Scholars who specialized in Middle East literature may well have begun to draw on European modes of literary analysis informed by one or another strand of poststructuralist thought earlier, but it is fair to say that it was Timothy Mitchell's 1988 book *Colonising Egypt* which most dramatically introduced poststructuralism into Middle East studies. Most older scholarly work on modern Egyptian history had understood Egypt's colonization to have begun with that country's occupation by British forces in 1882 and the imposition of an informal protectorate; more recent work influenced by political economy had tended to highlight the ways in which Egypt's integration into a Europe-centered world market during the nineteenth century had led to the British occupation. Mitchell used the term "colonizing" very differently: he understood it as the process whereby more or less the same new regime of power and knowledge whose emergence Foucault had explored in western Europe unfolded in nineteenth- and early twentieth-century Egypt. This process was manifested in new institutions (including a modern army, new public schools and hospitals, model villages for peasants, and the reconfiguration of urban space), new discourses (among them the moral reform and social uplift of the lower classes, new conceptions of political authority, and eventually Egyptian nationalism) and new practices (such as new modes of writing, learning and sociability). Mitchell also drew on the work of the French philosopher Jacques Derrida to argue that this process was crucially bound up with the elaboration of what he saw as a uniquely modern opposition between "reality" and its representation, which underpinned this new system of truth and order in Egypt as it had elsewhere.

Many scholarly reviewers hailed Mitchell's book as original, important and challenging, even if they did not agree with everything in it.[21] As one of the earliest attempts to explore how Foucault and Derrida might be used to understand non-Western histories and societies, *Colonising Egypt* was widely read and cited well beyond Middle East studies and facilitated the engagement of scholars in this and other fields with poststructuralism. At the same time, the new way of understanding modern Egyptian history which Mitchell proposed was drawn upon and developed in various ways.[22]

Colonial discourse and postcolonial theory

Even though, as we have seen, Said's *Orientalism* played a significant role in introducing elements of Foucault's thought to an American academic audience, it is nonetheless important to emphasize (as many of his critics pointed out) that in this book Said's embrace of Foucault was always partial and ambivalent. He acknowledged the influence of other thinkers, for example the English Marxist cultural critic Raymond Williams (1921–88) and the Italian Marxist theorist Antonio Gramsci (1891–1937), whose concept of "hegemony" Said drew on to explain the strength and durability of Orientalism – though as several critics noted, in *Orientalism* Gramsci was largely overshadowed by Foucault, and the two thinkers' approaches are in any case theoretically inconsistent, if not incompatible.

In the years that followed the publication of *Orientalism* Said tended to distance himself from poststructuralism's rather stark and bleak view of the human condition and of hope for a better world, instead embracing a more humanistic position that sustained human agency, active political engagement and the possibility of noncoercive, nondominating kinds of knowledge. For example, in an influential 1982 essay, "Traveling Theory," Said criticized what he characterized as Foucault's "overblown" conception of power and praised the insistence of the linguist (and political activist) Noam Chomsky on not only opposing repression and injustice in the present but also continuing to insist on the possibility of a more just future society – a utopian impulse that was absent from Foucault's vision of the world.[23]

Said's pioneering effort to understand Europe's encounter with the rest of the world by focusing on the question of representation, on the discourse(s) which shaped how Westerners perceived the non-West (and thus themselves as well), helped stimulate the development of two important new domains of scholarly inquiry. One of these revolved around the study of "colonial discourse" – what the editors of an important collection of writings on the subject defined as "the variety of textual forms in which the West produced and codified knowledge about non-metropolitan areas and cultures, especially those under colonial control."[24] Inspired in large measure by Said's analysis of the knowledge/power nexus at the heart of Orientalism, a host of scholars began to explore the ways in which European (and later American) scholars, travelers, officials and others had perceived the non-Western peoples and cultures over whom Western power was increasingly being exerted during the colonial era and after, leading to a veritable explosion of innovative work.

One could cite endless examples of scholarly work on colonial discourse from the 1980s onward, dealing with many parts of the world. Here I will mention only Peter Hulme's *Colonial Encounters: Europe and the Native Caribbean, 1492–1797*, whose focus is evident from its title, as well as work on India by such scholars as Ronald B. Inden and Bernard Cohn. In a 1986 article and then at much greater length in a 1990 book, *Imagining India*, Inden drew on Said's understanding of Orientalism as an apparatus by which Westerners had produced a certain representation of the Orient to show how, going back to the eighteenth century, Western Indologists had constructed a highly distorted image of Indian society that depicted caste as its central institution. For his part Cohn examined (among other things) the key role which British colonial censuses played in producing new ways of classifying India's population and in strengthening British control over it.[25]

Along the way scholars involved in the study of colonial discourse increasingly came to refine their analyses and incorporate new elements into them, building on Said's general approach but also rendering it more complex, nuanced and concrete in various ways. For one, there was a growing insistence that one could not look simply at what Westerners thought, said and did about the non-Westerners over whom they exercised power. A proper understanding of the "colonial encounter" also required attention to the ways in which colonial discourse, as well as the practices and institutions of colonial rule, were themselves profoundly shaped by what non-Western colonial subjects thought, said and did. By extension, just as colonized societies were profoundly affected by the imposition of foreign rule, so were the colonizers and their societies profoundly affected by empire, in ways that had rarely received much attention. Just as one could not really make sense of the elaboration of the notion of the West without taking proper account of the ways in which that notion had been profoundly shaped by the interactions which those who would come to see themselves as Westerners had with those who would come to be defined as non-Westerners, so the relations between colonized and colonizers had to be seen as always complex, contradictory and reciprocal.

To give just a few examples: Uday Mehta offered a new understanding of eighteenth- and nineteenth-century British liberalism by exploring the ways in which this purportedly universalistic ideology nonetheless justified the denial of political rights to certain categories of people, particularly colonial subjects in India. Susan Thorne challenged the downplaying of the significance of empire in conventional historical accounts of nineteenth-century England by examining how concepts of race and class intersected and helped shape each other, among other ways through the work of foreign and domestic evangelical Christian missions. Ann Laura Stoler argued that evolving definitions of national and racial identity in European countries were the product not only of contestation in the metropole but also crucially involved the proper categorization of European and "mixed-blood" populations in the colonies as well.[26] Numerous other scholars elucidated the ways in which the colonized were not mute victims but actively participated in shaping the modern world, through various forms of resistance to colonialism but also by selectively appropriating and recasting elements of European and colonial discourse and deploying them in unexpected ways. As two leading scholars of colonialism articulated the premises underpinning this approach: "[T]hinking about empire as much as the daily efforts to manage it were deeply affected in every dimension by the actions of the 'colonized,'" such that one had to question "the very dualism that divided colonizer from colonized" and explore "the processes by which they were mutually shaped in intimate engagement, attraction, and opposition."[27] Work in this emerging field was often distinguished by its interdisciplinarity and its strongly comparative character, with scholars feeling free to cross conventional intellectual boundaries to forge innovative theoretical concepts and research methods and to engage in wide-ranging scholarly conversations across the disciplines.

Edward Said himself would delve further into one key aspect of the complex and reciprocal relationship between "the West" and "the rest" in his 1993 book *Culture and Imperialism*.[28] We tend to assume, Said suggested, that "colonial undertakings were marginal and perhaps even eccentric to the central activities of the great metropolitan cultures." In fact, Said insisted, empire was central to modern European culture, and one could not make sense of that culture without taking it into account. Scholars of European literature thus had to locate the works they studied in relation to the broader historical contexts which had helped shape them. So, for example, a key chapter of *Culture and Imperialism* argued that a fuller understanding of a novel like Jane Austen's *Mansfield Park*, first published in 1814, required critical awareness of the fact that it was colonial slavery which produced the wealth that made possible the social

world Austen depicted – a reality only partially and indirectly acknowledged in the text itself yet central to it. The point was not to belittle
Austen as a writer or diminish the importance of her novels; it was rather
to encourage a deeper awareness of the links between the nineteenth- and
twentieth-century European novel (and European culture more broadly)
and contemporary European colonialism and imperialism. Building on
and extending the argument he had made in *Orientalism* fifteen years
earlier, Said thus demanded that scholars not treat the West and the rest
of the world as if they were separate worlds, each with its own distinctive
essence and historical trajectory, but instead explore the ways in which
they had powerfully influenced – indeed, constituted – each other in the
modern era.

As the study of colonialism flourished in the years that followed the
publication of *Orientalism*, scholars exploring domains first charted by
Said further developed, and inevitably modified, his approach in other
important ways. For example, perspicacious readers will have noted that
gender was not a central concern of *Orientalism*, though Said had certainly
pointed out how the Orient and Orientals were often not only eroticized
but also depicted as effeminate, weak and passive, in contrast with a West
portrayed as active, powerful and male, and he had also discussed various
writers' depictions of Oriental women. Yet *Orientalism* appeared just as
feminist theory, women's studies and the study of gender were beginning
to dramatically transform American academia, a trend that would gather
strength in the decades that followed. Increasingly, scholars engaged in
the study of colonialism would use gender as a key category of analysis,
which had the effect of rendering the critique of Orientalism much more
nuanced and complex.

A good part of the new work on women and gender in the Middle East
and the wider Muslim world discussed in Chapter 5 enriched colonial
discourse analysis in just this way. One relatively early example is the
Algerian writer Malek Alloula's 1986 book *The Colonial Harem*, which
creatively examined the ways in which (often lewd) picture postcards of
Algerian women sent by French settlers in or visitors to Algeria early in
the twentieth century manifested prevailing European ideas and fantasies
about these women and the lives they supposedly lived in the "harem."
Similarly, Sarah Graham-Brown's 1988 *Images of Women: The Portrayal
of Women in Photography of the Middle East 1860–1950* built on, but also
extended, Said's critique of Orientalism by exploring how the new technology of photography affected the depiction of Middle Eastern women.

Inevitably, some of the new feminist work on women and gender challenged aspects of Said's approach. Billie Melman, in her 1992 *Women's
Orients: English Women and the Middle East, 1718–1918*, lamented the

fact that women had been largely omitted from studies of Orientalism and imperialism, including Said's.[29] Her research into travel writing on the Middle East by English women in the eighteenth and nineteenth centuries convinced her that "Europe's attitude towards the Orient was neither unified nor monolithic. Nor did it progress (or regress) linearly. Nor did it necessarily derive from a binary vision sharply dividing the world into asymmetrical oppositions: male–female; West–East; white–nonwhite and Christian–Muslim, nor from that universal propensity to 'think in pairs.'" Rather, Melman argued, alongside the dominant, male, Orientalist and imperialist vision of the Middle East Said had accurately described, there developed an alternative view, found in many of the writings by women travelers, which often challenged "middle-class gender-ideology," led to "self-criticism rather than cultural smugness" and sometimes even produced "identification with the other that cut across the barriers of religion, culture and ethnicity."

In the preface to her book's second edition, Melman explicitly criticized Said for his "gender-blindness" in *Orientalism*. Happily, she went on, the ways in which "the colonies and the colonial experience constituted the gendered British identity and the experience of women and men, mainly of the middle classes," were now coming to be central to studies of Western society during the age of empire, even as "students of the colonial experience now begin to realise how useful the historical category of gender is to our comprehension of that central experience and its changing representations." Melman insisted that "Western knowledge of and knowledge about the Orient was not monolithic or systematically constructed; that there was not one and totalising view of the West's cultural other," as Said had seemed to suggest in *Orientalism*.

This line of argument was echoed by others, among them the literary scholar Lisa Lowe, who argued that "Orientalism is not a single developmental tradition but is profoundly heterogeneous," the product of many different (and sometimes discordant) discourses intersecting and interacting, leading to complexities and contradictions. Similarly, in his study of the reception of "Oriental" influences in nineteenth-century European culture, the British historian John MacKenzie criticized what he saw as the simplistic binary oppositions characteristic of the Saidian critique of Orientalism, which had thereby committed "that most fundamental of all historical sins, the reading back of contemporary attitudes and prejudices into historical periods." "The approach to the eastern Other can only be fully understood through a recognition of the complexity of the range of Others which constituted at once both threat and potential liberation [for the arts in Europe]." MacKenzie argued that "a fascination with Orientalism was as likely to be [politically as well as culturally] oppositional as consensual in relation to established power structures, a promoter of a ferment in ideas as in artistic innovation... It is difficult to discover in any of the arts at whatever period sets of clearly delineated binary oppositions, sharp distinctions between the moral Self and the depraved Other... In reality, Orientalism was endlessly protean, as often consumed by admiration and reverence as by denigration and depreciation."[30]

However one judges the various critiques, revisions, and elaborations of Said's original approach, it is clear that from the 1980s onward there was an explosion of innovative scholarly work – and vigorous debates – on colonialism and empire, in the metropole as well as in the colonies. This flourishing and strongly interdisciplinary field was increasingly characterized by the use of gender, along with class and race, as key analytical categories and by increasingly sophisticated work that sought to transcend simple binary oppositions and trace the mutually formative interactions which shaped many of the contours of the world we still live in today.[31]

This brings us to the second of the two domains of scholarly inquiry to which, as I suggested at the beginning of this section, Said's *Orientalism* had helped give birth and for which it was a central text. This was "postcolonial theory" or "postcolonial studies," which also emerged as a distinct intellectual enterprise in the 1980s and overlapped with (and for some even subsumed) colonial discourse analysis. It was (and remains) less a coherent, clearly defined theoretical position with a well-defined research agenda than an intellectual stance with a loosely knit set of interests, concerns and questions.

Postcolonial theory sought to develop intellectual tools that could be used to make sense of the world as it had evolved since the end of formal colonial rule – hence the "post" in its name – though it insisted on due attention to the enduring legacies of colonialism as well. However, as Leela Gandhi put it, while "postcolonialism has taken its place with theories such as poststructuralism, psychoanalysis and feminism as a major critical discourse in the humanities" and "has generated an enormous corpus of specialised academic writing... 'postcolonialism' itself remains a diffuse and nebulous term." While, Gandhi argued, postcolonial studies had "enabled a complex interdisciplinary dialogue within the humanities, its uneasy incorporation of mutually antagonistic theories – such as Marxism and poststructuralism – confounds any uniformity of approach. As a consequence, there is little consensus regarding the proper content, scope and relevance of postcolonial studies."[32]

Robert Young, the author of a recent book on postcolonial studies, described its intellectual aims this way:

First, investigating the extent to which not only European history but also European culture and knowledge was part of, and instrumental in, the practice of colonization and its continuing aftermath. Second, identifying fully the means and causes of continuing international deprivation and exploitation, and analysing their epistemological and psychological effects. Third, transforming those epistemologies into new forms of cultural and political production that operate outside the protocols of metropolitan traditions and enable successful resistance to, and transformation of, the degradation and material injustice to which disempowered peoples and societies remain subjected.[33]

Since this field is only tangentially related to the main themes of this book, I will not elaborate further, except to note once again that Said's *Orientalism* contributed significantly to the burgeoning of postcolonial theory, providing additional evidence of the tremendous intellectual impact of that work across the humanities.

Before concluding, it is important to reiterate one other important intellectual consequence of the focus on representation to which Said's *Orientalism* contributed so significantly. As I discussed in Chapter 5, much of the critique of Orientalism which had developed in the 1970s, *before* the publication of Said's book, was predicated on the belief that it was indeed possible to produce accurate knowledge of the Middle East and the Muslim world. This accurate knowledge – which, it was hoped, would not serve the interests of Western power over the region – was to be attained by using the analytical tools of political economy, thereby eschewing the cultural essentialism that characterized much of Orientalism and the simplistic teleology that characterized modernization theory. This meant giving explanatory primacy to such things as social structure, the local, regional and global dynamics of capitalist development, and political and social struggles in their historical contexts, rather than to questions of culture.

While Said was certainly aware of the critical work under way before *Orientalism*, he was in that book centrally focused on the question of representation, of how societies perceive and depict themselves and one another. And although this may not have been his intention, many read him as not only depicting Marx himself as an Orientalist but also as rejecting Marxian modes of historical explanation and social analysis, including political economy, in favor of the analysis of discourse. In the wave of scholarly writing on colonialism and the postcolonial world that followed along the path Said had marked out, often theoretically informed by one or another variant of poststructuralism or more broadly by the linguistic or cultural turn in the humanities, the kind of materialist analysis which had inspired much critical and innovative work in the late 1960s and 1970s was often shunted aside.

Marxian and political economy approaches came to be seen by many in the 1980s as too narrow in their insistence on the centrality of class as a category, too essentialist in their commitment to social-structural causation, and too teleological in their positing of large-scale and long-term historical trajectories.[34] They also seemed to ignore, or at least marginalize, discourse, culture, or more broadly questions of meaning, which were the key focus of the new work on representation. Nor (as I noted in Chapter 5) did such approaches initially seem able to offer adequate explanations of such phenomena as the persistence and politicization of religion, in the Middle East (the Iranian revolution, the rise of Islamist movements, the growth of messianic religious nationalism in Israel, etc.) or for that matter elsewhere (e.g., the growth of right-wing evangelical Protestantism in the United States).

As a consequence the influence of political economy-inspired approaches, including social and economic history, waned somewhat. Many younger scholars turned instead to the question of representation as the hot new thing, and pride of place was given to discourse analysis, to cultural studies and to cultural history. These were all worthwhile and often very productive approaches and generated much excellent work, but in some cases they were pursued exclusively through the critical reading of texts (literary, official, and so on) without sufficient interest in grounding those texts in the social, political and other contexts which had produced them and within which they did their "work." This trend was perhaps especially significant in literary studies, but it also afflicted at least some scholars in other disciplines who had embraced the linguistic turn. This was in part what prompted Aijaz Ahmad to be so critical of Said: though Said had himself been quite deeply politically engaged throughout the last three decades of his life, Ahmad held him (rather unfairly) in large measure responsible for launching an intellectual trend that had led to what he saw as a pernicious retreat from engagement with how the great bulk of the planet's population actually lived and struggled to survive, that is, with the realities of politics, economics, power and oppression, and an accompanying turn toward what he saw as the abstract, depoliticized and ahistorical analysis of texts.

Over time, as the first flush of excitement over the possibilities opened up by the linguistic turn waned and as academic sensibilities shifted, there was a growing sense that it was possible – indeed, intellectually necessary – to combine due attention to the question of representation with due attention to social and political dynamics, hierarchies of power and historical contexts, and to explore how these domains are intertwined. This was not to be accomplished by positing, as classical Marxism had done, that ideology and culture were merely reflections or expressions of society's "real" economic base, but by developing methods of analysis that took all meaningful human social activity, whether "material" or "discursive," as determinative, indeed mutually constitutive. Figuring out how to actually do this naturally proved much more difficult than specifying it as a goal, and many of the issues raised by the linguistic turn remained contentious into the twenty-first century.[35]

In an afterword written for the 1995 reprinting of *Orientalism*, Edward Said assessed the impact of his book and some of the responses to it. He began by expressing regret that some readers, especially in Arab and Muslim countries, had used his book to argue that the entire West was the enemy of Islam and the Arabs, or that Islam was perfect. His rejection of essentializing, Said insisted, applied just as much to Islamic fundamentalist claims about "true Islam" as it did to the Western representation of "the Orient" that he had criticized in *Orientalism*.

He went on to discuss the reception of the book in the Arab world where, he felt, much of the criticism to which it was subjected constituted "an accurate reflection of how decades of loss, frustration and the absence of democracy have affected intellectual and cultural life in the Arab region." Said insisted that *Orientalism* had been an effort to break down barriers, to open up new ways of thinking that critically transcended boundaries between cultures and forms of knowledge, to develop "a new way of conceiving the separations and conflicts that had stimulated generations of hostility, war, and imperial control."

Said concluded his assessment on a rather optimistic note. While "the animosities and inequities still exist from which my interest in Orientalism as a cultural and political phenomenon began," he wrote, "there is now at least a general acceptance that these represent not an eternal order but a historical experience whose end, or at least partial abatement, may be at hand. Looking back at it from the distance afforded by fifteen eventful years and the availability of a massive new interpretative and scholarly enterprise to reduce the effects of imperialist shackles on thought and human relations, *Orientalism* at least had the merit of enlisting itself openly in the struggle, which continues of course in 'West' and 'East' together."

Writing from the vantage point of the early years of the twenty-first century, it is perhaps a bit more difficult to share Said's optimism. But he was certainly right to note the profound transformations which scholarship in the humanities had experienced in the last decades of the twentieth century, transformations to which *Orientalism*, along with Said's other work, made no small contribution. This is not to say that *Orientalism* is flawless or that none of the criticisms made of it have any validity. I tend to agree with the assessment made by Sadik al-'Azm, and echoed by others who accept the book's central thrust, that sometimes "the stylist and polemicist in Edward Said . . . runs away with the systematic thinker." One could in fact make a good case that this is the main source of the book's shortcomings and lacunae. Nonetheless, *Orientalism*, taken together with Said's other work, can and should also be seen as a very necessary and timely critical (and political) intervention which not only assailed, and played a crucial role in undermining, a powerful and long-established way of conceptualizing the modern world but also offered a very fruitful alternative vision of how to think about it and operate in it.

Among other things, that vision called on intellectuals to take responsibility for, challenge and transcend some of the key boundaries and categories which had long been deployed to produce knowledge about large segments of the human race, often with pernicious consequences. Over the past generation that vision has proven enormously productive, opening the way for a host of scholars to build on – but also to question, modify and develop – some of Said's key insights and analyses, and thereby to enable us all to think differently about what we are doing and explore largely uncharted terrain in new ways. The scholarly work produced along the way has illuminated long ignored expanses of the human social world in the modern era and highlighted the extent to which neither West nor East (nor Islam) can usefully be understood as ontologically distinct entities but must be seen as constructed, and mutually constitutive, categories. It is testimony to *Orientalism*'s enduring importance and impact that scholars (as well as political activists, and those who see themselves as both) continue to be inspired, stimulated and provoked by engaging critically with its insights and arguments, and more broadly with Edward W. Said's legacy as a scholar and as a dissident intellectual.

7   After Orientalism?

Not everyone accepted the critique of Orientalism, of course. A good many scholars of Islam or the Middle East rejected it outright and lamented the fact that "Orientalist" had come to be widely used in a pejorative sense. Others found the whole controversy largely irrelevant to their work, continued much as they had always done, or embraced different ways of making sense of things. These included non-Marxist variants of political economy, for example John Waterbury's 1983 book *The Egypt of Nasser and Sadat: The Political Economy of Two Regimes* or Alan Richards and John Waterbury's 1990 *A Political Economy of the Middle East: State, Class, and Economic Development,* but also one or another of the new games in town.[1] For example, "rational choice theory" proliferated in American political science in this same period, sporting premises and methods that could not have been more incommensurate with those of colonial discourse analysis, postcolonial theory, poststructuralism, mainstream social science or even plain old Marxism – though perhaps it had somewhat less of an impact on political science work on the Middle East than it did elsewhere.[2]

Nonetheless, the critique of Orientalism gradually won widespread (if never universal) acceptance among students of the Middle East and Islam, and the rejection of cultural essentialism and of the radical dichotomization of East and West which lay at its heart eventually came to be taken as plain common sense by many in the field. In 1998 the Middle East Studies Association organized a special plenary session at its annual meeting to celebrate the twentieth anniversary of the publication of Edward Said's *Orientalism.* The praise heaped on Said on this occasion for his contribution to the field of Middle East studies was in sharp contrast to the dismay or disdain with which many senior scholars in Middle East and Islamic studies had greeted his book when it first appeared. This acclaim indicated the extent to which the field had changed, with a great many scholars who were broadly sympathetic to the intellectual thrust (if not to every aspect or detail) of the critiques advanced by Said and others – and in some cases to their politics as

well – now holding leadership positions within MESA and in the field as
a whole.

Islam and Islamism . . . again

Despite the widespread acceptance of the critiques of Orientalism and
modernization theory, however, the question of how to understand and
study Islam and predominantly Muslim societies continued to arouse
controversy into the early twenty-first century, in large measure because
of developments in the Middle East and the wider Muslim world which
bore directly on contemporary intellectual, political and policy concerns.
Among other things, scholars had to grapple with the continuing importance of Islam in contemporary Middle Eastern and other predominantly
Muslim societies, and more specifically with how best to explain the ability of parties, movements and regimes which rejected secularism and
instead called for the creation of what they deemed a properly Islamic
society and state to win the support of, and mobilize, substantial numbers of people. In short, they had to explain the emergence and continuing strength of Islamism, the derivation of a political ideology and
practice from the Islamic faith. Whole forests were sacrificed for the
paper needed to produce the hundreds of books and thousands of articles and conference papers that were produced on Islam and Islamism
from the 1970s onward, amidst ongoing debates about how to interpret
and explain this phenomenon – if indeed it could be characterized as a
single phenomenon. This is not the place to attempt a comprehensive
survey of this vast literature, but I will try to outline at least a few key
issues.

As I noted toward the end of Chapter 5, the "resurgence" of Islam
did not pose any great intellectual problem to those who, like Bernard
Lewis, regarded Islam as a more or less unchanging and monolithic
civilization which continued to govern the minds of its adherents. In
an article in the September 1990 issue of *The Atlantic Monthly* Lewis
restated, but also elaborated on, his explanation of "The Roots of Muslim Rage" which he saw as fueling Islamist movements worldwide.[3] The
issue's cover was adorned with an illustration of a stereotypically bearded,
turbaned, hook-nosed and scowling Muslim, with the bloodshot reflection of an American flag in each eyeball to show how enraged he was at
the United States; another lurid illustration appeared in the middle of
Lewis' essay. It was, presumably, the editors of *The Atlantic Monthly* rather
than Lewis himself who commissioned and approved these illustrations,
but such crude depictions of the angry, threatening, irrational Muslim –
portrayals of a kind which would be deemed racist or antisemitic if done of

African-Americans or Jews – actually fit the thrust of Lewis' analysis quite well.

Part of the Muslim world, Lewis asserted, was currently going through a period in which Islam "inspired in some of its followers a mood of hatred and violence." Though he began by insisting that "we [i.e., Westerners] share certain basic cultural and moral, social and political, beliefs and aspirations" with many, perhaps even most, Muslims, this qualification disappeared as Lewis began to speak of a "struggle between these rival systems [of Christendom, today Europe, and Islam] that has now lasted for some fourteen centuries." In this struggle "the Muslim" – Lewis now switched to the third-person singular form to denote all Muslims every-where – "has suffered [three] successive stages of defeat" at the hands of the West over the past three centuries or so. First "he" – Lewis' represen-tative Muslim now became male – lost to the advancing power of Russia and the West; then there was "the undermining of his authority in his own country, through an invasion of foreign ideas and laws and ways of life and sometimes even foreign rulers or settlers, and the enfranchisement of native non-Muslim elements."

The third – the last straw – was the challenge to his mastery in his own house, from emancipated women and rebellious children. It was too much to endure, and the outbreak of rage against these alien, infidel, and incomprehensible forces that had subverted his dominance, disrupted his society, and finally violated the sanctuary of his home was inevitable.

This produced "a feeling of humiliation – a growing awareness, among the heirs of an old, proud, and long dominant civilization, of having been overtaken, overborne, and overwhelmed by those whom they regarded as their inferiors." Eventually, this rage came to be directed primarily against the United States. This had little to do, Lewis insisted, with US support for authoritarian and oppressive regimes in the Muslim world, US support for Israel, US imperialism, or indeed anything else the United States had done or was now doing. It did perhaps have a bit to do with rabidly anti-American ideas derived from Marxism or romantic Third Worldism, but the main source of "Muslim rage" was simply Muslims' inability to tolerate "the domination of infidels over true believers." This was the real source of the "current troubles" in such places as Eritrea, Kashmir, Chinese-ruled Sinkiang and Kosovo.

"Islamic fundamentalism," Lewis went on, "has given an aim and a form to the otherwise aimless and formless resentment and anger of the Muslim masses at the forces which have devalued their tradi-tional values and loyalties and, in the final analysis, robbed them of their beliefs, their aspirations, their dignity, and to an increasing extent even their livelihood," channeling them against the secularism and modernity represented by the United States. "This is," Lewis summed up, "no less than a clash of civilizations – the perhaps irrational but surely historic reaction of an ancient rival against our Judeo-Christian heritage, our secular present, and the worldwide expansion of both." Given this, there was not much the West could do other than to try to achieve a better understanding of Islamic civilization and hope that more moderate, tolerant and open strains of Islam would eventually win out.

As I have noted, Lewis was nothing if not consistent: this 1990 article manifested more or less the same premises that had informed Lewis's writing going back to the 1950s. Yet it is surely inaccurate and misleading to explain the Eritrean struggle for independence from Ethiopia, waged by both Christians and Muslims on a thoroughly secular nationalist platform, or Albanian Kosovar demands for the restoration of the autonomy which Slobodan Milosevic's regime took from them to bolster his own postcommunist credentials as a Serbian nationalist, or Kashmiri opposition to that region's forcible inclusion within India, and so on, simply as manifestations of the rage which "the Muslim" feels about Islam's inferiority to Western civilization. To do so is to utterly ignore (if not distort) history, politics and complex local, regional and global contexts in the most reductionistic and simplistic way.

Nonetheless, articles such as this – in this case published just as the military forces of the United States and its allies were massing for the campaign that would expel Iraqi forces from Kuwait – offered Americans an accessible and satisfying explanation for why there was so much anger and resentment against the United States among Arabs and Muslims. It was not, at bottom, because of anything "we" in the West might have done or were doing, or even because of how our actions and policies were mistakenly perceived by others; it was due largely or even solely to a profound defect in Islamic civilization, a wound which remained unhealed and indeed could not really heal unless, apparently, Muslims stopped being Muslims.

Bernard Lewis had his even less subtle emulators. One was Thomas Friedman, at the time a *New York Times* correspondent but within a decade that newspaper's chief foreign affairs commentator and something of a media star. An op-ed piece he published in the *Times* in October 1990, during the run-up to the Gulf War, provides a good illustration of how, despite all the critiques to which it had been subjected, the kind of cultural essentialism which critics argued was central to the Orientalist tradition continued to be pressed into service, especially at moments of crisis.[4]

In this essay Friedman baldly asserted that the profound differences between the West and the Arab world could be highlighted by looking at the symbols that, he claimed, represented each. "The symbol of the West," Friedman declared, "is the cross – full of sharp right angles that begin and end. But the symbol of the Arab East is the crescent moon – a wide ambiguous arc, where there are curves, but no corners." What Westerners failed to understand, according to Friedman, was that Arabs just don't think like "we" do: whereas we are rational and say what we really mean, for Arabs things are often not what they seem; they say one thing but mean and do another. In the Middle East truth and reality are always relative, even dreamlike, just like the desert landscape. Unfortunately, the United States lacked enough trained and experienced foreign service and intelligence personnel who really understood how the Arabs think, leaving it at a disadvantage in its confrontation with the regime of Saddam Husayn in Iraq.

Friedman's dichotomization of the West and the Arab world, each neatly equipped with a symbol that purportedly expressed its essence, its core cultural attributes and fixed mentality, was no doubt crude and simplistic, even laughable; but at a critical moment it offered Americans an easy way both to make sense of a complicated and often confusing world and to reassure themselves about their innocence, righteousness and rationality.

While this perspective – sometimes termed "neo-Orientalist" because it recapitulated key elements of Orientalism in a contemporary setting – certainly had its adherents, many scholars offered a very different understanding of the spread of Islamism. For one, they insisted that the emergence of Islamist ideology and movements should not be seen as a "resurgence" of tradition or as an essentially reactionary "throwback" to premodern times, a manifestation of something antimodern inherent in an Islam which had not yet properly modernized itself. Rather, Islamism was, despite its claim to be a "return" to a pristine original Islam, actually very much a product of the modern world, a thoroughly modern development.

For example, Ayatollah Khomeini's argument that the Shi'i 'ulama should exercise political power directly, for which he claimed unchallengeable support in Shi'i theology and jurisprudence, was often characterized as a throwback to the premodern era; yet in fact it constituted a radical break with virtually all prior Shi'i political thought and could have been developed and won significant support only in the historical context of Iran in the second half of the twentieth century. In other words, this was an innovation in Shi'i thought that portrayed itself as a return to tradition.[5] Similarly, though Sunni Islamists sincerely saw themselves as seeking to realize a Muslim society modeled on the first Muslim community, that of the Prophet Muhammad and his companions and followers, in many respects their vision actually constituted a sharp break with, and rejection of, much of what most Muslims had for centuries taken to be normative Islam.

Moreover, these political and social visions, the terms in which they were put forth and the efforts to realize them would not only *not* have made sense to earlier generations of Muslims but reflected the appropriation and incorporation of many thoroughly modern concepts (like the nation-state, democracy, popular sovereignty, constitutionalism, social justice, anti-imperialism, science, etc.) and modern modes of political organization, propaganda and action (including the political party, the mass movement, mass protests, journalism, the audio cassette and the video tape). At the same time, adherents of this scholarly viewpoint argued, most of the thinkers, leaders and activists of Islamist movements had been educated in institutions of a kind which had not even existed a century earlier and had been shaped by the ideas, discourse and practices characteristic of modernity. Many scholars therefore argued that it was necessary to abandon the view, rooted in both Orientalism and modernization theory, that Islamist ideologies and movements were in any useful sense "traditional," even when they invoked (a certain vision of) Islamic tradition. They were in fact quite modern, very much products of the twentieth century, just as nationalisms which claimed ancient roots and used powerful language and symbols drawn from religious tradition (including Zionism and Arab nationalism, among others) were actually quite new and the forms of identity they advocated constituted a radical break with the past.

More broadly, adherents of this school argued, the time was past when one could simply treat "modern" and "Western" (or modernization and westernization) as synonyms or see modernity as one single thing. Modernity meant different things to different people in different places; it therefore did not make sense to assume, as much of social and political theory did, that there was only one modernity, that of the West, which should be regarded as the proper goal of all human social evolution and the norm against which everything else should be measured (and always found lacking). There were in fact many modernities, many different paths along which societies had developed in the modern era, with much complex mutual borrowing and interaction of ideas, practices and institutions among them.

From this perspective, though each claimed ancient roots and sought legitimation in an appeal to tradition, Islamism, Hindu nationalism, Sikh nationalism, messianic religious Zionism and right-wing evangelical Protestant Christianity in the United States in the last third of the twentieth century were all in fact thoroughly modern phenomena. Each

was the product of complex political, social, economic and cultural forces
operating in specific historical contexts and conjunctures, and none was
usefully viewed as a throwback to some earlier, premodern time or as a
vestige of tradition which had perversely persisted into the modern age.
So Islamism could not usefully be seen as the "resurgence" or "revival"
or "return" of a single thing called Islam; rather, it was a label for a heterogeneous set of phenomena, meaning many different things in different
places. While there were certainly important links, affinities, commonal-
ities and interactions among Islamist ideologies and movements (especially within distinctive Sunni and Shiʻi spheres, but across sectarian lines
as well), there were also significant differences rooted in local histories,
cultures and politics, and in any case they could not all be reduced to a
single "Islam."[6]

A related question that also attracted the attention of scholars studying
Islamism, especially in the 1990s, was whether at least certain versions
of Islamism, and certain Islamist parties, movements or groups, might
be compatible with democracy, an issue of obvious importance to policymakers in the United States and elsewhere. Authoritarian regimes in
the Arab countries had by the mid to late 1990s apparently crushed, or
at least contained, efforts by radical Islamist groups to violently overthrow them, while in Iran a growing reformist movement had emerged,
with support among prominent Shiʻi clergymen as well as among lay
people, advocating a more tolerant, open and democratic path for the
Islamic Republic. What did the existence of relatively moderate strains
of Islamism signify, and how should the United States and its local allies
deal with them?

On this issue two distinct camps might be discerned. Advocates of
what might be called the hard-line position followed Bernard Lewis in
seeing Islam as a wounded civilization and Islamism in all its forms as a
pathology and a potential threat to the West. I will discuss this perspective in more detail later; for now I will say only that in various books,
articles, op-ed pieces, public lectures and media appearances, its advocates argued through the 1990s that Islamism had replaced communism
as the gravest threat facing the West (and Israel) and that only a firm,
even aggressive stance, including the use of military force, could eradicate that threat. Attention to the political and social grievances that led
people in the Arab and Muslim world to join or support Islamist groups
was pointless, nor was it reasonable to expect that such groups would ever
be willing or able to abide by the rules of democracy, since Islam was
by its very nature autocratic and intolerant. Islamism was totalitarianism
and generated terrorism, plain and simple; there were no moderate or
potentially democratic Islamists worth talking about.

This hard-line position was opposed by what might be called the liberal camp, one of whose leading figures was John L. Esposito, founding director of the Center for Muslim–Christian Understanding at Georgetown University, established in 1993. One of Esposito's many books on Islam and Islamism, the 1996 *Islam and Democracy* (co-authored with the Center's associate director John Voll), used case studies of six Muslim countries to argue that Islamism was a diverse and multifaceted phenomenon. Esposito and Voll highlighted efforts by Muslim democrats to draw on elements within the Islamic tradition to develop an authentically Islamic version of democracy and argued that despite widespread Western images of Islamists as uniformly violent and radical, there were a significant number of Islamist activists and movements who eschewed revolution and violence and wanted to take their place in mainstream society and the democratic political process.[7]

The relatively optimistic stance of Esposito, Voll and others in this camp tended to coincide with arguments being made in these same years about the contribution which at least some of the more moderate Islamist groups might make to the flourishing of "civil society" in Arab and Muslim lands, an issue which had attracted the attention of a number of social scientists in Middle East studies (and other fields as well). The concept of "civil society" has long and complex roots in social and political theory, but in this context it was generally used to refer to the mass of voluntary associations, parties, clubs, trade unions and similar organizations which operated above the level of the individual, family or clan but were not part of the state either. US political scientists, sociologists and other scholars interested in this question deemed civil society to be a necessary buffer between citizen and state, fostering civility, popular participation and democracy, and its absence or weakness in Arab and Muslim lands was regarded as one of the prime causes of persistent authoritarianism, lack of respect for the rule of law, and weak loyalty to the nation-state.

Hence the importance of determining whether Islamist groups, with their parties, publishing houses and media outlets, social and cultural associations, and social service organizations should be reckoned as part of civil society or not. The answer to this question would bear on predictions about whether the democratization which had affected post-communist eastern Europe and other parts of the world might also ultimately transform the Middle East. It also had a bearing on policy questions, for example whether the US government should back the efforts of client-states like Egypt to crush or marginalize even moderate and nonviolent Islamist movements, or whether it should instead initiate contacts with them and encourage democratization, even if that might eventually mean permitting Islamist parties to come to power through the ballot box.

The largest scholarly effort to address these issues was the "Civil Society in the Middle East Project," funded by the Ford and Rockefeller foundations and directed by political scientist Augustus Richard Norton, which sponsored research, organized conferences and disseminated publications, culminating in the two-volume collection *Civil Society in the Middle East* (1994–95). Overall, scholarly research on civil society in the early to mid-1990s tended to paint a relatively optimistic picture of the prospects for the growth of civil society and the inclusion of moderate Islamists therein, and more broadly for movement toward political liberalization in the Middle East, prognoses which (as we will see) were not uncontroversial.[8]

The question of terrorism

In the 1990s the much-debated issue of whether Islam or Islamism was a threat to the West or not came to be increasingly bound up with the problem of terrorism. The term in something like its modern political sense goes back to the French Revolution, when it was used with reference to the campaign of the French revolutionary government to crush opposition by executing large numbers of those it deemed to be counterrevolutionaries (the "Reign of Terror" of 1793–94). By extension, it came to mean (as the Oxford English Dictionary puts it) "a policy intended to strike with terror those against whom it is adopted; the employment of methods of intimidation; the fact of terrorizing or condition of being terrorized."

In the late nineteenth and early twentieth centuries the term was sometimes used to denote the strategy pursued by some European revolutionaries and nationalists to undermine regimes or exact revenge by assassinating royalty and government officials. Later still, British officials came to use the term widely to describe anticolonial violence, whether directed against military and civilian agents of colonial rule or against civilians, in Ireland, India, Cyprus, Kenya and elsewhere. Similarly, the French depicted the anticolonial violence perpetrated during Algeria's struggle for independence (1954–62) as terrorism. Along the same lines the Russian government, from the 1990s into the twenty-first century, insisted on portraying its effort to crush secessionist rebels in largely Muslim Chechnya as a struggle against terrorism, exploiting the fact that *some* Chechens had used terrorism as a means of struggle to delegitimize Chechen nationalism altogether and perpetuate Russian domination.

In classifying anticolonial violence as terrorism plain and simple, as acts disconnected from any rational, comprehensible and possibly even legitimate grievances about oppressive conditions, colonial officials drew on the same discourse which led them to use terms like "riots," "disturbances," or "troubles" to denote various forms of anticolonial collective action. This had the effect of portraying such acts and episodes as irrational eruptions against peace and order, allegedly "incited" or perpetrated by a small minority of "troublemakers" and "outside agitators" against the wishes of the purportedly docile and largely happy majority of subjects, rather than as "revolts" or "rebellions," which might have implied recognition that such actions were essentially responses to perceived oppression and enjoyed some degree of popular support.

The Zionist movement in Palestine, and later the State of Israel, adopted much the same discourse with regard to Palestinian opposition to Zionism and, after 1967, to the Israeli occupation of the West Bank and Gaza. In mainstream Israeli historiography, for example, the 1936–39 Palestinian Arab revolt against British colonial rule and the Zionist state-building enterprise it protected and fostered was usually referred to as "the events" (*hame'ora'ot*), which made the revolt seem like a motley set of irrational eruptions rather than a popular nationalist insurrection. Similarly, into the early 1990s Israeli officials and nearly all of the Israeli media insisted on referring to all Palestinian nationalist militants and the organizations to which they belonged as terrorists (*mehablim*). They thereby lumped together all violent (and even some nonviolent) acts by Palestinians against Israelis – whether civilians within Israel, Jewish settlers in the occupied West Bank and Gaza, or military personnel – as terrorism.

This characterization certainly had some basis in reality: from the 1960s onward some Palestinian nationalist (and later Islamist) organizations *did* carry out terrorist attacks against Israeli civilians as well as others, including Jews in other countries. But as with British, French and other colonialisms earlier on, official Israeli insistence on depicting the Palestine Liberation Organization and the Palestinian nationalist movement it led as about nothing *but* terrorism was a way of deflecting attention away from the deeply rooted grievances and aspirations that motivated the Palestinians, including even those who perpetrated clearly immoral and reprehensible acts of terrorist violence, and from the conditions which had led them to adopt such a repugnant tactic. This portrayal thus served to bolster both Israel's self-image as the victim of irrational hatred and mindless violence and its campaign for international sympathy and support.

There is perhaps something particularly ironic about the Israeli case, because in the years just before Israel was established in 1948 the British colonial government of Palestine regarded some of those who would later be among Israel's pre-eminent political leaders as vicious terrorists. For example, two future prime ministers, Menahem Begin and Yitzhak Shamir, had in those years been hunted men, wanted by the British authorities for leading clandestine Jewish paramilitary organizations which had carried out what the British saw as brutal acts of terrorism: the assassination of British officials, the kidnapping and hanging of British soldiers, the bombing of British installations which led to civilian casualties, bomb attacks on innocent Arab civilians, and so on. Of course, many Jews in Palestine, and later in the State of Israel, regarded these men and their comrades-in-arms not as terrorists but as freedom fighters and patriots. The same is true of the Israeli intelligence agents who in 1954 planted bombs at US and British facilities in Egypt in an effort to disrupt that country's improving relations with the West and of the Israeli officials who in that same year ordered the seizure of a Syrian airliner in order to take hostages who could be traded for captured Israeli soldiers.[9]

When the shoe was on the other foot, of course, few Israelis would find it possible to understand how Palestinians whom they saw as vicious terrorists could be hailed by fellow Palestinians as freedom fighters; nor was there much comprehension that terrorism is a tactic, a means that many people (including Jews) have used when they felt they lacked more effective options to strike at a militarily superior enemy. Down to the present day, Israeli officials (especially those on the right) have sought to reduce the entire Palestinian struggle to terrorism, depicting Israel as a peace-loving state compelled to use drastic means to deter or suppress hate-filled, bloodthirsty "Arab" terrorists mindlessly bent on its destruction. (The term "Palestinian" did not win a place in the official Israeli political lexicon until the 1990s, since its use was long deemed to imply some recognition of the existence of a distinct Palestinian people with national rights in its own homeland; instead the generic "Arabs" was usually used.) That terrorism by Palestinians against Israeli civilians has its roots in ongoing occupation and dispossession and is likely to end only when Palestinians see some other way to realize their national aspirations remains difficult for many Israelis to grasp. Instead they have tended to accept Prime Minister Ariel Sharon's repeated assertion that "Israel has been fighting terrorism for a hundred years," thereby once again reducing all Palestinian opposition to Zionism – a comprehensible response, however one judges it politically, morally or otherwise – to irrational, fanatical hatred.[10]

My point here is not to single out Israel, which has by no means been unique in defining and explaining terrorism in self-serving ways. Such behavior has in fact been typical of most if not all states, which brings us back to the larger question of what terrorism is, an issue that would be of concern to many scholars and others engaged with the Middle East in the 1990s and beyond. If one wanted to be as neutral and objective as possible, one might today define terrorism as the use or threat of violence directed primarily against civilians in order to achieve some political aim. This definition is useful because it is based not on the identity, politics or motives of those who perpetrate terrorist acts but on the character of the acts themselves and of their victims – i.e., politically motivated violence against civilians. This definition also encourages us to condemn *all* terrorist acts as morally unacceptable, for if one starts to pick and choose, justifying or ignoring certain acts or forms of terrorism while condemning others, the inevitable result is a morally untenable double standard.

By this definition, terrorism has indeed been used by many organizations and movements, including the Palestinian organizations which carried out airplane hijackings, attacks on Israeli civilians and (since the mid-1990s) suicide bombings, as well as Zionist groups in pre-1948 Palestine, the Tamil Tigers in Sri Lanka, some European ultraleft groups, Chechen rebels against Russian rule and, unfortunately, many others. However, this definition also prohibits us from ignoring the many governments that have used terrorist means against their own people or others; hence the term "state terrorism," as opposed to terrorism carried out by political groups and movements challenging existing regimes. The long list of states which have practiced state terrorism would include such obvious candidates as Nazi Germany and Stalin's Soviet Union, but also (for example) Guatemala, Honduras and El Salvador, where for decades military regimes backed by the United States used murder, massacres and torture to crush even the most moderate and lawful efforts to seek social and political reform.

Unfortunately, tendentious definitions of terrorism and politically motivated double standards have characterized much of the work in what by the 1980s was the burgeoning field some facetiously called "terrorology" – the study of terrorism as a political, social, cultural and psychological phenomenon. One of the pioneers in this field was Yonah Alexander, who in 1977 was the founding editor of *Terrorism: An International Journal*, which devoted itself to the study of terrorism. When he launched his journal Alexander was based at the Institute for Studies in International Terrorism at the State University of New York in out-of-the-way Oneonta, but he would eventually make it into the world of

Washington DC think tanks by becoming senior fellow at the right-wing Potomac Institute for Policy Studies and director of its International Center for Terrorism Studies, founded in 1998.

Alexander's journal, and the work of most other self-proclaimed terrorism specialists, focused on terrorism by what might be called "the usual suspects," i.e. nonstate groups. State terrorism, which by any plausible count has claimed many more innocent lives than terrorism carried out by nonstate groups, was generally left out of the picture. Hence the irony of the second issue of *Terrorism*, which featured an article by Fereydoun Hoveyda, at the time ambassador to the United Nations from Iran, a country whose ruler, the shah, had won a well-earned international reputation for deploying a particularly brutal secret police to crush every demand for democracy and social justice and who regularly denounced armed attacks on his dictatorship by clandestine revolutionary groups as terrorism.

The same tendentious perspective informed Claire Sterling's influential 1981 book *The Terror Network*, which focused on alleged European and Middle Eastern terrorist groups and charged that the Soviet Union (along with Cuba and Libya) was behind most of them.[11] Though critics questioned Sterling's claims, which some felt were largely the product of CIA disinformation efforts, officials of the new Reagan administration hailed her book and cited it to support their hard-line anti-Soviet stance. Early on the Reagan administration had declared that the fight against "international terrorism" (meaning alleged terrorist groups and networks purportedly backed by the Soviets) would be "the soul of our foreign policy," replacing former President Jimmy Carter's avowed (but always rather selective) concern with human rights. Official rhetoric now characterized terrorism as an evil scourge spread by depraved opponents of civilization itself, a return to barbarism in the modern age.

This new official US stance had a lot to do with the fact that by the early 1980s, in the aftermath of the Iranian revolution and the 1982 Israeli invasion of Lebanon, US institutions and personnel, especially but not exclusively in the Middle East, had increasingly become prime targets of violent attacks. Government officials usually portrayed such attacks as disconnected from any historical, political or other context: rather than looking at why certain groups opposed to what they saw the United States doing used violent means to strike at US power, they depicted international terrorism as an expression of mindless, baseless hatred of the United States, part of the global communist conspiracy run from Moscow, or both.

What happened in Lebanon in 1983 is a case in point. US Marines had been sent to Lebanon the previous year as part of a multinational force charged with protecting the Palestinian civilian population after the massacres at the Sabra and Shatila refugee camps, perpetrated by right-wing Christian militiamen while their Israeli patrons who had occupied much of the country stood by and watched. But the US forces soon took sides in Lebanon's ongoing civil war, supporting the right-wing Christian government which had been installed by Israel during its invasion but which many Lebanese regarded as illegitimate. As a result, the United States became a prime target for the Lebanese Shi'i Hizbullah movement and associated groups, whose operatives are widely believed to have carried out both the April 1983 suicide bombing of the US embassy in Beirut, which killed 63 people (including most of the CIA personnel stationed there), and the October 1983 suicide bombings that killed some 241 Marines (as well as 58 French soldiers). The attacks led President Reagan to withdraw US forces from Lebanon, which is exactly what those who planned the attacks hoped to achieve.

Nonetheless, in this case as in others, US government officials treated violence of this kind not as a tactic, a morally questionable but often effective means of achieving some political goal, but as an inexplicable eruption of madness and hatred having nothing to do with anything "we" had done or were perceived to have done. This made it impossible to really understand why individuals and groups who lacked the tanks, helicopter gunships, warplanes and cruise missiles available to their much more powerful adversaries deemed it acceptable and expedient to use terrorism as a tactic or a strategy. Hence the common resort to pop psychology and crude cultural stereotypes, resulting in endless articles and television programs purporting to explain "the terrorist mindset" or why Arabs or Muslims embraced a "culture of death."

The politics which underpinned and sustained widespread and influential depictions of the threat allegedly posed by international terrorism were laid out clearly in one of the key texts of this period. This was the 1986 book *Terrorism: How the West Can Win*, edited by Benjamin Netanyahu.[12] Contributors to the volume included Bernard Lewis and various luminaries of the US neoconservative movement and of the European and Israeli right, and it can be seen as a manifestation of what I pointed to in Chapter 5 as the convergence of the (Jewish and non-Jewish) American right and the Israeli right around an anti-Soviet, anti-Palestinian, anti-Islamic and antiterrorist agenda.

Netanyahu had first gained public attention in Israel as the brother of Jonathan Netanyahu, who led the Israeli commandos who had rescued hijacked hostages held at Entebbe, Uganda, in 1976 and was killed during the operation; he would go on to a political career that would lead him to the prime ministership of Israel in 1996–1999, and again beginning in 2009. The Jonathan Institute which Netanyahu established soon after his brother's death sought to attract attention to the problem of terrorism, which Netanyahu depicted as "part of a much larger struggle, one between the forces of civilization and the forces of barbarism."

International terrorism for Netanyahu was "not a sporadic phenomenon born of social misery and frustration. It is rooted in the political ambitions and designs of expansionist states [like the Soviet Union and radical Arab states like Syria and Libya] and the groups that serve them [like the PLO]." In *Terrorism: How the West Can Win*, Netanyahu offered a definition of terrorism not very different from the one I proposed earlier, and he insisted that guerrillas and other irregular fighters were not the same as terrorists, who were to be distinguished by their deliberate targeting of civilians. But his real agenda was to discredit the PLO, which in that period was winning international recognition as sole representative of the Palestinians, by painting it as nothing but a terrorist organization and Soviet proxy. He sought thereby to combat a growing sense in Europe and elsewhere that Palestinian terrorism was a symptom rather than a root cause of the Israeli–Palestinian conflict and that no durable peace was possible without addressing Palestinian grievances and aspirations. At the same time, Netanyahu hoped to win Western support for a hardline Israeli policy toward Palestinian nationalism and the Arab world by weaving the PLO, Islam, Arab nationalism, Libya, Syria, Iran and Soviet communism into one seamless web of "international terrorism."

The US government also resorted to defining terrorism selectively and tendentiously. A good example of this can be found in *Terrorist Group Profiles*, published by the United States government in 1989. Though in his preface Defense Secretary Frank Carlucci pointed out that "terrorism is essentially a tactic – a form of political warfare designed to achieve political ends," the report featured short profiles of a very wide range of groups, parties and movements which the US government had declared to be terrorist organizations. These included almost all the Palestinian armed organizations, Hizbullah, the Irish Republican Army, the Armenian nationalist ASALA, the Basque separatist ETA, the Italian Red Brigades, the communist-led New People's Army of the Philippines, the Tamil Tigers of Sri Lanka, the Japanese Red Army and Sikh separatists in India as well as all the left-led guerrilla movements of Central America.

It may come as a surprise to some that the list also included the African National Congress, the main movement fighting for democracy and majority rule against South Africa's apartheid regime. For a period during the 1980s the ANC had in fact authorized bombings which took the lives of black and white civilians, but this tactic was soon abandoned.

In any case it was always obvious that the ANC was a mass movement which enjoyed the support of most black South Africans, a reality demonstrated a few months after *Terrorist Group Profiles* was published when the white minority regime released ANC leader Nelson Mandela after twenty-eight years of imprisonment and entered into negotiations with the ANC that would lead to a nonracial, democratic constitution and Mandela's election as the first president of a free South Africa.

As the case of the ANC illustrates, some of the organizations on the US government's terrorist list had indeed used terrorist means, but many could not reasonably be deemed nothing but terrorist organizations. While groups like the Red Brigades and Japanese Red Army were tiny, politically isolated, ultraleftist sects, many of the others had at least some popular support and terrorism was only one of the tactics they used, and often not the most important one. It would therefore seem that what got the ANC and many of the others onto this list was not so much the fact that they were sometimes guilty of targeting civilians as the perception that they posed a threat to US interests or had links to the Soviet Union – which did in fact extend support to the ANC, the PLO and some of the other "terrorist" organizations. The US also defined terrorism rather broadly, so that (for example) attacks by guerrilla movements in El Salvador on US military and intelligence personnel dispatched to assist local counterinsurgency campaigns were deemed terrorist acts.

Equally striking was who was left off the list: the brutal regimes in Central America which, armed and financed by the United States, had over decades killed vastly greater numbers of their own citizens than the guerrillas challenging them; the dictatorship of General Pinochet in Chile, which was installed with US support and went so far as to murder its opponents in the heart of Washington, DC; the regime of General Suharto in Indonesia, which engaged in brutal repression and mass murder in that country as well as in occupied East Timor; outfits like UNITA in Angola and RENAMO in Mozambique, which with US backing (and in the latter case, that of South Africa as well) used terrorism rather freely in their campaigns to topple governments the US saw as pro-Soviet; the Nicaraguan *contras* who, with funding and weapons supplied by the United States, sometimes used terrorist means in their campaign to overthrow the revolutionary Sandinista government; and, one might argue, even the Central Intelligence Agency itself, which is known to have carried out or facilitated its share of assassinations and bombings, probably including a 1985 car bombing in Beirut which missed its intended target, Hizbullah's spiritual leader Muhammad Husayn Fadlullah, but did kill seventy-five Lebanese civilians.

In the 1990s, as the Soviet Union and its client regimes ceased to exist, the use of terrorism by Europeans against other Europeans seemed to subside, and the PLO recognized and entered into negotiations with Israel, the specter of Soviet-sponsored "international terrorism" gave way to the specter of "Islamic terrorism." Ironically, US support for the resistance to the Soviet military intervention in Afghanistan that began in 1979 helped create this new and much more serious menace. Many Arab Islamists went to Afghanistan in the 1980s to help the Afghan resistance (massively armed and financed by the CIA) expel the godless communists. After the Soviets withdrew from Afghanistan in 1989, these trained and often radicalized volunteers hoped to return home and renew the struggle to topple their own corrupt and authoritarian regimes and install what they saw as a properly Islamic state and society. However, those regimes proved able to crush or contain the Islamist challenge, leading some of the most extreme groups to decide to target the United States instead.[13]

In fact, the most radical among them came to regard the United States as their main enemy. As they saw it, it was US political, military and financial support which propped up the local regimes they hated, in Saudi Arabia, Egypt and elsewhere. The 1991 Persian Gulf war and its aftermath further fueled the anger and hatred which extremist Islamist groups felt toward the United States. While Islamists had no love for the secularist and nationalist Ba'th party regime led by Saddam Husayn which ruled Iraq and which had occupied Kuwait in the summer of 1990, they opposed the US-led war which forced the Iraqis out of Kuwait as aggression against the Muslim world and saw the stationing of US forces on the sacred soil of Saudi Arabia for more than a decade after the end of that war as an abomination. The suffering of the largely Muslim people of Iraq under United Nations-imposed sanctions and, last but not least, the ongoing Israeli–Palestinian conflict also fostered resentment among many Muslims and rendered them sympathetic, or at least receptive, to radical Islamist denunciations of the United States as the prime enemy of Islam.

The result was a series of attacks from the later 1990s onward that targeted US embassies and the US military in Africa and the Middle East and culminated in the September 11, 2001 attacks on the World Trade Center in New York and the Pentagon in Washington DC. Beyond the symbolic and political dimensions of these attacks, and particularly September 11, it seems likely that the radical Islamists who perpetrated them hoped that they would provoke the kind of US response that would turn Muslim opinion against the United States, undermine pro-US governments in predominantly Muslim countries and eventually enable the Islamists to win power.

The threat of terrorism perpetrated by radical Islamist groups naturally came to loom increasingly large for policymakers and scholars alike by the late 1990s. Governments as well as nonstate groups had proven all too willing to kill, injure, mutilate and rape civilians to achieve their political and military ends, and now extremist Muslim groups – a tiny minority of the world's more than one billion Muslims, but all too effective and deadly – had targeted the United States in particular. As a result the question of how to understand "Islamic terrorism" and terrorism in general, and how to respond to them effectively, remained a subject of vigorous, sometimes rancorous, debate.

Those we might term hard-liners – generally on the political right – tended to argue that terrorism perpetrated by Muslims had strong roots in Islam as such, deemed attention to the motives and grievances expressed by the perpetrators irrelevant or even harmful, and emphasized the use of force to eradicate it, in part by attacking what they called "rogue states" (like Afghanistan under the Taliban, Iraq, Iran and Syria) which allegedly supported terrorism or harbored terrorists. The hard-liners argued that Muslim extremists hated the United States (and by extension the West as a whole) essentially because of what it *was* – that is, because of the values of democracy, tolerance and secularism which it espoused – and that there was therefore little the United States could do other than try to eradicate the terrorists by force.[14]

In contrast, others – mainly on the liberal and left side of the political spectrum – argued that the problem of terrorism could not be dealt with effectively by purely military or police methods. They generally agreed that it was necessary to apprehend or deter those who had launched or were planning terrorist attacks – though that would require a sustained commitment to multilateral consultation and international cooperation, a commitment to which the Bush administration seemed allergic. But a long-term solution to the problem also required attention to the factors which in this specific historical period had prompted a tiny minority of Muslims to engage in terrorism, and many more to deem it morally acceptable or even praiseworthy. These factors included the tyrannical, corrupt and/or ineffective regimes, often propped up by the United States, under which so many Muslims lived, endemic poverty, underdevelopment and lack of opportunity, and foreign economic and political domination. Only by addressing the legitimate grievances and aspirations of the vast majority of Muslims could their sympathies and support be enlisted and the extremist minority be politically isolated, marginalized and eventually neutralized.

Liberal and leftist scholars and observers thus pointed to the gap many Muslims (and others) saw between what the United States preached and what it practiced as a key factor in explaining why the extremists had

targeted the United States and why they enjoyed a degree of popular understanding and sympathy. They argued that the policies the
United States had pursued in the Arab and Muslim worlds – including unequivocal support for Israel, perceived by Arabs and Muslims as
the oppressor of the Palestinians, and more broadly American hegemony
over much of this part of the world, manifested in various ways – actually
had a great deal to do with the widespread perception among Muslims
(but also among many non-Muslims around the globe) that the United
States was a swaggering bully intent on using its massive military and
economic power to impose its will on the world. These policies, they
suggested, apart from being misguided, counterproductive and wrong,
gave ammunition to extremist groups like al-Qa'ida and bolstered their
claim that the United States was the prime enemy of Islam and hence
a legitimate target. So if some Muslims displayed approval, or at least
understanding, of extremist Islamist attacks on the United States, it was
not so much because of what the United States *was* or *stood for* (as the
right claimed) but because of what the United States actually *did* in that
part of the world, both its current policies and the bitter legacy left by
much of its long engagement in the region since the Second World War.[15]

The clash of civilizations

The ongoing debates over Islam, Islamism and terrorism in the 1990s and
beyond fed into, and were often fueled by, wider debates among scholars,
journalists and policymakers over how to think about the post-Cold War
world. In his 1990 article "The Roots of Muslim Rage," Bernard Lewis
had characterized the conflict between Islam and the West, allegedly dat-
ing back to the emergence of Islam fourteen centuries ago, as a "clash of
civilizations." Such images were very much in the air in the last decade of
the twentieth century. In the late 1980s the communist-ruled countries
of central and eastern Europe had broken free of Soviet control and
established new, more or less capitalist, formally democratic and pro-
Western regimes, and in 1991 the Soviet Union itself ceased to exist.
The end of communist rule in Russia and elsewhere also meant the end
of the Cold War, since the United States no longer had a rival for global
hegemony. This led observers to seek new ways of understanding the
fault lines and potential sources of conflict in the post-Cold War world,
and one of those ways involved a reversion to the old but still powerful notion that the world was divided into fundamentally different and
clashing civilizations. Though Bernard Lewis and others had long relied
on this model, it was Samuel Huntington who in the 1990s probably did
most to generalize and popularize this conception of the world.

We last met Huntington in Chapter 5, where we saw that during the 1960s this prominent but controversial Harvard professor was a leading advocate of the US war in Vietnam and a vigorous proponent of massive bombardment of the countryside; this, he predicted, would drive the peasants into government-controlled territory and deprive the communist-led insurgents of their mass base. The advice which some of his former students offered the shah of Iran in the 1970s was equally effective: drawing on Huntington's theories about social change and political order, they advised the shah to establish a political party (the only one allowed) which could be used to mediate between the masses and the state and mobilize the former to better implement the latter's programs. What followed only deepened popular alienation from, and opposition to, the shah's regime and contributed to the onset of the crisis that ultimately toppled the shah in 1979. Despite this, or perhaps because of it, by the early 1990s Huntington was the Eaton Professor of the Science of Government at Harvard and director of its John M. Olin Institute for Strategic Studies, named for (and funded by) a right-wing industrialist.

Huntington laid out his vision of the postcommunist world in an article, "The Clash of Civilizations?," published in the summer 1993 issue of *Foreign Affairs*, the influential journal of the Council on Foreign Relations and a key link between scholars and policymakers.[16] Huntington argued starkly that in the period ahead, the fundamental sources of conflict in the world would not be "primarily ideological or primarily economic. The great divisions among humankind and the dominating source of conflict will be cultural . . . [T]he principal conflicts of global politics will occur between nations and groups of different civilizations. The clash of civilizations will dominate global politics. The fault lines between civilizations will be the battle lines of the future."

During the Cold War the world had been divided along geopolitical lines, into the First, Second and Third Worlds – that is, the West, the communist bloc, and everyone else. But now, Huntington argued, it was more useful to see the world as divided into distinct civilizations, defined by such things as language, history and religion but also by how people identified themselves. "The people of different civilizations," Huntington explained, "have different views on the relations between God and man, the individual and the group, the citizen and the state, parents and children, husband and wife, as well as differing views of the relative importance of rights and responsibilities, liberty and authority, equality and hierarchy." These differences, "the product of centuries," were much more deeply rooted and important than ideology, and despite facile talk of globalization, regionalism along civilizational lines was growing.

Huntington identified seven or eight major civilizations: the West (including western Europe and the United States); Slavic-Orthodox civilization, encompassing Russia and much of eastern and southeastern Europe; Islam, with its Arab, Turkic and Malay subdivisions; Confucian civilization, meaning largely China; Japan; Hindu civilization; Latin America; and "possibly African civilizations," to which Huntington did seem to not attribute much importance. It was precisely where these civilizations rubbed up against one another, Huntington argued, that conflict was most likely: hence the turmoil and violence in the Balkans, where the West, Slavic-Orthodoxy and Islam were all in conflict; in the Caucasus, where Orthodoxy and Islam clashed; and in South Asia, where the Hindu and Islamic civilizations contended for dominance. Huntington also predicted the emergence of a Confucian–Islamic alliance, based on common opposition to the West. In the long run, the West should maintain its economic and military superiority and perhaps try to incorporate part or all of Latin America, even as it sought to achieve a better understanding of the other civilizations with which it would have to co-exist.

Huntington's "clash of civilizations" thesis aroused a great deal of controversy. One of the many rebuttals came from Roy Mottahedeh, the Harvard historian of Islam.[17] "Not only," Mottahedeh argued, "is the 'empirical' basis of [Huntington's] thesis a matter for dispute, but the theoretical structure proposed to explain the relation between 'culture' and political behavior seems to the present author very much open to question." He rejected Huntington's portrait of relations between Islam and the West and his frequent use of the terms "Arabs" and "Islamic" as if they were interchangeable, and pointed out that despite Huntington's assertion that all Muslims belonged to a single civilization, Muslims in South Asia, the Arab lands, Turkey and Indonesia all had very different political cultures. Mottahedeh showed that civilization as a category simply did not work well as an explanation either for conflict or for the identities, views and actions of its purported members. For example, Mottahedeh noted,

large elements of Western culture introduced by colonialism, imposition or mere imitation have developed deep and authentic roots in non-Western societies, to a degree that these societies often no longer sense these elements to be alien. Nothing in the premodern Islamic tradition drives modern Muslims to give the vote to women, and many Muslim conservatives opposed the enfranchisement of women. But in countries such as Turkey, Egypt, and Iran the overwhelming majority of Islamists – advocates of the reintroduction of some measure of Islamic law – would now never raise a whisper against votes for women, who form an important part of their constituents.

Mottahedeh went on to point out that "it was once commonly said . . . that democracy could only live fully in Protestant countries . . . It was 'self-evident' to many Protestants that Catholics were obedient to the Pope and could not be true democratic participants . . . To distrust the ability of sincere Catholics to be true democrats seems as quaint and fanciful to us at the end of the twentieth century as will seem, in a generation, our present distrust of the ability of sincere Muslims to be true democrats."

For Mottahedeh Huntington's thesis also ignored differences among Muslims. There was certainly a minority which sought the imposition of a rigid interpretation of Islamic law and regarded the West as an alien civilization, but there were many more who did not share either the Islamists' vision or their political and social agenda. For Mottahedeh the "clash of civilizations" hypothesis seemed "far more a description (and prescription) than an explanatory system. It offers a long list of things that the West is – the bearer of individualism, liberalism, democracy, free markets and the like – but, by and large, just tells us that the non-Western, in the great American language of the multiple-choice test, is 'none of the above.'" However, it was an "extraordinary assumption" that Muslims' normative religious beliefs (which were in reality quite diverse) determined the behavior of those who formally ascribed to them. As a Christian, Mottahedeh noted, "in order for me to believe that Christians when abused are supposed to turn the other cheek, I must forget the example of almost all the Christians I have ever met." Huntington's claims thus lacked any solid empirical basis and recalled the "mania for order" which had led "theorists like Toynbee [see Chapter 3] to strain the evidence in order to discover lists of traits that 'essentially' characterize the units they call 'civilizations.'"

The end of area studies?

Even as Huntington and others were arguing that humanity was fundamentally divided into essentially different and clashing civilizations, a significant number of scholars, journalists and writers were coming to the opposite conclusion. They saw the post-Cold War world as undergoing what came to be called "globalization" – an increasing degree of economic, political and even cultural integration which was breaking down old barriers and fostering new forms of openness, exchange and interaction. Globalization came to be one of the buzz-words of the 1990s, the subject of numerous books and scholarly and popular articles and op-ed pieces discussing whether, and if so how, the world was becoming more integrated, as well as the possible consequences of this process or set of processes.

Some of the prognoses made by enthusiasts of globalization were hardly worth the paper they were printed on: for example, that the entire world would inexorably meld into a liberal democratic capitalist utopia; that the nation-state would disappear as beneficent transnational corporations assumed ever greater power; that the global spread of McDonald's would ensure world peace; or that the "digital revolution" and the Internet would somehow alleviate poverty and promote good will and mutual understanding everywhere. Other analyses were more sober and sought to figure out what, if anything, was actually going on. Some pointed out that overly rosy visions of the future were nothing new and no more likely to be realized now than they had been in the past. In the late nineteenth century, for example, global economic integration reached unprecedented proportions and many were convinced that an era of permanent peace, prosperity and social progress was at hand. Yet this era culminated in the catastrophic First World War, followed by decades which witnessed devastating warfare in many parts of the globe, genocide, new forms of tyranny, and social turmoil.

The end of the Cold War and growing interest in globalization inevitably led to a reconsideration of area studies as a framework for organizing (and funding) the production of knowledge. As we saw in Chapter 4, area studies (including Middle East studies) had emerged during and after the Second World War in large measure as a way of providing US policymakers with the kind of knowledge they needed to successfully conduct American foreign policy in the Cold War. Hence the large-scale funding which foundations, and then the taxpayers, provided to universities and other institutions to facilitate the study of "strategic" languages (including Arabic, Persian and Turkish) but also of the politics, cultures and histories of places which few Americans could actually locate on a map. Now, with the Cold War over and a new focus on problems and processes that seemed to transcend national and regional boundaries, some asked whether the time had come to abandon area studies, predicated as it was on the existence of distinct world areas, and instead develop new ways of producing and organizing knowledge that would help make sense of the dynamics of globalization.

It was this kind of thinking which in 1993 led the Ford and Mellon foundations to reduce funding for regionally focused research and training and instead launch a joint globalization project. A year later the president of the Social Science Research Council – one of the midwives of area studies after the Second World War – proposed (and partially implemented) the dismantling of many of its regional committees, which for decades had overseen the disbursement of funding for dissertation and postdoctoral research and had sought (with limited success) to set research agendas for their fields. Instead, the SSRC created a new dissertation research fellowship program to which graduate students planning research on any part of the world could apply, which meant that those specializing in the Middle East would be competing for all too limited funding with others specializing in East Asia or Africa or even Eastern Europe. Selection of awardees would be made not by specialists in one area studies field but by scholars drawn from a range of fields. Along similar lines, the SSRC launched new committees and projects which fostered research on broad themes of global import, for example international migration and sexuality. Needless to say, these moves aroused considerable controversy within the SSRC and across the area studies fields.

But area studies proved more resilient than some had expected early in the 1990s. The federal funds originally allocated under Title VI of the 1958 National Defense Education Act continued to flow to area studies centers at various universities, supporting research, language training and courses on specific world regions as well as public outreach and teacher training, and while foundation funding for area studies declined it did not altogether cease. (In the 2000–02 funding cycle, the sixteen Middle East national resource centers received a total of $2.6 million to support language and other teaching, outreach and teacher training, plus another $1.5 million for what were originally called National Defense Foreign Language fellowships but which in the late 1970s were given the more benign name of Foreign Language and Area Studies fellowships.) Recognizing that "local knowledge" remained essential, the SSRC eventually created smaller (and less well-funded) "regional advisory panels" to replace the defunct regional committees.[18]

At the same time, the various area studies organizations, including the Middle East Studies Association, remained relevant by providing scholars increasingly well trained and well grounded in their disciplines with a venue for intellectual as well as social interaction with others interested in the same part of the world. The continued viability of area studies was perhaps also sustained by its interdisciplinary character, which seemed to resonate with a widespread intellectual (if not always institutional) interest in American academia in fields and endeavors that crossed conventional disciplinary boundaries – for example, the study of women, gender and sexuality, cultural studies, and urban studies – along with a renewed commitment to empirical and theoretical work that was strongly comparative.

The growing attention at many US colleges and universities to (controversial) issues of diversity and to multiculturalism, a product of the continuing salience of racial and ethnic divisions and conflicts in American society, along with worries that Americans remained poorly informed about the rest of the world, the need to offer "world civilization" courses and a burgeoning "world history" movement, may also have bolstered the standing of area studies, though its relation with the expanding field of international studies on college campuses remained uncertain. Last but not least, the ongoing and often troubled involvement of the United States in many parts of the world outside the West highlighted the continuing need for people who had some solid knowledge of those places. Facile talk of globalization was all very well, but in a crunch one needed to know about the politics, histories and cultures of specific locales, and over the previous half-century area studies had to a large extent provided the institutional framework for producing people equipped with such knowledge.

It may be too soon to tell, but from the vantage point of the first years of the twenty-first century it would seem that area studies had weathered the storms of the immediate post-Cold War period. In large part this may have been because these fields, including Middle East studies as practiced in the United States, were by the 1990s not what they had been thirty years earlier. The sharp decline (within academia, at least) of once dominant paradigms like a cultural-essentialist Orientalism and modernization theory resulted in the dissipation of the intellectual coherence which had characterized the field in its first decades. But the kind of intellectual fragmentation that had come to characterize Middle East studies was the norm across a great many other fields and disciplines and was counter-balanced, probably even outweighed, by the fact that many Middle East specialists, perhaps especially younger scholars, were now not only well versed in the theoretical and methodological issues and debates of their own disciplines but also routinely engaged with innovative work that cut across or transcended disciplinary boundaries. They could thus increasingly manage, without any great difficulty, to participate in productive scholarly conversations with their disciplinary colleagues (fellow historians, political scientists, anthropologists, literature specialists, etc.) but also with scholars from other disciplines interested in this part of the world and in others as well. At the same time, even as getting revised doctoral dissertations and scholarly monographs published by financially strapped university presses grew more difficult, numerous Internet-based listservs as well as journals and websites enabled scholars to share information, exchange opinions and disseminate book reviews and articles more effectively. A number of new print journals also appeared, for example the *Arab Studies Journal*, founded and run by graduate students at Georgetown University (and later New York University as well).

Moreover, because so many scholars working on the Middle East were participants in the scholarly conversations and debates that had transformed broad segments of the humanities and the social sciences in recent decades, Middle East studies had to a considerable extent overcome its insular and rather backward character and was now much more open to, and engaged with, the wider intellectual world than had once been the case. The developments of the last two or three decades, including the critiques of Orientalism and modernization theory, the broad range of new work on colonialism, innovative approaches to historical, social and cultural analysis influenced by anthropology, and more broadly heightened interaction among disciplines and fields had given many within Middle East studies a new set of common languages that facilitated productive intellectual exchange. This was also a much more intellectually and politically self-aware and self-critical field than was once the case. As a result the best of the new work in this field was by the beginning of the twenty-first century very much on a par with the best produced in other area studies fields, and scholars specializing in the Middle East were being read and listened to by scholars specializing in other parts of the world as never before.[19]

That this was the case also owed something to two other factors. Thirty years ago the academic study of the Middle East was conducted in the United States largely by American-born white males. Over the decades since, the gender balance in this field as in many other domains shifted dramatically, a shift that also certainly contributed to increased scholarly attention to gender as a key analytical category. And although statistics are hard to come by, it would also seem that a significantly higher proportion of the faculty and graduate students in Middle East studies was now of Middle Eastern background or origin than had been the case earlier on. Among them were native speakers of Middle Eastern languages who may also already have had a deep familiarity with one or more societies in the region.

Of course, American-born students with no Middle Eastern roots whatsoever had long shown themselves to be perfectly capable of mastering the languages of the region and achieving important insights into its societies and cultures; indeed, it can be argued that while foreigners must work hard to understand local ways, they have the advantage of not being so steeped in those ways that they find it difficult to achieve the critical distance necessary for scholarly analysis. In any case, the demographic contours of the field had certainly changed over the last quarter of the twentieth century, with growing numbers of students and faculty with roots in, and personal as well as scholarly links with, the region they were studying. This development had largely positive effects on the quality of knowledge produced – though as we will see this was not an assessment accepted by all.

In conjunction with a generally higher level of mastery of relevant languages and the use of innovative theoretical and methodological approaches, scholars in the field were by the late twentieth century also making use of a broader range of sources than in the past. A case in point is work on the history of the Arab provinces of the Ottoman empire. Students and scholars with a command of both Arabic and Ottoman Turkish made increasing use not only of the vast Ottoman imperial archives in Istanbul but also of local Islamic court records and family papers, along with more traditional sources like the writings of European consuls and travelers, to produce unprecedentedly in-depth and complex portraits of social, political, economic and cultural life in these lands in the last four hundred years of Ottoman rule.[20]

These studies helped to undermine what was once conventional wisdom in late Ottoman history, that these lands were economically, socially and culturally stagnant before Napoleon's army landed in Egypt in 1798, that they were uniformly characterized by despotism, the oppressive and retrograde imposition of Islamic law, and the rigorous segregation and subordination of non-Muslims, and that all real change was induced by contact with the West. Instead, the newer scholarship began to elucidate indigenous sources and dynamics of change while also showing how this region was part of the broader sweep of world history long before the nineteenth century and the onset of westernization or modernization as conventionally understood. As a result of these scholarly advances, Ottoman historians often came to have much broader and more fully comparative perspectives than historians of early modern Europe, many of whom had only recently come to understand that they needed to overcome their own provincialism by addressing the ways in which developments in Europe were not utterly *sui generis* but were often bound up with larger patterns and dynamics of change that affected large stretches of Eurasia.

Scholars and the state

If the preceding assessment is accurate, it would be fair to say that the changes which had transformed Middle East studies in the United States over the last several decades of the twentieth century had made it a more intellectually productive and interesting scholarly field. However, as I noted briefly at the end of Chapter 5, this development was accompanied by a growing gap between academics studying the Middle East and the officials, agencies and institutions of the United States government, and a corresponding decline in the influence of university-based scholars on the shaping of foreign policy and on the media, the main purveyor of information, images and attitudes about the region to the broad public.

For one, a good many (though by no means all) students and scholars in this field were less than happy with US government policies toward the Middle East in the 1980s and beyond. Hard evidence is lacking, but it is probably safe to suggest that much of the membership of the Middle East Studies Association, the field's main professional organization, was not enthusiastic about US support for Saddam Husayn's regime in its war against Iran in the 1980s, the US-led Gulf War of 1991, the sanctions regime imposed on Iraq thereafter, the US-led invasion of Iraq in 2003 or, more broadly, the extent to which successive US administrations countenanced Israel's ongoing occupation of the West Bank, Gaza and East Jerusalem, its continuing implantation of Jewish settlements there, and its rejection of a Palestinian state in those territories as endorsed by virtually the entire international community. There was a widespread (though never universal) sense that the policies pursued by the United States in the Middle East were hindering, rather than contributing to, peace, democracy, human rights, development and progress in the region.

This disaffection from official policy and the premises which underpinned it did not mean that US-based scholars studying the Middle East were unwilling to share their perspectives on, and try to influence, US policy toward the region. In fact, many devoted a great deal of time and effort to trying to educate the broader public, through informal meetings, lectures, articles, op-ed pieces, radio and television interviews and the like, and to convey their views to elected officials; not a few were also quite willing to meet with State Department and intelligence agency personnel. It is rather that the shared vision of the world, and of the place of the United States within it, that had once linked the world of academia with the world of policymaking had faded, and many scholars no longer spoke the same language as policymakers.

Adding to this sense of distance and alienation was a new and much more critical understanding of the proper relationship between scholars and the state – not a surprising development in the aftermath of a period in which the pernicious ends to which scholarly knowledge could be put had been made all too visible, in Vietnam but elsewhere as well. As we saw in Chapter 4, in the first decades of the Cold War a good many scholars in this as in other area studies fields, especially social scientists working on contemporary issues, saw no problem with conducting research on behalf of the government and cooperating with intelligence agencies, because they were all part of the good fight against communism. By the 1980s those who were assuming the leadership in US Middle East studies were by and large much more wary about their sources of funding and the ends to which their training and research, and that of their students, might be put. Fewer scholars were willing to allow what they knew about the region to be used in the service of a state about whose policies they were often at least dubious, for example by conducting research for agencies like the CIA or by encouraging promising students to enter government service. There developed a widespread sense that to allow one's research agenda to be determined by the needs of the state or serve potentially pernicious ends was not only a betrayal of one's integrity as a scholar but might also compromise one's ability to conduct research in the Middle East, where by the 1980s real or alleged CIA connections had gotten Americans and others denounced, kidnapped or worse.

At issue was not government funding per se: since the passage of the National Defense Education Act in 1958 (see Chapter 4), a great many students and scholars working on the Middle East had happily made use of NDFL/FLAS and other government fellowships for language training, graduate study, and research. A large proportion of the budgets of the centers for Middle East studies at universities around the country also came from the federal government. But because this individual and institutional funding came through the US Department of Education it was deemed morally and politically acceptable even by those who most vociferously disagreed with US government policies in the Middle East. Similarly, additional government funding for graduate student and faculty research on the Middle East first made available by the 1992 Near and Middle East Research and Training Act – originally channeled through the Social Science Research Council and later through the Council of American Overseas Research Centers – was not seen as posing a problem, because the funding was allocated first through the US Information Agency and then through the State Department budget.

The real issue was which part of the US government was supplying the funding, for what ends and with what conditions. As early as 1985 the Middle East Studies Association had asked "university-based international studies programs to refrain from responding to requests for research contract proposals from the Defense Academic Research Support Program [established by the Defense Department to fund academic research on issues of interest to the military] or from other intelligence entities and calls upon its members to reflect carefully upon their responsibilities to the academic profession prior to seeking or accepting funding from intelligence sources."

Some years later MESA also criticized the new National Security Education Program, created by the National Security Education Act of 1991. The NSEP sought to bolster the teaching of "less commonly taught" languages (including Arabic, Persian and Turkish), thereby enabling (as the program's website put it) "the nation to remain integrally involved in global issues related to US National Security" as well as to "develop a cadre of professionals with more than the traditional knowledge of language and culture who can use this ability to help the US make sound decisions on and deal effectively with global issues related to US National Security."[21] Unlike other programs funding research and training on the Middle East, the NSEP was housed in the Department of Defense, intelligence agency officials sat on its oversight board, and recipients of the funding it offered were required to work for a government agency involved in national security affairs after their fellowship or scholarship was completed.

In a 1993 resolution endorsed by a referendum of its membership, MESA joined with the African Studies Association and the Latin American Studies Association to "deplore the location of responsibility in the US defense and intelligence community for a major foreign area research, education, and training program... This connection can only increase the existing difficulties of gaining foreign governmental permissions to carry out research and to develop overseas instructional programs. It can also create dangers for students and scholars by fostering the perception of involvement in military or intelligence activities, and may limit academic freedom." MESA called on the government to establish a peer and merit review process for funding applications that would be independent of military, intelligence and foreign policy agencies and to broaden the service requirement so that it would include a much wider range of jobs, including those outside government service.

Until its concerns were met, MESA urged that "its members and their institutions not seek or accept program or research funding from NSEA..." Three years later MESA adopted yet another resolution reiterating its rejection of NSEP because the law appropriating funding for the program now required that all recipients of fellowships agree to work for the Defense Department or some intelligence agency for at least two years, or else repay the cost of their fellowship.[22] (This last requirement was later relaxed somewhat so that recipients who could not find employment with a national security agency despite a "good faith effort" to do so could fulfill the service requirement by working in higher education.) MESA would voice the same concerns about other outgrowths of the NSEP, for example the 2002 National Flagship Language Initiative – Pilot Program (NFLI-P), launched to address what were seen as "America's extraordinary deficiencies in languages critical to national security."[23] Many (though by no means all) Middle East studies faculties adopted MESA's perspective on this issue, declining to seek NSEP funding for themselves or their institutions.

The disinclination by MESA and many of its individual and institutional members to cooperate with the government in ways that had been common in the 1950s and 1960s was certainly not shared by everyone in the field. Yet it is instructive that when in the 1980s reports surfaced of questionable links between academics and intelligence agencies, the most vocal response among scholars in the field was condemnation. A case in point is the scandal surrounding Nadav Safran, whom we met in Chapter 4 as a young political scientist whose first book set forth an analysis of modern Egyptian history informed by modernization theory and who by the mid-1980s was director of Harvard University's Center for Middle Eastern Studies. The scandal erupted when it became known that Safran had taken $45,700 from the Central Intelligence Agency to fund a major international conference he was hosting at Harvard on "Islam and Politics in the Contemporary Muslim World" – a hot topic at the time and one of obvious interest to the CIA. Not only had Safran secretly used CIA funding for this conference, he had not told the invitees, a number of whom were coming from the Middle East, that the CIA was picking up the tab – a decision that could have gotten some of them into very hot water back home. It then came out that Safran had also received a $107,430 grant from the CIA for the research project that led to his 1985 book *Saudi Arabia: The Ceaseless Request for Security*.[24] Safran's contract with the CIA stipulated that the agency had the right to review and approve the manuscript before publication and that its role in funding the book would not be disclosed. And indeed, the book as published made no mention of the fact that the research for it had been partially funded by the CIA.

When the scandal broke, about half of the invitees to Safran's conference withdrew, and many of the faculty and students associated with Harvard's Center for Middle Eastern Studies publicly expressed their unhappiness with what Safran had done. A month later the Middle East Studies Association censured Safran, on the grounds that his actions had violated its 1982 resolution calling on scholars to disclose their sources of research funding. Safran intimated that his critics were motivated by antisemitism, but after an internal investigation at Harvard he agreed to step down as center director at the end of the academic year.[25] Safran was surely not the only academic to have secretly or openly solicited or accepted funding from an intelligence agency for his research in this period, and no doubt such relationships persisted long after this scandal, but the reaction to it – unimaginable in the early decades of US Middle East studies – does indicate how the relationship between academia and the state had changed.

Think tanks and talking heads

But there was a price to be paid for the gap that had opened up between the world of Middle East scholarship and the world of policymaking. If many college- and university-based academics no longer entirely shared the worldview that prevailed in Washington or no longer felt the need to shape their research agenda so that it was relevant to the policies that flowed from that worldview, there were others who stood ready to meet the demand for knowledge that would serve the state. Many of these were based not in institutions of higher education but in the host of think tanks that had proliferated from the 1970s onwards – privately funded institutions oriented toward the production and dissemination of knowledge designed to inform and influence public policy, for our purposes mainly the foreign policy of the United States.

Some of these institutions and organizations went back a long way. The Carnegie Endowment for International Peace, for example, was founded in 1910 to advance international cooperation, while the Council on Foreign Relations, publisher of the influential journal *Foreign Affairs*, was established in 1921, originally as a sort of elite dinner club. The liberal Brookings Institution was established in 1927, supported by Carnegie and Rockefeller funding, while the conservative American Enterprise Institute was founded in 1943 to promote "limited government," "free enterprise" and a "strong foreign policy and national defense." After the Second World War contractors like the huge RAND Corporation entered the field to produce or fund research for the military and intelligence and other government agencies concerned with foreign policy (see Chapter 4). Another wave beginning in the 1960s had witnessed the establishment of a large number of what one observer called "advocacy" think tanks, like the Center for Strategic and International Studies (1962), the Heritage Foundation (1973) and the Cato Institute (1977), which combined "policy research with aggressive marketing techniques" as they struggled to secure funding and influence in an increasingly competitive marketplace. There are now also many "legacy-based" institutions, like the Carter Center in Atlanta and the Nixon Center for Peace and Freedom in Washington, DC. By the end of the twentieth century there were an estimated 2,000 organizations engaged in policy analysis based in the US, a substantial proportion of them focused on foreign policy and international relations.[26] The 1970s also witnessed the establishment of what Lisa Anderson called "a new generation of professional graduate schools of public policy," many of whose graduates went on to work for policy oriented think tanks rather than in colleges and universities.[27]

The Middle East was a relative backwater for the think tank industry until the 1980s. The Middle East Institute, which as I mentioned in Chapter 4 had been founded in 1946, published a journal and organized conferences but exercised relatively little political clout. By contrast, the Washington Institute for Near East Policy (WINEP), founded in 1985, quickly achieved a much higher profile and much greater influence. Describing itself as "a public educational foundation dedicated to scholarly research and informed debate on US interests in the Middle East," WINEP emerged as the leading pro-Israel think tank in Washington. Its founding director, Martin Indyk, had previously worked at the American Israel Public Affairs Committee (AIPAC), founded in 1959 and by the 1970s by far the most well-funded, visible and effective pro-Israel lobbying organization.[28]

Indyk and his colleagues at WINEP worked hard to strengthen Israel's standing in Washington as the key US ally in the Middle East and to ensure that US policy in the region coincided with the policies and strategies of the Israeli government. During the late 1980s and early 1990s this meant trying to foil US recognition of the PLO and US pressure on Israel to halt settlement activity in the West Bank and Gaza and enter serious negotiations. In the 1990s WINEP expanded its purview to encompass the entire Middle East, but its focus always remained on Israel, for which it tried to build support by arguing that Israel and the United States faced a common threat from Islamic radicalism and terrorism, defined rather broadly to encompass virtually all of Israel's enemies, state and non-state. Various other think tanks also began or stepped up research and advocacy on Middle East issues in the late 1990s and early 2000s. These included the Haim Saban Center for Middle East Policy, launched by the Brookings Institution in 2002, and the conservative American Enterprise Institute, but also several new right-wing think tanks.

During the Clinton administration a substantial number of WINEP alumni served in key foreign policy positions, including Martin Indyk himself, appointed as Special Assistant to the President and Senior Director for Near East and South Asian Affairs at the National Security Council and, later, as US Ambassador to Israel. They and other Clinton administration officials promulgated the policy of "dual containment," whereby the United States would seek to isolate, and if possible eliminate, the governments of both Iraq and Iran, not coincidentally perceived as two of Israel's most serious enemies. By the late 1990s, however,

WINEP would itself be outflanked by newer rivals which unlike WINEP openly aligned themselves with the stances of the Israeli right (or even far right) and argued for aggressive US action against Israel's enemies, including the overthrow of the regime of Saddam Husayn in Iraq.

The policies these and other explicitly right-wing think tanks advocated during the Clinton years, when they were in the political wilderness, were initially regarded as extreme and outlandish. But many of them would eventually be adopted by the George W. Bush administration, in which their architects assumed key posts. Among them were Vice President Richard Cheney; Defense Policy Board member (and for a time chair) Richard Perle, a key advocate of war against Iraq; Deputy Defense Secretary Paul Wolfowitz; Undersecretary of State John Bolton; and Undersecretary of Defense Douglas Feith. Before assuming power these men and their colleagues had, through such right-wing organizations as the Project for a New American Century and the Jewish Institute for National Security Affairs, called for the use of US military power to dominate the world, massive increases in military spending, and unequivocal support for the policies of the Israeli right.[29] After the attacks of September 11, 2001, President George W. Bush openly embraced much of their agenda, tacitly supporting Israel's effort to crush the Palestinian uprising by force and in March–April 2003 invading and occupying Iraq.

The first years of the twenty-first century thus witnessed an unprecedented convergence in positions of supreme power in Washington of right-wing (and in some cases Christian fundamentalist) zealots and neo-conservative American Jews united by a common vision of securing permanent and unchallengeable US global hegemony, with a strong focus on the Middle East and a close embrace of Israel, a vision to be achieved by military force if necessary. The war against Iraq was in a sense the pilot project for this radical vision. As Michael Ledeen, in 2003 "resident scholar in the Freedom Chair" at the American Enterprise Institute and long a fixture among right-wing foreign-policy activists, was reported to have put it, crudely but not inaccurately: "Every ten years or so, the United States needs to pick up some small crappy little country and throw it against the wall, just to show the world we mean business."[30] More specifically, a reconstructed, oil-rich Iraq was seen as a valuable new base for US power in the Middle East, enabling the United States to terminate its problematic relationship with Saudi Arabia and compel the Arabs (including the Palestinians) to make peace with Israel on the latter's terms. That the vast majority of the international community, including a great many Americans, vehemently rejected the use of military force to achieve this vision made no difference whatsoever to its advocates.[31]

There were certainly voices raised, in academia, the think tank world and elsewhere, in opposition to this agenda and the understanding of the world which underpinned it, as there had been voices offering alternative views about US policy toward the Middle East at other critical junctures. But during the 1980s, 1990s and early years of the twenty-first century these voices received relatively little attention, and university-based scholars seemed to play a decreasing role in influencing foreign policy. Critics of US foreign policy also found it difficult to make themselves heard through the mass media. It is striking that the great bulk of the "talking heads" who appeared on television to offer their opinions on the 1990–91 Gulf crisis, on the 2003 Iraq war and on other issues relating to the Middle East and US policy toward it seemed to come not from academia but from among professional pundits, from people associated with think tanks or with one of the public policy schools, and from retired military personnel. Whatever their knowledge (or lack thereof) of the languages, politics, histories and cultures of the Middle East, these people spoke the language and shared the mind-set of the Washington foreign policy world in a way few university-based scholars did. They were also used to communicating their perspective in effective sound bites, whereas academics were often put off by the ignorance and political conformism of much (though by no means all) of American mass-media journalism and its tendency to crudely oversimplify complex issues and transform everything (even war) into a form of entertainment.

Of course, this helped bring about a considerable narrowing of the perspectives available to the public and the consolidation of a powerful, indeed almost impenetrable, consensus about the Middle East that encompassed most of the political class and the punditocracy. Republicans and Democrats argued mainly over how best to maintain US hegemony in the region, leaving very little room for those who envisioned a fundamentally different foreign policy founded on peace, democracy, human rights, mutual security, multilateral disarmament, nonintervention and respect for international law. It is, however, worth noting that despite the virtual absence of such views in the mass media, they were embraced by a good many Americans, as evidenced by the massive demonstrations that preceded the US attack on Iraq in March 2003 and the polls which indicated substantial public opposition to war, partly because of the new modes and channels of communication and organizing made possible by the Internet.

Nonetheless, with much of the American public reeling in shock in the aftermath of September 11, critical (and even moderate) voices were largely drowned out by the right, which quickly and effectively moved to implement its global agenda by exploiting public outrage against the

Islamist extremists who had perpetrated the September 11 attacks. They succeeded in "selling" first military intervention in Afghanistan (justified by the fact that the Taliban regime had allowed al-Qa'ida to operate in that country and refused to hand over those responsible for organizing the September 11 attacks) and then war against Iraq, despite the fact that no one was able to produce any credible evidence that the regime of Saddam Husayn had had anything to do with the September 11 attacks or still possessed weapons of mass destruction. In this effort conservative scholars like Bernard Lewis played a significant part, graphically illustrating their continuing, even enhanced, clout in right-wing policymaking circles long after their standing in scholarly circles had declined, as well as the durability and power of some very old Orientalist notions many had mistakenly thought dead as a doornail.

Soon after September 11 Lewis was invited to meetings with President Bush, Vice President Cheney, and members of the Defense Department's key Defense Policy Board, to whom he offered his understanding of the Middle East and the Muslim world and of the role that the United States could and should play in them. Lewis now endorsed the use of US military power to overthrow Saddam Husayn's regime and assured his listeners that after that was accomplished, the United States could without any great difficulty remold Iraq into a democracy which would serve as a beacon and model for the entire region.[32] His larger vision of Islamic history was laid out in his book *What Went Wrong?: Western Impact and Middle Eastern Response*. Though the book was written before the September 11 attacks, it offered a distressed and perplexed American public an explanation for those attacks and Bush administration policymakers a rationale for their response.

As in most of his other work going back half a century, in this book Lewis painted with a very broad brush, writing of "the Islamic world" and "the West" as if they were self-evidently distinct and monolithic entities. Indeed, the book was replete with the kinds of sweeping generalizations and unsupported assertions that scholarship on Islam and the Middle East had moved away from long before, in favor of careful, nuanced, fine-grained analyses well grounded in local histories and contexts. Islam as portrayed by Lewis was always and everywhere introverted, uninterested in other cultures, and imbued with a sense of superiority that would in the nineteenth century be rudely challenged by the superior technology, weaponry and ideas of the West. Virtually ignoring the impact of colonialism, various Muslim societies' complex and quite different engagements with the transformations of the modern era, and unpleasant aspects of Western history, Lewis concluded that Muslims had essentially failed to respond properly to the challenges of modernity.

Instead they had remained religious, inclined to authoritarianism, and full of irrational resentment and anger. A postscript added to the book after the September 11 attacks described them as "the latest phase in a struggle [between Islam and Christendom/the West] that has been going on for more than fourteen centuries."[33]

In yet another book, *The Crisis of Islam: Holy War and Unholy Terror*, written after September 11 and published early in 2003, Lewis once again rehashed the arguments and material he had used in so many of his publications over the previous half-century. Here too his basic argument was that Islam and the Middle East had failed to modernize; hence Islamism and terrorism. Though he faulted the United States for its ties with unpleasant and undemocratic regimes in the Middle East, he also insisted that US policy had been basically successful. One might reasonably conclude from Lewis's analysis that there was really not much the United States or other Western powers could do to fix the problems of the Middle East or Muslim world, since they had had so little to do with creating them in the first place. But despite the essentially pessimistic assessment of the state of the Arab and Muslim worlds manifested in these books, Lewis had by this time become a leading academic advocate of the view that by occupying and reshaping Iraq the United States could lead the Arabs toward democracy, progress and modernity, and the book argued for a vigorous Western military response to the threat posed by "Muslim rage." Since Lewis never really engaged with his critics, he was never compelled to reconcile this apparent contradiction; nor did it much bother those in government and the media whose favorite Middle East expert he had become. As one reviewer put it in 2003, these two books "are well on their way to becoming the standard accounts of the us-and-them, war-of-the worlds, believers-and-infidels conception of the Muslim mind."[34]

Lewis was not alone in his views, of course, though his age, much trumpeted erudition, magisterial style and very British air of authority enhanced his stature. There were others whose perspective on the Middle East also coincided neatly with, and bolstered, the neoconservative foreign policy agenda in the 1990s and early 2000s. Notable among them was the Lebanese-born political scientist Fouad Ajami, of the School of Advanced International Studies in Washington, DC, which boasted one of the country's premier graduate programs in foreign and military policy. Though Ajami's later scholarly work had been roundly criticized within academia because of his sweeping and questionable assertions about what he saw as the self-induced pathologies of Arab culture and politics, his Arab origins and his endorsement of the agenda of the US and Israeli right opened doors in Washington and made him a media star, someone whose role it was (as the author of one magazine profile put it) "to unpack the unfathomable mysteries of the Arab and Muslim world and to help sell America's wars in the region." Ajami's pronouncements, like those of Bernard Lewis, were solicited and cited by high officials of the Bush administration. For example, in an August 2002 speech to the Veterans of Foreign Wars laying out the case for war against Iraq and the overthrow of Saddam Husayn's regime, Vice President Dick Cheney declared that, "as for the reaction in the Arab street, the Middle East expert Professor Fuad Ajami predicts that after liberation, the streets in Basra and Baghdad are sure to erupt in joy in the same way throngs in Kabul greeted the Americans."[35]

Rough politics: blacklisting and the silencing of dissent

Luminaries like Ajami and Lewis were seconded by a number of less well-known but more vociferous bulldogs of the right who, in the aftermath of September 11, seized the opportunity to try to delegitimize and silence those who disagreed with them. They were by no means the first to go after their opponents in this manner. As political divisions within the field of Middle East studies had become more intense from the 1970s onward, especially over the Israeli–Palestinian conflict, various unpleasant accusations about anti-Arab or anti-Israel (or even antisemitic) bias had been bandied about, particularly by nonacademic organizations which sought to influence the academic study of the Middle East by narrowing the range of opinions deemed legitimate.

Especially vocal and effective were organizations that defined themselves as pro-Israel, including AIPAC and the Anti-Defamation League (ADL), founded by the Jewish fraternal organization Bnai Brith in 1913 to combat antisemitism and other forms of bigotry. Among other things, these organizations claimed that Saudi and other Arab money was being used to fund new positions and programs at US universities and thereby insinuate an unwholesome pro-Arab bias into Middle East studies. These concerns were not inherently invalid: many colleges and universities have faced legitimate questions about whether large donations come with strings attached, visible or invisible, that might affect faculty appointments, curriculum and programming, and several US universities did in fact accept donations from wealthy Arabs, including members of some of the ruling families of the oil-rich Gulf states, to fund chairs or programs in Arab studies. But it is not clear that these donations had any untoward influence on scholarship or teaching at those institutions, and in any case American universities also accepted, without much controversy, large donations for Jewish and Israeli studies programs from people (Jews and non-Jews) strongly supportive of Israel.

Such controversies did not always involve Arabs and Jews. For example, in the 1990s Armenian-Americans and others in the United States sounded the alarm when the Turkish government offered to fund new chairs in Ottoman and Turkish studies at leading American universities. Their fears seemed to be borne out when evidence surfaced that the scholar appointed to a Turkish-funded chair at Princeton University had advised the Turkish ambassador to the United States on how to combat Armenian demands that Turkey acknowledge that hundreds of thousands of Armenians had been massacred in the Ottoman empire during the First World War. Bernard Lewis would also get caught up in this issue: in June 1995, following lawsuits filed by Armenian and antiracist organizations, a French court found that Lewis had "failed in his duty of prudence and objectivity" by making "erroneous" statements that denied or downplayed the Armenian genocide. Lewis was required to pay a symbolic one franc in damages.[36]

In the 1980s AIPAC and the ADL compiled and circulated material accusing various scholars of being anti-Israel propagandists and pro-Arab apologists, and there is evidence that efforts were also made to try to prevent otherwise qualified scholars (some of them Jews) from securing academic positions because they were deemed critical of Israeli policies. There were also claims that antisemitism was rampant in Middle East studies. Some of these organizations' targets, as well as other critics, responded by pointing out that these organizations defined antisemitism so broadly as to encompass virtually all criticism of Israel, and that in fact a good many American and Israeli Jews held views these organizations denounced as antisemitic. They argued that the real threat to academic freedom came from efforts by AIPAC, the ADL and similar organizations intent on defending the official Israeli line to suppress open debate about Israeli policies and the "special relationship" between Israel and the United States by intimidating and silencing those perceived as critical of Israel. The compilation and circulation by these organizations of "blacklists" reminded many of the tactics used during the McCarthy-era anticommunist "Red Scare" and led to the ADL and AIPAC being censured by the Middle East Studies Association.[37]

This does not seem to have deterred the ADL, because in 1993 a police raid on the ADL's San Francisco office revealed that, with the help of a member of the San Francisco Police Department's intelligence unit who had access to police and FBI files, the ADL had for years been collecting information on Palestine solidarity groups and Jewish critics of Israel in the San Francisco area, as well as on local activists in the campaign against

South Africa's apartheid regime and on many other organizations and individuals. Subsequent investigations and lawsuits revealed that some of the data on anti-apartheid organizing collected for the ADL had been made available to the South African government. Though it continued to insist it had done nothing wrong, the ADL eventually paid a substantial sum to settle a suit brought by the city of San Francisco over charges that it had illegally acquired confidential government information and disbursed additional sums to settle other lawsuits.[38]

Edward Said, probably the most outspoken and visible advocate for the Palestinian cause in the United States, was the target of several scurrilous attacks apparently intended to besmirch his character and intimidate critics of Israel. In 1989, for example, the neoconservative Jewish magazine *Commentary* published an exercise in character assassination titled "Professor of Terror." Its author, Edward Alexander, accused Said of leading a "double career as literary scholar and ideologue of terror," because Said had allegedly defended the punishment of Palestinians who collaborated with the Israeli occupation during the first Palestinian *intifada*, but more broadly because for Alexander the PLO (of whose Palestine National Council Said was then a member) was nothing but a terrorist organization, so that anyone who supported it was *ipso facto* a terrorist or, at best, an apologist for terrorism.[39]

As we saw in our discussion of terrorism, this was an argument which the Israeli right and its allies in the United States propagated widely. A decade later *Commentary* returned to the fray by publishing an article accusing Said of lying about his own life story by claiming that he had spent his childhood in Jerusalem rather than in Cairo. The author's real goal seems to have been to undermine Said's credibility and that of the Palestinian cause as a whole, in keeping with the Israeli right's ultimately successful effort to discredit and derail Israeli–Palestinian negotiations which might have led to Israeli withdrawal from the occupied territories, the dismantling of Jewish settlements and the establishment of a Palestinian state in the West Bank and Gaza.[40]

After the September 11 attacks, some on the far-right end of the Middle East studies spectrum decided to exploit this apparently propitious moment to launch an assault on scholars in Middle East studies who did not kowtow to the views of the Bush administration and those of the Israeli right. A key figure in this campaign was Daniel Pipes, who received his Ph.D. in medieval Islamic history from Harvard in 1978 but soon began to focus on contemporary issues. In various articles and in his 1983 book, *In the Path of God: Islam and Political Power*, Pipes argued that the "Islamic revival" of recent years was attributable largely to the vast sums expended by the Saudi and Libyan regimes, enriched by the post-1973 rise in oil prices, to disseminate and promote their versions of Islam. As a result, Pipes predicted, "current waves of Islamic activism would die along with the OPEC boom."[41] Pipes' thinking apparently evolved in the years that followed, when oil prices dropped but Islamist movements flourished, for on his own website he would later tout himself as "one of the few analysts who understood the threat of militant Islam."

Pipes taught at various universities for short stints and held minor government posts but never secured a permanent academic position; instead he made something of himself in right-wing foreign policy circles. He served as editor of the conservative foreign policy journal *Orbis* and by 1990 had become director of his own small think tank, the Philadelphia-based Middle East Forum, whose goal was to "define and promote American interests" in the Middle East. Those interests were defined as "strong ties with Israel, Turkey, and other democracies as they emerge," human rights, "a stable supply and a low price of oil," and "the peaceful settlement of regional and international disputes."[42]

In the 1990s Pipes carved out a small but moderately successful niche for himself in the world of right-wing punditry, disseminating his views through op-ed pieces, magazine articles, books, public lectures and appearances on television and radio talk shows, as well as through his own publication, *Middle East Quarterly*. By the mid-1990s Pipes was arguing that militant Islam posed a grave threat to the United States and its allies, especially Israel. This threat should be met, Pipes believed, not by acknowledgement or accommodation of essentially baseless Muslim grievances but by a tough, indeed aggressive stance to undermine or eradicate the militants and the states which supposedly fostered them – the same kind of stance which the Republican right believed had won the Cold War and which it now wanted to serve as the foundation for US foreign policy in the post-Cold War world. For Pipes this also meant promoting the views and policies of the Israeli right, which rejected the kind of peace settlement (with the Palestinians but also with Syria) that most of the world (including many Israelis) regarded as reasonable and instead sought to use Israel's military superiority (and if possible America's as well) to impose its terms for peace on the Arabs.

Like others on the American Jewish right, and increasingly also the non-Jewish right, Pipes argued that the interests of Israel and the United States had converged: militant Islam had replaced the Soviet Union and its allies as the gravest threat to both, and they should work together to confront this threat by all means necessary. Along the way Pipes acquired a reputation in Muslim-American circles as an "Islamophobe" and "Muslim basher" whose writings and public utterances aroused fear and suspicion toward Muslims. Pipes claimed that he was not against Muslims or Islam but was only opposed to Islamism, which distorted Islam and used terrorism to attack the United States and its allies. Yet the tone and often the content of much of what he had to say could plausibly be understood as inciting suspicion and mistrust of Muslims, including Muslim-Americans, and as derogatory of Islam.[43]

In his campaign against radical Islam – critics said Islam period – Pipes sometimes collaborated with journalist Steven Emerson, whose main focus during the 1990s was to sound the alarm about the threat Muslim terrorists posed to the United States. By the end of that decade Emerson was describing himself as a "terrorist expert and investigator" and "Executive Director, Terrorism Newswire, Inc." Along the way, critics charged, Emerson had sounded many false alarms, made numerous errors of fact, bandied accusations about rather freely, and ceased to be regarded as credible by much of the mainstream media.[44] The September 11 attacks seemed to bear out Emerson's warnings, but his critics would probably respond that even a broken clock shows the right time twice a day. Pipes' association with Emerson and others like him did not enhance his standing among either scholars or more balanced journalists and commentators.

A year after the September 11 attacks, Pipes and his Middle East Forum launched a new initiative directly targeting academic Middle East studies. This was a website called Campus Watch, ostensibly established to "review and critique Middle East studies in North America, with an aim to improving them." Campus Watch initiated its campaign against those who did not share Pipes's right-wing views by attacking eight professors of Middle East or Islamic studies from institutions around the country for what Pipes deemed unacceptable views about Islam, Islamism, Palestinian rights, and/or US policy in the region; the website also cited fourteen universities for similar sins. Among those attacked was Professor John Esposito of Georgetown University, who was characterized as an apologist for Islamic and Palestinian terrorism, apparently because he had urged attention to the grievances that led some Muslims to perpetrate suicide bombings and many more to applaud or tolerate them, and also advocated the scholarly study of Islamism rather than blanket denunciation. Campus Watch also invited college students and others to monitor their professors and send in classroom statements which they deemed anti-Israel or anti-American, helping Campus Watch compile "dossiers" on suspect faculty and academic institutions.

The attacks prompted a storm of protest: over one hundred professors from around the country sent messages denouncing Campus Watch for its crude attempt to silence debate about the Middle East and the airing of critical views by insinuating that the scholars under attack had been apologists for terrorism or were somehow unpatriotic. To show solidarity with their beleaguered fellow scholars, many of the protestors demanded that they too be added to Campus Watch's blacklist.[45] Campus Watch thereupon compounded the damage it had already done by listing the names of those who had written to protest its smear campaign under a heading which stated that they had done so "in defense of apologists for Palestinian violence and militant Islam."

This was of course an egregious falsehood, because those who had written Campus Watch in protest did not for a minute accept Campus Watch's original allegation that the first eight scholars it had attacked were apologists for terrorism. They had written to denounce Campus Watch for launching what they saw as a vicious attack, by means of distortion and innuendo, on respectable scholars and to uphold academic freedom, the right of free speech and the importance to a democratic society of open discussion of issues of public concern. The protests and considerable media interest (and criticism) apparently led Campus Watch to back down and remove the web pages attacking the eight scholars as well as pages containing dossiers on individual professors. But it persisted in its mission of rooting out purported anti-Americanism, antisemitism, extremism, and apologetics for terrorism among academics.

In what may have been a reward for his vigorous advocacy of US military intervention in the Muslim world and his vociferous attacks on critics of official policy, in April 2003 President Bush nominated Pipes to the board of directors of the United States Institute of Peace, a federally funded institution dedicated to preventing, managing and peacefully resolving international conflicts. This appointment struck many as rather ironic, not only because Pipes opposed even the Bush administration's rather half-hearted and inconsistent efforts to restart Israeli–Palestinian negotiations but also because Pipes had expressed himself in favor of resolving conflicts through the use of superior military force rather than through negotiations. Muslim-American groups were outraged by the appointment of someone they believed had deliberately sought to spread fear and suspicion about Islam and Muslims, but so were moderate scholars who regarded Pipes as extreme in his views as well as in how he expressed them and therefore not suitable for a position on the board of this kind of institution. The liberal *Washington Post* called the Pipes nomination "salt in the wound" and a "cruel joke" for US Muslims and urged that it be rescinded by the White House or rejected by Congress.[46] When the nomination came before a Senate committee in July 2003, a number of Democratic senators expressed opposition and the session ended without a vote; the following month President Bush bypassed

Congress and installed Pipes as a member of the USIP board by means of a recess appointment, valid until the Congressional session ended in January 2005.

Critique from the right

Daniel Pipes was not alone in seeing academic Middle East studies as a cesspool of error, fuzzy thinking and anti-Americanism. Soon after the September 11 attacks the Washington Institute for Near East Policy published a book by Martin Kramer titled *Ivory Towers on Sand: The Failure of Middle Eastern Studies in America.*[47] Whereas Pipes's Campus Watch specialized in attacking scholars and academic institutions, Kramer's book claimed to offer a detailed and comprehensive critique of US Middle East studies from the right and therefore merits serious discussion.

After receiving his doctorate from Princeton University, Martin Kramer moved to Israel where he served as a research associate at Tel Aviv University's Moshe Dayan Center for Middle Eastern and African Studies, and then as the center's associate director (1987–95) and director (1995–2001). The Dayan Center, which describes itself as "an interdisciplinary research center devoted to the study of the modern history and contemporary affairs of the Middle East," is of course named after the famous Israeli general and politician, but it incorporated and superseded an older institution, the Shiloah Institute, named after Reuven Shiloah, the founder of Israel's intelligence and security apparatus. Both the old and new names reflect the Center's ongoing role as not merely a scholarly institution (though there have certainly been some serious scholars associated with it) but also a key site where senior Israeli military, foreign policy and intelligence officials can interact with academics working on policy-relevant issues.[48] It would seem that the Dayan Center provided Martin Kramer with his ideal model of the proper relationship between the world of scholarship and the world of policymaking, for the main complaint Kramer voiced in *Ivory Towers* was that US-based scholars of the Middle East had failed, or refused, to meet the US government's need for useful knowledge and accurate predictions about the region.

Kramer's basic argument was that Middle East studies is, to put it simply, a miserable failure. "America's academics have," he asserted, "failed to predict or explain the major evolutions of Middle Eastern politics and society over the past two decades. Time and again, academics have been taken by surprise by their subjects; time and again, their paradigms have been swept away by events. Repeated failures have depleted the credibility of scholarship among influential publics. In Washington, the mere mention of academic Middle Eastern studies often causes eyes to roll."[49]

To explain how this came about, Kramer offered his interpretation of the development of Middle East studies in America, portrayed as a fall from (relative) grace largely attributable to the pernicious influence of one bad doctrine and its chief propagator, Edward W. Said.

Kramer began by briefly recounting the origins and early history of Middle East studies in the United States. Despite promising beginnings, things did not go well. Too many scholars were in the grip of overly optimistic notions like modernization theory, which posited that the entire world (including the Middle East) could and would be remade in the image of the United States of the 1950s. In the 1970s the Lebanese civil war and then the Iranian revolution shattered this illusion, revealing the field's intellectual bankruptcy and leaving it without a dominant paradigm. Even worse, scholarly standards were appallingly low, which allowed "tenured incompetents" to secure many of the all too scarce academic positions, breeding resentment among new graduates and graduate students. Government and foundation funding dropped, exacerbating the sense of crisis in the field.

For Kramer it was this crisis which accounted for the success of Said's *Orientalism* and the transformation it almost single-handedly wrought in US Middle East studies. Despite that book's grave flaws, it served perfectly as a weapon in the hands of insurgents pushing a radical political and theoretical agenda. By delegitimizing established scholars and scholarship and providing an alternative theory and politics, it helped the academic left – and especially the Arabs and Muslims among them – achieve intellectual and institutional hegemony in US Middle East studies. Kramer attributed what he saw as the abject failure of most scholars to resist the onslaught of Said and his acolytes to a loss of self-confidence, stemming from the failure of the models in which they had earlier put so much faith.

The damage *Orientalism* wreaked on US Middle East studies was considerable, in Kramer's assessment: "*Orientalism* made it acceptable, even expected, for scholars to spell out their own political commitments as a preface to anything they wrote or did. More than that, it enshrined an acceptable hierarchy of political commitments, with Palestine at the top, followed by the Arab nation and the Islamic world. They were the long-suffering victims of Western racism, American imperialism, and Israeli Zionism – the three legs of the orientalist stool."[50] Said's *Orientalism* also allegedly licensed political and ethnic tests for admission to the field: one had to be a leftist or, even better, an Arab or Muslim, whose numbers now increased dramatically. However, despite their pretensions to intellectual superiority, Said's acolytes who seized control of US Middle East studies in the 1980s failed to do any better than their discredited predecessors in predicting or explaining the dynamics of Middle Eastern politics, precisely because their predictions were driven by their radical politics and trendy postmodernist theorizing, not by careful observation of the real world.

For example, Kramer argued, the Saidian left utterly failed to anticipate or account for the rise of Islamism; all they could manage were denunciations of purported American bias against Islam and Muslims. In the 1990s, liberals like John Esposito who understood that Said's message and tone were too radical and off-putting for the American mainstream developed an accessible, upbeat, softened image of Islam and Islamism, downplaying their violent and threatening dimensions. Esposito and others seized on a string of would-be "Muslim Luthers" who could be touted as the forerunners of an imminent Islamic "reformation," all the while failing to notice the ways in which authoritarian Arab states were successfully promoting secularization and blocking the Islamist challenge. Similarly, because they were convinced that the Arab regimes were fragile and lacked legitimacy and social roots, liberal and leftist scholars had grossly underestimated those regimes' durability; all the scholarly attention and foundation funding devoted to the study of "civil society" in the Arab world were thus based on vain illusions and missed what was really going on in the region. Overall, Kramer charged, US Middle East scholars, misled by their political agenda and arcane theories, had failed to take the real history and culture of the region into account. As a result, their prognoses were mistaken and of decreasing interest to policymakers.

Kramer went on to attack the Social Science Research Council for its alleged failure – even refusal – to use the government funding it received to support policy-relevant research, and the Middle East Studies Association for its rejection of the National Security Education Program. The "new mandarins" who had assumed leadership of the field lost the confidence of official Washington because of their haughty disdain for policymakers and their squandering of public funds on empty theorizing and worthless research projects. "In the centers of policy, defense, and intelligence," Kramer asserted, "consensus held that little could be learned from academics – not because they knew nothing, but because they deliberately withheld their knowledge from government, or organized it on the basis of arcane priorities or conflicting loyalties."[51]

The self-inflicted crisis of academic Middle East studies was further manifested, Kramer argued, in the growing recourse that government and the media had to Middle East experts based in think tanks rather than those in academia. It was, Kramer claimed, the "intolerant climate" in academia that had led many talented people to gravitate to the think tanks, where their work "often surpassed university-based research in clarity, style, thoroughness, and cogency." Even within universities, however, Middle East studies was in decline, since all the resources invested in it over the decades had yielded little worthwhile knowledge, making deans and departments reluctant to replace retiring faculty in this field, much less hire new faculty and expand programs.

"What will it take to heal Middle Eastern studies," Kramer asked in his conclusion, "if they can be healed at all?" Here Kramer explicitly counterposed the theorizing in which too many academics had indulged to the empirical study of "the Middle East itself," while also advocating renewed attention to "the very rich patrimony of scholarly orientalism." "Orientalism had heroes," Kramer continued. "Middle Eastern studies have none, and they never will, unless and until scholars of the Middle East restore some continuity with the great tradition," a continuity ruptured by the foolish social-science models of the 1950s and 1960s and then by the destruction wrought by Said and his postmodernist devotees. In the longer run, despite the resistance of the radical mandarins and the inertia of the SSRC and the foundations, "breakthroughs will come from individual scholars, often laboring on the margins. As the dominant paradigms grow ever more elaborate, inefficient, and insufficient, they will begin to shift. There will be more confessions [of failure] by senior scholars, and more defections by their young protégés."[52]

To hasten this process, Kramer suggested that the federal government reform the process it used to decide which Title VI-funded national resource centers, including centers for Middle East studies, received funding, by including government officials in the review process and encouraging more attention to public outreach activities. More broadly, Congress should hold hearings "on the contribution of Middle Eastern studies to American public policy," with testimony not only from academics but from government officials, directors of think tanks and others as well. While such steps might help, Kramer concluded, ultimately the field would have to heal itself by overcoming its irrelevance and its intolerance of intellectual and political diversity. Its new leaders would have to forge a different kind of relationship with "the world beyond the campus," based on the principle that "the United States plays an essentially beneficent role in the world."

Some of the criticisms of US Middle East studies which Kramer set forth in *Ivory Towers* may seem to resonate with those set forth in this book. For example, Kramer depicted modernization theory as flawed, though he ignored the Cold War context which produced it and explained its popularity in psychological terms, as the product of Americans' missionary zeal and naïve optimism. Some of the prognoses offered by scholars in the early and mid-1990s about the moderation and fading away of Islamism were indeed overly broad, though it is also worth noting that in some countries (Turkey, for example) Islamist parties did in fact evolve in a democratic and moderate direction. And Kramer was correct to note that both mainstream and political economy-oriented Middle East scholars generally failed to anticipate the rise of Islamist movements in the 1970s, though he ignored the sophisticated analyses subsequently advanced by scholars.

As a history of Middle East studies as a scholarly field, however, Kramer's approach was deeply flawed. Kramer simplistically blamed Edward Said and *Orientalism* for everything that he believed had gone wrong with Middle East studies from the late 1970s onward, utterly ignoring both the extensive critiques of modernization theory and Orientalism that preceded the publication of that book (see Chapter 5) and the complex and often critical ways in which Said's intervention was received (see Chapter 6). As *Ivory Towers* tells the story, every scholar in Middle East studies either lost his or her critical faculties and slavishly embraced every pronouncement that fell from the lips of Edward W. Said, or else cringed in terror and kept silent. This is clearly a caricature: as we saw, for the most part scholars in the field did not simply swallow Said's take on Orientalism hook, line and sinker but engaged with it critically, accepting what seemed useful and rejecting, recasting or developing other aspects. And Kramer's psychologizing account of why so many scholars and students in Middle East studies were receptive to critiques of the field's hitherto dominant paradigms was shallow and inadequate, as well as tendentious.

All too often Kramer resorted to cheap shots and epithets instead of serious analysis. For example, it was no doubt good fun for Kramer to characterize the scholars of the Middle East and Islam at my own institution, New York University, as "post-orientalist fashion designers," but this does not really tell us much about what actually goes on there. More broadly, as Juan Cole of the University of Michigan has shown, such right-wing attacks on Middle East scholars as "postmodernist, leftist, anti-American terrorist-coddlers" have little basis in reality. By way of example Cole pointed out that of the fourteen senior professors of Middle East political science teaching at federally funded national resource centers as of early 2003, only one could plausibly be characterized as a postmodernist, few would define themselves as leftists, and none could reasonably be called anti-American (whatever that means) or apologists for terrorism.[53]

Kramer claimed in *Ivory Towers* that US Middle East scholars had repeatedly made predictions that did not come true. In some instances his accusations were on-target; in others he took quotations out of context or misconstrued them. But he was also rather selective: for example, in *Ivory Towers* we do not find Kramer taking his colleague Daniel Pipes to task for inaccurately predicting in the early 1980s that Islamist activism would decline as oil prices fell, nor is it likely that he would see fit to criticize mentors like Bernard Lewis and Fouad Ajami for predicting that virtually all Iraqis would welcome invading US forces and happily accept American occupation.[54] Nor has Kramer's long-time institutional base, the Dayan Center in Tel Aviv, been especially successful at predicting significant developments, for example the outbreak of the first Palestinian *intifada* against Israeli occupation in 1987.

More broadly, however, Kramer's fixation on accurate prediction as the chief (or even sole) gauge of good scholarship is itself highly questionable. Most scholars do not in fact seek to predict the future or think they can do so; they try to interpret the past, discern and explain contemporary trends and, at most, tentatively suggest what *might* happen in the future if present trends continue, which they very often do not. Of course, governments want accurate predictions in order to shape and implement effective policies, but Kramer's insistence that the primary goal of scholarship should be the satisfaction of that desire tells us a great deal about his conception of intellectual life and of the proper relationship between scholars and the state.

As I suggested earlier, Kramer's model of what US Middle East studies should be seems to be based on the institution with which he was affiliated for some two decades, the Dayan Center. Just as many (though by no means all) of the Israeli scholars associated with the Dayan Center have seen themselves as producing knowledge that will serve the security and foreign policy needs of Israel, so American scholars of the Middle East should, Kramer suggested, shape their research agendas to provide the kinds of knowledge the US government will find most useful. His book demonstrated no interest whatsoever in the uses to which such knowledge might be put or in the question of the responsibility of intellectuals to maintain their independence and "speak truth to power," or indeed in what scholarship and intellectual life should really be about. His real complaint was that US Middle East studies had failed to produce knowledge useful to the state. Yet by ignoring larger political and institutional contexts, Kramer could not understand or explain why so many scholars had grown less than enthusiastic about producing the kind of knowledge about the Middle East the government wanted – or conversely, why it was that the government and the media now routinely turned to analysts based in think tanks, along with former military and intelligence personnel, for policy-relevant knowledge rooted in the official consensus about what constitutes America's "national interest" in the Middle East.

But there is a larger issue at stake here. At the very heart of Kramer's approach is a dubious distinction between the trendy, arcane "theorizing" of the scholarship he condemned as at best irrelevant and at worst pernicious, on the one hand, and on the other the purportedly hard-headed, clear-sighted, theory-free observation of, and research on, the "real Middle East" in which he and scholars like him see themselves as engaging. Kramer was not wrong to suggest that there has been some trendy theory-mongering in academia, including Middle East studies. But he went well beyond this by now banal observation, and beyond a rejection of poststructuralism, to imply that all theories, paradigms and models are distorting and useless, because they get in the way of the direct, unmediated, accurate access to reality that he seemed to believe he and those who think like him possess.

This seems to me an extraordinarily naive and unsophisticated understanding of how knowledge is produced, one that few scholars in the humanities and social sciences have taken seriously for a long time. Even among historians, once the most positivist of scholars, few would today argue that the facts "speak for themselves" in any simple sense. Almost all would acknowledge that deciding what should be construed as significant facts for the specific project of historical reconstruction in which they are engaged, choosing which are more relevant and important to the question at hand and which less so, and crafting a story in one particular way rather than another all involve making judgments that are, at bottom, rooted in some sense of how the world works – in short, in some theory or model or paradigm or vision, whether implicit or explicit, whether consciously acknowledged or not. Kramer's inability or refusal to grasp this suggests a grave lack of self-awareness, coupled with an alarming disinterest in some of the most important debates scholars have been having over the past four decades or so.

It is moreover a stance which Kramer did not – indeed, could not – maintain in practice. His assertions throughout the book were in fact based on a certain framework of interpretation, even as he insisted that they were merely the product of his acute and hard-headed powers of observation, analysis and prediction. It is for example striking that at the very end of *Ivory Towers* Kramer explicitly set forth what is obviously a political and moral judgment rooted in his own (theoretical) vision of the world: his insistence that a healthy, reconstructed Middle East studies must accept that the United States "plays an essentially beneficent role in the world." He never explained *why* we should accept this vision of the US role in the world as true, nor did he even acknowledge that it may be something other than self-evidently true. The assertion nonetheless undermined his avowed epistemological stance and graphically demonstrated its untenability.

Similarly, though this is largely implied rather than clearly asserted, Kramer seemed to regard Bernard Lewis' notion of the "return" of an ever-present, wounded and enraged "Islam" as the best way of explaining Islamism as a sociopolitical phenomenon. Yet it should be obvious that that interpretation can hardly be taken as simple common sense, as the product of empirical observation untainted by theory. It is rather the product of a specific framework of interpretation which one may accept or reject, embrace or question, but which definitely rests upon certain assumptions about the proper category and method of analysis to be used in order to elucidate the phenomenon being studied. So while Kramer had a good time attacking others for their theorizing, he did not seem to realize that he was doing a fair bit of theorizing himself.

I have treated *Ivory Towers Built on Sand* here as if it were a serious intellectual exercise. Yet it was clearly written and published as a politically motivated polemic, an attack on MESA and the "Middle Eastern studies establishment" designed to further Kramer's political agenda. It is noteworthy that in the same year *Ivory Towers* was published, Martin Kramer assumed the post of editor of *Middle East Quarterly*, published by Daniel Pipes' Middle East Forum. From this perspective, Pipes' McCarthyesque assault on mainstream, liberal and leftist scholars of Middle East studies by means of his Campus Watch website and Kramer's intellectually simplistic and tendentious critique of US Middle East studies can be seen as complementary. One might even go so far as to portray Kramer and Pipes as, respectively, the "good cop" and "bad cop" of the far-right end of the Middle East studies spectrum.

The Campaign against Middle East Studies

The attacks which Pipes and Kramer launched on MESA and Middle East studies in the United States after the September 11 attacks were quickly picked up by the conservative and neoconservative media, yielding a spate of articles in such magazines as *National Review* and on right-wing websites. Echoing Pipes and Kramer, right-wing commentators attacked MESA because its annual meeting allegedly featured too many scholarly panels on topics they deemed esoteric and irrelevant, and not enough panels on al-Qa'ida, Palestinian suicide bombings and "anti-American incitement." Such denigration of anything scholars do that does not produce knowledge that is immediately and directly useful to the government suggests a worrisome anti-intellectualism as well as a gross misunderstanding of the role scholars and institutions of higher education play in a democratic society. Moreover, as Juan Cole has noted, there have in fact been endless academic publications, panels and conferences on Islamism over the past quarter-century, and insisting that MESA (which is in any case supported not by the federal government but by its members' dues) devote itself exclusively to this topic would be like "insisting that Italian historians work only on the Cosa Nostra."[55] It is also worth noting that many Middle East scholars, including some who have been vocal critics of US policy in the region, have always been quite willing to share their expertise and perspectives with government officials and agencies, and their numbers have probably grown since September 11 – though it is not clear that official Washington has been very interested in engaging with critical perspectives.

Some right-wing critics went beyond Kramer's proposals for "reform" of the Title VI program and called for federal funding of Middle East studies to be reduced or cut off. Others urged that the Department of Education use its control over Title VI funding to mandate "balance" and "diversity" in teaching about the Middle East, and particularly about the Arab-Israeli conflict. In this context balance and diversity seemed to be code words for pressuring colleges and universities to muzzle critics of US and Israeli policies and promote viewpoints more congenial to those of the Bush administration and the Israeli government. This was made explicit in proposals put forward by a number of right-wing members of Congress. In April 2003, for example, Senator Rick Santorum, Republican of Pennsylvania, announced plans to introduce legislation that would cut off federal funding to American colleges and universities that were deemed to be permitting faculty, students and student organizations to openly criticize Israel, since Santorum seemed to regard all such criticism as inherently antisemitic. Meanwhile, Santorum's colleague Senator Sam Brownback of Kansas proposed the creation of a federal commission to investigate alleged antisemitism on campus – again defined rather broadly to include virtually all criticism of Israeli policies.[56]

This campaign to use the power of the federal government to reshape the academic study of the Middle East began to bear fruit in June 2003. Responding to right-wing allegations about the abuse of Title VI funding by "extreme" and "one-sided" critics of US foreign policy, the Select Education Subcommittee of the House of Representatives' Committee on Education and the Workforce convened brief hearings on "International Programs in Higher Education and Questions of Bias" at which a conservative critic repeated allegations that Title VI-funded Middle East centers were infested by anti-American acolytes of Edward Said.[57] Over the months that followed this committee formulated, and the

(Republican-controlled) House of Representatives passed, legislation to extend Title VI funding which for the first time mandated that programs "foster debate on American foreign policy from diverse perspectives." The bill also provided for the creation of a new International Higher Education Advisory Board with the power to monitor and evaluate federally funded area studies programs; four of the board's seven members would be appointed by congressional leaders and at least two of the remaining three members would represent national security agencies. This and similar proposals were for several years blocked by Senate Democrats who were concerned that they might open the door to an unprecedented degree of partisan political intrusion into university-based area studies, particularly Title VI-funded Middle East studies centers. These proposals were also opposed by a broad range of groups involved in higher education, which perceived them as part of a campaign to stifle critical voices and as a threat to the autonomy of American institutions of higher education and long-established principles of academic freedom. Thanks to persistent lobbying, however, allegations about "bias" in Middle East studies and proposals to amend Title VI in order to promote "diversity" continued to surface every time the program came up for Congressional reauthorization.

In the summer of 2008 critics of the Title VI program finally achieved a measure of success: Congress passed, and President Bush signed, a bill that reauthorized the program but for the first time included a requirement that institutions applying for Title VI funding explain "how the activities funded by the grant will reflect diverse perspectives and a wide range of views and generate debate on world regions and international affairs." Applicants were also required to describe how they would encourage students to enter government service in "areas of national need," to be determined by the Secretary of Education after consultation with a wide range of federal agencies. It remains to be seen what impact these provisions will actually have on the allocation of Title VI funding and on the direction and character of the program.[58]

Partisans of the US and Israeli right, and critics of mainstream Middle East studies, continued to pursue their agenda in a variety of other arenas as well through the end of the Bush presidency. For example, in 2006 the United States Commission on Civil Rights issued a briefing report entitled "Campus Anti-Semitism," and somewhat later its findings and recommendations on the issue. Based on a rather cursory and partisan "factfinding" process, the report and findings seemed to conflate criticism of Zionism and Israel with antisemitism while accepting at face value questionable assertions concerning alleged antisemitic incidents on university campuses. It would seem that the real purpose of this exercise

was not to combat actual antisemitism on university campuses but to
censor and delegitimize certain opinions expressed by faculty by tarring
them with the brush of antisemitism.[59]

At the state level David Horowitz, a 1960s radical turned ultracon-
servative, orchestrated a campaign to induce state legislatures to enact a
"Student Bill of Rights" that would combat the allegedly pervasive indoctrination of innocent college students by leftist faculty. As of 2008 no state
had actually adopted such legislation, but through his online magazine
FrontPage, and its associated Jihad Watch website, Horowitz and his allies
(like Pipes and his acolytes at Campus Watch, along with other groups)
continued vociferously to accuse scholars who argued for a complex and
historically grounded understanding of Islam and Islamism, or who were
critical of US or Israeli policies, of being "anti-American" and support-
ers of terrorism. Middle East studies centers, programs and departments
were accused of lacking balance and diversity, or of harboring critics
of Israel (often depicted as antisemites). There were also instances in
which invitations to scholars for speaking engagements were withdrawn
by the sponsors after pressure from outside groups, usually because
of the invitees' actual or purported positions on the Israeli–Palestinian
conflict.

One particularly egregious incident, in which a local government
agency actually blacklisted a respected Middle East scholar on the basis
of his purported political views, was reminiscent of the "Red Scare"
of the late 1940s and 1950s, when schoolteachers and college faculty
(among others) who had been accused of communist affiliations, or who
refused to testify about their political beliefs or sign "loyalty oaths,"
were driven from their jobs or denied employment. Early in 2005 the
right-wing *New York Sun,* along with a vote-seeking candidate in the
Democratic primary for mayor of New York City, went after Professor
Rashid Khalidi of Columbia University for criticisms he had allegedly
voiced of Israeli policies toward the Palestinians. Without giving Khalidi
any opportunity to respond to the allegations against him, the chancellor
of the New York City public schools barred Khalidi from participating in a professional development program that Columbia, like other
universities with Title VI centers, had been running for city schoolteachers. To its credit Columbia University defended Khalidi's First Amend-
ment rights, rebuked the chancellor and severed its connection with the
teacher-training program.[60]

It is worth noting that David Horowitz, maestro of *FrontPage* and
the Student Bill of Rights, was also one of the chief purveyors of the
term "Islamofascism." Along with Paul Berman, Christopher Hitchens
and several other formerly left-leaning intellectuals who had embraced

some or all of the Bush agenda, as well as many neoconservatives, Horowitz used this term to denote a broad range of avowedly Islamic regimes, groups and trends that were supposedly very similar to the European fascist and Nazi movements and regimes of the interwar years and should therefore be fought just as vigorously. This identification of (a very loosely defined) radical Islamism with fascism seems to have been intended to help whip up public support for the Bush administration's policies, among other things by portraying the invasion of Iraq (and the open-ended and apparently permanent "global war on terror") as the moral equivalent of the Second World War. However, most scholars and observers of Islam and Islamist movements rejected the equation of Islamism and fascism as historically and analytically inaccurate and misleading, in part because it unhelpfully lumped together regimes and movements as different from (and as often in conflict with) one another as Hizbullah, al-Qa'ida, the Islamic Republic of Iran, Hamas, the Taliban in Afghanistan, the Muslim Brothers in Egypt, and Saudi Arabia – the latter, of course, a close ally of the United States.

In the post-September 11 period, groups based outside of academia also stepped up efforts to deny jobs, tenure or promotion to scholars they deemed excessively critical of Israel or of US foreign policy in the Middle East. Through scurrilous media and website attacks, by letter-writing and email campaigns, by threatening to withhold donations and by other means, these groups sought to pressure colleges and universities to make decisions based not on a fair and objective peer review of a current or prospective faculty member's record of scholarship, teaching and service but on his or her purported political views. University administrators were not always resolute in resisting such pressures, despite demands by organizations like the Middle East Studies Association and the American Association of University Professors that they vigorously defend their faculty's academic freedom and the integrity and independence of their institutions.[61]

Such campaigns, and the broader right-wing offensive against Middle East studies of which they were a part, cumulatively had something of a chilling effect on scholars of the Middle East and Islam, many of whom understandably felt that they were being monitored, and even sometimes threatened, harassed or persecuted, by apparently well-funded and highly partisan zealots based outside of academia who used every means at their disposal to denounce and defame those with whom they disagreed. Graduate students applying for academic jobs and younger scholars not protected by tenure felt especially vulnerable, knowing that they might be judged on the basis not of their scholarly work and teaching skills but of their real or alleged political views.

More broadly, it was quite plausible to see the often vicious attacks launched against Middle East scholars, against Middle East studies as an academic field, and against the institutions at which that field was based as a campaign directed against knowledge, expertise and scholarship, designed to marginalize or silence those who actually knew something about the region so that the Bush administration and its allies could pursue their manifestly disastrous policies with as little public debate and opposition as possible. (Continuing a trend that, as we have seen, began decades earlier, the Bush administration usually drew its Middle East specialists not from universities but from conservative foreign-policy think tanks.) There was considerable irony in this situation, given that developments in Iraq and elsewhere in the Middle East in the post-September 11 years suggested that it was the targets of this right-wing offensive, and not its perpetrators and their mentors, who were by far the more productive and innovative scholars and who possessed the more accurate and reliable understanding of what was actually going on in the region and beyond.

Nonetheless, in the fall of 2007 a group of scholars and others who had long been alienated from the Middle East Studies Association, for four decades the pre-eminent learned society in North American Middle East studies, announced the establishment of an organization of their own, on the model of other small splinter groups formed over the years in several academic fields by disgruntled conservative scholars. The Association for the Study of the Middle East and Africa (ASMEA) declared itself "a new academic society dedicated to promoting the highest standards of research and teaching in Middle Eastern and African studies, and related fields . . . first and foremost, a community of scholars concerned to protect academic freedom and promote the search for truth to reach new heights in inquiry."[62]

Rather predictably, the new organization's Academic Council featured Bernard Lewis (then ninety-one years old) as chairman and Fouad Ajami as vice-chairman. ASMEA's founders proclaimed it to be a strictly scholarly and apolitical alternative to an irredeemably politicized MESA. It was, however, telling that, as of early 2009, its Academic Council included, alongside several *bona fide* academics whose scholarly work actually focused on the Middle East, at least two people who had achieved prominence outside academia, in the world of policymaking: former Secretary of State George P. Schultz, an economist by training but hardly a noted scholar of either the Middle East or Africa, and Leslie

Gelb, who served as a Pentagon official during the Vietnam War and in the State Department during the Carter administration, was a diplomatic correspondent for the *New York Times*, and then became president and eventually president emeritus of the Council on Foreign Relations. Perhaps coincidentally, both Schultz and Gelb had also been vocal advocates of the invasion of Iraq.[63] Given ASMEA's obvious political bent and partisan agenda, it seemed very unlikely that it would pose a serious challenge to MESA's status as the leading professional and scholarly organization in this field any time soon.

The assaults to which US Middle East studies was subjected in the post-September 11 period certainly did not make it easier for scholars of the modern and contemporary Middle East and Muslim world to pursue their work. Nor did the tense atmosphere enhance the likelihood that Americans would acquire a better understanding of what was going on in the Middle East and the Muslim world, or facilitate a more informed, intelligent and reasoned discussion of the involvement of the United States in those regions, past, present or future. It was understandable that many scholars of the Middle East and Islam could feel themselves and their field to be under siege, even if such attacks were not, as discussed earlier in this chapter, entirely unprecedented. But it should also be said that, despite this, most US-based scholars of the Middle East and the Muslim world continued to go about their business, and the work they produced remained by and large not only impressively high in quality but also in more sustained and productive dialogue with scholars, methods and ideas in other fields than perhaps it had ever been.

It was also the case that September 11 and its aftermath led to a surge of public interest in the Middle East and Islam, to which scholars (among others) responded with a flood of books and articles, many of them of excellent quality and some of which were also highly accessible to a non-academic public. The period also witnessed dramatically increased enrollments in college courses taught by specialists on the Middle East and Islam, including language courses, and increased hiring in these fields. There was at the same time a heightened awareness in Congress and beyond that the United States urgently needed to expand the number of Americans who knew something about the languages, history and cultures of the region, which led to several new federally funded programs, especially for language pedagogy.

So, despite the nasty assaults to which scholars and their organizations and institutions were subjected, and notwithstanding (or perhaps partly because of) the very grim situation in much of the Middle

East, it might be argued that university-based Middle East studies in the United States flourished both intellectually and institutionally in the years after September 11.[64] Yet it also seemed clear that, given the very fraught historical conjuncture, and given the fact that this was an academic field focused on a strife-torn region in which the United States was likely to remain deeply and often painfully involved for the foreseeable future, the character, direction and funding of Middle East studies in the United States would continue to arouse controversy and conflict.

Afterword

As I was completing this book in November 2003, US military forces were still struggling to control and pacify occupied Iraq. Basic services were still not functioning properly in many parts of that country and the massive task of reconstruction had hardly begun. It was not clear when or how US officials would transfer substantive power to Iraqis, attacks on US occupation forces were on the rise, and the United States (and Britain, its junior partner in the invasion and occupation of Iraq) remained thoroughly isolated in the world community.

In the months that followed the overthrow of the Ba'thist regime which had ruled Iraq for thirty-five years, it became clear not only that the American public had been misled about the rationale for going to war in Iraq but also that Bush administration officials had given inadequate thought to what would happen in the wake of military victory. Lacking any very deep understanding of the complex realities of Iraqi society and politics and willingly lulled by the optimistic forecasts of pro-war scholars and experts, those officials envisioned a scenario in which the vast majority of Iraqis would enthusiastically welcome their country's occupation and, under the benign tutelage of the United States, happily go about creating a stable, peaceful, free-market democracy in the heart of the Arab world. They were thus grossly unprepared for what actually ensued. That the United States, by far the strongest military power on earth, could defeat Iraq's armed forces and conquer that country was never in doubt; whether the United States could successfully put Iraq back together afterward in anything like the way it imagined remains highly uncertain. And it will take years, if not decades, for all the consequences of the US conquest and occupation of Iraq – many of them unintended and unpredictable – to fully unfold.

Just this kind of disconnect between vision and reality, between policy and consequence, has frequently characterized America's involvement with the Middle East over the past half century. It seems rather late in the day to argue that this is primarily the result of insufficient expert knowledge about the region. As we have seen, the decades after the Second

274

World War witnessed the investment of substantial private and public funds to develop expertise about the Middle East in the United States, largely to help establish, maintain and enhance US political, economic and military interests and commitments in this crucial arena of the Cold War. Yet the policies pursued by the United States have repeatedly proven counterproductive even in terms of their avowed goals.

Hostility to Arab nationalism in the 1950s and 1960s enhanced the stature of leaders like Nasser and discredited pro-US regimes; the CIA's overthrow of Iran's parliamentary government in 1953 and Washington's close embrace of the shah generated widespread anti-American sentiment and helped set the stage for the shah's downfall and the coming to power of a vociferously anti-US revolutionary regime a quarter-century later; support for extremist Islamist forces fighting the Soviets in Afghanistan, coupled with indifference to the unraveling of that country once the Soviets withdrew, allowed the Taliban to achieve power and helped give rise to the groups and networks that produced al-Qa'ida in the 1990s; US support for Saddam Husayn's war of aggression against Iran in the 1980s set the stage for Iraq's occupation of Kuwait in 1990 and all that followed; and so on. It did not bode well for the future that within days of the US conquest of Iraq, some of the same politicians and commentators who had so vociferously beat the drums for war against Iraq had already begun to call for action against both Syria and Iran, echoed a bit more faintly by Bush administration officials.

One might explain these errors of judgment and failures as a consequence of what some used to call, with reference to the disastrous US intervention in Vietnam, "the arrogance of power." From this perspective, having dominion over others tends to render one oblivious to what is actually going on, and in particular to those forces and factors which seek to challenge those in power. One thinks of Winston Churchill, then Britain's Colonial Secretary, in the early 1920s dismissing Arab demands for independence and insisting that his subjects' children's children would still be living under British rule. More generally, one can see how deluded British, French and other colonial officials were to believe that India or Indochina or Algeria would remain under their control indefinitely, and what an illusion it was for the Afrikaners who dominated apartheid South Africa to convince themselves that that system could last forever. The conviction of US officials – supposedly "the best and the brightest" of their generation – that there was no way that the vastly superior military power of the United States could be thwarted by a ragtag army of sandal-wearing Vietnamese is another case in point. To put it crudely, it can be argued that overweening power often makes those who exercise it stupid, preventing them from accurately comprehending what is going on around them and leading them to grossly underestimate the resolution and capabilities of those who oppose them.

But there is clearly something else involved here as well. While a generalized arrogance of power may well often lead to miscalculation and failure, there are always specific understandings of the world also at work, particular forms of knowledge which can lead to a distorted grasp of reality and unexpected (often disastrous) consequences. This is, in a sense, exactly what we have been exploring in much of this book, with specific reference to the Middle East: the interpretive frameworks, produced and reproduced within certain political and cultural contexts, which have to a considerable extent shaped how policymakers, but also many others in the West, have understood Islam and the Middle East. As we saw, the Orientalist depiction of Islam as a unitary civilization in decline, modernization theory's conception of the character and trajectory of social, cultural and political change in the Third World, and various combinations of the two have played important roles in shaping how officials, the media and the public made sense of the Middle East and the Muslim world and thereby influenced the policies which the United States pursued in them.

This is not to suggest for a moment that social interests have played no part in determining policy: had the Middle East lacked massive petroleum reserves, for example, it would undoubtedly have been deemed of much less geopolitical importance to policymakers. Yet how one defines those interests is itself a question of differing, indeed conflicting, perceptions and agendas. For example, it has long been the policy of the United States to use all means necessary to ensure that relatively cheap oil continues to flow from the Persian Gulf region. Yet it could be argued that reliance on cheap oil is in fact economically, socially and ecologically detrimental to the United States and that a coherent set of policies aimed at weaning this country from its addiction to fossil fuels would serve us much better in the long run, among many other things by eliminating much of the rationale for the massive US military presence in the Middle East and repeated interventions there. So how one defines the interests of the United States in the Middle East (or anywhere else) is itself a highly contentious issue, entailing consideration of exactly *whose* interests – those of the transnational energy companies, of what President Eisenhower called "the military-industrial complex," of powerful elites in the countries that produce and consume petroleum, of other segments of their populations, and so on – are served by one or another definition of "the national interest." Which brings us right back to where this book began, to the question of the politics of knowledge.

As we have seen, conflicts among scholars about how to understand this part of the world are often not simply academic exercises: they take place within, and are influenced by, broader contexts, and they can have real-world consequences, as the debates about how to assess the "Islamic threat" to the United States and how to respond to the September 11 attacks showed. Differing frameworks of interpretation, some with deep historical roots, offer conflicting ways of making sense of the world; they not infrequently cite the same data but interpret them very differently and draw quite different conclusions from them.

This book has tried to trace, in broad outline, what I see as important dimensions of the development of the Western study of Islam and later of the Middle East, with particular attention to the United States over the past half-century or so. As I acknowledge in the Introduction, there are other ways this story could be told. This book has inevitably been shaped by the context in which it was written, as well as by my own interests and concerns. I have no doubt that a decade or two or three from now, the period through which we are now living will look very different than it does to us now, and much of what we today take to be urgent issues, unbridgeable differences of opinion and cutting-edge scholarship may seem passé.

Nonetheless, I hope that this book and the analysis of Middle East studies it lays out will be useful, particularly to readers in the United States. What we know and don't know about the Middle East and the Muslim world has become increasingly crucial. There was a time when the consequences of the use (or misuse) of American power in that region were felt only dimly and indirectly in the United States. The Iranian hostage crisis of 1979–1981 aroused very strong feelings, but for most Americans it was something that happened "over there" and did not lead to any serious re-assessment of US policy toward Iran, past or present. Even the deaths of several hundred American soldiers in Beirut in 1983, in the context of a failed intervention in Lebanon's tortured political conflicts, failed to have much impact.

In one sense, the September 11 attacks in New York and Washington changed all that: Americans now understand that there are organized groups in the world which are ready, willing and able to indiscriminately kill American civilians, among others. In another sense, however, very little has changed: only a minority of Americans have troubled themselves to ask why it is that there are people whose hatred for the United States is such that they could bring themselves to murder large numbers of Americans, and (possibly even more importantly) to wonder if perhaps the fact that we did not even know enough to realize that they hated us, or why, should be a cause for concern, and for self-scrutiny.

These are not questions which the government of the United States, many experts on the Middle East or the Muslim world, or the mainstream media have encouraged Americans to ask or helped us answer. Instead, we are urged to be satisfied with stock depictions of bloodthirsty, fanatical Muslim terrorists who want to do us harm because they are evil and hate our way of life. Indeed, some do hate many of the things most Americans cherish about their country, and of course nothing justifies terrorism and murder. But we also very much need to understand what it is that motivates such people, what enables them to appeal for support and sympathy to a much larger number of Muslims, and why even a substantial number of non-Muslims in various parts of the world seemed to feel that September 11 was something the United States had coming to it.

As I suggested at the outset, we cannot any longer afford not to know, if we ever could. The costs of the historical amnesia, willful ignorance and crude misunderstandings about the rest of the world and our place in it that pervade American society, culture and politics are only likely to rise, and it is the innocent here and abroad who will by and large pay the price.

I do not seek to offer any profound conclusion to this book because the issues it addresses are still very much with us and likely to loom even larger in the years ahead, especially given the course our leaders have so far chosen to follow. No closure is possible, or even desirable; there is only the imperative to question, to learn, to engage and, I hope, to rethink where we have been historically, where we are today and where we are headed, so that we as a society might one day stand in some more beneficent and sustainable relation to the rest of the world – and to our better selves.

Notes

While the publisher has made every attempt to ensure that the website addresses in these notes are accurate and up to date, it cannot be held responsible for their content.

INTRODUCTION

1. For further discussion of these issues, see Peter Novick, *That Noble Dream: The Objectivity Question and the American Historical Profession* (Cambridge: Cambridge University Press, 1988) and Robin Blackburn, ed., *Ideology in Social Science: Readings in Critical Social Theory* (New York: Pantheon Books, 1972).

1 IN THE BEGINNING

1. In his controversial 1987 book *Black Athena: the Afroasiatic Roots of Classical Civilization*, Martin Bernal argued that the great debt which ancient Greek culture owed to neighboring Egypt had been ignored or concealed by nineteenth-century European scholars, who saw ancient Greece as "the cradle of the West" and could not tolerate the thought that the Greeks had borrowed heavily from the "Semitic" – or even worse, African – Egyptians. Bernal came under strong attack from classicists for his highly revisionist (and, his critics argued, wildly inaccurate) reading of ancient history.

   On the whole it seems fair to suggest that much of Bernal's analysis of how nineteenth-century scholarly views of ancient Greece and Egypt were colored by contemporary racial theories – an analysis which clearly draws inspiration from Edward W. Said's critique of Orientalism, about which I will have a great deal to say in Chapter 6 – is on target. However, the revisionist reconstruction of ancient history he proposes seems doubtful and his depiction of ancient Egyptian culture as "African" or "black" is as essentialist as the traditional view he criticizes. See Martin Bernal, *Black Athena: The Afroasiatic Roots of Classical Civilization*, 2 vols. (New Brunswick: Rutgers University Press, 1987, 1991). For a critique of Bernal, see Mary R. Lefkowitz and Guy MacLean Rogers, eds., *Black Athena Revisited* (Chapel Hill: University of North Carolina Press, 1996); but see also Bernal's response to his critics, in David Chioni Moore, ed., *Black Athena Writes Back: Martin Bernal Responds to his Critics* (Durham, NC: Duke University Press, 2001). For more balanced discussions of the merits and flaws of Bernal's work see *Talanta* (Proceedings of the Dutch Archaeological and Historical Society) 48–49 (1996–97), and Walter Burkert, *The Orientalizing Revolution: Near Eastern Influence on Greek Culture in the Early Archaic Age* (Cambridge, MA: Harvard University Press, 1992).

2. The quotations from Aristotle and Strabo can be found in Martin W. Lewis and Kären E. Wigen, *The Myth of Continents: A Critique of Metageography* (Berkeley: University of California Press, 1997), pp. 23, 214. See also Denys Hay, *Europe: The Emergence of an Idea* (Edinburgh: Edinburgh University Press, 1957), pp. 1–6.

3. See for example Patricia Springborg, *Western Republicanism and the Oriental Prince* (Austin: University of Texas Press, 1992).

4. Hay, *Europe*, p. 4.

5. Quoted in Thierry Hentsch, *Imagining the Middle East* (Montreal: Black Rose Books, 1992), p. 13.

6. For a lengthier discussion of this issue see Hentsch, *Imagining*, pp. 14–20. See also Peregrine Horden and Nicholas Purcell, *The Corrupting Sea: a Study of Mediterranean History* (Oxford: Blackwell, 2000).

7. Hay, *Europe*, pp. 14–15. See too Benjamin Braude, "The Sons of Noah and the Construction of Ethnic and Geographical Identities in the Medieval and Early Modern Periods," *William and Mary Quarterly* 54 (1997): 105–142.

8. Donald F. Lach has produced the most extensive study of ancient Greek, Roman and medieval knowledge (and ignorance) of Asia, particularly India and China, in his *Asia in the Making of Europe, I: The Century of Discovery* (Chicago: University of Chicago Press, 1965).

9. In Robert G. Hoyland, *Seeing Islam as Others Saw It: A Survey and Evaluation of Christian, Jewish and Zoroastrian Writings on Early Islam* (Princeton: The Darwin Press, 1997), p. 23. Hoyland's book is the richest and most comprehensive compilation and evaluation of non-Muslim writings on the emergence of Islam and thus an invaluable source. Jews who had formerly been under Byzantine rule also found Muslim rule a great improvement. Unlike the Byzantine state and its official church, which had reviled, persecuted and sometimes tried to forcibly convert the Jews, the Muslims (like the Sasanians before them) were generally tolerant and granted the Jews considerable autonomy.

10. In Hoyland, *Seeing Islam*, pp. 535–536.

11. Norman Daniel, *Islam and the West: The Making of an Image* (Edinburgh: Edinburgh University Press, 1960), and R. W. Southern, *Western Views of Islam in the Middle Ages* (Cambridge, MA: Harvard University Press, 1962). Norman Daniel would later publish a second book, *The Arabs and Medieval Europe* (London: Longman, 1975), which covered much of the same ground from a different angle. For a more recent study see John V. Tolan, *Saracens: Islam in the Medieval European Imagination* (New York: Columbia University Press, 2002).

12. Hoyland, *Seeing Islam*, pp. 218–219.

13. Southern, *Western Views*, pp. 14–15.

14. On Arculf see Hoyland, *Seeing Islam*, pp. 219–223.

15. Quoted in Southern, *Western Views*, p. 21.
16. Maxime Rodinson, *Europe and the Mystique of Islam*, trans. Roger Veinus (Seattle: University of Washington Press, 1987; first published in French in 1980), 6.
17. From William of Malmesbury's account of Urban's message at Clermont, quoted in Hay, *Europe*, pp. 32–33.
18. Southern, *Western Views*, p. 36.
19. Daniel, *The Arabs*, p. 245.
20. Ibid., p. 54.
21. Quoted in Rodinson, *Europe*, p. 16.
22. Ibid., pp. 22–23. See too Daniel, *The Arabs*, pp. 185–187.
23. Dorothee Metlitzki, *The Matter of Araby in Medieval England* (New Haven: Yale University Press, 1977), p. 249.
24. Maria Rosa Menocal, *The Arabic Role in Medieval Literary History: A Forgotten Heritage* (Philadelphia: University of Pennsylvania Press, 1987), pp. xii–xiii, 1–2.
25. Southern, *Western Views*, p. 28. See too Dionisius A. Agius and Richard Hitchcock, eds., *The Arab Influence in Medieval Europe* (Reading: Ithaca Press, 1994).
26. Daniel, *The Arabs*, p. 242.
27. Quoted in Southern, *Western Views*, p. 31. The fullest discussion of this question can be found in Norman Daniel's *Islam and the West*.
28. For more recent scholarly work on medieval European images of Islam, see Michael Frassetto and David R. Blanks, eds., *Western Views of Islam in Medieval and Early Modern Europe: Perception of Other* (New York: St. Martin's Press, 1999).

2 ISLAM, THE WEST AND THE REST

1. Norman Daniel, *Islam and the West: The Making of an Image* (Edinburgh: Edinburgh University Press, 1960), p. 307.
2. William Rainolds, author of *Calvino-Turcismus*, quoted in Albert Hourani, *Europe and the Middle East* (Berkeley: University of California Press, 1980), p. 26.
3. *The Turkish Letters of Ogier Ghiselin de Busbecq*, trans. Edward Seymour Forster (Oxford: Clarendon Press, 1927), pp. 59–61.
4. Quoted in Lucette Valensi, *The Birth of the Despot: Venice and the Sublime Porte*, trans. Arthur Denner (Ithaca, NY: Cornell University Press, 1993), p. 64.
5. Ibid., p. 58.
6. Quoted in Thierry Hentsch, *Imagining the Middle East* (Montreal: Black Rose Books, 1992), pp. 65–66.
7. Valensi, *Birth of the Despot*, p. 71. See also Springborg, *Western Republicanism*.
8. See Janet L. Abu-Lughod, *Before European Hegemony: The World System, A.D.1250–1350* (New York: Oxford University Press, 1989).

9. Donald F. Lach, *Asia and the Making of Europe, I: The Century of Discovery* (Chicago: University of Chicago Press, 1965), p. xii.

10. For a recent discussion of some of the issues, see the forum on "Asia and Europe in the World Economy" in *American Historical Review* 107 (April 2002).

11. See also the works discussed or cited below and in Chapter 5, and from a very different perspective David S. Landes, *The Wealth and Poverty of Nations: Why Some Are So Rich and Some So Poor* (New York: W. W. Norton, 1998).

12. For a recent discussion of this issue see Şevket Pamuk, "The Price Revolution in the Ottoman Empire Reconsidered," *International Journal of Middle East Studies* 33 (2001): 68–89.

13. See J. G. A. Pocock, "What Do We Mean by Europe?," *The Wilson Quarterly* 21 (1997): 12–29.

14. Eric L. Jones, *The European Miracle* (Cambridge: Cambridge University Press, 1981).

15. For a survey and critique of many of these approaches, see J. M. Blaut, *The Colonizer's Model of the World: Geographical Diffusionism and Eurocentric Theory* (New York: The Guilford Press, 1993). See also Janet Abu-Lughod, "On the Remaking of History: How to Reinvent the Past," in *Remaking History*, ed. Barbara Kruger and Phil Mariani (Seattle: Bay Press, 1989), pp. 111–129.

16. J. M. Blaut offers a strong statement of this perspective. But see also the work of Immanuel Wallerstein, André Gunder Frank and Samir Amin cited in Chapter 5. For a recent discussion of these issues, see the essays on Alfred W. Crosby's book *Counting and Power* in *American Historical Review* 105 (2000).

17. For a sampling of recent work that bears on these issues, see Sidney Mintz, *Sweetness and Power: The Place of Sugar in Modern History* (New York: Viking Penguin, 1985); Ann Laura Stoler, "Rethinking Colonial Categories: European Communities and the Boundaries of Rule," in *Colonialism and Culture*, ed. Nicholas B. Dirks (Ann Arbor: University of Michigan Press, 1992), and also Stoler's *Race and the Education of Desire: Foucault's History of Sexuality and the Colonial Order of Things* (Durham, NC: Duke University Press, 1995); Paul Rabinow, *French Modern: Norms and Forms of the Social Environment* (Cambridge, MA: MIT Press, 1989); Timothy Mitchell, *Colonising Egypt* (Cambridge: Cambridge University Press, 1988); and Frederick Cooper and Ann Laura Stoler, eds., *Tensions of Empire: Colonial Cultures in a Bourgeois World* (Berkeley: University of California Press, 1997).

18. Norman Daniel, *Islam, Europe and Empire* (Edinburgh: Edinburgh University Press, 1966), p. 20.

19. Quoted in Billie Melman, *Women's Orients: English Women and the Middle East, 1718–1918* (Ann Arbor: University of Michigan Press, 1992), pp. 86–87. Lady Mary Wortley Montagu also used her popularity as a writer to promote the practice of inoculation against smallpox, which she first witnessed being practiced among the Ottomans; this method was used widely in Europe and beyond until replaced by vaccination at the beginning of the nineteenth century.

3   ORIENTALISM AND EMPIRE

1. Raymond Schwab, *The Oriental Renaissance: Europe's Rediscovery of India and the East, 1680–1880,* trans. Gene Patterson-Black and Victor Reinking (New York: Columbia University Press, 1984); first published in France in 1950.
2. Quoted in ibid., pp. 12–13.
3. See for example John M. MacKenzie, *Orientalism: History, Theory and the Arts* (Manchester: Manchester University Press, 1995) and James Stevens Curl, *The Egyptian Revival: An Introductory Study of a Recurring Theme in the History of Taste* (London: George Allen & Unwin, 1982).
4. Maxime Rodinson, *Europe and the Mystique of Islam,* trans. Roger Veinus (Seattle: University of Washington Press, 1987), p. 59.
5. Norman Daniel, *Islam and the West: The Making of an Image* (Edinburgh: Edinburgh University Press, 1960), p. 36.
6. See Hilton Obenzinger, *American Palestine: Melville, Twain and the Holy Land Mania* (Princeton: Princeton University Press, 1999), and John Davis, *The Landscape of Belief: Encountering the Holy Land in Nineteenth-Century American Art and Culture* (Princeton: Princeton University Press, 1996).
7. On travelers' accounts, see Billie Melman, *Women's Orients: English Women and the Middle East, 1718–1918* (Ann Arbor: University of Michigan Press, 1992). On photographic depictions of women, see Sarah Graham-Brown, *Images of Women: The Portrayal of Women in Photography of the Middle East 1860–1950* (New York: Columbia University Press, 1988) and Malek Alloula, *The Colonial Harem* (Minneapolis: University of Minnesota Press, 1986). For a recent survey and evaluation of Orientalism in nineteenth-century British culture, see MacKenzie, *Orientalism.*
8. Rodinson, *Europe,* p. 60.
9. Quoted in a letter to the editor by John R. Lenz, *The New York Times Book Review,* November 8, 1998.
10. Lothrop Stoddard, *The Rising Tide of Color Against White World-Supremacy* (New York: Charles Scribner's Sons, 1921), pp. 299–300. On racism in this period see George W. Stocking, *Race, Culture, and Evolution: Essays in the History of Anthropology* (New York: The Free Press, 1968) and *Victorian Anthropology* (New York: The Free Press, 1987); and Elazar Barkan, *Retreat of Scientific Racism: Changing Concepts of Race in Britain and the United States between the World Wars* (Cambridge: Cambridge University Press, 1992).
11. In Ernest Renan, *The Poetry of the Celtic Races, and Other Studies,* trans. William G. Hutchison (Port Washington: Kennikat Press, 1970), pp. 84–108.
12. See Lawrence I. Conrad, "Ignaz Goldziher on Ernest Renan: From Orientalist Philology to the Study of Islam," in *The Jewish Discovery of Islam: Studies in Honor of Bernard Lewis,* ed. Martin Kramer (Tel Aviv: The Moshe Dayan Center for Middle Eastern and African Studies, 1999), pp. 137–180.
13. For a brief biography of Blunt see Albert Hourani, *Europe and the Middle East* (Berkeley: University of California Press, 1980), ch. 5.
14. The full text of Jamal al-Din's letter can be found in Nikki R. Keddie, ed., *An Islamic Response to Imperialism: Political and Religious Writings of Sayyid*

Jamal al-Din "al-Afghani" (Berkeley: University of California Press, 1968). It is worth noting that al-Afghani made sure that his letter was not translated and published in the Middle East, for fear that it would scandalize Muslim opinion and undermine his political goals. My thanks to Juan Cole for reminding me of this.

15. In Robert C. Tucker, ed., *The Marx–Engels Reader* (New York: W. W. Norton, 1972), pp. 577–588.
16. Ibid., p. 339.
17. In Lewis S. Feuer, ed., *Karl Marx and Friedrich Engels: Basic Writings on Politics and Philosophy* (Garden City, NY: Anchor Books, 1959), p. 451.
18. Bryan S. Turner, *Weber and Islam: A Critical Study* (London: Routledge & Kegan Paul, 1974), p. 3. See also Bryan S. Turner, *Marx and the End of Orientalism* (London: Allen & Unwin, 1978).
19. For an introduction to the Russian case, see Daniel R. Browe and Edward J. Lazzerini, eds., *Russia's Orient: Imperial Borderlands and Peoples, 1700–1917* (Bloomington: Indiana University Press, 1997).
20. See the report on the conference published in *The Moslem World* 1 (1911): 55.
21. E. Mercier, *La Question indigène* (Paris, 1901), p. 220, quoted in Lothrop Stoddard, *The New World of Islam* (New York: Charles Scribner's Sons, 1921), p. 145.
22. Marnia Lazreg, "The Reproduction of Colonial Ideology: The Case of the Kabyle Berbers," *Arab Studies Quarterly* 5 (1983): 380–395, and Patricia M. E. Lorcin, *Imperial Identities: Stereotyping, Prejudice and Race in Colonial Algeria* (London: I. B. Tauris, 1995).
23. Marwan Buheiry, "Colonial Scholarship and Muslim Revivalism in 1900," *Arab Studies Quarterly* 4 (1982): 1–16; emphasis in the original.
24. The Earl of Cromer, *Modern Egypt*, 2 vols. (New York: MacMillan, 1908).
25. See too Cromer's article "The Government of Subject Races," *Edinburgh Review* 207 (1908): 1–27, which argued that the Christian morality which buttressed British imperialism would enable the British empire to escape the fate which befell the Roman empire.
26. Victor Kiernan, *The Lords of Human Kind: European Attitudes to Other Cultures in the Imperial Age* (London: Serif, 1995; first published 1969), p. 29.
27. Valentine Chirol, *The Middle Eastern Question; or, Some Political Problems of Indian Defence* (London: J. Murray, 1903), p. 5.

4 THE AMERICAN CENTURY

1. Lothrop Stoddard, *The New World of Islam* (New York: Charles Scribner's Sons, 1921), p. 355. Stoddard's sympathy for Muslim renewal and his criticism of colonialism stemmed from his strong advocacy of white supremacy. In another book published the same year, *The Rising Tide of Color Against White World-Supremacy*, from which I quoted in Chapter 3, Stoddard warned that the white race was in imminent danger of being debased by mixture with the "colored" races, especially Asians. To prevent this, Stoddard argued, it was necessary to keep the races separate, by prohibiting the immigration of

Asians into predominantly white lands but also by abandoning the dream of permanent white rule over, and settlement in, Asian lands.

2. Palestine was of course the great exception to decolonization and national self-determination in the region. During the First World War Britain had committed itself to fostering the creation of a "national home" for the Jewish people in Palestine, in keeping with the goals of the Zionist movement, which sought to create a Jewish majority and a Jewish state in that land, despite the fact that its population was at the time overwhelmingly Arab. As the mandatory power Britain facilitated Jewish immigration and land purchases and suppressed the Palestinian Arab majority, which demanded the country's independence as an Arab state. In 1948 the Jewish community in Palestine (by then one-third of the population) was able to defeat both the Palestinian Arabs and forces from the neighboring Arab countries who came to their aid and establish a Jewish state in three-quarters of the country. In the process half of the Palestinians fled or were expelled from their homes, becoming refugees, and no Palestinian state emerged. For decades after the Palestinians and most Arabs elsewhere denounced Israel as an illegitimate colonial-settler enclave and demanded that the Palestinians be allowed to return to their homes and exercise their right to national self-determination.

3. Maxime Rodinson, *Europe and the Mystique of Islam*, trans. Roger Veinus (Seattle: University of Washington Press, 1987), p. 69.

4. "Editorial," *The Moslem World* 1 (1911): 1. Decades later the journal changed its name to *The Muslim World*.

5. Reminiscing about his "brief encounter with orientalism" as a student at Oxford in the 1930s, the economic historian Charles Issawi described studying with the eminent D. S. Margoliouth: "His erudition was fantastic, but I had never heard anything resembling the sounds that issued from his throat when he spoke Arabic – which means that I had never met an orientalist. I cannot say that I was wildly excited by the course (especially since he omitted all the juicy bits [of the Arabic texts they read] saying, 'That is not a nice passage') . . . " In *Paths to the Middle East: Ten Scholars Look Back*, ed. Thomas Naff (Albany: State University of New York Press, 1993), p. 144.

6. On the early history of the study of the ancient Near East in the United States, see Bruce Kuklick, *Puritans in Babylon: the Ancient Near East and American Intellectual Life, 1880–1930* (Princeton: Princeton University Press, 1996).

7. "Problems of Modern Middle Eastern History," *Report on Current Research* (Washington, DC: Middle East Institute, Spring 1956), reprinted in Hamilton A. R. Gibb, *Studies on the Civilization of Islam* (Boston: Beacon Press, 1962), p. 336.

8. The political scientist Robert Vitalis has argued that one can in fact trace the emergence of what would later be called "international studies" (and thus to some extent area studies as well) back to the pre-First World War period, a development inextricably bound up with questions of race at home and abroad as well as with the acquisition by the United States of a formal colonial empire; see his article "International Studies in America," in *Items & Issues* (a publication of the Social Science Research Council) 3 (2002). His argument makes eminent sense, and more research on that period as well as on the

interwar years is certainly needed. But it is my impression that relatively little of the work done in the United States in this emerging field dealt with the Middle East, so that it remains plausible to see the Second World War as marking a significant turning point in both intellectual and institutional terms – a topic which I will discuss in detail shortly. See also Jacob Heilbrunn, "The News from Everywhere," *Lingua Franca* (May–June 1996): 49–56.

9. Albert Howe Lybyer, *The Government of the Ottoman Empire in the Time of Suleiman the Magnificent* (Cambridge, MA: Harvard University Press, 1913; reprinted 1978), p. 9.

10. See for example Hamilton A. R. Gibb, *Studies on the Civilization of Islam* (Boston: Beacon Press, 1962). Albert Hourani published a sympathetic portrait of Gibb in his *Europe and the Middle East* (Berkeley: University of California Press, 1980), ch. 6. But see too William Polk, "Sir Hamilton Gibb Between Orientalism and History," *International Journal of Middle East Studies* 6 (1975): 131–139.

11. Sir Hamilton Gibb and Harold Bowen, *Islamic Society and the West: A Study of the Impact of Western Civilization on Moslem Culture in the Near East*, vol. I, parts 1–2 (London: Oxford University Press, 1950, 1957), pp. 44–45.

12. Ibid., vol. I, part 2, pp. 70, 77.

13. H. A. R. Gibb, *Modern Trends in Islam* (Chicago: University of Chicago Press, 1947; reprinted 1972 by Octagon Books, New York), pp. 5, 7.

14. Ibid., p. 123.

15. Quoted in Noam Chomsky, *The Fateful Triangle: The United States, Israel and the Palestinians* (Boston: South End Press, 1983), p. 17. Chomsky's source for this quote is Joyce and Gabriel Kolko, *The Limits of Power* (New York: Harper & Row, 1972), p. 242.

16. William Stivers, *America's Confrontation with Revolutionary Change in the Middle East, 1948–83* (New York: St. Martin's Press, 1986), p. 3.

17. Quoted in Irene Gendzier, *Managing Political Change: Social Scientists and the Third World* (Boulder: Westview Press, 1985), p. 27.

18. On the United States in the Middle East see Stivers, *America's Confrontation*; Miles Copeland, *The Game of Nations: the Amorality of Power Politics* (London, Weidenfeld & Nicolson, 1969); Wilbur Crane Eveland, *Ropes of Sand: America's Failure in the Middle East* (New York: W. W. Norton, 1980); David W. Lesch, *Syria and the United States: Eisenhower's Cold War in the Middle East* (Boulder: Westview Press, 1992); Irene Gendzier, *Notes from the Minefield: United States Intervention in Lebanon and the Middle East, 1945–1958* (New York: Columbia University Press, 1997); Nathan J. Citino, *From Arab Nationalism to OPEC: Eisenhower, King Saʿud, and the Making of US–Saudi Relations* (Bloomington: Indiana University Press, 2002); and Douglas Little, *American Orientalism: the United States and the Middle East since 1945* (Chapel Hill: University of North Carolina Press, 2002). For a survey of CIA operations worldwide, see William Blum, *The CIA: A Forgotten History – US Global Interventions since World War 2* (London: Zed Books, 1986).

19. The most comprehensive English-language study of the 1953 coup in Iran and its aftermath is Mark J. Gasiorowski, *US Foreign Policy and the Shah: Building a Client State in Iran* (Ithaca, NY: Cornell University Press, 1991);

but see too Ervand Abrahamian, "The 1953 Coup in Iran," *Science & Society* 65 (2001): 182–215. The coup was planned and overseen by CIA official Kermit Roosevelt, grandson of Theodore Roosevelt and cousin of Franklin Roosevelt. In his book *Countercoup: The Struggle for the Control of Iran* (New York: McGraw-Hill, 1979), Roosevelt speciously claimed that the United States intervened only to prevent a planned communist takeover of Iran. A 1953 report to the National Security Council laid out the post-coup scene in blunt terms: military aid to Iran "has great political importance apart from its military impact. Over the long term, the most effective instrument for maintaining Iran's orientation toward the West is the monarch, which in turn has the Army as its only real source of power. US military aid serves to improve Army morale, cement Army loyalty to the shah, and this will consolidate the present regime and provide some assurance that Iran's current orientation toward the West will be perpetuated." Quoted in Gendzier, *Managing Political Change*, p. 69.

20. Robert B. Hall, *Area Studies: With Special Reference to their Implications for Research in the Social Sciences* (New York: Social Science Research Council, 1947), p. 84.

21. Robert A. McCaughey, *International Studies and Academic Enterprise: A Chapter in the Enclosure of American Learning* (New York: Columbia University Press, 1984), pp. 114–115.

22. McGeorge Bundy, 1964, quoted in Bruce Cumings, "Boundary Displacement: Area Studies and International Studies During and After the Cold War," in *Universities and Empire: Money and Politics in the Social Sciences During the Cold War*, ed. Christopher Simpson (New York: The New Press, 1998), p. 163. Timothy Mitchell has plausibly suggested that what would later become known as "area studies" had significant pre-Second World War roots which have not been adequately acknowledged or explored; see "The Middle East in the Past and Future of Social Science," in *The Politics of Knowledge: Area Studies and the Disciplines*, ed. David Szanton (forthcoming; currently available at http://escholarship.cdlib.org/ias/szanton.html).

23. Hall, *Area Studies*, pp. 22, 81–82. On the history of the SSRC see Kenton W. Worcester, *Social Science Research Council, 1923–1998* (New York: Social Science Research Council, 2001).

24. Quoted in Immanuel Wallerstein, "The Unintended Consequences of Cold War Area Studies," in *The Cold War and the University: Toward an Intellectual History of the Postwar Years*, ed. Noam Chomsky (New York: The New Press, 1997), p. 205.

25. J. C. Hurewitz, in Naff, *Paths*, pp. 96–97.

26. McCaughey, *International Studies*, pp. 192, 195.

27. Ibid., pp. 140, 200, 250.

28. See Hourani, *Europe*, pp. 127–129; Edward W. Said, *Orientalism* (New York: Pantheon Books, 1978), p. 53; and Nancy Elizabeth Gallagher, ed., *Approaches to the History of the Middle East: Interviews with Leading Middle East Historians* (Reading: Ithaca Press, 1994), interview with Albert Hourani.

29. Quoted in Said, *Orientalism*, p. 275.

30. Hamilton Gibb, "Area Studies Reconsidered," quoted in Wallerstein, "Unintended Consequences," pp. 214–216. See also Said, *Orientalism*, p. 106.

31. Bernard Lewis, "Communism and Islam," *International Affairs* (January 1954): 1–12.

32. Bernard Lewis, "Islamic Concepts of Revolution," in *Revolution in the Middle East and Other Case Studies*, ed. P. J. Vatikiotis (London: Allen and Unwin, 1972), ch. 2.

33. For a thoughtful assessment of Hodgson's work, see Edmund Burke, III, "Islamic History as World History: Marshall Hodgson, 'The Venture of Islam,'" *International Journal of Middle East Studies* 10 (1979): 241–264.

34. Daniel Lerner, *The Passing of Traditional Society: Modernizing the Middle East* (New York: The Free Press, 1958), p. 50.

35. Ibid., p. 47.

36. Ibid., p. 402.

37. Gendzier, *Managing Political Change*, pp. 132–133.

38. Ibid., pp. 255–257.

39. Nadav Safran, *Egypt in Search of Political Community: an Analysis of the Intellectual and Political Evolution of Egypt, 1804–1952* (Cambridge, MA: Harvard University Press, 1961).

40. Ibid., pp. 3–4.

41. Ibid., p. 165.

42. Lucien Pye, *Guerrilla Communism in Malaya*, quoted in Gendzier, *Managing Political Change*, p. 59.

43. Samuel Huntington, "The Bases of Accomodation," *Foreign Affairs* 46 (1968): 642–656. For a rather positive assessment of Huntington's career, see Robert D. Kaplan, "Looking the World in the Eye," *The Atlantic Monthly* (December 2001). For an interesting discussion of Huntington's role in the evolution of modernization theory, see Colin Leys, *The Rise and Fall of Development Theory* (London: James Currey, 1996), ch. 3.

44. Quoted in Gendzier, *Managing Political Change*, p. 62.

45. Manfred Halpern, *The Politics of Social Change in the Middle East and North Africa* (Princeton: Princeton University Press, 1963).

46. See Hurewitz's contribution to Naff, *Paths*.

47. Quoted in *MERIP Reports* no. 38 (June 1975): 9.

5   TURMOIL IN THE FIELD

1. Anouar Abdel-Malek, "Orientalism in Crisis," *Diogenes* 44 (1963): 103–140. The Italian Orientalist Franceso Gabrieli published a response to Abdel-Malek in which he defended the great majority of Orientalists as disinterested scholars engaged in the search for truth; see "Apology for Orientalism," *Diogenes* 50 (1965): 128–136. Around this same time the Palestinian historian A. L. Tibawi also published a critique of Orientalism, largely for what he saw as its enduring legacy of Christian polemics against Islam; see his "English-Speaking Orientalists," *Islamic Quarterly* 8 (1964): 25–45.

2. On Rodinson, see Nancy Elizabeth Gallagher, ed., *Approaches to the History of the Middle East: Interviews with Leading Middle East Historians* (Reading: Ithaca Press, 1994), ch. 5; see also Maxime Rodinson, *Cult, Ghetto, and State: The Persistence of the Jewish Question* (London: Al Saqi Books, 1983), ch. 2 ("Self-Criticism"). On Samir Amin, see his *Re-Reading the Postwar Period: An Intellectual Itinerary*, trans. Michael Wolfers (New York: Monthly Review Press, 1994), chs. 2–4. See also Abdallah Laroui, *The Crisis of the Arab Intellectual: Traditionalism or Historicism*, trans. Diarmid Cammell (Berkeley: University of California Press, 1976); chapter 5 of Laroui's book, "Marxism and the Third World Intellectual," was first published in 1958. Other early and at least somewhat critical French-language studies of Orientalism include Raymond Schwab, *La Renaissance oriental* (Paris: Editions Payot, 1950), cited earlier as *The Oriental Renaissance*, and Jean-Jacques Waardenburg, *L'Islam dans le miroir de l'Occident* (The Hague: Mouton, 1962).

3. Norman Daniel, *Islam, Europe and Empire* (Edinburgh: Edinburgh University Press, 1966), p. xiii. See also Norman Daniel, *The Arabs and Mediaeval Europe* (London: Longman, 1975).

4. Norman Itzkowitz, "Eighteenth Century Ottoman Realities," *Studia Islamica* 16 (1958): 73–94.

5. On Islamic history, see "A Vision of History: an Examination of Professor Toynbee's Ideas," in Albert Hourani, *A Vision of History: Near Eastern and Other Essays* (Lebanon: Khayat, 1961); "Islam as a Historical Problem in European Historiography," in *Historians of the Middle East*, ed. Bernard Lewis and P. M. Holt (London: Oxford University Press, 1962); "Islam and the Philosophers of History," *Middle Eastern Studies* 3 (1967), 206–268; and *Islam in European Thought* (Cambridge: Cambridge University Press, 1991). On the Ottoman period, see "The Changing Face of the Fertile Crescent in the XVIIIth Century," *Studia Islamica* 7 (1957), also published as "The Fertile Crescent in the Eighteenth Century," in Hourani, *Vision*; "The Ottoman Background of the Modern Middle East," in Albert Hourani, *The Emergence of the Modern Middle East* (Berkeley: University of California Press, 1981); and "Ottoman Reform and the Politics of Notables," in *Beginnings of Modernization in the Middle East*, ed. William R. Polk and Richard L. Chambers (Chicago: University of Chicago Press, 1968), ch. 2.

6. Originally published in *Catalyst* (Summer 1967): 20–73, and republished in James D. Cockcroft, André Gunder Frank and Dale L. Johnson, *Dependence and Underdevelopment: Latin America's Political Economy* (Garden City, NY: Anchor Books, 1972).

7. See for example "The Development of Underdevelopment" and "Economic Dependence, Class Structure, and Underdevelopment Policy," in Cockcroft et al., *Dependence*, chs. 1–2.

8. Though there were critiques emerging from other, non-Marxist directions as well; see for example Dean C. Tipps, "Modernization Theory and the Comparative Study of Societies: A Critical Perspective," in *Comparative Modernization*, ed. Cyril E. Black (New York: The Free Press, 1976), pp. 62–88.

9. See Samir Amin's classic *Accumulation on a World Scale: a Critique of the Theory of Underdevelopment*, trans. Brian Pearce (New York: Monthly Review

Press, 1974), first published in French in 1970, and his numerous other books. André Gunder Frank has published far too many books, book chapters and articles to list here; over the decades he has continued to vigorously criticize Eurocentric approaches to world history and insist on the long-term centrality of Asia to the global economy, a brief period of European hegemony notwithstanding.

10. For important early Marxist critiques of Gunder Frank and Wallerstein, see Ernesto Laclau, "Capitalism and Feudalism in Latin America," *New Left Review* 67 (1971): 19–38, and Robert Brenner, "The Origins of Capitalist Development: a Critique of Neo-Smithian Marxism," *New Left Review* 104 (1977): 25–92. For a broader discussion of policy economy approaches, see Peter Evans and John D. Stephens, "Studying Development since the Sixties: the Emergence of a New Comparative Political Economy," *Theory and Society* 17 (1988): 713–745. For an interesting discussion of dependency theory and Middle East studies, see Robert Vitalis, "The End of Third Worldism in Egyptian Studies," *Arab Studies Journal* 4 (1996): 13–33.

11. Barrington Moore, Jr., *The Social Origins of Dictatorship and Democracy: Lord and Peasant in the Making of the Modern World* (Boston: Beacon Press, 1966), p. 486.

12. For the record: I have been associated with MERIP for many years, as a member of its editorial committee and later as a contributing editor.

13. See *Forbidden Agendas: Intolerance and Defiance in the Middle East* (London: Al Saqi Books, 1984).

14. Roger Owen, "Studying Islamic History," *Journal of Interdisciplinary History* 4 (1973): 287–298.

15. Talal Asad, "Two European Images of Non-European Rule," in *Anthropology and the Colonial Encounter*, ed. Talal Asad (Amherst, NY: Humanity Books, 1973).

16. See Bryan S. Turner, *Weber and Islam: A Critical Study* (London: Routledge and Kegan Paul, 1974).

17. Bryan S. Turner, *Marx and the End of Orientalism* (London: Allen & Unwin, 1978), p. 85. See too Turner's *Capitalism and Class in the Middle East: Theories of Social Change and Economic Development* (London: Heinemann, 1984).

18. Laroui, *Crisis*, ch. 3.

19. For a brief introduction to the *Annales* school, see Stuart Clark, "The *Annales* Historians," in *The Return of Grand Theory in the Human Science*, ed. Quentin Skinner (Cambridge: Cambridge University Press, 1985), ch. 10.

20. First published in 1974 as *Capitalist Agriculture and the Origins of the European World-Economy in the Sixteenth Century*, the book was republished under its new title by New York's Academic Press. Wallerstein would go on to publish numerous books and articles elaborating on, and further developing, his approach to modern world history.

21. *Arabia Without Sultans: A Political Survey of Instability in the Arab World* (New York: Vintage Books/Randon House, 1975). See also Helen Lackner, *A House Built on Sand: A Political Economy of Saudi Arabia* (London: Ithaca Press, 1978).

22. "Why ASQ?," *Arab Studies Quarterly* 1 (1979): 1.

23. "The Roots of the Ulama's Power in Modern Iran," in *Scholars, Saints, and Sufis: Muslim Religious Institutions since 1500*, ed. Nikki R. Keddie (Berkeley: University of California Press, 1972), p. 229. Keddie's chapter in this book was immediately followed by another on the same topic, by Hamid Algar, who came to a very different (and though his formulation may be questioned, more accurate) conclusion: "Yet it would be rash to predict the progressive disintegration of the political role of the ulama. Despite all the inroads of the modern age, the Iranian national consciousness still remains wedded to Shi'i Islam, and when the integrity of the nation is held to be threatened by internal autocracy and foreign hegemony, protests in religious terms will continue to be voiced, and the appeals of men such as Ayatullah Khumayni to be widely heeded." See Algar, "The Oppositional Role of the Ulama in Twentieth-Century Iran," in Keddie, *Scholars*, p. 255.

24. See for example the volume edited by George Lenczowski, *Iran under the Pahlavis* (Stanford: Hoover Institution Press, 1978). Lenczowski's own contribution, a chapter on Iranian politics, not only avoided mentioning the CIA's crucial role in organizing the coup that in 1953 overthrew parliamentary government and restored the shah to absolute power but also obsequiously glorified the shah as a strong and wise (but not dictatorial) leader committed to dragging his backward people into the modern world.

25. For examples of relatively early and more sophisticated work on this topic, see Edmund Burke, III, and Ira M. Lapidus, eds., *Islam, Politics, and Social Movements* (Berkeley: University of California Press, 1988).

26. Bernard Lewis, "The Return of Islam," *Commentary* (January 1976): 39–49.

27. "Area Studies: A Critical Reassessment," in *The Study of the Middle East: Research and Scholarship in the Humanities and the Social Sciences*, ed. Leonard Binder (New York: John Wiley & Sons, 1976).

28. (Austin: University of Texas Press, 1977), xi. In 1965 Fernea had published *Guests of the Sheik* (Garden City, NY: Doubleday, 1965), which focused on the lives of village women in southern Iraq where her husband, the anthropologist Robert Fernea, was conducting research.

29. Lois Beck and Nikki Keddie, eds., *Women in the Muslim World* (Cambridge, MA: Harvard University Press, 1978), p. 1.

30. Since the gap between conceiving a research project and publishing what results from it in book form often takes as much as a decade, it was not until the mid-1980s that the trickle of new work broadened into a flood. One example of a pioneering work conceived in the mid-1970s but only published years later is Judith Tucker, *Women in Nineteenth-Century Egypt* (Cambridge: Cambridge University Press, 1985), which positioned itself at the intersection of the new women's history and the new social history and broke new ground by making extensive use of Islamic court archives to reconstruct women's lives. See too Nikki Keddie and Beth Baron, eds., *Women in Middle Eastern History: Shifting Boundaries in Sex and Gender* (New Haven: Yale University Press, 1991), which featured innovative research by (generally younger) historians and reflected the evolution of the field since the 1970s, especially a focus on gender as

a central dimension of social relations rather than on the initial feminist project of retrieving and reconstructing the lives of hitherto marginalized women.

31. Hanna Batatu, *The Old Social Classes and the Revolutionary Movements of Iraq: A Study of Iraq's Old Landed and Commercial Classes and of its Communists, Ba'thists, and Free Officers* (Princeton: Princeton University Press, 1978).

32. Ervand Abrahamian, *Iran Between Two Revolutions* (Princeton: Princeton University Press, 1978).

33. Peter Gran, *Islamic Roots of Capitalism* (Austin: University of Texas Press, 1978).

34. The most hard-hitting critique was authored by F. De Jong; see *International Journal of Middle East Studies* 14 (1982): 381–399, with Gran's response. Gran would offer a more fully developed version of his approach in *Beyond Eurocentrism: A New View of Modern World History* (Syracuse: Syracuse University Press, 1996).

6   SAID'S *ORIENTALISM*: A BOOK AND ITS AFTERMATH

1. For an insightful introduction to Said's life and work, and a collection of some of his writings, see Moustafa Bayoumi and Andrew Rubin, eds., *The Edward Said Reader* (New York: Vintage, 2000). Readers may also be interested in Said's autobiographical *Out of Place: A Memoir* (New York: Knopf, 1999).

2. Aijaz Ahmad, "*Orientalism* and After: Ambivalence and Metropolitan Location in the Work of Edward Said," *In Theory: Classes, Nations, Literatures* (London: Verso, 1992); Roger Owen, "The Mysterious Orient," *Monthly Review* 31 (1979): 58–63.

3. Ontology is the branch of philosophy that deals with being; here "ontological" refers to what Said saw as Orientalism's dichotomization of the Orient and the West. Epistemology deals with the nature and origins of knowledge; Said means that Orientalism assumed that understanding the Orient required using different premises and methods than could be used to understand the West.

4. Edward W. Said, *Orientalism* (New York: Pantheon Books, 1978), pp. 2–3. Henceforth the page numbers in the text will refer to this edition, the first in paperback.

5. This diverse intellectual trend was termed "poststructuralism" because in part it developed as a rejection of French structuralist thought; similarly, "postmodernism" saw itself as superseding modernist modes of thought and social analysis. For an introduction to some of these issues, see Quentin Skinner, ed., *The Return of Grand Theory in the Human Sciences* (Cambridge: Cambridge University Press, 1985), especially chs. 1, 8 and 9.

6. For a short introduction to Foucault's thought see Mark Philp, "Michel Foucault," in ibid., ch. 4.

7. On images of the Arabs in the United States see Edmund Ghareeb, ed., *Split Vision: The Portrayal of Arabs in the American Media* (Washington, DC:

The American–Arab Affairs Council, 1983); Jack Shaheen, *The TV Arab* (Bowling Green, OH: Bowling Green State University Popular Press, 1984); and Michael W. Suleiman, *The Arabs in the Mind of America* (Brattleboro, VT: Amana Books, 1988). For a broader exploration of depictions of the Middle East in the United States, see Melani McAlister, *Epic Encounters: Culture, Media, and US Interests in the Middle East, 1945–2000* (Berkeley: University of California Press, 2001) and Douglas Little, *American Orientalism: the United States and the Middle East since 1945* (Chapel Hill: University of North Carolina Press, 2002).

8. Bernard Lewis, "The Question of Orientalism," *The New York Review of Books*, June 24, 1982.
9. Edward W. Said, "Orientalism: An Exchange," *The New York Review of Books*, August 12, 1982.
10. J. H. Plumb, *The New York Times Book Review*, February 18, 1979.
11. For a discussion of historians' response to *Orientalism*, see the essays in "Orientalism Twenty Years On," a special section of *The American Historical Review* 105 (2000).
12. *International Review of Middle East Studies* 12 (1980): 544–547.
13. Maxime Rodinson, *Europe and the Mystique of Islam*, trans. Roger Veinus (Seattle: University of Washington Press, 1987), pp. 130–131, n. 3.
14. See "The Road to Morocco," Albert Hourani's review of *Orientalism*, in *The New York Review of Books*, March 8, 1979, but also Gabriel Piterberg's chapter on Hourani and Orientalism in *Middle Eastern Politics and Ideas: A History from Within*, ed. Moshe Ma'oz and Ilan Pappé (London: I. B. Tauris, 1997); Owen, "The Mysterious Orient," cited in n. 2 above.
15. Sadik Jalal al-'Azm, "Orientalism and Orientalism in Reverse," *Khamsin* 8 (1981): 5–26.
16. Ahmad, "*Orientalism* and After."
17. James Clifford, "On *Orientalism*," *The Predicament of Culture: Twentieth-Century Ethnography, Literature, and Art* (Cambridge, MA: Harvard University Press, 1988), ch. 11.
18. Edward W. Said, "Orientalism Reconsidered," in *Europe and its Others*, ed. Francis Barker, Peter Hulme, Margaret Iversen and Diana Loxley, vol. I (Colchester: University of Essex, 1985); also published in *Race & Class* 27 (1985): 1–15, and in Alexander Lyon Macfie, ed., *Orientalism: A Reader* (New York: New York University Press, 2000), ch. 35.
19. John E. Toews, "Intellectual History after the Linguistic Turn: The Autonomy of Meaning and the Irreducibility of Experience," *American Historical Review* 92 (1987): 881–882. For a more recent discussion of these issues, see Ronald Gregor Suny, "Back and Beyond: Reversing the Cultural Turn?," *American Historical Review* 107 (2002): 1476–1499.
20. For a relatively early example of the impact of the linguistic turn on social history, see Gareth Stedman Jones, "Rethinking Chartism," *Languages of Class: Studies in English Working Class History, 1832–1982* (Cambridge: Cambridge University Press, 1983), ch. 3, but also Joan Wallach Scott, *Gender and the Politics of History* (New York: Columbia University Press, 1988), especially

the Introduction and ch. 3. For a poststructuralist discussion of the question of experience, see Joan Wallach Scott, "The Evidence of Experience," *Critical Inquiry* 17 (1991): 773–797.

21. See for example Sami Zubaida, "Exhibitions of Power," *Economy and Society* 19 (1990): 359–375, and Charles Hirschkind, "'Egypt at the Exhibition': Reflections on the Optics of Colonialism," *Critique of Anthropology* 11 (1991): 279–298.

22. See for example Khaled Fahmy's *All the Pasha's Men: Mehmed Ali, his Army and the Making of Modern Egypt* (Cambridge: Cambridge University Press, 1997), which acknowledged its intellectual debt to *Colonising Egypt* but insisted on the necessity of a detailed investigation of how Egyptians themselves participated in shaping the institutions, discourses and practices whose emergence Mitchell outlines. See too Mitchell's latest book, *Rule of Experts: Egypt, Techno-Politics, Modernity* (Berkeley: University of California Press, 2002).

23. This essay and others appeared in Edward W. Said, *The World, the Text and the Critic* (Cambridge, MA: Harvard University Press, 1983).

24. Patrick Williams and Laura Chrisman, eds., *Colonial Discourse and Post-Colonial Theory: A Reader* (New York: Columbia University Press, 1994), p. 5.

25. Ronald Inden, "Orientalist Constructions of India," *Modern Asian Studies* 20 (1986) and *Imagining India* (Oxford: Basil Blackwell, 1990); for some of Bernard Cohn's work, see his *An Anthropologist among the Historians and Other Essays* (Delhi: Oxford University Press, 1987). See also Nicholas B. Dirks, ed., *Colonialism and Culture* (Ann Arbor: University of Michigan Press, 1992).

26. Uday Singh Mehta, *Liberalism and Empire: A Study in Nineteenth-Century British Liberal Thought* (Chicago: University of Chicago Press, 1999); Susan Thorne, *Congregational Missions and the Making of an Imperial Culture in Nineteenth-Century England* (Stanford: Stanford University Press, 1999); Ann Laura Stoler, *Race and the Education of Desire: Foucault's* History of Sexuality *and the Colonial Order of Things* (Durham, NC: Duke University Press, 1995) and *Carnal Knowledge and Imperial Power: Race and the Intimate in Colonial Rule* (Berkeley: University of California Press, 2002).

27. See Fred Cooper and Ann Laura Stoler, eds., *Tensions of Empire: Colonial Cultures in a Bourgeois World* (Berkeley: University of California Press, 1997), pp. viii, ix.

28. Edward W. Said, *Culture and Imperialism* (New York: Knopf, 1993).

29. Billie Melman, *Women's Orients: English Women and the Middle East, 1718–1918* (Ann Arbor: University of Michigan Press, 1992), Preface to the second edition, Introduction.

30. Lisa Lowe, *Critical Terrains: French and British Orientalisms* (Ithaca, NY: Cornell University Press, 1991); MacKenzie, *Orientalism*, pp. 209–215. See also Mark Crinson, *Empire Building: Orientalism and Victorian Architecture* (London: Routledge, 1996).

31. For an excellent collection that manifests the concerns and methods of innovative recent work on colonialism, see Julia Clancy-Smith and Frances Gouda, eds., *Domesticating the Empire: Race, Gender, and Family Life in French and Dutch Colonialism* (Charlottesville: University Press of Virginia, 1998).

32. Leela Gandhi, *Postcolonial Theory: A Critical Introduction* (New York: Columbia University Press, 1998), pp. viii, 3. See too Williams and Chrisman, *Colonial Discourse*.

33. Robert J. C. Young, *Postcolonialism: An Historical Introduction* (Oxford: Blackwell, 2001), p. 69. See too Ella Shohat, "Notes on the 'Post-Colonial,'" *Social Text* 31/32 (1992). For Young's assessment of Said's *Orientalism*, see Robert Young, *White Mythologies: Writing History and the West* (London: Routledge, 1990), ch. 7.

34. For an interesting discussion of some of these issues, see Gyan Prakash, "Writing Post-Orientalist Histories of the Third World: Perspectives from Indian Historiography," *Comparative Studies in Society and History* 32 (1990): 383–408.

35. A key text here is Raymond Williams, *Marxism and Literature* (Oxford: Oxford University Press, 1977). As noted earlier, Said had been much influenced by Williams' (and Gramsci's) writings on culture and society, though in *Orientalism* it had been Foucault who seemed to occupy center stage.

7   AFTER ORIENTALISM?

1. John Waterbury, *The Egypt of Nasser and Sadat: The Political Economy of Two Regimes* (Princeton: Princeton University Press, 1983); Alan Richards and John Waterbury, *A Political Economy of the Middle East: State, Class, and Economic Development* (Boulder: Westview Press, 1990).

2. Rational choice theory is uninterested in such things as meaning, symbols, self-definition and collective action and interaction; instead, its methodological starting point is the individual and his or her interests. Individuals are presumed to act rationally to achieve their preferences, given the opportunities or constraints they face, calculating the likely costs and benefits of any action before making the choices that they expect will allow them to attain what they want. With the proper (mathematical) models, therefore, one can predict what individuals (and by extension groups) are likely to do in a given situation. For a critique of this (to my mind rather impoverished) approach to understanding human social life, which had its roots in economics but has been embraced by a substantial number of political scientists and sociologists, see for example Donald P. Green and Ian Shapiro, *Pathologies of Rational Choice Theory: A Critique of Applications in Political Science* (New Haven: Yale University Press, 1996), and Margaret S. Archer and Jonathan Q. Tritter, eds., *Rational Choice Theory: Resisting Colonization* (London: Routledge, 2000).

3. Bernard Lewis, "The Roots of Muslim Rage," *The Atlantic Monthly*, September 1990.

4. Thomas Friedman, "A Dreamlike Landscape, A Dreamlike Reality," *The New York Times*, October 28, 1990.

5. For a cogent exposition of this view, see Sami Zubaida, *Islam, the People and the State* (London: I. B. Tauris, 1989), chs. 1–2.

6. See ibid.; Joel Beinin and Joe Stork, eds., *Political Islam* (Berkeley: University of California Press, 1997); Aziz al-Azmeh, *Islams and Modernities* (London: Verso, 1993); Dale F. Eickelman and James Piscatori, *Muslim Politics* (Princeton: Princeton University Press, 1996).

7. John L. Esposito and John O. Voll, *Islam and Democracy* (New York: Oxford University Press, 1996). For a similar argument see Noah Feldman, *After Jihad: America and the Struggle for Islamic Democracy* (New York: Farrar, Straus & Giroux, 2003).

8. See Augustus Richard Norton, ed., *Civil Society in the Middle East*, 2 vols. (Leiden: E. J. Brill, 1994, 1995); for a short introduction to this approach, see Jillian Schwedler, ed., *Toward Civil Society in the Middle East? A Primer* (Boulder: Lynne Rienner, 1995). For a more critical discussion of the concept's utility, see James Gelvin, ed., *The Civil Society Debate in Middle Eastern Studies* (Los Angeles: UCLA Near East Center, c. 1996).

9. For a recent discussion of this issue, see Joel Beinin, "Is Terrorism a Useful Term for Understanding the Middle East and the Israeli-Palestinian Conflict?," *Radical History Review* 85 (2003): 12–23.

10. See for example Sharon's November 11, 2001 video message to the General Assembly of the United Jewish Communities, in which he said that Israel had been fighting terrorism for 120 years – i.e., since the beginnings of proto-Zionist Jewish immigration to Palestine in the early 1880s – at http://www.mfa.gov.il/mfa/go.asp?MFAH0kpo0

11. Claire Sterling, *The Terror Network: The Secret War of International Terrorism* (New York: Holt, Rinehart and Winston, 1981). For a critique see Edward S. Herman, *The Real Terror Network: Terrorism in Fact and Propaganda* (Boston: South End Press, 1982).

12. Benjamin Netanyahu, ed., *Terrorism: How the West Can Win* (New York: Farrar, Straus & Giroux, 1986). The quotations from Netanyahu in the following two paragraphs come from pp. ix and 7 of his book, respectively.

13. In this context it is also worth recalling that in the early 1980s the Israeli authorities tolerated and even encouraged the Palestinian Islamist elements in the West Bank and Gaza who would later form Hamas, in the hope that they would form a counterweight to the secular-nationalist PLO.

14. For a recent statement of this perspective, see Daniel Pipes, *Militant Islam Reaches America* (New York: W. W. Norton, 2002).

15. See for example Fred Halliday, *Islam and the Myth of Confrontation: Religion and Politics in the Middle East* (London: I. B. Tauris, 1996) and *Two Hours that Shook the World – September 11, 2001: Causes and Consequences* (London: Saqi, 2002), and John L. Esposito, *Unholy War: Terror in the Name of Islam* (New York: Oxford University Press, 2002).

16. Samuel P. Huntington, "The Clash of Civilizations?," *Foreign Affairs* 72 (1993): 22–49. Huntington expanded this article into a book from whose title the question mark had disappeared: *The Clash of Civilizations and the Remaking of World Order* (New York: Simon and Schuster, 1996). In his original article Huntington quoted approvingly from Bernard Lewis's "The Roots of Muslim Rage."

17. Roy P. Mottahedeh, "The Clash of Civilizations: An Islamicist's Critique," *Harvard Middle Eastern and Islamic Review* 2 (1996): 1–26.
18. For an overview of some of these debates, see Jacob Heilbrunn, "The News from Everywhere," *Lingua Franca* (May–June 1996).
19. For a useful but now somewhat dated discussion of research, trends and issues in Arab studies, see Hisham Sharabi, ed., *Theory, Politics and the Arab World: Critical Responses* (New York: Routledge, 1990).
20. See for example Beshara Doumani, *Rediscovering Palestine: Merchants and Peasants in Jabal Nablus, 1700–1900* (Berkeley: University of California Press, 1995) and Dina Rizk Khoury, *State and Provincial Society in the Ottoman Empire: Mosul, 1540–1834* (Cambridge: Cambridge University Press, 1997). See too Ariel Salzmann, "An Ancien Régime Revisited: 'Privatization' and Political Economy in the Eighteenth-Century Ottoman Empire," *Politics & Society* 21 (1993): 393–423.
21. See the NSEP website at http://www.ndu.edu/nsep/
22. See the MESA website at http://w3fp.arizona.edu/mesassoc/resolutions.htm
23. See the National Foreign Language Center, letter of April 1, 2002 to potential grant recipients, at www.nflc.org/flagship/application/NFLI-P.pdf
24. Nadav Safran, *Saudi Arabia: The Ceaseless Request for Security* (Cambridge, MA: Harvard University Press, 1985).
25. For details see *The Harvard Crimson*, October 1985–January 1986. In the interests of full disclosure, I should note that I was one of a group of Harvard faculty and research fellows affiliated with the Center for Middle Eastern Studies who publicly dissociated themselves from Safran's conference and insisted that neither the center nor anyone who might be seen as acting in its name should solicit or accept funding from the CIA or any other intelligence agency.
26. The term "think tank" seems to go back to the Second World War and originally referred to a "secure room or environment where defense scientists and military planners could meet to discuss strategy." See Donald E. Abelson, "Think Tanks and US Foreign Policy: An Historical Perspective," in *US Foreign Policy Agenda* (the "Electronic Journal of the US Department of State"), November 2002, at http://usinfo.state.gov/journals/itps/1102/ijpe/ijpe1102.htm
27. See Lisa Anderson, "The Scholar and the Practitioner: Perspectives on Social Science and Public Policy," Leonard Hastings Schoff Memorial Lecture, Fall 2000, School of International and Public Affairs, Columbia University (unpublished), p. 21.
28. On AIPAC see Lee O'Brien, *American Jewish Organizations and Israel* (Washington, DC: Institute of Palestine Studies, 1986), ch. 4, and Edward Tivnan, *The Lobby: Jewish Political Power and American Foreign Policy* (New York: Simon and Schuster, 1987).
29. By way of example see "A Clean Break: A New Strategy for Securing the Realm," a 1996 strategy paper prepared for Benjamin Netanyahu based on ideas formulated by a group that included Richard Perle and other future Bush administration officials. It is available at http://www.israeleconomy.org/strat1.htm

30. Quoted in Jonah Goldberg, "Baghdad Delenda Est, Part Two," *National Review Online*, April 23, 2002, at http://www.nationalreview.com/goldberg/goldberg042302.asp

31. For a fuller discussion see Joel Beinin, "Pro-Israel Hawks and the Second Gulf War," *Middle East Report Online* (April 2003), at http://www.merip.org/mero/mero040603.html

32. See Robert Blecher, "'Free People Will Set the Course of History': Intellectuals, Democracy and American Empire," *Middle East Report Online* (March 2003), at http://www.merip.org/mero/interventions/blecher_interv.html

33. See Juan R. I. Cole's review in *Global Dialogue* 4 (2002), available at http://www.juancole.com/essays/review.htm
    See also Riaz Hassan, *Faithlines: Muslim Conceptions of Islam and Society* (Oxford: Oxford University Press, 2002), which offers a comparative survey of what Muslims in four different countries actually believe and thereby undermines Lewis' portrait of contemporary Islam as static and monolithic.

34. On Lewis' influence after September 11, see Michiko Kakutani "How Books Have Shaped US Policy," *The New York Times*, April 5, 2003, and Clifford Geertz, "Which Way to Mecca?," *The New York Review of Books*, June 12, 2003. See too Kenneth Pollack's review of *The Crisis of Islam* in *The New York Times Book Review*, April 6, 2003. Pollack, a vocal advocate of the invasion of Iraq, expressed admiration for Lewis but was exasperated by Lewis' reliance on his own authority to support his broad assertions, instead of providing evidence or even detailed arguments.

35. See Adam Shatz's critical but poignant assessment of Ajami's career, "The Native Informant," in *The Nation*, April 28, 2003; for the full text of Cheney's speech see *The Daily Standard* at http://www.theweeklystandard.com/Content/Public/Articles/000/000/001/573whsry.asp

36. On the Princeton case see Amy Magaro Rubin, "Critics Accuse Turkish Government of Manipulating Scholarship," *Chronicle of Higher Education*, October 27, 1995, and Roger W. Smith, Eric Markusen and Robert Jay Lifton, "Professional Ethics and the Denial of Armenian Genocide," *Holocaust and Genocide Studies* 9 (1995): 1–22. On the Lewis case see *Le Monde*, June 23, 1995.

37. See *The New York Times*, January 30, 1985, and the *MESA Newsletter* vol. 7 no. 1 (Winter 1985): 5–7.

38. See the stories and sources cited at http://www.adlwatch.org/

39. Edward Alexander, "Professor of Terror," *Commentary* (December 1989): 49–50.

40. Justus Reid Weiner, "'My Beautiful Old House' and Other Fabrications by Edward Said," *Commentary* (September 1999): 23–31.

41. Daniel Pipes, *In the Path of God: Islam and Political Power* (New York: Basic Books, 1983); the quoted passage is from Daniel Pipes, "Oil Wealth and Islamic Resurgence," in *Islamic Resurgence in the Arab World*, ed. Ali E. Hillal Dessouki (New York: Praeger, 1982), ch. 2, where the argument is put even more crudely.

42. See the Middle East Forum's website at http://www.meforum.org/ as well as Pipes' own website, at www.danielpipes.org

43. Material critical of Pipes can be found on the website of the Council on American Islamic Relations, at www.cairnet.org
   But see too Pipes' own website, cited above.

44. On Emerson see for example http://www.fair.org/extra/9901/emerson.html

45. I should note that I was one of those who wrote Campus Watch in protest and asked that my name be added to its blacklist, in solidarity with the scholars under attack.

46. See *The Forward*, April 11, 2003, and "Fueling a Culture Clash," *The Washington Post*, April 19, 2003.

47. Martin Kramer, *Ivory Towers on Sand: The Failure of Middle Eastern Studies in America* (Washington, DC: Washington Institute for Near East Policy, 2001). Kramer became Wexler-Fromer Fellow at the Washington Institute for Near East Policy, in 2006 he was appointed a Senior Fellow at the right-wing Shalem Center in Israel, and in 2007 he became an Associate of the John M. Olin Institute for Strategic Studies at Harvard, founded in 1989 by Samuel Huntington.

48. For a somewhat dated but still interesting discussion of Middle East studies in Israel, see Shukri Abed, *Israeli Arabism: the Latest Incarnation of Orientalism* (Washington, DC: International Center for Research and Public Policy, 1986). See also Gil Eyal, *The Disenchantment of the Orient: Expertise in Arab Affairs and the Israeli State* (Stanford: Stanford University Press, 2006).

49. Kramer, *Ivory Towers*, p. 2.

50. Ibid., p. 37.

51. Ibid., p. 97.

52. The quotations in this paragraph are drawn from ibid., pp. 122–124.

53. Juan R. I. Cole, "Why Are Arch-Conservatives Ganging Up on the Middle East Studies Association?," *History News Network*, January 20, 2003, at http://hnn.us/articles/1218.html

54. In a friendly and positive review of Pipes' *In the Path of God* soon after it was published, Kramer had noted what he termed "an unwarranted boldness in the author's predictions," particularly his forecast that a fall in oil prices would result in the decline of Islamist activism. See *The American Spectator* (July 1984), pp. 38–40; also available at
   http://www.geocities.com/martinkramerorg/PathofGod.htm
   But Pipes' inaccurate prediction went unmentioned in *Ivory Towers*, suggesting that Kramer was disinclined to judge him (or other ideological allies) by the same standards he applied to scholars with whom he disagreed. It should be noted that in the preface to the 2002 edition of his book, Pipes acknowledged that his explanation of the trajectory of Islamism had been excessively monocausal.

55. Juan R. I. Cole, "Why Are Arch-Conservatives Ganging Up on the Middle East Studies Association?," *History News Network*, January 20, 2003, at http://hnn.us/articles/1218.html

56. See, for example, http://nc.indymedia.org/news/2003/04/5151.php

57. See, for example, the *National Review Online* articles by Stanley Kurtz at www.nationalreview.com/kurtz/kurtz061603.asp (June 16, 2003) and www.nationalreview.com/kurtz/kurtz200310140905.asp (October 14, 2003).

58. The full text of the Higher Education Opportunity Act of 2008 can be found at http://frwebgate.access.gpo.gov/cgi-bin/getdoc.cgi?dbname=110_cong_public_laws&docid=f:publ315.110.pdf

59. The commission's briefing report can be found at www.uscer.gov/pubs/08150campusantibrief07.pdf, while the findings and recommendation can be found at www.uscer.gov/pubs/050306FRUSCCRRCAS.pdf. The letter of concern released by the Middle East Studies Association's Committee on Academic Freedom can be found on the organization's website, www.mesa.arizona.edu/

60. See Joyce Purnick, "Some Limits on Speech in Classrooms," *The New York Times*, February 28, 2005; "N.Y. School Board Bans a Controversial Arab Professor," *The Forward*, February 25, 2005.

61. Letters from the Middle East Studies Association's Committee on Academic Freedom protesting infringements of academic freedom can be found at http://mesa.wns.ccit.arizona.edu/caf/caf_letters.htm#.
For the record: I served as president of the Middle East Studies Association in 2006–2007.

62. See the ASMEA website at www.asmeascholars.org/index.php?option=com_content&view=article&id=2&Itemid=3

63. Even stranger (and more telling) was the presence of General Çevik Bir on ASMEA's Academic Council at the organization's inception. Bir, formerly deputy chief of staff of the Turkish armed forces, was a leading advocate of the Turkish–Israeli strategic alliance, but he was also notorious in his home country as a key architect both of the July 1997 "soft coup" that removed Prime Minister Necmettin Erbakan from power and of what an International Commission of Jurists report described as a secret plan developed by the Turkish military "to initiate a smear campaign against certain journalists, politicians, and human rights activists and organisations in order to discredit them publicly by associating them with the Kurdish Workers' Party (PKK)." Bir subsequently disappeared from the ASMEA Academic Council roster. See the section of the ICJ report titled "The Military" at http://www.icj.org/news.php3?id_article=2692&lang=en

64. For a fuller discussion of this and related issues, see my response to the question "Did the Events of 9/11 Change the Field of Middle East Studies," in *International Journal of Middle East Studies* 39 (2007), and my 2007 MESA presidential address, in *Middle East Studies Association Bulletin* 42 (2008): 5–15.

Bibliography

Abdel-Malek, Anouar. "Orientalism in Crisis." *Diogenes* 44 (1963): 103–140.

Abed, Shukri. *Israeli Arabism: the Latest Incarnation of Orientalism.* Washington, DC: International Center for Research and Public Policy, 1986.

Abrahamian, Ervand. *Iran Between Two Revolutions.* Princeton: Princeton University Press, 1978.

"The 1953 Coup in Iran." *Science & Society* 65 (2001): 182–215.

Abu-Lughod, Janet L. *Before European Hegemony: The World System, A.D. 1250–1350.* New York: Oxford University Press, 1989.

"On the Remaking of History: How to Reinvent the Past." In *Remaking History*, edited by Barbara Kruger and Phil Mariani, 111–129. Seattle: Bay Press, 1989.

Agius, Dionisius A., and Richard Hitchcock, eds. *The Arab Influence in Medieval Europe.* Reading: Ithaca Press, 1994.

Ahmad, Aijaz. *In Theory: Classes, Nations, Literatures.* London: Verso, 1992.

Alexander, Edward. "Professor of Terror." *Commentary* (December 1989): 49–50.

Alloula, Malek. *The Colonial Harem.* Translated by Myrna Godzich and Wlad Godzich. Minneapolis: University of Minnesota Press, 1986.

Amin, Samir. *Accumulation on a World Scale: A Critique of the Theory of Underdevelopment.* Translated by Brian Pearce. New York: Monthly Review Press, 1974.

Eurocentrism. New York: Monthly Review Press, 1988.

Re-Reading the Postwar Period: An Intellectual Itinerary. Translated by Michael Wolfers. New York: Monthly Review Press, 1994.

Archer, Margaret S., and Jonathan Q. Tritter, eds. *Rational Choice Theory: Resisting Colonization.* London: Routledge, 2000.

Asad, Talal, ed. *Anthropology and the Colonial Encounter.* Amherst, NY: Humanity Books, 1973.

al-'Azm, Sadik Jalal. "Orientalism and Orientalism in Reverse." *Khamsin* 8 (1981): 5–26.

al-Azmeh, Aziz. *Islams and Modernities.* London: Verso, 1993.

Barkan, Elazar. *Retreat of Scientific Racism: Changing Concepts of Race in Britain and the United States between the World Wars.* Cambridge: Cambridge University Press, 1992.

Barker, Francis, Peter Hulme, Margaret Iversen and Diana Loxley, eds. *Europe and its Others*, vol. I. Colchester: University of Essex, 1985.

Batatu, Hanna. *The Old Social Classes and the Revolutionary Movements of Iraq: A Study of Iraq's Old Landed and Commercial Classes and of its Communists, Ba'thists, and Free Officers*. Princeton: Princeton University Press, 1978.

Bayoumi, Moustafa, and Andrew Rubin, eds. *The Edward Said Reader*. New York: Vintage, 2000.

Beck, Lois, and Nikki Keddie, eds. *Women in the Muslim World*. Cambridge, MA: Harvard University Press, 1978.

Beinin, Joel. "Is Terrorism a Useful Term for Understanding the Middle East and the Israeli-Palestinian Conflict?" *Radical History Review* 85 (2003): 12–23.

Beinin, Joel, and Joe Stork, eds. *Political Islam*. Berkeley: University of California Press, 1997.

Bernal, Martin. *Black Athena: The Afroasiatic Roots of Classical Civilization*, 2 vols. New Brunswick: Rutgers University Press, 1987, 1991.

Binder, Leonard. "Area Studies: A Critical Reassessment." In *The Study of the Middle East: Research and Scholarship in the Humanities and the Social Sciences*, edited by Leonard Binder. New York: John Wiley & Sons, 1976.

Blackburn, Robin, ed. *Ideology in Social Science: Readings in Critical Social Theory*. New York: Pantheon Books, 1972.

Blaut, J. M. *The Colonizer's Model of the World: Geographical Diffusionism and Eurocentric Theory*. New York: The Guilford Press, 1993.

Blum, William. *The CIA: A Forgotten History – US Global Interventions since World War 2*. London: Zed Books, 1986.

Braude, Benjamin. "The Sons of Noah and the Construction of Ethnic and Geographical Identities in the Medieval and Early Modern Periods." *William and Mary Quarterly* 54 (1997): 105–142.

Brenner, Robert. "The Origins of Capitalist Development: a Critique of Neo-Smithian Marxism." *New Left Review* 104 (1977): 25–92.

Browe, Daniel R., and Edward J. Lazzerini, eds. *Russia's Orient: Imperial Borderlands and Peoples, 1700–1917*. Bloomington: Indiana University Press, 1997.

Buheiry, Marwan. "Colonial Scholarship and Muslim Revivalism in 1900." *Arab Studies Quarterly* 4 (1982): 1–16.

Burke, III, Edmund. "Islamic History as World History: Marshall Hodgson, 'The Venture of Islam.'" *International Journal of Middle East Studies* 10 (1979): 241–264.

Burke, III, Edmund. and Ira M. Lapidus, eds. *Islam, Politics, and Social Movements*. Berkeley: University of California Press, 1988.

Burkert, Walter. *The Orientalizing Revolution: Near Eastern Influence on Greek Culture in the Early Archaic Age*. Cambridge, MA: Harvard University Press, 1992.

Chirol, Valentine. *The Middle Eastern Question; or, Some Political Problems of Indian Defence*. London: J. Murray, 1903.

Chomsky, Noam. *The Fateful Triangle: The United States, Israel and the Palestinians*. Boston: South End Press, 1983.

Citino, Nathan J. *From Arab Nationalism to OPEC: Eisenhower, King Sa'ud, and the Making of US–Saudi Relations*. Bloomington: Indiana University Press, 2002.

Clancy-Smith, Julia, and Frances Gouda, eds. *Domesticating the Empire: Race, Gender, and Family Life in French and Dutch Colonialism*. Charlottesville: University Press of Virginia, 1998.

Clifford, James. *The Predicament of Culture: Twentieth-Century Ethnography, Literature, and Art*. Cambridge, MA: Harvard University Press, 1988.

Cockcroft, James D., André Gunder Frank and Dale L. Johnson. *Dependence and Underdevelopment: Latin America's Political Economy*. Garden City, NY: Anchor Books, 1972.

Cohn, Bernard. *An Anthropologist among the Historians and Other Essays*. Delhi: Oxford University Press, 1987.

Conrad, Lawrence I. "Ignaz Goldziher on Ernest Renan: From Orientalist Philology to the Study of Islam." In *The Jewish Discovery of Islam: Studies in Honor of Bernard Lewis*, edited by Martin Kramer. Tel Aviv: The Moshe Dayan Center for Middle Eastern and African Studies, 1999.

Cooper, Fred, and Ann Laura Stoler, eds. *Tensions of Empire: Colonial Cultures in a Bourgeois World*. Berkeley: University of California Press, 1997.

Copeland, Miles. *The Game of Nations: the Amorality of Power Politics*. London: Weidenfeld & Nicolson, 1969.

Crinson, Mark. *Empire Building: Orientalism and Victorian Architecture*. London: Routledge, 1996.

Cromer, the Earl of (Evelyn Baring). "The Government of Subject Races." *Edinburgh Review* 207 (1908): 1–27.

Modern Egypt, 2 vols. New York: MacMillan, 1908.

Cumings, Bruce. "Boundary Displacement: Area Studies and International Studies During and After the Cold War." In *Universities and Empire: Money and Politics in the Social Sciences During the Cold War*, edited by Christopher Simpson. New York: The New Press, 1998.

Curl, James Stevens. *The Egyptian Revival: An Introductory Study of a Recurring Theme in the History of Taste*. London: George Allen & Unwin, 1982.

Daniel, Norman. *The Arabs and Medieval Europe*. London: Longman, 1975.

Islam and the West: The Making of an Image. Edinburgh: Edinburgh University Press, 1960.

Islam, Europe and Empire. Edinburgh: Edinburgh University Press, 1966.

Davis, Eric. *Challenging Colonialism: Bank Misr and Egyptian Industrialization, 1920–1941*. Princeton: Princeton University Press, 1983.

Davis, John. *The Landscape of Belief: Encountering the Holy Land in Nineteenth-Century American Art and Culture*. Princeton: Princeton University Press, 1996.

De Jong, F. "On Peter Gran, *Islamic Roots of Capitalism: Egypt, 1760–1840*." *International Journal of Middle East Studies* 14 (1982): 381–399.

Dirks, Nicholas B., ed. *Colonialism and Culture*. Ann Arbor: University of Michigan Press, 1992.

Doumani, Beshara. *Rediscovering Palestine: Merchants and Peasants in Jabal Nablus, 1700–1900*. Berkeley: University of California Press, 1995.

Eickelman, Dale F., and James Piscatori. *Muslim Politics*. Princeton: Princeton University Press, 1996.

Esposito, John L. *Unholy War: Terror in the Name of Islam*. New York: Oxford University Press, 2002.

Esposito, John L., and John O. Voll. *Islam and Democracy*. New York: Oxford University Press, 1996.

Evans, Peter, and John D. Stephens. "Studying Development since the Sixties: The Emergence of a New Comparative Political Economy." *Theory and Society* 17 (1988): 713–745.

Eveland, Wilbur Crane. *Ropes of Sand: America's Failure in the Middle East*. New York: W. W. Norton, 1980.

Eyal, Gil. *The Disenchantment of the Orient: Expertise in Arab Affairs and the Israeli State*. Stanford: Stanford University Press, 2006.

Fahmy, Khaled. *All the Pasha's Men: Mehmed Ali, his Army and the Making of Modern Egypt*. Cambridge: Cambridge University Press, 1997.

Feldman, Noah. *After Jihad: America and the Struggle for Islamic Democracy*. New York: Farrar, Straus & Giroux: 2003.

Feuer, Lewis S., ed. *Karl Marx and Friedrich Engels: Basic Writings on Politics and Philosophy*. Garden City, NY: Anchor Books, 1959.

Forbidden Agendas: Intolerance and Defiance in the Middle East. London: Al Saqi Books, 1984.

Frank, André Gunder. "Sociology of Development and Underdevelopment of Sociology." *Catalyst* (Summer 1967): 20–73.

Frassetto, Michael, and David R. Blanks, eds. *Western Views of Islam in Medieval and Early Modern Europe: Perception of Other*. New York: St. Martin's Press, 1999.

Friedman, Thomas. "A Dreamlike Landscape, A Dreamlike Reality." *The New York Times*, October 28, 1990.

Gabrieli, Francesco. "Apology for Orientalism." *Diogenes* 50 (1965): 128–136.

Gallagher, Nancy Elizabeth, ed. *Approaches to the History of the Middle East: Interviews with Leading Middle East Historians*. Reading: Ithaca Press, 1994.

Gandhi, Leela. *Postcolonial Theory: A Critical Introduction*. New York: Columbia University Press, 1998.

Gasiorowski, Mark J. *US Foreign Policy and the Shah: Building a Client State in Iran*. Ithaca, NY: Cornell University Press, 1991.

Gelvin, James, ed. *The Civil Society Debate in Middle Eastern Studies*. Los Angeles: UCLA Near East Center, c. 1996.

Gendzier, Irene. *Managing Political Change: Social Scientists and the Third World*. Boulder: Westview Press, 1985.

Notes from the Minefield: United States Intervention in Lebanon and the Middle East, 1945–1958. New York: Columbia University Press, 1997.

Ghareeb, Edmund, ed. *Split Vision: The Portrayal of Arabs in the American Media*. Washington, DC: The American–Arab Affairs Council, 1983.

Gibb, Hamilton A. R. *Modern Trends in Islam*. Chicago: University of Chicago Press, 1947; reprinted 1972 by Octagon Books, New York.

Studies on the Civilization of Islam. Boston: Beacon Press, 1962.

Gibb, Hamilton A. R., and Harold Bowen. *Islamic Society and the West: A Study of the Impact of Western Civilization on Moslem Culture in the Near East*, vol. I, parts 1–2. London: Oxford University Press, 1950, 1957.

Graham-Brown, Sarah. *Images of Women: The Portrayal of Women in Photography of the Middle East 1860–1950*. New York: Columbia University Press, 1988.

Gran, Peter. *Beyond Eurocentrism: a New View of Modern World History*. Syracuse: Syracuse University Press, 1996.

Islamic Roots of Capitalism: Egypt, 1760–1840. Austin: University of Texas Press, 1978.

Green, Donald P., and Ian Shapiro. *Pathologies of Rational Choice Theory: A Critique of Applications in Political Science*. New Haven: Yale University Press, 1996.

Hajjar, Lisa, and Steve Niva. "(Re)Made in the USA: Middle East Studies in the Global Era." *Middle East Report* 74 (October–December 1997).

Hall, Robert B. *Area Studies: With Special Reference to their Implications for Research in the Social Sciences*. New York: Social Science Research Council, 1947.

Halliday, Fred. *Arabia Without Sultans: A Political Survey of Instability in the Arab World*. New York: Vintage Books/Random House, 1975.

Islam and the Myth of Confrontation: Religion and Politics in the Middle East. London: I. B. Tauris, 1996.

Two Hours that Shook the World – September 11, 2001: Causes and Consequences. London: Al Saqi, 2002.

Halpern, Manfred. *The Politics of Social Change in the Middle East and North Africa*. Princeton: Princeton University Press, 1963.

Hassan, Riaz. *Faithlines: Muslim Conceptions of Islam and Society*. Oxford: Oxford University Press, 2002.

Hay, Denys. *Europe: The Emergence of an Idea*. Edinburgh: Edinburgh University Press, 1957.

Heilbrunn, Jacob. "The News from Everywhere." *Lingua Franca* (May–June 1996).

Herman, Edward S. *The Real Terror Network: Terrorism in Fact and Propaganda*. Boston: South End Press, 1982.

Hirschkind, Charles. " 'Egypt at the Exhibition': Reflections on the Optics of Colonialism." *Critique of Anthropology* 11 (1991): 279–298.

Hodgen, Margaret T. *Early Anthropology in the Sixteenth and Seventeenth Centuries*. Philadelphia: University of Pennsylvania Press, 1964.

Horden, Peregrine, and Nicholas Purcell. *The Corrupting Sea: A Study of Mediterranean History*. Oxford: Blackwell, 2000.

Hourani, Albert. *A Vision of History: Near Eastern and Other Essays*. Lebanon: Khayat, 1961.

"The Changing Face of the Fertile Crescent in the XVIIIth Century." *Studia Islamica* 7 (1957).

The Emergence of the Modern Middle East. Berkeley: University of California Press, 1981.

Europe and the Middle East. Berkeley: University of California Press, 1980.

"Islam as a Historical Problem in European Historiography." In *Historians of the Middle East*, edited by Bernard Lewis and P. M. Holt. London: Oxford University Press, 1962.

Islam in European Thought. Cambridge: Cambridge University Press, 1991.

"Islam and the Philosophers of History," *Middle Eastern Studies* 3 (1967): 206–268.

"Ottoman Reform and the Politics of Notables." In *Beginnings of Modernization in the Middle East*, edited by William R. Polk and Richard L. Chambers. Chicago: University of Chicago Press, 1968.

Hoyland, Robert G. *Seeing Islam as Others Saw It: A Survey and Evaluation of Christian, Jewish and Zoroastrian Writings on Early Islam*. Princeton: The Darwin Press, 1997.

Hulme, Peter. *Colonial Encounters: Europe and the Native Caribbean, 1492–179*. London: Methuen, 1986.

Huntington, Samuel. "The Bases of Accomodation." *Foreign Affairs* 46 (1968): 642–656.

"The Clash of Civilizations?" *Foreign Affairs* 72 (1993): 22–49.

The Clash of Civilizations and the Remaking of World Order. New York: Simon and Schuster, 1996.

Hurewitz, J. C. *Middle East Politics: the Military Dimension*. New York: Council on Foreign Relations, 1969.

Inden, Ronald. *Imagining India*. Oxford: Basil Blackwell, 1990.

"Orientalist Constructions of India." *Modern Asian Studies* 20 (1986).

Islamoglu, Huri, and Çaglar Keyder. "Agenda for Ottoman History." *Review* 1 (1977): 31–55.

Itzkowitz, Norman. "Eighteenth Century Ottoman Realities." *Studia Islamica* 16 (1958): 73–94.

Jones, Eric L. *The European Miracle*. Cambridge: Cambridge University Press, 1981.

Jones, Gareth Stedman. *Languages of Class: Studies in English Working Class History, 1832–1982*. Cambridge: Cambridge University Press, 1983.

Keddie, Nikki R., ed. *An Islamic Response to Imperialism: Political and Religious Writings of Sayyid Jamal al-Din "al-Afghani"*. Berkeley: University of California Press, 1968.

Scholars, Saints, and Sufis: Muslim Religious Institutions since 1500. Berkeley: University of California Press, 1972.

Keddie, Nikki R., and Beth Baron, eds. *Women in Middle Eastern History: Shifting Boundaries in Sex and Gender*. New Haven: Yale University Press, 1991.

Khoury, Dina Rizk. *State and Provincial Society in the Ottoman Empire: Mosul, 1540–1834*. Cambridge: Cambridge University Press, 1997.

Kiernan, Victor. *The Lords of Human Kind: European Attitudes to Other Cultures in the Imperial Age*. London: Serif, 1995.

Kramer, Martin. *Ivory Towers on Sand: The Failure of Middle Eastern Studies in America*. Washington, DC: Washington Institute for Near East Policy, 2001.

Kuklick, Bruce. *Puritans in Babylon: the Ancient Near East and American Intellectual Life, 1880–1930*. Princeton: Princeton University Press, 1996.

Lach, Donald F. *Asia in the Making of Europe, I: The Century of Discovery.* Chicago: University of Chicago Press, 1965.

Lackner, Helen. *A House Built on Sand: A Political Economy of Saudi Arabia.* London: Ithaca Press, 1978.

Laclau, Ernesto. "Capitalism and Feudalism in Latin America." *New Left Review* 67 (1971): 19–38.

Landes, David S. *The Wealth and Poverty of Nations: Why Some Are So Rich and Some So Poor.* New York: W. W. Norton, 1998.

The Crisis of the Arab Intellectual: Traditionalism or Historicism. Translated by Diarmid Cammell. Berkeley: University of California Press, 1976.

Lazreg, Marnia. "The Reproduction of Colonial Ideology: The Case of the Kabyle Berbers." *Arab Studies Quarterly* 5 (1983): 380–395.

Lesch, David W. *Syria and the United States: Eisenhower's Cold War in the Middle East.* Boulder: Westview Press, 1992.

Lefkowitz, Mary R., and Guy MacLean Rogers, eds. *Black Athena Revisited.* Chapel Hill: University of North Carolina Press, 1996.

Lenczowski, George. *Iran under the Pahlavis.* Stanford: Hoover Institution Press, 1978.

Lerner, Daniel. *The Passing of Traditional Society: Modernizing the Middle East.* New York: The Free Press, 1958.

Lewis, Bernard. "Communism and Islam." *International Affairs* (January 1954).

The Crisis of Islam: Holy War and Unholy Terror. New York: Modern Library, 2003.

"The Question of Orientalism." *The New York Review of Books,* June 24, 1982.

"The Return of Islam." *Commentary* 61 (January 1976): 39–49.

"The Roots of Muslim Rage." *The Atlantic Monthly* 266 (September 1990).

What Went Wrong?: Western Impact and Middle Eastern Response. New York: Oxford University Press, 2002.

Lewis, Martin W., and Kären E. Wigen. *The Myth of Continents: A Critique of Metageography.* Berkeley: University of California Press, 1997.

Leys, Colin. *The Rise and Fall of Development Theory.* London: James Currey, 1996.

Little, Douglas. *American Orientalism: The United States and the Middle East since 1945.* Chapel Hill: University of North Carolina Press, 2002.

Lorcin, Patricia M. E. *Imperial Identities: Stereotyping, Prejudice and Race in Colonial Algeria.* London: I. B. Tauris, 1995.

Lowe, Lisa. *Critical Terrains: French and British Orientalisms.* Ithaca, NY: Cornell University Press, 1991.

Lybyer, Albert Howe. *The Government of the Ottoman Empire in the Time of Suleiman the Magnificent.* Cambridge, MA: Harvard University Press, 1913; reprinted 1978.

Macfie, Alexander Lyon. *Orientalism.* Edinburgh: Pearson Education, 2002.

ed., *Orientalism: A Reader.* New York: New York University Press, 2000.

MacKenzie, John M. *Orientalism: History, Theory and the Arts*. Manchester: Manchester University Press, 1995.

Ma'oz, Moshe, and Ilan Pappé, eds. *Middle Eastern Politics and Ideas: A History from Within*. London: I. B. Tauris, 1997.

McAlister, Melani. *Epic Encounters: Culture, Media, and US Interests in the Middle East, 1945–2000*. Berkeley: University of California Press, 2001.

McCaughey, Robert A. *International Studies and Academic Enterprise: A Chapter in the Enclosure of American Learning*. New York: Columbia University Press, 1984.

Mehta, Uday Singh. *Liberalism and Empire: A Study in Nineteenth-Century British Liberal Thought*. Chicago: University of Chicago Press, 1999.

Melman, Billie. *Women's Orients: English Women and the Middle East, 1718–1918*. Ann Arbor: University of Michigan Press, 1992.

Menocal, Maria Rosa. *The Arabic Role in Medieval Literary History: A Forgotten Heritage*. Philadelphia: University of Pennsylvania Press, 1987.

Metlitzki, Dorothee. *The Matter of Araby in Medieval England*. New Haven: Yale University Press, 1977.

"Middle East Studies Network in the United States." *MERIP Reports* 38 (1975): 3–26.

Mintz, Sidney. *Sweetness and Power: The Place of Sugar in Modern History*. New York: Viking Penguin, 1985.

Mitchell, Timothy. *Colonising Egypt*. Cambridge: Cambridge University Press, 1988.

——. "The Middle East in the Past and Future of Social Science." In *The Politics of Knowledge: Area Studies and the Disciplines*, edited by David Szanton. Forthcoming; currently available at http://escholarship.cdlib.org/ias/szanton.html.

——. *Rule of Experts: Egypt, Techno-Politics, Modernity*. Berkeley: University of California Press, 2002.

Moore, Jr., Barrington. *The Social Origins of Dictatorship and Democracy: Lord and Peasant in the Making of the Modern World*. Boston: Beacon Press, 1966.

Moore, David Chioni, ed. *Black Athena Writes Back: Martin Bernal Responds to his Critics*. Durham, NC: Duke University Press, 2001.

Mottahedeh, Roy P. "The Clash of Civilizations: An Islamicist's Critique." *Harvard Middle Eastern and Islamic Review* 2 (1996): 1–26.

Naff, Thomas, ed. *Paths to the Middle East: Ten Scholars Look Back*. Albany: State University of New York Press, 1993.

Netanyahu, Benjamin, ed. *Terrorism: How the West Can Win*. New York: Farrar, Straus & Giroux, 1986.

Norton, Augustus Richard, ed. *Civil Society in the Middle East*. 2 vols. Leiden: E. J. Brill, 1994, 1995.

Novick, Peter. *That Noble Dream: The Objectivity Question and the American Historical Profession*. Cambridge: Cambridge University Press, 1988.

Obenzinger, Hilton. *American Palestine: Melville, Twain and the Holy Land Mania*. Princeton: Princeton University Press, 1999.

O'Brien, Lee. *American Jewish Organizations and Israel*. Washington, DC: Institute of Palestine Studies, 1986.

Owen, Roger. *Cotton and the Egyptian Economy, 1820–1914: A Study in Trade and Development.* Oxford: Clarendon Press, 1969.

"The Mysterious Orient." *Monthly Review* 31 (1979): 58–63.

"Studying Islamic History." *Journal of Interdisciplinary History* 4 (1973): 287–298.

Pamuk, Şevket. "The Price Revolution in the Ottoman Empire Reconsidered." *International Journal of Middle East Studies* 33 (2001): 68–89.

Pipes, Daniel. *In the Path of God: Islam and Political Power.* New York: Basic Books, 1983.

Militant Islam Reaches America. New York: W. W. Norton, 2002.

"Oil Wealth and Islamic Resurgence." In *Islamic Resurgence in the Arab World,* edited by Ali E. Hillal Dessouki. New York: Praeger, 1982.

Slave Soldiers and Islam: The Genesis of a Military System. New Haven: Yale University Press, 1981.

Pocock, J. G. A. "What Do We Mean by Europe?" *The Wilson Quarterly* (Winter 1997).

Polk, William. "Sir Hamilton Gibb Between Orientalism and History." *International Journal of Middle East Studies* 6 (1975).

Prakash, Gyan. "Writing Post-Orientalist Histories of the Third World: Perspectives from Indian Historiography." *Comparative Studies in Society and History* 32 (1990): 383–408.

Rabinow, Paul. *French Modern: Norms and Forms of the Social Environment.* Cambridge, MA: MIT Press, 1989.

Renan, Ernest. *The Poetry of the Celtic Races, and Other Studies.* Translated by William G. Hutchison. Port Washington: Kennikat Press, 1970.

Richards, Alan, and John Waterbury. *A Political Economy of the Middle East: State, Class, and Economic Development.* Boulder: Westview Press, 1990.

Rodinson, Maxime. *Cult, Ghetto, and State: The Persistence of the Jewish Question.* London: Al Saqi Books, 1983.

Europe and the Mystique of Islam. Translated by Roger Veinus. Seattle: University of Washington Press, 1987.

Roosevelt, Kermit. *Countercoup: The Struggle for the Control of Iran.* New York: McGraw-Hill, 1979.

Safran, Nadav. *Egypt in Search of Political Community: An Analysis of the Intellectual and Political Evolution of Egypt, 1804–1952.* Cambridge, MA: Harvard University Press, 1961.

Saudi Arabia: The Ceaseless Request for Security. Cambridge, MA: Harvard University Press, 1985.

Said, Edward W. *Culture and Imperialism.* New York: Knopf, 1993.

Orientalism. New York: Pantheon Books, 1978.

"Orientalism: An Exchange." *The New York Review of Books,* August 12, 1982.

"Orientalism Reconsidered." *Race & Class* 27 (1985): 1–15.

Out of Place: A Memoir. New York: Knopf, 1999.

The World, the Text and the Critic. Cambridge, MA: Harvard University Press, 1983.

Salzmann, Ariel. "An Ancien Régime Revisited: 'Privatization' and Political Economy in the Eighteenth-Century Ottoman Empire." *Politics & Society* 21 (1993): 393–423.

Schwab, Raymond. *The Oriental Renaissance: Europe's Rediscovery of India and the East, 1680–1880.* Translated by Gene Patterson-Black and Victor Reinking. New York: Columbia University Press, 1984.

Schwedler, Jillian, ed. *Toward Civil Society in the Middle East? A Primer.* Boulder: Lynne Rienner, 1995.

Scott, Joan Wallach. "The Evidence of Experience." *Critical Inquiry* 17 (1991): 773–797.

Gender and the Politics of History. New York: Columbia University Press, 1988.

Shaheen, Jack. *The TV Arab.* Bowling Green, OH: Bowling Green State University Popular Press, 1984.

Sharabi, Hisham, ed. *Theory, Politics and the Arab World: Critical Responses.* New York: Routledge, 1990.

Shatz, Adam. "The Native Informant." *The Nation,* April 28, 2003.

Shohat, Ella. "Notes on the 'Post-Colonial.' " *Social Text* 31/32 (1992).

Skinner, Quentin, ed. *The Return of Grand Theory in the Human Sciences.* Cambridge: Cambridge University Press, 1985.

Smith, Roger W., Eric Markusen and Robert Jay Lifton. "Professional Ethics and the Denial of Armenian Genocide." *Holocaust and Genocide Studies* 9 (1995): 1–22.

Southern, R. W. *Western Views of Islam in the Middle Ages.* Cambridge, MA: Harvard University Press, 1962.

Sterling, Claire. *The Terror Network: The Secret War of International Terrorism.* New York: Holt, Rinehart and Winston, 1981.

Stivers, William. *America's Confrontation with Revolutionary Change in the Middle East, 1948–83.* New York: St. Martin's Press, 1986.

Stocking, George W. *Race, Culture, and Evolution: Essays in the History of Anthropology.* New York: The Free Press, 1968.

Victorian Anthropology. New York: The Free Press, 1987.

Stoddard, Lothrop. *The New World of Islam.* New York: Charles Scribner's Sons, 1921.

The Rising Tide of Color Against White World-Supremacy. New York: Charles Scribner's Sons, 1920.

Stoler, Ann Laura. *Carnal Knowledge and Imperial Power: Race and the Intimate in Colonial Rule.* Berkeley: University of California Press, 2002.

Race and the Education of Desire: Foucault's History of Sexuality and the Colonial Order of Things. Durham, NC: Duke University Press, 1995.

Suleiman, Michael W. *The Arabs in the Mind of America.* Brattleboro, VT: Amana Books, 1988.

Thorne, Susan. *Congregational Missions and the Making of an Imperial Culture in Nineteenth-Century England.* Stanford: Stanford University Press, 1999.

Tibawi, A. L. "English-Speaking Orientalists." *Islamic Quarterly* 8 (1964): 25–45.

Tipps, Dean C. "Modernization Theory and the Comparative Study of Societies: A Critical Perspective." In *Comparative Modernization,* edited by Cyril E. Black. New York: The Free Press, 1976.

Tivnan, Edward. *The Lobby: Jewish Political Power and American Foreign Policy.* New York: Simon and Schuster, 1987.

Toews, John E. "Intellectual History after the Linguistic Turn: The Autonomy of Meaning and the Irreducibility of Experience." *American Historical Review* 92 (1987): 881–882.

Tolan, John V. *Saracens: Islam in the Medieval European Imagination.* New York: Columbia University Press, 2002.

Tucker, Judith. *Women in Nineteenth-Century Egypt.* Cambridge: Cambridge University Press, 1985.

Tucker, Robert C., ed. *The Marx–Engels Reader.* New York: W. W. Norton, 1972.

The Turkish Letters of Ogier Ghiselin de Busbecq. Translated by Edward Seymour Forster. Oxford: Clarendon Press, 1927.

Turner, Bryan S. *Capitalism and Class in the Middle East: Theories of Social Change and Economic Development.* London: Heinemann, 1984.

Marx and the End of Orientalism. London: Allen & Unwin, 1978.

Weber and Islam: A Critical Study. London: Routledge & Kegan Paul, 1974.

Valensi, Lucette. *The Birth of the Despot: Venice and the Sublime Porte.* Translated by Arthur Denner. Ithaca, NY: Cornell University Press, 1993.

Vatikiotis, P. J., ed. *Revolution in the Middle East and Other Case Studies.* London: Allen & Unwin, 1972.

Vitalis, Robert. "The End of Third Worldism in Egyptian Studies." *Arab Studies Journal* 4 (1996): 13–33.

"International Studies in America." *Items & Issues* (a publication of the Social Science Research Council) 3 (2002).

Waardenburg, Jean-Jacques. *L'Islam dans le miroir de l'Occident.* The Hague: Mouton, 1962.

Wallerstein, Immanuel. *The Modern World-System: Capitalist Agriculture and the Origins of the European World-Economy in the Sixteenth Century.* New York: Academic Press, 1974.

"The Unintended Consequences of Cold War Area Studies." In *The Cold War and the University: Toward an Intellectual History of the Postwar Years,* edited by Noam Chomsky. New York: The New Press, 1997.

Waterbury, John. *The Egypt of Nasser and Sadat: The Political Economy of Two Regimes.* Princeton: Princeton University Press, 1983.

Weiner, Justus Reid. " 'My Beautiful Old House' and Other Fabrications by Edward Said." *Commentary* (September 1999).

Williams, Patrick, and Laura Chrisman, eds. *Colonial Discourse and Post-Colonial Theory: A Reader.* New York: Columbia University Press, 1994.

Williams, Raymond. *Marxism and Literature.* Oxford: Oxford University Press, 1977.

Worcester, Kenton W. *Social Science Research Council, 1923–1998.* New York: Social Science Research Council, 2001.

Young, Robert J. C. *Postcolonialism: An Historical Introduction.* Oxford: Blackwell, 2001.

White Mythologies: Writing History and the West. London: Routledge, 1990.

Zubaida, Sami. "Exhibitions of Power." *Economy and Society* 19 (1990): 359–375.

Islam, the People and the State. London: I. B. Tauris, 1989.

Index

Abdel-Malek, Anouar, 149–150, 191
Abrahamian, Ervand, 180
Abu-Lughod, Ibrahim, 172, 183
al-Afghani, Jamal al-Din, 82–83, 93, 284
Afghanistan, 232, 233, 251, 270, 275
Africa, 11, 18, 279–280
African National Congress, 230–231
Ahmad, Aijaz, 199–200, 213
Ajami, Fouad, 251, 252–253, 264, 271
al-'Azm, Sadik Jalal, 196–199, 214
Alexander, Yonah, 227–228
Algeria, 67, 71–72, 90–91, 117, 209, 224
Alloula, Malek, 209
Alternative Middle East Studies Seminar, 171
American Enterprise Institute, 247, 248
American Israel Public Affairs Committee (AIPAC), 248, 253, 254–255, 297
American Oriental Society, 68, 128
Amin, Samir, 150, 159
Anthropology and the Colonial Encounter, 168
Anti-Defamation League, 253, 254–255
antisemitism, 253, 254, 268–269
Arab-Americans, 172–173
"Arab mind", *see* Semites
Arabs, 20
Arab Studies Journal, 241
Arab Studies Quarterly, 172
area studies, 122–129, 237–241, 243
Armenia, Armenians, 23, 101, 254
"Aryans," 59, 80, 105
Asad, Talal, 167, 168
Asia, conceptions of, *see* "East," the
Association of Arab-American University Graduates, 172–173
Association for Middle East Women's Studies, 180
Association for the Study of the Middle East and Africa, 271–272
Austen, Jane, 208

Baring, Evelyn, *see* Cromer, Earl of
Batatu, Hanna, 180
Beck, Lois, 179
Becker, Carl, 90, 102
Berger, Morroe, 129
Bernal, Martin, 279–280
Binder, Leonard, 146, 179
Blunt, Wilfred Scawen, 82, 95
Bodin, Jean, 43
Britain
   expansion in Aden and Persian Gulf, 73
   in Egypt, 72–73, 93–95
   Middle East studies in, 129–130
Brookings Institution, 247, 248
Browne, Edward, 92
Busbecq, Ogier Ghiselin de, 43
Bush, George W. (and Bush administration), 175, 233, 249, 258, 268, 270, 271, 274
Byzantines (Eastern Roman Empire), 16–18, 21, 22, 27, 40

Cambridge History of Islam, 164–165, 190
Campus Watch, 257–258, 266
Carnegie Foundation, 125
Carter, Jimmy, 228
Caucasians, *see* "Aryans"
Center for Strategic and International Studies, 247
Central Intelligence Agency (CIA), 115, 121, 123, 139, 145, 146, 229, 231, 244, 246–247, 275
Champollion, Jean-François, 67, 71
Charlemagne, 16
Chechens (and Chechnya), 224, 227
Chomsky, Noam, 206
Churchill, Winston, 275
civilization
   concept of, 9, 11, 62–63, 74–77
   decline of, 62–63, 104–108
civil society, 223–224
"clash of civilizations," 219, 234–237

312

Made in United States
North Haven, CT
05 October 2022

25040794R00211